"Reading Bernard Williams collects the work of many fine philosophers who have read Bernard Williams with great profit and provides an ideal point of entry for those who have not yet had that pleasure. Since Williams' work is often more difficult than it appears, it is extremely helpful to have a book that offers so many clear-eyed critical explications of his ideas."

Kwame Anthony Appiah, Princeton University

READING BERNARD WILLIAMS

When Bernard Williams died in 2003, *The Times* newspaper hailed him as "the greatest moral philosopher of his generation." This outstanding collection of specially commissioned new essays on Williams' work will be essential reading for anyone interested in Williams, ethics and moral philosophy and philosophy in general.

Reading Bernard Williams examines the astonishing scope of his philosophy from metaphysics and philosophy of mind to ethics, political philosophy and the history of philosophy. An international line-up of outstanding contributors conduct a wide-ranging discussion of the central aspects of Williams' work, including:

- Williams' challenge to contemporary moral philosophy and his criticisms of "absolute" theories of morality
- Reason and rationality
- The good life
- The emotions
- Williams and the phenomenological tradition
- Philosophical and political agency
- Moral and political luck
- Ethical relativism

Contributors: Simon Blackburn; John Cottingham; Frances Ferguson; Joshua Gert; Peter Goldie; Charles Guignon; Sharon Krause; Christopher Kutz; Daniel Markovits; Elijah Millgram; Martha Nussbaum; and Carol Rovane.

Daniel Callcut is Assistant Professor of Philosophy at the University of North Florida. His doctoral thesis was titled *Bernard Williams and the End of Morality* (Johns Hopkins, 2003). He has since published a number of articles indebted to themes and ideas from Williams.

READING BERNARD WILLIAMS

Edited by
Daniel Callcut

Routledge
Taylor & Francis Group

LONDON AND NEW YORK

This edition published 2009
by Routledge
2 Park Square, Milton Park, Abingdon, Oxon, OX14 4RN

Simultaneously published in the USA and Canada by Routledge
270 Madison Ave, New York, NY 10016

Routledge is an imprint of the Taylor & Francis Group, an informa business

Typeset in Goudy by
Taylor & Francis Books
Printed and bound in Great Britain by
TJ International Ltd, Padstow, Cornwall

British Library Cataloguing in Publication Data
A catalogue record for this book is available from the British Library

Library of Congress Cataloging in Publication Data
Reading Bernard Williams / edited by Daniel Callcut.
p. cm.
Includes bibliographical references and index.
1. Williams, Bernard Arthur Owen. 2. Ethics. 3. Philosophy,
Modern–20th century. I. Callcut, Daniel.
BJ604.W553R43 2008
192—dc22
2008017896

ISBN13: 978-0-415-77189-4 (hbk)
ISBN13: 978-0-415-77190-0 (pbk)
ISBN13: 978-0-203-88259-7 (ebk)

CONTENTS

CONTENTS

CONTRIBUTORS

Simon Blackburn is Professor of Philosophy at the University of Cambridge. His books include *Spreading the Word* (1984), *Essays in Quasi-Realism* (1993), *The Oxford Dictionary of Philosophy* (1994), *Ruling Passions* (1998), *Think* (1999), *Being Good* (2001), *Lust* (2004), *Truth: A Guide* (2005), and *Plato's Republic* (2007).

Daniel Callcut is Assistant Professor of Philosophy at the University of North Florida. His doctoral thesis was titled *Bernard Williams and the End of Morality* (Johns Hopkins, 2003). He has since published a number of articles indebted to themes and ideas from Williams.

John Cottingham is Professor of Philosophy at the University of Reading. He is editor of *Ratio*, an international journal of analytic philosophy. His many books include *Descartes* (1986), *Philosophy and the Good Life* (1998), *On the Meaning of Life* (2003), and *The Spiritual Dimension: Religion, Philosophy and Human Value* (2005). His *Cartesian Reflections* is published by Oxford University Press (2008), and a multi-authored collection of papers discussing his own work on ethics and religion, *The Moral Life*, ed. N. Athanassoulis and S. Vice, is published by Palgrave Macmillan in 2008.

Frances Ferguson is Mary Elizabeth Garrett Professor in Arts and Sciences and Professor of English at Johns Hopkins University, Baltimore, MD. She has written on a variety of eighteenth- and nineteenth-century topics, and on literary theory. Her books include *Wordsworth: Language as Counter-spirit* (1977), *Solitude and the Sublime: Romanticism and the Aesthetics of Individuation* (1992), and *Pornography: The Theory* (2004).

Joshua Gert is Associate Professor of Philosophy at Florida State University and Co-editor of the journal *Social Theory and Practice*. He is the author of *Brute Rationality: Normativity and Human Action* (2004) and also of numerous articles on reasons and rationality, ethics, and the philosophy of color.

Peter Goldie is Samuel Hall Chair in Philosophy at the University of Manchester. He is the author of *The Emotions: A Philosophical Exploration*

(2000), *On Personality* (2004), and numerous articles on topics in philosophy of mind, ethics, and aesthetics.

Charles Guignon is Professor of Philosophy at the University of South Florida. His many books and essays address topics in historiography, literary theory and psychotherapy, existentialism, phenomenology and postmodern theory, and hermeneutics. His most recent work includes *On Being Authentic* (2004) and the second edition of the *Cambridge Companion to Heidegger* (2006).

Sharon R. Krause is Associate Professor of Political Science at Brown University. She is the author of *Liberalism with Honor* (2002) and *Civil Passions: Moral Sentiment and Democratic Deliberation* (2008), and numerous essays on topics in classical and contemporary liberalism.

Christopher Kutz is Professor of Law and Director of the Kadish Center for Morality, Law, and Public Affairs at the University of California at Berkeley. His work includes *Complicity: Ethics and Law for a Collective Age* (2000), and essays on democratic theory, the law of war, the metaphysics of criminal law, and the nature of political legitimacy.

Daniel Markovits is Professor of Law at Yale Law School. He is the author of *A Modern Legal Ethics: The Law, Morals, and Politics of Adversary Advocacy in a Democratic Age* (2008), and numerous essays on contract law, legal ethics, distributive justice, democratic theory, and other-regarding preferences.

Elijah Millgram is E.E. Ericksen Professor of Philosophy at the University of Utah. He is the author of *Practical Induction* (1997), of *Ethics Done Right: Practical Reasoning as a Foundation for Moral Theory* (2005), and the editor of *Varieties of Practical Reasoning* (2001).

Martha C. Nussbaum is Ernst Freund Distinguished Service Professor of Law and Ethics in the Department of Philosophy, Law School, and Divinity School at the University of Chicago. Her most recent works include *Sex and Social Justice* (1998), *Women and Human Development* (2000), *Upheavals of Thought: The Intelligence of Emotions* (2001), *Hiding from Humanity: Disgust, Shame, and the Law* (2004), *Frontiers of Justice: Disability, Nationality, Species Membership* (2006), *The Clash Within: Democracy, Religious Violence, and India's Future* (2007), and *Liberty of Conscience: In Defense of America's Tradition of Religious Equality* (2008).

Carol Rovane is Professor of Philosophy and Chair of the Philosophy Department at Columbia University. She is the author of *The Bounds of Agency: An Essay in Revisionary Metaphysics* (1998), *For and Against Relativism* (forthcoming), and essays on several interrelated topics: problems of the first person, personal identity, relativism, the foundations of value, and questions of group vs. individual responsibility.

ACKNOWLEDGEMENTS

I would like to thank all the contributors both for their essays and for the enjoyable correspondence. Elijah Millgram was especially supportive at a point when I was not sure that the project would get off the ground.

The staff at Routledge have been terrific. Tony Bruce, in particular, has been a wonderful source of encouragement and ideas. I would also like to thank Christopher Hook, Adam Johnson, Sonja van Leeuwen, and Amanda Lucas for their very helpful assistance.

I am very grateful for the support of the Philosophy Department and the Ethics Center of the University of North Florida. Jennifer Lawson, a UNF graduate student, has been a superb research assistant. I also thank the Department of Philosophy at Georgia State University for inviting me to participate in a conference on Bernard Williams in March 2006 (not least because I first met Patricia Williams at this conference and she has been enormously encouraging ever since). I am also grateful for the support and stimulation I received in the summer of 2005 (at Yale Law School) and 2006 (at the Berlin-Brandenburgische Akademie der Wissenschaften) as a SIAS Summer Institutes Fellow. Thanks to all the SIAS crew.

Finally, I would like to thank (for reasons they all know) Rita Callcut, Roy Callcut, Jennifer Fisher, Christopher Grau, Brenda Heideman, David Knowles, Jerry Schneewind, and Susan Wolf.

INTRODUCTION

Daniel Callcut

So we come to a point where most of my efforts have been concentrated: to make *some* sense of the ethical as opposed to throwing out the whole thing because you can't have the idealized version of it.[1]

The only serious enterprise is living.[2]

Bernard Williams' writings arguably constitute the most important and most cited body of work in contemporary Anglophone moral philosophy: it would be hard to pick up a survey or anthology of contemporary ethical theory without seeing a very large number of references to his work. He has published groundbreaking work in many areas of philosophy: on moral luck (a term he coined), on internal and external reasons (terms also coined by Williams), on moral objectivity, on integrity and authenticity, on personal identity, on theory and anti-theory, on ethical reflection, on shame, on truth and truthfulness, on genealogy, and in other areas too. Some of the terms coined by Williams now constitute the names of research topics and certain phrases (such as "one thought too many"[3]) look well on their way to achieving a kind of philosophical immortality. Contemporary philosophy would look very different without Williams' contributions. Contemporary moral philosophy has been so profoundly altered by Williams that if one subtracted his influence, it is hard to imagine the shape of what would be left.

The extent of Williams' impact can easily be underestimated since it is spread across many of the distinct subfields that now constitute professional philosophy. Yet it is also the case that, in spite of his influence, Williams remained throughout his life something of a renegade within English-language philosophy: his ideas generated many a research program but there has not been a large amount of philosophy conducted in what one might call a Williamsian spirit. One of the things that distinguishes Williams' work from that of many of his contemporaries is the way that he brings together aspects of moral philosophy that tend to get separated by

1

the distinction between metaethics and normative ethics. His work explores the implications for ethics of truths *about* the ethical (historical, cultural, political, psychological, biological, and so on). His work is thus able to reveal and wrestle with what would otherwise remain merely latent tensions between influential positions in metaethics and normative ethics. His doubts about moral theory and everyday moral thought led him "to try to find out – often by the crude method of prodding it – which parts of moral thought seemed ... to be actually alive."[4] His work is, as a result, marked by a rich and ambivalent relationship with moral skepticism.

Williams' work, not surprisingly, thus offers a deep engagement with themes and ideas that have become emblematic of modernism. He interrogates and recasts, as Elijah Millgram observes in Chapter 7 of this volume, ideas that have become philosophical clichés. Moreover, Williams was brilliant at spotting when the intellectual, cultural, and emotional implications of an idea had only been half-absorbed. He worked, for example, to clarify some of the intuitions underlying a conception of value that was not only central to much twentieth-century philosophy but one which also arguably has become a central tenet of much contemporary life: namely, the view that there is no objective moral reality, and that ethical norms are projections on to an in itself valueless world. Williams emphasized the point that if evaluative thought is to be understood as a projection, then some sense needs to be made of what is "there anyway."[5] Projection, to adapt a phrase of his, requires a screen. Thus, Williams' interest in making sense of an "absolute conception" of reality (i.e. a conception of what is there anyway) was, as Simon Blackburn makes clear in Chapter 1, fueled in part by his interest in making room for the significance of the claim that ethical norms are *not* there anyway. Blackburn argues that pragmatists who reject Williams' metaphysics will nonetheless need to find ways to retain and rearticulate his basic insights and distinctions. Millgram, by contrast, presents a sustained argument for the view that Williams' focus was, from a practical point of view, on the wrong distinctions, and that (ironically) Williams' brilliant explorations of the fact/value and science/ethics distinctions should ultimately help liberate philosophers from the kind of worldview within which such distinctions are important.

Williams did not think that rejection of the idea of moral reality (in the "there anyway" sense) meant an end to (at least not entirely) the notions of ethical knowledge or ethical truth. More specifically, he argued that we should think of ethical concepts as vehicles with which we construct ethical reality, a reality of which we can then (sometimes rightly) claim to have knowledge. But Williams doubted whether current forms of ethical self-understanding could easily accommodate this constructivist model of ethical knowledge. He was thus far more interested than many of his contemporaries in the revisionary implications of a 'projectivist' or 'dispositionalist' conception of value: how should we personally, socially, and politically accommodate the fact that any ethical way of life (in Williams' words) "is only one of many that are equally compatible with human nature"?[6] Williams took the serious versions of ethical relativism seriously. How could he not, given his view that values and obligations are, as Charles Guignon puts it in Chapter 8, "projections of our culturally conditioned commitments"? Carol Rovane, in Chapter 3, explains both Williams' "distinctive and influential contribution to the topic of relativism" and her own account of the truth in relativism.

Williams, then, was interested in the question of "what needs to be, and what can be, restructured in the light of a reflective and nonmythical understanding of our ethical practices."[7] He argued that what must be achieved by an adequate conception of ethics is a robust enough sense of the importance of ethical concerns. Williams explored ways to understand the kind of importance typically accorded to ethical concerns even if the various traditional justifications for morality failed. He stressed the importance of getting over the recoil idea, associated most prominently with existentialism, that if ethical norms have no importance from a cosmic or God's eye point of view, then they lose their importance. This response, Williams argues powerfully in "The Human Prejudice," is itself part of a worldview "not yet thoroughly disenchanted."[8] He was constantly engaged with the question of what it means to come deeply to inhabit (or reinhabit, after disenchantment) a meaningful and ethical life lived within not just a human but an historically and culturally situated point of view. Nonetheless, one can certainly see moments of what John Cottingham in Chapter 2 calls a "lingering dismay" at the human cosmological condition. Cottingham explores to what extent Williams' difficulties are generated by the fact that, for Williams, human dispositions are the sole and ultimate support of human value and meaning.

Thick concepts, as Peter Goldie explains in Chapter 5, play a central role for Williams in providing the texture of ethical, cultural, and emotional life. Williams thinks of thick ethical concepts as the prime vehicles of ethical knowledge: they embody agreement on an historically contingent but shared form of ethical life. The conditions of modernity, however, mean that ways of life that would have once been simply inherited are increasingly transferred into the realm of conscious choice. Williams defended (in characteristically nuanced fashion) the idea that this can be a liberation. But it can also mean that personal and cultural confidence, in the form expressed by practical know-how within a way of life, is challenged or undermined by the sheer variety of different modes of life on offer. Thus the question of which thick concepts to "live" (in the sense explained by Goldie) can be plagued with cultural and personal uncertainty and worries about arbitrariness (in the sense explained by Cottingham). Williams' later work increasingly dwelt on the philosophical and ethical significance of the cultural history that has brought such questions of contingency and identity to the fore.

3

Williams was keenly aware that one way to be skeptical about morality is simply to consider it not very important. Hedonists need not deny that they have moral obligations: they just do not let them get in the way of their pleasure. This is part of what Williams was getting at when he writes that "an ethical skeptic is not necessarily the same as someone who doubts whether there is any ethical knowledge" and that "to be skeptical about ethics is to be skeptical about the force of ethical considerations."[9] Williams, for the most part, seems to defend such skepticism as (at the very least) perfectly coherent and intelligible. This is not an argument that ethical life is necessarily irrational: see Joshua Gert's exploration of the complex questions involved in interpreting Williams' views on reasons and rationality in Chapter 4. Nor is Williams denying that for many people the happy life will be (will need to be, in light of who they are) an ethical one. Indeed, his forceful criticism of what he called the "morality system" stems precisely from a concern to overcome a conception of ethics that encourages the idea that the ethical life and the happy life are in opposition. The problem with morality, in Williams' pejorative sense, is that (as Daniel Markovits explains in Chapter 6) it constructs ethical life as a "form of subjugation" and that it leaves the individual (as Frances Ferguson puts it in Chapter 9) owing "her soul or his to a company store so large as to include the world." Williams argued powerfully that if ethical norms are to have authority, then they must integrate into a life worth living.

One can then see why Williams thought that in many ways novelists and playwrights offered more useful moral insight than moral theorists. The traditional moral theories seemed made for a world that had the kind of metaphysical and moral order that he believed it lacked. Williams saw the absence of such order as casting doubt on the rationale for normative moral theory, which he tended to identify with metaphysically ambitious attempts to ground a universalistic, systematic morality. He thought of much moral theory, as Ferguson points out, "as a kind of pseudo-science." To model ethical theory on (a certain understanding of) scientific theory only made sense if one could make good on the claim that moral beliefs track a structured ethical reality in the same way that scientific beliefs track the structure of empirical reality. Williams thought that too much moral philosophy was built on this illusion. Moral philosophy needed to find styles and methodologies that managed better to accommodate the fact that ethical norms live in human dispositions. Williams explored the ways in which moral philosophy might do this without falling prey to an "inert mixture of relativism and conservatism."[10] Too much ethical theory was too ahistorical, too utopian, and too abstracted from concrete human life to provide intelligent guidance. Moral philosophy needed to involve itself more in (in a phrase that Sharon Krause develops into a term of art in Chapter 12) "the actual."

Many of Williams' most influential discussions – including his critique of utilitarianism and his acclaimed discussion of moral luck – grow out of an extraordinary ability to articulate the emotional reality of ethical life. In Chapter 6, Markovits highlights Williams' keen sense of the untenable psychological implications of consequentialist or Kantian accounts of morality: their demand for impersonality is, as Markovits puts it, "inconsistent with … the conditions for the development of an (integrated) moral character." Williams had a novelist's sense of the human weight of things and used this sense to test moral theories against what he thought of as both more realistic and more appealing conceptions of ethical life. (In Chapter 8, Guignon explains the affinities between this approach and methodologies employed within the phenomenological tradition.) Williams was particularly adept at registering the way that the human significance of actions exceeds their intentions. There is "in the story of one's life," as he puts the point in his discussion of *Oedipus Tyrannus*, "an authority exercised by what one has done, and not merely by what one has intentionally done."[11] The fact that the meaning of an action can be determined by what happens, in a way that goes beyond intention and control, is just one instance of the way that human life is hostage to luck. Christopher Kutz, in Chapter 11, extends Williams' insights with regard to the role of luck in political life while warning of the "normative gamble" that this recognition can encourage.

Williams suggested that much moral philosophy offered a naïve 'good news' view of the world, devoid of an appreciation of conflict, tragedy, and loss. Williams was fond of pointing out (in Nietzschean fashion) what one might call 'the bad in the good': the discomfort that much actual moral (and aesthetic) achievement should produce given the historical conditions of creation. Martha Nussbaum suggests, in Chapter 10, that Williams offers a corrective to the kind of philosophy that offers a "flight from reality." But she also argues that Williams' corrective itself stands in need of correction: the recognition of inevitable tragedy and loss needs to be integrated into a fuller picture that recognizes both the good in life (despite the existence of tragedy) and the often unappreciated extent to which much of the tragic can be avoided or at least diminished by human effort. Krause concurs with this while endorsing (as Nussbaum does) Williams' recognition of the fact that "internal dividedness on moral questions and the feeling of regret are common."

Williams argued, in words that were prescient as well as still pertinent, that it is a mistake "to detach the spirit of liberal critique from the concept of truth."[12] His work became increasingly occupied with the question of which existing ethical concepts could (in some form) emerge from genealogical and social critique, and his late work pointed towards a style of ethical philosophy that encouraged conceptual creativity in ethical theory and practice. Thus his interest in preserving a sense of the importance of ethical concerns should not be equated with the concern to defend 'traditional' morality. Indeed, one of the most important casualties of a nonmythical conception of ethics is the idea that ethical norms all stand or fall together. His writing on these issues is enriched by the fact that there are wider cultural concerns about the 'status' of values and, particularly in a secular context, wider concerns about how to understand and sustain the deliberative priority traditionally accorded to ethical concerns. Moreover, Williams' historicist conception of ethics means that the philosophical and ethical questions cannot be neatly separated from the cultural questions. Williams is quite self-aware about all this, and the self-awareness adds a further layer of richness to his work. I think that his work is best read as working towards a response to outright ethical skepticism: what he shows is that ethical skepticism can be rejected by rejecting the implicit conception of ethics on which it depends. But don't listen to me: read Bernard Williams!

Notes

1 Interview with Bernard Williams, *The Harvard Review of Philosophy*, Vol. XII (Spring 2004), p. 86.
2 Bernard Williams, *Ethics and the Limits of Philosophy* (Cambridge, MA: Harvard University Press, 1985), p. 117.
3 Bernard Williams, "Persons, Character and Morality," in *Moral Luck* (Cambridge: Cambridge University Press, 1981), p. 18.
4 Preface to *Moral Luck*, p. x.
5 See Williams, *Ethics and the Limits of Philosophy*, Chapter 8.
6 Ibid., p. 52.
7 Ibid., p. 194.
8 Bernard Williams, "The Human Prejudice," in A. W. Moore (ed.), *Philosophy as a Humanistic Discipline* (Princeton, NJ: Princeton University Press, 2006), p. 137.
9 Williams, *Ethics and the Limits of Philosophy*, p. 25.
10 Bernard Williams, *Truth and Truthfulness: An Essay in Genealogy* (Princeton, NJ: Princeton University Press, 2002), p. 220. See also "Pluralism, Community and Left Wittgensteinianism," in *In the Beginning Was the Deed* (Princeton, NJ: Princeton University Press, 2005).
11 Bernard Williams, *Shame and Necessity* (Berkeley, CA: University of California Press, 1993), p. 69.
12 Bernard Williams, *Truth and Truthfulness*, p. 4.

Part I

ETHICS AND METAPHYSICS

1

THE ABSOLUTE CONCEPTION

Putnam vs Williams

Simon Blackburn

Science deals exclusively with things as they are in themselves; and art exclusively with things as they affect the human sense and human soul. Her work is to portray the appearances of things, and to deepen the natural impressions which they produce upon living creatures. The work of science is to substitute facts for appearances, and demonstrations for impressions. Both, observe, are equally concerned with truth; the one with truth of aspect, the other with truth of essence. Art does not represent things falsely, but truly as they appear to mankind. Science studies the relations of things to each other: but art studies only their relations to man.

(John Ruskin, *Stones of Venice*, 11.47–8)

Williams wrote that his "notion of an absolute conception can serve to make effective a distinction between 'the world as it is independent of our experience' and 'the world as it seems to us'".[1] It does this by understanding "the world as it seems to us" as "the world as it seems peculiarly to us"; the absolute conception will, correspondingly, be "a conception of the world that might be arrived at by any investigators, even if they were very different from us".[2] It contrasts with parochial or "perspectival" or what Williams calls "peculiar" conceptions, ones available only to a more or less restricted set of subjects, who share a contingent sensory apparatus, or culture or history. The question that I want to discuss first is whether this gives us a reliable distinction.

On the same page, Williams goes on to say that "The substance of the absolute conception ... lies in the idea that it could nonvacuously explain how it itself, and the various perspectival views of the world, are possible."[3] This is a different, and apparently a more ambitious claim.[4] One might think, for instance, that any sufficiently advanced investigators of a world like ours, even if they are very different from us, might converge on, say, something like Newton's laws of motion, or even on subsequent physics and mathematics. But there is no evident reason why that should equip them to explain how our perspectival view of the world is possible, if only

9

because they may not be equipped to understand our view of the world or to know what it is. Indeed, Williams' well-known and highly developed sense of history suggests that his view ought to be that often they will *not* be equipped to understand some of our social, political, and ethical concepts, precisely because these are the contingent growths of our peculiar history, and need to be understood in historical terms. Williams himself says as much.[5] There is a tension here in his thought, or even an outright inconsistency, and Hilary Putnam and others are right to notice it.[6]

Williams' distinction is a cousin, at least, of the primary/secondary quality distinction. It is sometimes suggested that this in turn was the child of a particular historical time, the result of one phase of science, but with no claim on those before, or by implication those of us now past, that time. This is not true, for some version of the distinction long precedes seventeenth-century science. It was widely found in the classical world, being a side-product of ancient atomism, and implicit in the standard tropes of scepticism.[7] It remains true, of course, that the distinction was very much highlighted in the seventeenth century, not only because of the resurgence of materialism and atomism, but also with the Copernican recognition of the role of the observer. It is also highly debatable how that distinction was to be drawn, and both Locke's arguments for the distinction, and the distinction itself, were rapidly contested.[8] Berkeley, perhaps following Pierre Bayle, who in turn credited Simon Foucher, denied that the distinction had any substance at all.[9] Notably, he did this by using a precursor of Putnam's "entanglement" arguments (Berkeley puts it in terms of hostility to "abstraction") to urge that we could have no idea of a world conceived in purely primary quality terms. Berkeley argues that if we take away the features that relate to our specific senses in the way, whatever it may be, that colour is specific to sight, we are left with no conception of an object at all, and hence no conception of the bearer of some reduced set of primary qualities.

In Berkeley, a conception, or what he calls an idea, is of course an empirically tinged notion, identified with a presentation in the imagination, so it may be that a Lockean can evade the argument by admitting that even if we have no conception by these standards of a purely primary qualitied object, we can nevertheless perfectly well understand the notion. For what follows, it is important as well to notice that while Locke's distinction is in essence *metaphysical*, or at least physical, Berkeley's objection is in terms of what we can *conceive* of, or what we have an idea of, or can represent to ourselves. We should also notice that Locke defended his distinction by calling on the relative *stability* of primary quality perception compared to the potential *variability* of secondary quality perception, and this asymmetry, whatever it may come to, does not require that anyone can conceive of the world in purely primary terms. The asymmetry is denied by Berkeley, but it is hard not to feel that there is something to it.[10] So something like Williams' contrast has an initial appeal. It is not implausible to suppose that rational Martians would, if intelligent and scientific enough, come to share with us the scientific framework we employ, deploying thoughts about spatial configuration, temporal passage, velocity, mass, energy, electric charge, and no doubt others, while there would be less presumption that they would taste as we do, smell the same smells, feel heat or cold as we do, or respond to colours in our way. There is just as little presumption that they would have anything like our moral sensibilities or our political or normative sensibilities, any more than we should expect them to share our senses of humour. Everyone knows that in these areas variations of sensibility are to be expected.

Williams updates Locke in terms of descriptions of the world that have some claim to represent what is "there anyway" as opposed to ones that are "peculiar", that is, that are available to us only as creatures with particular constitutions and modes of perception, which we could not suppose to be shared by all rational enquirers. But this introduces a crucially different issue, since we ought to wonder whether at least some concepts that are in his sense peculiar might enable us to represent what is just there anyway, attributing things *properties* which are just there anyway, but which we pick out or respond to in our own parochial, peculiar way. We can get a vivid sense of this possibility if we think of Nagel's problem with imagining what it is like to be a bat. The bat's *take* on the world, if Nagel is right, remains always opaque to us, for we are not equipped to share it. But what the bat does is certainly to detect things that are just there anyway – solid three-dimensional things, since that's what echolocation is for. Nagel may not be right about the inevitable opacity to us of the bat's take on things. But even his prima facie case for this shows that there is a crucial distinction between the property represented, and the conceptions enabling this representation to occur, and it is one that also opens Williams to Putnam's attack, to which I now turn.[11]

I

In *Renewing Philosophy*, Putnam opens his opposition to Williams by considering two cases where our modes of receptivity seem to be to the fore, namely heat and colour. In each case he rejects the idea that our responses in any sense determine the properties we perceive. In the case of heat, he directs us to the scientifically central concept of temperature. In the case of colour, he draws on the approach of Jonathan Westphal. A surface is green just in case it *refuses* to reflect a significant percentage of red light relative to light of other colours, including green. This enables Putnam to write:

> the view that green is a perfectly good property of things, one which is relational in the sense of involving the relations of the

surface to light, but not relational in the sense of involving the relations of the surface to *people*, is alive and well.[12]

He urges, and we should agree, that whatever dispositionality appears in these accounts is no bar to the idea of these properties appearing in the best scientific conception of the world – our best approximation to Williams' absolute conception.

But this is a question of a *property* appearing in the scientific understanding of the world. Williams' concern initially seemed aimed at a contrast between *social and ethical thinking* and *scientific thinking*. We might put it by saying that while Putnam can follow Westphal in putting *reference*, colour properties themselves, and properties of heat and temperature, firmly into the scientific sphere, that leaves the question of *sense*, or what above I called different subjects' *take* on things, open. Someone feeling heat does not usually feel it *as* motion, and somebody thinking of colour, unless he is especially well educated, is unlikely to think of it in terms of refusal of light. Rather, his tactile or visual system substitutes for any need to theorize, delivering a phenomenology instead, a view of the world that indeed selects the properties Westphal and Putnam talk about, but in a way that, for all we can yet see, may be peculiar to us, or peculiar to those of us who have unimpaired tactile and visual systems.

There is, of course, no single story about the relationship between concept and property. For instance, Putnam here diverges from John McDowell, whose writings on these matters he has otherwise tended to endorse. McDowell says outright that the concept of a sensory quality "cannot be understood in abstraction from the sensory character of experience. What it is for something to be red, say, is not intelligible unless packaged with an understanding of what it is for something to look red."[13] It is important that McDowell here writes not only of our phenomenological conception of red colour, but of the property or quality itself. But Putnam's approach to redness purely in terms of the relation between a surface and incident light appears to leave out altogether the fact that redness is a *perceptible* property, for us, or any implications for the *concept* that arise from that fact.

Perhaps Williams could leave McDowell and Putnam to wrestle over what is to be said about the *property* of being red. For *some* of his purposes, he could even side with Putnam, so far as that is concerned. For, to repeat, it is enough for some of Williams' purposes if the *concept*, linked at least to the mode of presentation or mode of experience associated with heat or colour, is peculiar to us. And that might be so whatever our best theory of the property of being coloured or hot turned out to be.

Putnam writes as though if we are talking of our conception of heat or colour, given by experience, the subject has in effect become the *sensation* of heat and colour, and he points out that Williams offers no arguments for denying that sensations are brain processes.[14] But it is not clear at all whether this interpretation of a sense-reference distinction is justified, nor how the point about the possibly material nature of sensations relates to Williams' concerns. To take the second point first, put in terms of sensations, when he is talking of a peculiar *conception* of the world, Williams' concern is not to defend any particular ontology of sensations or qualia, but to defend the idea of a special or peculiar kind of judgement, that is enabled by the experience, or by the sensation if we talk that way. It does not matter in the least whether the sensation is a brain process. This special kind of judgement is what has subsequently become familiar as a perceptual demonstrative thought, the kind of thought that would be voiced when we say "*that* red is too sombre" or "that smell is still lingering". What matters is that the perceptual demonstrative thought is *peculiarly* ours, and perhaps can only be ours at some evolutionary or historical or cultural juncture. The question is whether having this element of subjectivity enables us to make a specific kind of judgement, and one that could not be made by creatures with a different subjectivity. If having the subjectivity is itself a matter of being in a particular brain state, the distinction and the defence still remain. After all, our brains themselves are peculiarly ours, and peculiarly configured by evolution, history and culture.

Perhaps thinking further about the different sensory modality of smell will make the matter clearer. Scientists interested in olfactory perception study the influence of emotion and mood on such perception, and how alongside things like associative learning, gender, and even according to some researchers sexual orientation, they influence the hedonic tone and the sensory threshold for different odours. The experience of smelling is substantially different depending on these factors. The odorant itself, i.e. the pheromone or other chemical, remains identical, and just like the reflectance properties of a surface, can be scientifically isolated and described, in this case chemically. So can the specialized proteins in the olfactory receptors that bind odorant molecules, just as the differential wavelength sensitivities of different cones in the eye can be found. But the experience of smelling requires more. It requires that the brain generates an organized response to the arrival of those molecules, just as it must respond to levels and differences in energy at the short, medium and long end of the light spectrum in ways that can only be approximated by a quite complex algorithm (which is one reason for caution about a casual notion of 'red light'). Currently the science of smell tells us that different odorants set up different patterns of spatial activity in the glomerular layer of the olfactory bulb, suggesting a combinatorial mechanism for olfactory coding. With different subjects, different patterns of activity arise, and then the take or the phenomenology of odour perception is altered. Nobody doubts that this 'take' or phenomenology is in some sense brain located, and certainly brain-dependent. But the point is that it gives different subjects different takes on the one chemical (the thing that is just there, anyway), up to the point where one subject has no olfactory experience at all, smells nothing, in circumstances in which the other does. Goodman's description of the situation in terms of different worlds seems especially apt: it is natural to think that the dog's olfactory world is entirely distinct from mine, and in many respects mine may be distinct from yours. We have, on this account, no reason to think in terms of one world of smells, from which different creatures make different selections. There is one chemical world, perhaps many different combinations of philia and receptors, and different spatial and combinatorial algorithms, set by other factors, before we smell anything in our own distinctive, or as Williams would put it, peculiar, ways. No doubt, similar things are true of taste, and the different ways things taste to different people, or the same person at different times, is a matter of everyday remark.

I do not think that everything about smells generalizes to colour or heat: for a start, the scientific underpinnings of different smellings are chemicals themselves, not properties of other things, such as a disposition not to reflect red light. But the example illustrates the overwhelming importance of keeping conception apart from property. With this in hand, let us ask: why did Putnam think it necessary to confine the property of being coloured to having a relationship to light, rather than, for instance, having a three-way relationship to light and us, such as having the power to reflect or to refuse to reflect a kind of light apt to strike us in one way or another? Obviously enough, once the possibility of mind–brain identity is on the board, it clearly makes no difference to the *scientific* status of colour or smell whether they are best analyzed without invoking any relation to us, or whether such a relation is central to them. Since we are part of the same scientific world, a relation to us is as good a scientific property as, say, being poisonous to us.

This three-way relation can do justice to the thought developed by Jonathan Bennett, that you can change a thing's secondary qualities, but not its primary qualities, by changing us rather than it.[15] At present, phenol-thio-urea (and, apparently, Brussels sprouts) taste bitter to some proportion of people, and insipid to others. Genetic drift or evolutionary advantage means that we *could* change so that phenol-thio-urea (or Brussels sprouts) become insipid or tasteless, or so that they become bitter or astringent. There is no reason why the same kind of structure should not exist with colour or sound, tactile feelings, or odours. And where a change in us produces a change in a property, we will naturally want either to analyze it in relational terms, or at least to give an account of how it supervenes on some scientific truth which may concern reflectance and light but also concerns us. The only alternative would be to try the heroic ploy of holding that after such a change, Brussels sprouts remain *really* bitter, although everyone finds them bland. But that way, I take it, lies a general scepticism about our knowledge of secondary qualities that few would want to hold.[16]

We can say more about how firmly we get into the picture if we look in a little more detail at the teleology of the senses: what they are for. So, for example, with smell we get a very different story than with colour constancy. Smells are provoked by events. The electrical energy passed from the receptors in the cilia is greatest just *when* the original binding takes place. Hence, we habituate to them quite quickly: witness the smoker who does not realize the fug he carries around with him. This is presumably how people could bear to live in medieval cities and castles. Colours, by contrast, are perceived as the same for as long as we care to look, and through large variations of incident light, and therefore through large variations of patterns of energy falling on us.[17] It is therefore tempting, and I think correct, to speculate that smells essentially alert us to things and especially things likely to affect us. This is their function, and once they have done this job, they die away. The teleology of colour perception is different. It is not the registration of locations in the spectrum of reflected light, for if it were, we would be much more sensitive to features such as intensity of light, and colour temperature, as both film and digital cameras are. Instead, we ourselves are concerned with the discrimination and tracking of objects by their surfaces. It matters to us when surfaces change: at sunset we don't want to be misled into thinking that the berries are ripening just because the ambient light temperature has got warmer, for example. Tracking things is what colour vision is *for*. By contrast the teleology of smell is essentially one of warning us, in this case of the presence of the kinds of substances that carry effects on our well-being, for good or ill. Again, there is no prospect of an account that makes sense of any of that without bringing us ourselves firmly into the relationship. But as I have insisted, that does nothing to impugn the scientific or objective status of the relations that science discovers.

II

Perhaps Putnam's most serious objection to Williams is that he needs an "absolute notion of 'absoluteness'", yet cannot on his own grounds sustain it. This is because "*his* denial that semantic relations could figure in any purely scientific conception – not *mine* – leaves Williams with only a *perspectival* notion of absoluteness, not an absolute one".[18] And there is no doubt that Williams does say things that deny him an absolute notion of 'absoluteness', for Putnam's reasons. These can be summarized as follows. The question of whether some conception features in an absolute account of the world is the question whether we can expect convergence upon it from sensorily diverse, but rational, investigators. But the question whether we have such convergence will inevitably be a question of interpretation, and such questions are only settled by the best, most *reasonable*, interpretations that can be given of the different communities of investigators. In

Quinean terms, that leaves them open to indeterminacies of translation: within the perspective afforded by one way of taking some investigators (one translation manual) there may be convergence, but within another there may be none. Hence, the question of absoluteness is itself perspectival, and there is no "absolute notion of 'absoluteness'".

The argument is sufficiently strong in its own right, but is particularly difficult for Williams, since as Putnam makes plain, Williams is himself committed to its premises. Williams accepts a Quinean or Davidsonian view of interpretation, and the corollary of semantic indeterminacy. He may have been wrong to do so: several philosophers have argued that the various doctrines of semantic indeterminacy are much more difficult to make sense of than is usually acknowledged, and I incline to agree with them. In my view it is a non-negotiable truth that 'cats' in my mouth, and in yours too, refers to cats, and furthermore this is one determinate truth, so that we do not just have one sentence that can with equal propriety be interpreted as expressing any of an indefinite and vast number of different truths. But without adjudicating that, what of the other part? What is the argument that Williams does need a concept of 'absoluteness' that would itself feature in a scientific view of the world, or even a view of the world "couched in the language of mathematical physics"?

This is much less certain. As we have already remarked, when Williams talks of the powers of the absolute conception, it is in terms of its ability to explain all manner of things, including how it is itself possible, and also how the various perspectival conceptions we have are also possible. This is where its substance is said to lie.[19] And he happily concedes that such explanations will be "to some degree perspectival":[20] this is the part where he concedes that they would *not* themselves be available to any investigator, since others may lack a capacity to grasp the conception which we ourselves, through possessing it, can grasp. These other investigators would therefore lack an adequate conception of the explanandum (for instance, having no sense of smell, they would be unable to explain scientifically how our sense of smell works – Williams is less explicit about what kind of explanation of this, doing full justice to the explandandum, we would ourselves ever be able to mount, however much science we learn). So it seems that wearing one hat at least, he is himself happily committed to a perspectival conception of absoluteness, and the question is whether this indeed vitiates his position, as Putnam claims.

Putnam's only argument that it does so, in the paper replying to Williams, is that even Rorty could agree to a perspectival conception of absoluteness, yet Rorty has no time for the spectrum that Williams is offering. Perhaps Putnam is right that Rorty could have agreed, but one of Williams' complaints about him is that in fact he did not. Here is the passage in which he expresses what he calls the second fault in Rorty's account, the first being that he fails entirely to explain why the picture of the world being 'already there' and helping to control our descriptions of it, is so compelling. Williams writes:

> [This] leads directly to the second fault in Rorty's account: it is self defeating. If the story he tells were true, then there would be no perspective from which he could express it in this way. If it is overwhelmingly convenient to say that science describes what is already there, and if there are no deep metaphysical or epistemological issues here but only a question of what is convenient (it is "simply because" of this that we speak as we do), then what everyone should be saying, including Rorty, is that science describes a world already there. But Rorty urges us not to say that, and in doing so, in insisting, as *opposed* to that, on our talking of what it is convenient to say, he is trying to reoccupy the transcendental standpoint outside human speech and activity, which is precisely what he wants us to renounce.[21]

Anyone going this way becomes a 'perspectival absolutist': someone who goes around saying that science describes what is just there, anyway, but who regards themselves as a pragmatist, reserving a place for further comment, about our own involvement in attaining the scientific perspective. Williams' objection is not that this position is untenable, but that it is in fact not the one Rorty is advocating, while the one he is advocating instead is unavailable to him by his own lights. Earlier pragmatists had in fact noticed the problem, and embraced the position that Williams thinks Rorty ought to hold. The Oxford pragmatist F.C. Schiller wrote that:

> Realism manifestly is a theory of very great pragmatic value. In ordinary life we all assume that we live in an "external" world, which is "independent" of us, and peopled by other persons as real and as good, or better, than ourselves. And it would be a great calamity if any philosophy should feel it its duty to upset this assumption. For it works splendidly, and the philosophy which attacked it would only hurt itself.[22]

This is Williams' position as well. It is therefore not at all clear that Putnam can frighten Williams by dangling the spectre of Rorty in front of him, when on Williams' own account there is clear water between himself and Rorty, which enables him to escape the problems he poses for the latter.

There is indeed a remaining question whether perspectival absolutism is a coherent position, and without invoking the spectre of Rorty, Putnam might certainly claim that it is not, although the rhetorical tone of his discussion suggests that he thinks it is coherent but trivial. It may be difficult to prove incoherence, if we remember how perspective got into the picture in the first place. It was not by insisting on a peculiarly human or parochial element in our perception and thought about shape or mass, motion or temperature, for instance. It was only by insisting on the indeterminacy of interpretation, meaning that whether *other* people or other creatures are thought to be similarly responsive to shape, mass, or the rest is assessed only perspectivally. And that difference of focus surely leaves a coherent position that contrasts the lack of 'peculiarity' of judgements of shape or mass, while allowing the 'peculiarity' of interpretation. Or, the position might move in David Lewis's direction, supposing that the absolute status of shape or mass, their position as privileged properties, itself serves to diminish, perhaps to vanishing point, any indeterminacy of interpretation that a more catholic or egalitarian attitude to properties allows.[23] On that view, Williams was conceding too much to Quine and Davidson when he talked of interpretation, but was entirely on the right track when he talked about science.

A subsidiary reason for supposing that this might be the best line for Williams to follow is also mentioned by Putnam. This is that in doffing his cap to Davidson, in particular, Williams should remember that Davidson believes he has a transcendental argument that there are some concepts that all rational creatures must have in their repertoire: concepts such as belief, and truth and falsity. For rational creatures must manage to communicate, which implies interpreting each other, which implies the deployment of just these concepts. Yet Williams does not want to say that truth or belief belong to the absolute conception of the world, marking out the equivalent of Lockean primary qualities. This is awkward, certainly, but Williams could reply with a distinction. In the cases of scientific primary qualities, he may say, what we can properly expect is convergence not only in possession of those concepts, but in their application. We would not expect Martian scientists to work in terms of mass, but systematically diverge from us about whether one body has greater mass than another. But if Quine and Davidson are right, while we may expect the Martians to have concepts of truth and belief, there is no expectation at all that they will apply them just as we do. Their different perspective on sayings may be quite intractable, unless Lewis is right and we can expect their judgements of interpretation to be, like ours, governed by the privileged universals that are instanced in the world around us and whose instancings have a monopoly in explaining things.

III

The upshot is that Williams has room to defend his distinction as one among our concepts. He can continue to hold that the modes of thought that our sensibilities give us are more peculiarly tied to the contingent nature of those sensibilities in some cases than others. And he might do well to tiptoe past the issue of whether the reference of these modes of thought, the properties of things that they represent, are always things, properties, powers or dispositions of things that are also visible to fundamental science, and in that sense 'just there anyway'. But it is quite clear that for both him and Putnam the central issue is not with heat, colour, or odour, but with concepts that help to structure our social and moral worlds. It is the concepts of the human sciences rather than bare empirical concepts that excites both authors.

Why is Putnam opposed? He has often claimed solidarity with those Oxford philosophers, from Philippa Foot and Elizabeth Anscombe onwards, who have sought safety from wicked prescriptivists and emotivists by highlighting the place of so-called 'thick' concepts in our sayings about people and things. Thick concepts knead together 'facts' and 'values' in one package, and many writers, including Putnam and Williams alike, think that they resist disentangling into two separable components: the facts and the values. Putnam frequently uses this amalgamation, and the impossibility of disentangling *any* description of the world from some tinge of valuation, to generate his own response to Williams' spectrum. Yet this is a surprising ploy, for thick concepts are just the ones whose perspectival and often peculiar or parochial identities are most apparent. Their contingent, historical and cultural peculiarity is written on their face, as it were. I shall illustrate the problem by drawing upon a piece of history.

The noted historian Quentin Skinner details some of the rhetorical strategies employed at the beginning of the seventeenth century, by the newly emergent commercial class, in order to legitimize their activities, and deflect the opprobrium that was then easily expressed against wicked usurers, "city cormorants", and the practitioners of ungodly worldly activities in general.[24] His analysis works entirely against a background of shifting forces contending for the possession of 'thick' terms – terms which in Skinner's analysis "perform an evaluative as well as a descriptive function in our language".[25] The strategies available to the new "innovating ideologists"[26] include extending or refiguring the descriptive background to an acknowledged positive term in such a light that it could be seen to extend to the questionable activity that the ideological innovators were seeking to legitimize. Thus the innovators would co-opt religious terms with an established positive ring, for instance, by representing commercial ability as *provident*, or *prudent*, and representing commercial activity in terms of a *dedicated* life, a worldly *asceticism*, or *devotion to a calling*. Sometimes their course included taking hitherto neutral terms and adding a positive gloss: *discerning* and *penetrating* – neither of which name aristocratic virtues – begin at this time to emerge as terms of approbation, for example. And sometimes hitherto negative words were taken and revalued: *ambitious* is a good example. Conversely, hitherto positive terms such as *profligate*, *obsequious* or *condescending* – each of them actually used as *commendations* in the courtly, hierarchical and aristocratic society that was gradually being replaced – began to gain their current load of disapproval and even resentment.

In other words, the new social forces bent and adapted both the evaluative and descriptive bases for socially important terms, bringing the questionable activities within their orbit, and exploiting, or when necessary changing, their evaluative load in order to align the favourable ring with the intended application.

Now proponents of entangling and of thick concepts are quite coy about telling us when one thick concept gives way to another, as I have complained before.[27] Are we to say that at the beginning of the seventeenth century one set of concepts disappeared, and quite different ones, unfortunately expressed in homophonic terms, replaced it? The real question for anyone such as Putnam, pleased to call himself a pragmatist or sympathizer with pragmatism, is how can an equivalently interesting, insightful description of how the new ideology generated the innovation be given, without first recognizing the lynchpin of Skinner's account, the interpenetration of description, which is one thing, and evaluation, which is another, however often they happen together? It is no accident that the 'new' concepts arrived, nor that the particular appropriations took the form that they did. If historical analysis had to stop short with the vacuous commentary that what happened at the beginning of the seventeenth century was the replacement of one set of concepts by another, historical understanding would be stopped in its tracks.

It is, in one respect, worse than this. Historical understanding would not be so much stopped as smothered, prevented from getting underway at all. For, in general, diversity of concept does not imply disagreement. There are many different compatible descriptions of any one subject matter, as of course Goodman and Putnam have often reminded us. So if the change at the beginning of the seventeenth century was simply to be described as the gradual displacement of one set of thick concepts by another, there would be no reason to see the change as involving conflict: it would in principle be open to someone to conjoin both descriptions without there being any necessary reason to see a tension between them. But if *that* is where we remained, we would lose sight of the essential historical fact, which is that the change was indeed one of ideological conflict. The displacement was not unmotivated; it was not one of random conceptual drift, but the deliberate deployment of persuasive speech to foment a revaluation of different activities and qualities that they demanded. You simply cannot say that, without noticing that we are in the domains of both description and evaluation, the same things differently valued and differently compared to other paradigms of virtue or vice.

A final remark about this example may also help. If we say we are in the conceptual domain, and leave it there, then via the rule following considerations, the practices of those applying the terms pre-seventeenth century followed a rule: where there is a concept, there is a rule of application. And the ideological innovators broke rules. But I do not think that's true, at least in any interesting sense. They introduced new practices, like someone who bakes a cake a new way, or takes a new route for a journey, but such people do not break rules. They are more like someone who in some context stretches a vague term a little further or less far than some statistical majority. You can call a suitcase heavy, if you are tired, even if to the majority who are not it would be regarded as reasonably light.

The peculiarity, in Williams' sense, in perception of odour is not a philosopher's construct, but a matter of everyday experience as we notice habituation and change in ourselves. As my example shows, the similar peculiarity of *thick* thinking is similarly visible not only to philosophers, but to historians. They not only can recognize change, but also can chart the different rhetorical strategies employed by people deliberately driving change. In the period Skinner is considering, it was words like 'godly', 'pious', 'ambitious', 'prudent', that were pulled into the service of legitimizing the new commercial order. At another time we might chart the rise and fall of terms like 'cad' or 'gentleman', of virtues like politeness and courtesy, and of the various extensions and importances accorded to being saved, pure, provident, or godly. These vary historically, just as olfactory perception varies with personal factors.

This example suggests that thick terms are richly peculiar. It also suggests that Williams' spectrum should be deeply congenial to pragmatism. As Huw Price has recently written, pragmatism is essentially in the business of substituting anthropology and genealogy for metaphysics.[28] It avoids "representation" because it sees it as empty. We do not get a theory, or add to theory, but only set off down a blind alley if we hope for a story whereby we can pat ourselves on the backs, complacently content that the term "cad" refers to caddishness, and so on for all our thick terms. Rather, pragmatism looks to the relation between the term and practice. The genealogy lies in the practices of a society in which, for example, being a gentleman was a passport to status, and being a cad was the dishonourable failure to live up to the gentlemanly code. It is the *opponents* of pragmatism, the metaphysical realists, who find it important to talk of receptivity and representation, of qualities in the world that merit the application of the term, or who think of more or less static rules governing its application, in place of the fluid and contested realities which historians chart.

Out-and-out pragmatists such as Rorty or Price, think that what is true of these historically mutable terms is true of everything. Representation is always the enemy and our practice in making judgements is always the right focus to substitute for it. Williams, evidently, held that in the case of common sense and at least what we might call the inshore waters of science, this was otherwise. One reason for thinking he was right is that genealogy and anthropology, like Skinner's piece of history, can only go on against

21

the background of a shared world. We need to suppose things about the environment within which adaptation took place and practice was moulded in order to give a historical narrative, or even the sketchiest just-so stories about the evolution of a way of thought. So we would again find ourselves respecting something bearing some resemblance to Williams' spectrum: not necessarily put in terms of 'an absolute conception', but rather in terms of explanatory depth and explanatory importance. If these concepts themselves import 'perspective', or are themselves peculiar to a point of view, as Putnam's semantic argument suggests, then that neither renders them unfit for purpose nor redundant for pragmatists.

There is a general view among many philosophers that, somehow, the rule following considerations put an obstacle in front of this way of distinguishing a bare, primary-qualitied reality from anything more richly described. But this is also not an easy case to make. Suppose we agree that there is a moral to be drawn from those considerations, along the lines that representation is not to be thought of as a two-way traffic between single subject and a (part of) the world, but as a normative transaction governed by some kind of rule or convention tying us to a language, to the interpretive strategies of other people, or to a *practice*. This way we might arrive somewhere in the vicinity of Richard Rorty and think of truth being supplanted by solidarity, or we might find ourselves nearing those authors who put a constitutive role for the *consentium gentium* in determining the rightness of application of any term, and who believe that this much presence of the human serpent flattens out any interesting distinction along Williams' lines.

We might, but if so, we will certainly have left Wittgenstein somewhere behind. Wittgenstein does not emphasize conformity with others, still less any kind of Rortian solidarity or self-absorption, but a *technique*. It was engineering, not social solidarity, that the misanthropic Wittgenstein had in his blood. And in the first instance techniques give us abilities and successes explained by the intractable physical properties of things: their size, shape, elasticity, friction, charge, mass, velocity and acceleration. Again, the moral is going to be that there is no getting started on more indirect or interesting teleologies for particular parts of our judgemental repertoires without standing firm on the fact that we are situated as we are. And Williams remains correct that the terms in which that situation can be the most barely presented must occupy a special role in any of our explanatory endeavours.[29]

Notes

1 Bernard Williams, *Ethics and the Limits of Philosophy* (London: Collins, 1985), p. 139.
2 Ibid., p. 139.
3 Ibid., p. 139.

4 Bernard Williams, *Descartes: The Project of Pure Inquiry* (Harmondsworth: Penguin Books, 1978), p. 246.

5 Ibid., pp. 301–2.

6 Putnam pounces on the inconsistency in *Renewing Philosophy* (Cambridge, MA: Harvard University Press, 1992), p. 99. See also Gideon Rosen, "Objectivity and Modern Idealism", in Michaelis Michael and John O'Leary Hawthorne (eds), *Philosophy in Mind* (Dordrecht: Kluwer, 1994).

7 See, for example, R.J. Hankinson, *The Sceptics* (London: Routledge, 1995), pp. 155–92.

8 A.D. Smith, "Of Primary and Secondary Qualities", *Philosophical Review*, 99, 1990, 221–54.

9 George Berkeley, *Principles of Human Knowledge*, §9–10; Pierre Bayle, *Historical and Critical Dictionary*, entry for 'Pyrrho'.

10 Berkeley, *Principles*, §14–15.

11 Also noticed by Rosen, "Objectivity and Modern Idealism", p. 307.

12 Hilary Putnam, *Renewing Philosophy*, p. 96

13 John McDowell, *Mind and World* (Cambridge, MA: Harvard University Press, 1996), p. 29.

14 Putnam, *Renewing Philosophy*, p. 94.

15 Jonathan Bennett, "Substance, Reality and Primary Qualities", *American Philosophical Quarterly*, 2, 1965, 1–17.

16 Although I have heard this Über-realism defended on occasion, and it presumably lies behind Bertrand Russell's view in *Problems of Philosophy* that it would be "favouritism" to suppose that what we see as blue is actually blue. Putnam's emphasis on there being a *correct* way to perceive colour, raises the question of how he himself would respond to Bennett's case.

17 The classic account is C.L. Hardin, *Colour for Philosophers* (Indiana: Hackett, 1988).

18 Hilary Putnam, "Reply to Bernard Williams's Philosophy as a Humanistic Discipline", *Philosophy* 76, 2001, p. 608.

19 Williams, *Ethics and the Limits*, p. 139.

20 Ibid., p. 140.

21 Ibid., pp. 137–8.

22 F.C.S. Schiller, *Studies in Humanism* (London: Macmillan, 1907), p. 459.

23 David Lewis, "New Work for a Theory of Universals", *Australasian Journal of Philosophy* 61, 1983, 343–77.

24 Quentin Skinner, *Visions of Politics*, Vol. 1 (Cambridge: Cambridge University Press, 2002), Chapter 8.

25 Ibid., p. 146.

26 Ibid., p. 148.

27 Simon Blackburn, "Through Thick and Thin", *Proceedings of the Aristotelian Society*, Supplementary Volume 66, 1992, 285–99.

28 Huw Price and David MacArthur, "Pragmatism, Quasi-realism and the Global Challenge", in Cheryl Misak (ed.), *The New Pragmatists* (Oxford: Oxford University Press, 2007), pp. 91–120.

29 I have developed this argument at greater length in "Pragmatism, All or Some?" forthcoming. For evidence that Wittgenstein has a very nuanced attitude to these issues, see my "Wittgenstein's Irrealism", in Rudolph Haller and Johannes Brandl (eds), *Wittgenstein: Towards a Re-Evaluation* (Vienna: Verlag Hölder-Adler-Tempsky, 1990), pp. 13–26.

2

THE GOOD LIFE AND THE "RADICAL CONTINGENCY OF THE ETHICAL"

John Cottingham

The past is a foreign country: they do things differently there.

(L.P. Hartley)[1]

I Introduction

It is hard to deny that things might easily have been different.[2] A fervent Catholic in Belfast may reflect that she might easily have been a Protestant had she been brought up a few streets away. An urbane modern European who regards human sacrifice as inconceivably abhorrent might well have regarded it as quite the done thing had he been born in ancient Mesopotamia or Peru. How disturbed should we be by this apparent *contingency* in our deepest beliefs and attitudes? This will be the question I shall mostly be concerned with in this chapter. The way we answer that question has crucial implications for the ancient philosophical project of trying to determine how one should live. Bernard Williams was very pessimistic about the viability of that project, at least in anything like its traditional ambitious form; and the eloquent articulation of the grounds for such pessimism – centring on the problem of contingency – was among his most potent philosophical legacies. For those among us who harbour the hope that the ancient project is still one we can reasonably address, it is a matter of some importance to see if we can find a way of defusing that pessimism.

II Contingency and genealogy

In the last book published in his lifetime, Williams summed up one of the recurring themes in his philosophy by speaking of the "radical contingency in our current ethical conceptions", namely that "they might have been different from what they are".[3] This observation coheres with Williams' interest in the aetiology of ethics, and its subversive potentialities. Friedrich

Nietzsche, whose ruminations on the 'genealogy' of ethics had a certain fascination for Williams, evidently intended those ruminations to be unsettling: the claims of Christian morality to command universal allegiance, for example, are supposed to be undermined once we see its origins as stemming from the craven desire of the herd to protect themselves against those of superior energy and power.[4] In similar, albeit rather more nuanced, vein, Williams made the striking point that in ethics (unlike science) "reflection can destroy knowledge".[5] And the kind of reflection he had in mind was aetiological and historical.

To uncover the historical roots of a cultural phenomenon is not, of course, necessarily to show it is suspect. The subversive forays of Nietzsche in ethics (or Freud, in religion) would be less troubling than they are if they rested merely on a crude genetic fallacy. Williams himself, moreover, was quite clear that the availability of a plausible genealogical story need not necessarily be demoralizing (he cites Hume's account of the genesis of the 'artificial' virtue of justice as an example of a historical or quasi-historical story that has no real tendency to undermine our commitment to that virtue, and to its value).[6] So the contingency that he took to be disturbing is not merely a function of the contingencies of history. We came to where we now are by a historical path that might, presumably, have been otherwise; but there may still be respects in which the path can be judged to be a productive and worthwhile one – one that has traversed fruitful territory and led us to a place where we are glad to have arrived.[7]

Though the fact that our ethics has a history need not necessarily unsettle us, the historian's perspective does characteristically involve a certain distancing, and this feature may take us nearer to discerning what it is that bears the weight of Williams' worries. His pejorative use of the term 'local' is highly significant in this connection. Caught up in the everyday discourse of the 'local culture' to which they belong, people may subscribe to certain ethical values; indeed, some of the very concepts they use (what Williams famously called the 'thick' ethical concepts)[8] may embody certain implicit judgements about what is to be admired or condemned. But the cultural historian, from a more detached perspective, may be able, while fully understanding the discourse and its rules, to prescind from its implicit values: he may even be able to "see a whole segment of the local discourse as involving a mistake."[9] From this there arises a possible threat to our *own* current conceptions, which can be extrapolated, as it were, from our ability to apply such a critique to previous cultures. Witch-hunting provides a convenient paradigm: we can now, when we look back, identify the cultural milieu in which 'witches' were persecuted as embodying pervasive errors.[10] Such errors, to our present eyes, did not simply involve particular misjudgements – burning the wrong people from time to time – but rather arose from the fact that the entire segment of discourse relating to witches embodied (we can now see) deeply suspect concepts and unfounded classifications.

Cashed out in this way, however, the worry appears to be not so much about contingency as about *error*. The fact that our ethical discourse might have been otherwise is not in itself the problem, so much as the fact that it might be mistaken. If we can retrospectively condemn segments of past ethical systems as unstable, because they can now be seen to have rested on mistakes, might not future generations be able to pass similar scathing judgement on our own ways of talking and judging, indeed on whole chunks of our current moral discourse, and its associated array of concepts and classifications?

Yet on further reflection this thought does not, in itself, seem any more unsettling than the thought that our current scientific discourse, for example, might one day be seen to embody pervasive errors. Simple induction leads us to suppose that some, perhaps a great deal, of our current science will in the course of time need revising, perhaps radically. Yet that possibility, or even likelihood, seems not so much a reason for despair or paralysing anxiety as a reason to bear in mind our fallibility, and meanwhile do the best we can – taking care not just to apply our concepts as carefully as possible, but to keep a wary critical eye on the concepts themselves, and to be prepared to probe the presuppositions which they encapsulate.

Such recommendations are hardly new: it was Socrates who famously urged that "the unexamined life is not worth living",[11] thereby inaugurating the very process of critical philosophical inquiry. Admittedly Socrates was seen as a stingray;[12] but the paralysis he produced was not supposed by him or anyone else to be the inevitable result of critical distancing *per se*, but simply a result of his success in spotlighting actual confusions and inconsistencies in the beliefs and attitudes of his interlocutors. Perhaps Williams' heightened awareness of the possibilities of error in our current ethical discourse can be construed as Socratic in spirit; but if so, it does not in itself seem enough to justify his ethical pessimism. For why should not the very reminder of the possibility of error serve as a stimulus for scrutiny and improvement, rather than a generator of permanent paralysis?

III Levels of contingency

Our preliminary conclusions do not so far seem to give much support to Williams' view of the contingency of our ethical conceptions as something with disturbing implications. But before rushing to judgement, it will be useful to explore in more detail what exactly such alleged contingency amounts to.

Things might have been different. At the most basic level, this may be construed *biologically*. We human beings might have been different. We might have been tigers; we might have been lambs. Actually, of course, that makes no sense. A single evolutionary process, we may grant, led to the rise of species like the sheep and the tiger, and us, but the branch of the 'tree' of

26

life to which we humans belong diverged so far ago from that which produced these other mammals that it is incoherent to suppose that *we* might have been such creatures.

Nonetheless, there are concerns that do seem to be raised once we adopt a biologically informed genealogical perspective on our origins. Our human nature came into being, let us grant, as a result of various complex evolutionary pressures, which might, under different circumstances, have produced creatures very similar to us but with slightly different characteristics. This Darwinian thought may seem to put pressure on the comfortable Aristotelian conception of a determinate human nature, oriented towards a goal that represents the good for its kind. If species are fluid, capable of modification under the influence of random mutation and selective environmental pressure, then a slightly different creature, with presumably different 'goals' and 'goods' might easily have replaced us (or might still do so). So the good for humankind seems to lose its exalted status as a kind of lodestar to guide the course of our lives, and becomes instead but one of many possible patterns of flourishing for creatures of our type, liable in due course to be superseded.

Such worries turn out under scrutiny to be of negligible force. To begin with, the evolutionary changes here invoked are going to be ones that operate over many millions of years. We do not know exactly when 'modern' *homo sapiens* came into existence, but there is good reason to suppose that our species has remained biologically stable for many millennia. And certainly the human beings with whom Aristotle or the Buddha or Jesus were concerned were, in all respects relevant to biological flourishing, pretty much identical with us. Even if there were not ample scientific proof of this (including, for example, that from DNA analysis), the indirect evidence from a whole range of literary texts, such as the epic poetry and drama of the ancient world, provides an overwhelming case for supposing that its inhabitants were beings for whom the basic biological determinants of well-being were no different from what they are for us today. If there is any contingency that threatens the equilibrium of our ethical conceptions, it is not going to be found by looking at the realm of biology and the alleged instabilities to be discovered there.

Culture is a different matter. Here we see massive and recognizable changes over historically manageable periods of time. It is not just, as Williams himself so eloquently demonstrated, that if we go back far enough, for example, to classical times, we find ethical appraisal and its associated virtues arranged around rather different priorities (for example, concerns about shame and honour) than those which receive primacy in later ethical writers.[13] Even if we go back a generation or two, to the world of our own parents or grandparents, we find conceptions of a good human life incorporating models of what sort of behaviour is to be admired and emulated that are very different from our own. As but one example, influential in the

27

childhoods of many born around the middle of the twentieth century, one may consider the virtues which are taken for granted as characterizing an admirable life in C.S. Forrester's novels about the imaginary British naval hero Horatio Hornblower – a character whose exploits are set in the Napoleonic wars, but whose conceptions of virtue unmistakeably reflect the 'stiff upper lip' ideals of the British officer of the Second World War period and its aftermath. The standards Hornblower sets himself include the firm suppression of the emotions and an even firmer ban on their overt expression, rigid adherence to obligations associated with rank and station, punctilious observance of accepted norms of military and class deportment, and a disdain for, or at least a constant willed subordination of, private and family concerns as against those of professional duty. It is an ethos which we can recognize, and perhaps admire; but even in the relatively short time that has elapsed since those books were written (the 1950s), a host of social and cultural developments have eroded its attraction as an unquestionable model for the good life – or at the very least its appeal has ceased to be able to operate upon us in quite the way it did then.

Humans are ingenious, versatile creatures – that is our strength. We seldom rest content with existing ways of doing things, but constantly devise, from generation to generation, new patterns of living, new models of conduct, new modes of social interaction. We are also, of course, powerfully shaped by inherited tradition, however much we might want to deny it. But traditions, if they are living traditions, are constantly subject to reinterpretation and modification as each generation responds to changing social and environmental pressures. There does indeed seem to be a radical contingency here, and one whose implications can seem unsettling. The code that guided a character such as Hornblower gained its strength and authority over him from a certain aura of necessity. For such a person, deviations might, under the pressure of fatigue or hardship, sometimes have seemed tempting, but they were immediately ruled out: in the kind of phrase that recurs throughout the novels, "however much he might have wanted to, he could not, simply *could* not, bring himself to contemplate it". This *given-ness* of an ethical code, the sense that it provides the fixed framework for ethical deliberation, rather than being itself a possible subject of deliberation, is precisely what seems threatened by reflection about its contingent historical origins and its likely future modification, or even demise.

IV Variety and convergence

Ethical contingency, as understood at the stage of the argument we have now reached, draws its disruptive power not just from the fact of there being conceivable alternatives to our present ways of doing things, nor from the possibility that some of our ethical practices and beliefs may involve error, but from the actual existence, in our recent or earlier history, of alternative ethical codes to our current ones.[14] These alternative codes, moreover, though they may not present themselves as live options for our allegiance, are not ones we can airily dismiss as 'primitive' or 'obsolete' (Williams was adamant about the dangers of such 'patronizing' attitudes).[15] On the contrary, they may contain many elements we can recognize as perfectly serviceable in their own terms, and indeed even admirable, or able to teach us something. All this throws our own current conceptions into relief: instead of constituting a self-evidently appropriate way of mapping out the domain of the ethical, they appear as simply a map of one local part of the territory, which has no intrinsic title to qualify as a better dwelling place than any of the others.

Yet perhaps this result is not as troubling as it first seems. To see this, it is worth opening our eyes to the variety of conceptions of the good life already to be found, not diachronically, by looking back over time, but synchronically, within our own contemporary culture. There are many lives we already count as good: the life of the scholar, the life of the craftsman, the life of the farmer, the life of the musician, the life of the teacher, the life of the doctor. Different individual talents and circumstances call for different models of virtue, and the contingency here seems entirely benign; for whoever supposed that talk of 'the good for humankind' demands a 'one size fits all' account of excellence. To think that the good life must require a monolithic account of virtue would be as absurd as insisting that everyone in society should try to cultivate the excellences of the brain surgeon. Many different patterns of living can be good, and there is nothing unsettling, for the accomplished painter who happens to be unmusical, in the thought that had things been different she might better have cultivated the skills of the violinist. Even types of calling which we might now often look on with a dubious eye – the life of the recruiting sergeant, for example, or the life of the sharpshooter – may be lives towards which under certain circumstances (e.g. when the nation is threatened by invaders) we may feel admiration and gratitude. Again, different circumstances call for different visions of how one should live, and the contingency here seems entirely benign.

Nevertheless (and this perhaps brings us closer to Williams' underlying worries about ethical discourse), in order for us to decide whether all these different particular modes of life can count as ethically admirable, we seem to need more than a long shopping list of particular activities and excellences. We seem to want them to fit into, or at least be consistent with, some more general template, by reference to which we can say that they are all authentic forms of human flourishing. That requirement seems to be equally if not more pressing when we do not merely consider the variety of roles and excellences within our own society, but start to look across, from the 'local' ethical culture, towards other culturally diverse societies elsewhere on the planet, or at the ethical cultures of past ages.

One way of meeting the 'general template' requirement would be to find sufficient overlap between all the various local human cultures and epochs to be able to say that all the different ethical discourses converged on certain universal ethical values. Perhaps all human beings have certain typical needs and desires that underlie the apparent differences in the way their various cultures are structured and these might supply the wherewithal for a non-local grounding of ethics. Williams, however, was very pessimistic about this possibility. A project of basing an objective ethics on agreed considerations regarding human nature is, he warned, "not very likely to succeed", given the wide variety in human societies and forms of life, and the "many and various forms of human excellence which will not all fit together into a one harmonious whole".[16]

But what exactly is the worry here? Talk of the incommensurability of various forms of human excellence calls to mind Williams' famous 'Gauguin problem' (a problem he devised to explore the phenomenon of 'moral luck', but which, like so many of his fertile ideas, has many philosophical ramifications).[17] If artistic success may be achieved at the cost of abandoning moral commitments, and there is an incommensurability about the goods involved here, then the philosophical project of providing a rational map of the good life faces an impasse – unless of course we cede to the 'morality' system its demand for universal precedence (something that Williams saw no rational reason to do). Against this, however, I have argued elsewhere that the Gauguin case is not made out. Certainly there is no evidence that artistic excellence can be achieved *only* at the cost of sacrificing moral values. But more to the point, the very idea of some kind of inherent conflict here seems doubtful; for in so far as great art involves the full engagement of our human sensibilities and responsiveness to others, there is every reason to suppose that the cultivation of artistic and of moral sensibility are intricately interlinked. This is not to deny that many great artists have led highly egotistical lives (what might be called the 'Ingmar Bergman syndrome'); it is merely to reject the romantic, self-exculpatory fantasy that addressing such failings might have threatened their artistic achievement.[18]

Of course, it may not be possible for a given human being to pursue everything that has value in such a way as to fit all those pursuits into a "harmonious whole". Yet this seems as much as anything a problem of time and resources: we are often forced to choose, and to make sacrifices, in order to achieve part of the excellence of which we are capable. This is perhaps not an ideal state of affairs: indeed, George Harris has in a recent book spent several chapters portraying it as a deeply tragic aspect of the human condition: "our values are pursued in a world that is very unfriendly and hostile to our efforts and … our own deepest values war against each other with tragic results".[19] But at the risk of seeming unsympathetic to Harris's grief, we need to remember that many, perhaps most value-conflicts are hardly catastrophic: a comfortable Western academic bewailing how his recreational hiking was cutting into the time available for wine-tasting might reasonably expect the response 'Get over it!'[20] More seriously, it is of course true and important that we cannot achieve everything of which we are capable; but this seems to be a point about human finitude rather than about some intractable tangle of incommensurability. Our human mortality, and our weakness, put severe limits on the good that any one person can achieve in a lifetime,[21] and one result of this is that any plausible blueprint for the good life will have to find space for the concept of sacrifice. But a study of the psycho-dynamics of sacrifice (something, as far as I know, that few if any moral philosophers have undertaken) would I suspect fall very far short of establishing that it is an inherently negative item on the balance sheet of human existence.[22] *Omnia praeclara sunt difficilia*, Spinoza reminds us: fine things are hard.[23] And the difficulty, the struggle, so far from being something always to be deplored from the standpoint of the good life, can surely be, for finite beings, a way of achieving a heightened awareness of the very preciousness of those goods we pursue.

As for Williams' broader worry about the wide variation in human societies and ethical systems, this is an important fact, and can readily be conceded. And in the light of that, it can also be conceded that it is implausible to suppose a general account of 'human nature' will generate a single distinctive pattern for human flourishing. But working this up into a dire problem is surely rather like bewailing the fact that the specification of a particular species (e.g. the rose) will not in itself be able to determine all the properties that must be present in any flourishing variety of that species. The various different types of rose tended by the horticulturalist may all constitute valid examples of flourishing for that species; and what is more, despite their distinctive virtues and splendours they all have something in common – that characteristic form that makes them instantly recognizable as roses.

In analogous fashion, it seems to me that we can contemplate the fascinating variety in human cultures and ethical systems yet at the same time see all or many of them, in their different ways, as satisfying or approaching the conditions for human fulfilment. One of the achievements of the Mexican director Alejandro Gonzalez Inarritu and his screenwriter Guillermo Arriaga in their film *Babel* (2006) is to portray characters embedded in vastly different societies and cultures (the subsistence Moroccan herdsman, the Japanese middle-class schoolgirl, the poor Mexican domestic worker and the wealthy American tourist), yet at the same time to disclose those diverse cultures as differing vehicles for the development of a common humanity, manifested in deep underlying common needs and desires – for physical security, for protection against vulnerability, for the development of personal relationships, for love and affection and family loyalty, and so on.

This is not the naïve claim that all varieties of human society are equally good. Just as varieties of plant may be judged failures, because of susceptibility to disease, or limited tolerance to variations in climate or soil, so there are ethical systems that do not satisfactorily serve the needs of their members, or which may even exclude whole groups within society from the chance of developing their talents properly. But this brings us back to the point that some ethical systems, and their associated 'thick' concepts, may embody mistakes. And that, as we have seen, is a different concern from the concern about contingency as such. As far as the latter worry is concerned, our conclusion from this section must be that the manifest variety in ethical systems, and the fact that our own happens to be but one among many, need have no inherently unsettling force, provided we have good reason to think that the ethical system to which we belong subserves an authentic form of human flourishing.

V Ultimate contingency and meaning

Our conclusions so far, while moving further than Williams would have countenanced in the direction of human essentialism (the idea of necessary and universal aspects of human nature), nevertheless does not escape the idea of contingency at a deeper level. Ultimately, we all share certain capacities and sensibilities because, quite simply, that is the way our species is, the way it has evolved. Must acknowledging this residual element of ultimate or 'bedrock' contingency be a cause for anxiety for the ethicist or the theorist of the good life?[24]

An example of a thinker who seems able to take such contingency on board with relative equanimity is David Wiggins:

> In philosophy as it is, there is a tendency for a first-order morality to be conceived as a structured array of propositions or judgments. But [it is better] to conceive of such an ethic more dispositionally, as a nexus of distinctive sensibilities, cares, and concerns that are expressed in distinctive patterns of emotional and practical response ... Such a nexus will be conceived by a Neo-Humean genealogist or aetiologist as something with a prehistory and a history as well as a present and a possible future.[25]

Wiggins is not unsettled by the terminus of contingency reached by these aetiological reflections, since he does not accept the widespread philosophical doctrine that, in order to be sound, our ethics require theoretical justification. The "title to correctness" of our ethical understanding, he argues, "does not depend on its degree or articulacy or the immediate availability to the moral subject of propositional grounds adduced for it".[26] The fact is that we inherit a certain nature, are inducted into a certain

ethical culture, and develop sensitivities and capacities for practical appreciation and judgement; when to these are added certain frameworks of
reciprocity and solidarity that naturally arise out of human beings needing
to interact together in stable and productive ways, then, so runs the argument, we have all that we need, or should desire, to justify an ethical
system. That does not mean that ethical disagreements cannot arise; but in
our attempts to resolve those disagreements, once we have delved down to
the bedrock level of our "distinctive sensibilities, cares and concerns", then
there is no more to say.

Could we rest content, as Wiggins suggests we should, with an ethics, a
theory of the good life, grounded on this ultimately contingent base?
Towards the end of his life, Williams appeared, against the dominant tone
of his writings, to allow that this might be possible. In his Royal Institute
Lecture of the year 2000, "Philosophy as a Humanistic Discipline", he
canvassed a defusing strategy that would apparently enable us to swallow
ultimate contingency without any fear of resulting dyspepsia:

> In fact ... once one goes *far enough* in recognizing contingency, the
> problem ... does not arise at all ... The supposed problem comes
> from the idea that a vindicatory history of our outlook is what we
> would really like to have, and the discovery that [our outlook] has
> the kind of contingent history that it does have is a disappoint-
> ment, which leaves us with at best a second best. But ... why
> should we think that? Precisely because we are not unencumbered
> intelligences selecting in principle among all possible outlooks, we
> can accept that this outlook is ours just because of the history that
> has made it ours, or, more precisely, has both made us, and made
> the outlook as something that is ours. We are no less contingently
> formed than the outlook is, and the formation is significantly the
> same. We and our outlook are not simply in the same place at the
> same time. If we really understand this, deeply understand it, we can
> be free of what is indeed another scientistic illusion, that it is our
> job as rational agents to search for ... a system of political and ethical
> ideas which would be the best from an absolute point of view.[27]

The defusing strategy is presented with great elegance, but it is not clear
that it succeeds in allaying the disquiet that arises from confrontation with
ultimate contingency. Both Wiggins and Williams represent that disquiet as
at root an epistemic one, about the "title to correctness" of our ethical
understanding (as Wiggins puts it), or about the (misguided) hankering for
an absolute perspective to validate our ethical ideas (as for Williams). But
suppose we lay aside such allegedly confused epistemic worries, and accept
that there is nothing more to be had by way of ethical knowledge than what
arises from the "first order activity of acting and arguing" within the

framework of ethical ideas we happen to have, coupled with the second order philosophical activity of "reflecting on those ideas at a more general level and trying to make better sense of them" and "the historical activity of understanding where they came from".[28] What would there be left to be anxious about?

A life lived within the framework so described could surely meet most of the requirements of a good life. Consider an individual inducted into a given ethical culture, in the way envisaged by Wiggins and Williams; let us assume that circumstances of her life are such as to provide all the basic biological and social preconditions for human flourishing, such as being healthy, well nourished, emotionally nurtured, free from repression or exploitation, able to make her own decisions without interference, and so on. The social and ethical culture in which she finds herself allows, let us assume, for the flowering of a significant range of her talents and capacities, and also for the cultivation not just of a variety of enjoyable and satisfying activities, but also for the development of those moral sensibilities and dispositions that are indispensable for human beings if they are to live together in a stable and mutually fulfilling way.

None of these various elements of a good human life seem likely to be undermined, for its subject, by reflecting on the fact that the ethical framework which structures her life is, in the various ways we have explored, ultimately contingent. But there is a further component of a good human life that does seem more vulnerable to such reflection, and that is *meaningfulness*. A good life for human beings needs to be not merely one that is healthy and flourishing and productive and morally sound, but also one that provides a sense of meaning or purpose. The twentieth-century French existentialists were expert at describing that sense of dislocation, or disorientation that arises when meaning ebbs away, and we are face to face with absurdity or futility. That mere contingency, mere 'facticity', threatens meaning is a worry that is not easily brushed aside.[29]

The nature of the worry can be seen by looking back to the more secure outlooks that obtained before modern anxieties about loss of meaning gained a foothold.[30] Within the teleological frameworks that informed much of the pre-modern Western ethical tradition, human life is held to be meaningful in virtue of a kind of fit or harmony between our human nature and the nature of the cosmos. In the Platonic and the Stoic traditions, for example, the world is fashioned in accordance with principles of order and rationality, and we, who are part of that ordered cosmos, achieve the best of which we are capable by aligning ourselves with that rational order. In Christian cosmology, itself owing not a little to these Platonic and Stoic roots, our lives achieve their meaning and purpose when oriented towards that ultimate reality that is the source of all goodness and value.[31]

The ethical pessimism discernible in the bulk of Williams' work derives, it seems to me, from a certain lingering dismay at what one might call the

'cosmological' contingency with which we are confronted when such transcendent sources of meaning and value are rejected. To speak of existential
Angst would be a trifle overblown for a writer of Williams' lightness of
touch and disdain for grandiloquence. But his dominant pessimism about
the ethical project seems to signal that even while urging himself to embrace
contingency, he still has a residual hankering for a worldview that offers
something more. Acknowledging that in the end "things merely *are*" (to
borrow the apt title phrase from a recent book by Simon Critchley)[32] – in
other words, abandoning any hope of a teleological framework to give our
human lives a purpose and meaning – leads Williams in his mainstream
work to what is finally a tragic view of the human condition. As he put it in
his masterpiece, *Shame and Necessity*, it is a view that "refuses to present
human beings [as] ideally in harmony with their world", and which "has no
room for a world that, if it were understood well enough, could instruct us
how to be in harmony with it".[33]

Williams, in the spirit of Nietzsche, closes the door here on the possibility of a supernatural or transcendent basis for meaning and harmonious
living. Nietzsche himself, of course, imagined that the resulting impasse
could be circumvented by some kind of act of will whereby humans (of an
exalted type) could somehow create meaning and value for themselves – a
confused fantasy that Williams, to his credit, was never tempted by.[34] I
cannot, of course, make something valuable by choosing or willing it (as if I
could make cardboard nutritious by deciding to eat it); indeed, this idea
precisely puts the cart before the horse, since in truth my choices or acts of
will can be worthwhile only in so far as their objects already have independent value.[35] What emerges from Williams' rejection of transcendence
seems instead to be a kind of resigned acquiescence, an acceptance that we
have to rest content in the prospect of a life grounded in no more than how
things "merely are". Yet there is a tension here, since the very acknowledgement implicit in that 'merely' carries with it a concealed yearning for
more. Even as we insist on our finitude, at that very moment, as Pascal and
Descartes remind us, we implicitly acknowledge the idea, at least, of something beyond it.[36] To construct a 'closed' theory of the good life, grounded
in no more than how we actually are, can seem like a wilful attempt to
assimilate us to beings without transcendent aspirations. Yet the ineradicable 'restlessness' of which Augustine eloquently spoke,[37] that powerful
desire to reach beyond the given which Pascal referred to when he declared
that "humankind transcends itself",[38] are but two expressions of a per-
ennial theme: it is the glory, or the wretchedness, of human beings never
wholly to acquiesce in the confines that structure our existence. Thomas
Nagel has put the resulting paradox with characteristic succinctness:

> Given that the transcendental step is natural to us humans, can we
> avoid absurdity by refusing to take that step and remaining entirely

within our sublunar lives? Well, we cannot refuse consciously,
for to do that we would have to be aware of the viewpoint we
were refusing to adopt. The only way to avoid the relevant self-
consciousness would be either never to attain it or to forget it –
neither of which can be achieved by the will.[39]

To make our ethical home within an entirely closed and contingent cosmos,
and pretend that we are wholly comfortable so doing, seems a violation of
our human nature. The options now seem severely limited. One would be a
kind of ethical quietism, the attempt at a sort of willed complacency in the
face of brute facticity. Another, equally evasive, would be the attempt to
detach ourselves from our plight and pretend it doesn't really matter
much – the strategy of irony.[40] A third option would be defiance – the kind
of response pioneered by Nietzsche and later perfected by Camus.[41] Yet to
this there is a severe cost. Simon Critchley, focusing (in the book mentioned above) on the poems of Wallace Stephens, which so eloquently
celebrate the 'mereness of things', ends up, with commendable honesty,
acknowledging something of the self-defeating nature of such a defiant
celebration of contingency:

> [A]t the moment of saying "God is dead, therefore I am", it is
> utterly unclear in what the "I am" consists. It is a mere leaf blown
> by the wind, a vapour, an ember, a bubble. The moment of the
> ego's assertion, in swelling up to fill a universe without God, is also
> the point at which it shrinks to insignificance.[42]

VI Coda: Confidence, hope and ethical necessity

Bernard Williams ended his most systematic reflections on the nature of
ethics by appealing to the need to have *confidence* in our ethical practices in
the face of radical contingency.[43] It is fair to say that this appeal, and the
nature of the confidence involved, have largely mystified his critics and
interpreters.[44] But (if a final aetiological hypothesis may be allowed) that
aspiration to confidence seems very likely to be a wan, ghostly trace of the
ancient theological virtue of *hope*. That virtue makes sense, for the believer,
because it has, or is taken to have, an object; but if, by contrast, all you
have is that "things merely are" – that we and the universe are "just there",
as Bertrand Russell[45] once put it – then confidence appears arbitrary. At
worst, indeed, it would seem to be incoherent; for what, precisely, is the
confidence supposed to be *about*? We already know the natural world is
there – that, for the secularist,[46] is a matter of bleak awareness, rather than
confidence. What is also presumably known or believed by the secularist is
that the world is in no way hospitable to our activities or aspirations
except, as it were, temporarily and purely by accident. He or she may,

presumably, wish that it would continue to be hospitable for as long as possible to whatever she or he wants or plans to do; but has no particular reason to think the tiny window that has opened for the furthering of her projects, or those of her associates, will not at any moment close, irreversibly and finally, for her and them, as it will inevitably, for the whole planet, sooner or later.

The shape of the difficulty finally emerges if one contrasts Williams' authentic pessimism with his later espousal of the 'defusing' strategy for accommodating contingency. In the defusing strategy, we are supposed to gain comfort from the thought that the same collection of random forces and circumstances that generated us human beings also generated the outlook we have: "we are no less contingently formed than our outlook". The authentic earlier pessimism, by contrast, mourned the loss of "a world that, if it were understood well enough, could instruct us how to be in harmony with it". Yet a faint trace of the earlier aspiration to harmony recurs in the defusing strategy: a certain sort of *fit* is still claimed to exist, since our (utterly contingent) outlook is no less contingent than our (utterly contingent) existence. "We and our outlook are not just in the same place at the same time", as Williams somewhat enigmatically puts it. But of course there is no real harmony here, just a concatenation of contingencies. We happen to be a certain way, we happen to have certain desires, and to value things in a certain way, and that is all there is to say. This is something we can perhaps learn to put up with, or perhaps try heroically to celebrate in the manner of Nietzsche, before he went mad, or Sisyphus, before his torments broke him; but *confidence* seems sadly out of place.

So if confidence doesn't work, and we wish to put aside irony and despair, then what remains is hope. Since hope, unlike confidence, is a theological virtue, it takes us beyond those 'limits of philosophy' which are the implicit and explicit theme of so much of Williams' work. For those who can espouse it, hope enables us to reach forward, beyond the contingent circumstances of our situation, and aspire to align ourselves with objective, non-contingent values that represent the best that humanity can become. Though many aspects of our outlook may, to be sure, be dependent on the manifold contingencies that shaped us, we are nevertheless, on this traditional religious picture, innately endowed with glimmerings of eternal and necessary values – for example, that cruelty is wrong, or compassion good, in all possible worlds. As G. K. Chesterton phrased it (albeit in characteristically mannered fashion):

> Reason and justice grip the remotest and the loneliest star ... You can imagine any mad botany or geology you please. Think of forests of adamant with leaves of brilliants ... But don't fancy that all that frantic astronomy would make the smallest difference to the reason and justice of conduct. On plains of opal, under cliffs cut

out of pearl, you would still find a notice-board, "Thou shalt not steal."[47]

These claims of universality and necessity are rhetorically phrased; but with the (perhaps surprising) current revival of various forms of ethical objectivism they are by no means so philosophically outlandish as they might have seemed during the heyday of ethical subjectivism in the middle of the twentieth century.[48] At all events, what turns out to obtain, on the traditional religious picture of a divinely-grounded ethics, is not, after all, the radical contingency of the ethical but its complete opposite – the radical necessity of the ethical: ethical truths, eternally generated by a necessarily existing source of goodness, obtain in all possible worlds.[49]

Such a worldview, if coherent, has obvious implications for the significance of human existence. The script, as it were, so far from being just a randomly assembled one that we have to make what sense of we may, instead becomes resonant with meaning.[50] Though it may take hard work to discern, and even harder work to pursue properly, there will be an objective teleological framework for human life; and if a pattern for the good life has been laid down for us,[51] then we have something to reach forward to, in the faith that our efforts need not be in vain. This does not imply some naïve supposition of guaranteed success; the human condition is such that in the pursuit of the good life there are always hostages to fortune along the way. But without hope in a non-contingent structure that grounds our human existence, and underlies our moral aspirations, the threat of futility or absurdity seems hard to banish completely. Some of our activities, to be sure, may still be satisfying, or achieve worthwhile things, and perhaps that is all we can, or should, aim for. But unless humans, *per impossibile*, find a way of stilling their transcendent aspirations, there will remain the background fear that all the frantic endeavours of those "imbecile worms of the earth", as Pascal called us,[52] cannot succeed in making our lives as a whole ultimately meaningful. And in the absence of meaningfulness, we will lack one of the most basic ingredients of the good life for humankind.

Acknowledgements

A version of part of this chapter was given at the University of Birmingham, May 2007, as the opening keynote address for the Royal Institute of Philosophy one-day conference on "Happiness and the Meaning of Life". I am grateful to many participants for helpful comments on that occasion, especially to Jimmy Lenman and Thad Metz. I am also most grateful to Adrian Moore for his valuable comments on the penultimate draft of this chapter, and to comments from him and from Anita Avramides, Robert Frazier, Penelope Mackie and Howard Robinson at a discussion group at Oxford. I should also like to thank Daniel Callcut for his encouragement and for his perceptive comments, and John Kekes, for his thoughtful reflections which, while coming from a different perspective from my own, have nonetheless stimulated me to think further about my position.

Notes

1 *The Go-Between* (London: Hamish Hamilton, 1953), Prologue, opening sentence.
2 Hard to deny, but not, of course, impossible, as witnessed, for example, by the metaphysical system of Spinoza.
3 Bernard Williams, *Truth and Truthfulness* (Princeton, NJ: Princeton University Press, 2002), p.20.
4 Friedrich Nietzsche, *Towards the Genealogy of Morals* [*Zur Genealogie der Moral*, 1887], Essay 1.
5 Bernard Williams, *Ethics and the Limits of Philosophy* (London: Collins, 1985), p. 148.
6 *Truth and Truthfulness*, p. 36.
7 To put it another way, history and genealogy may sometimes provide what Peter Railton has called a *vindicatory explanation* as opposed to a *debunking explanation*. See Railton, "Morality, Ideology and Reflection", in Edward Harcourt (ed.), *Morality, Reflection and Ideology* (Oxford: Oxford University Press, 2000), p. 141.
8 *Ethics and the Limits of Philosophy*, pp. 129–30.
9 Ibid., p. 148.
10 The issue is by no means of merely antiquarian interest, as may be seen for example from the troubled history of the South African Suppression of Witchcraft Act (1959). See J. Hund, "African Witchcraft and Western Law, Psychological and Cultural Issues", *Journal of Contemporary Religion*, 19(1) (2004), 67–84.
11 Plato, *Apology* [*c.* 399 BC], 38a.
12 Plato, *Meno* [c.380 BC], 79e.
13 Bernard Williams, *Shame and Necessity* (Berkeley, CA: University of California Press, 1993).
14 Compare Nietzsche:

> Just because our moral philosophers knew the facts of morality only very approximately in arbitrary extracts or in accidental epitomes – for example as the morality of their environment, their class, their church, the spirit of their time, their climate and part of the world – just because they were poorly informed and not even very curious about different peoples, times and past ages – they never laid eyes on the real problems of morality; for these emerge only when we compare *many* moralities. In all 'science of morals' so far one thing was *lacking*, strange as it may sound: the problem of morality itself; what was lacking was any suspicion that there was something problematic here. What the philosophers called 'a rational foundation for morality' and tried to supply was, seen in the right light, merely a scholarly variation of the common *faith* in the prevalent morality; a new means of *expression* for this faith; and thus just another fact within a particular morality; indeed, in the last analysis a kind of denial that this morality might ever be considered problematic – certainly the very opposite of an examination, analysis, questioning, and vivisection of this very faith.
> (Friedrich Nietzsche, *Beyond Good and Evil* [*Jenseits von Gut und Böse*, 1886], §186, trans. W. Kaufmann (New York: Random House, 1966))

15 *Shame and Necessity*, p. 10.
16 *Ethics and the Limits of Philosophy*, p. 153.
17 See Bernard Williams, *Moral Luck* (Cambridge: Cambridge University Press, 1981), Chapter 2.
18 See further J. Cottingham, *On the Meaning of Life* (London: Routledge, 2003), Chapter 1.
19 George Harris, *Reason's Grief* (Cambridge: Cambridge University Press, 2006), pp. 15–16.
20 The example is of course unfairly trivial. It should be noted in justice to Harris that he produces an interesting argument to show that any compromise strategy – one aimed at living the best life available to you given your interests and abilities – would still leave a "value deficit" (in the sense that that the rejected, second best, life would contain goods not included in the best life; *Reason's Grief*, p. 216). As will be clear from what follows, I would not dispute the ineliminable element of sacrifice in the best human life, merely its interpretation as tragic.
21 The point is exponentially multiplied when we consider the problems of organizing our collective arrangements in an attempt to accommodate the competing goals of different individuals: Harris's worries about intractable value-conflicts certainly gain momentum when applied in the political and social dimension. (Compare, for example, the discussions of the tension between liberty and security: "the greatest system of freedom from constraint cannot be realized in the safest possible world"; *Reason's Grief*, p. 218.)
22 There seems to be a difference between merely missing out on something (unavoidably, I have to miss the cricket match if I want to go to the rugby), and sacrificing in the richer sense of consciously deciding to give up something important for the sake of some higher good (I owe this point to Daniel Callcut). There may, moreover, be goods (for example, goods connected with moral growth and interpersonal development) whose very realization is inherently bound up with a measure of sacrifice on the part of the agents involved.
23 Benedict Spinoza, *Ethics* [*Ethica more geometrico demonstrata*, c. 1665], final sentence.
24 Compare Kant's famous worry: "If all value were conditional, and thus contingent, then no supreme principle could be found for reason at all." Immanuel Kant, *Groundwork for the Metaphysics of Morals* [*Grundlegung zur Metaphysik der Sitten*, 1785], Chapter 2, §32 (AK IV 428), trans. Thomas E. Hill Jr and Arnulf Zweig, *The Moral Law* (Oxford: Oxford University Press, 2002). 'AK' denotes the Akademie edition of *Kants gesammelte Schriften* (Berlin: Reimer/De Gruyter, 1900–).
25 David Wiggins, *Ethics* (London: Penguin, 2006), p. 236.
26 Ibid., p. 237.
27 Bernard Williams, "Philosophy as a Humanistic Discipline" (2000), in the volume of collected essays of the same title, ed. A. W. Moore (Princeton, NJ: Princeton University Press, 2006), pp. 193–4.
28 Ibid., p. 192.
29 The term 'facticity' is variously used by different writers, but I have in mind something like Heidegger's sense, when he associates it with a feeling of being "thrown" into the world; Martin Heidegger, *Being and Time* [*Sein und Zeit*, 1927], trans. J. Macquarrie and E. Robinson (New York: Harper and Row, 1962), §29. (The term is used somewhat differently by Jean-Paul Sartre in his account of the nature of human freedom (*L'Etre et le Néant* [1943], trans. H. E. Barnes (London: Methuen, 1957), Part IV, Chapter 1, §iii).
30 Though such anxieties of course have a long pedigree; witness the famous words of the 'preacher' in Ecclesiastes, Chapter 1.

31 For more on some of these themes, see Stephen Menn, *Descartes and Augustine* (Cambridge: Cambridge University Press, 1998), pp. 87–8; Catherine Wilson, "Soul, Body, and World: Plato's *Timaeus* and Descartes's *Meditations*", in S. Hutton and D. Hedley (eds), *Platonism at the Origins of Modernity* (Dordrecht: Springer, 2007), pp. 177–91; J. Cottingham, "Plato's Sun and Descartes's Stove: Contemplation and Control in Cartesian Philosophy", in M. Ayers (ed.), *Rationalism, Platonism and God: A Symposium on Early Modern Philosophy* (OUP/ Proceedings of the British Academy, 2007), 15–44.

32 Simon Critchley, *Things Merely Are: Philosophy in the Poetry of Wallace Stevens* (London: Routledge, 2005).

33 *Shame and Necessity*, p. 164. Part of Williams' project is to trace the antecedents of this tragic view to classical Greece.

34 Nietzsche envisages a "new philosopher" with a spirit "strong enough to revalue and invent new values". Friedrich Nietzsche, *Beyond Good and Evil* [*Jenseits von Gut und Böse*, 1886], trans. W. Kaufmann (New York: Random House, 1966), §203.

35 The 'anti-Nietzschean' argument sketched here would of course require an entire paper to articulate and defend properly. I raise some of the relevant considerations in *The Spiritual Dimension* (Cambridge: Cambridge University Press, 2005), Chapter 3, especially §2. See also Section 2 of J. Cottingham, "Impartiality and Ethical Formation", forthcoming in J. Cottingham, B. Feltham and P. Stratton-Lake (eds), *Partiality and Impartiality in Ethics*.

36 Blaise Pascal, *Pensées* [c. 1660], ed. L. Lafuma (Paris: Editions du Seuil, 1962), no. 131; René Descartes, *Meditations on First Philosophy* [1641], Third Meditation, ed. J. Cottingham (Cambridge: Cambridge University Press, 2nd edn, 1996), p. 35.

37 St Augustine, *Confessiones* [c. 398], Book I, Chapter 1: "*fecisti nos ad te, et inquietum est cor nostrum donec requiescat in te*" ("You have made us for yourself and our heart is restless until it finds repose in you").

38 Pascal, *Pensées*, no. 131: "*L'homme passe l'homme.*"

39 Thomas Nagel, "The Absurd", *Journal of Philosophy* Vol. LXIII, no. 20 (1971), §VI. Reprinted in Nagel, *Mortal Questions* (Cambridge: Cambridge University Press, 1979).

40 Pursued, for example, by Thomas Nagel, for whom it is enough to "approach our absurd lives with irony", and to give up trying to "dragoon an unconvinced transcendent consciousness into the service of an immanent, limited enterprise like a human life" ("The Absurd"). See also Richard Rorty, *Contingency, Irony and Solidarity* (Cambridge: Cambridge University Press, 1989).

41 See Friedrich Nietzsche, *Thus Spake Zarathustra* [*Also Sprach Zarathustra*, 1891], Part I; Albert Camus, *Le Mythe de Sisyphe* (Paris: Gallimard, 1942), final chapter.

42 Critchley, *Things Merely Are*, p. 87.

43 Williams, *Ethics and the Limits of Philosophy*, p. 169.

44 See, for example, Mark P. Jenkins, *Bernard Williams* (Chesham: Acumen, 2006), p. 184.

45 In his 1948 Third Programme debate with F. C. Copleston, reprinted in *Why I Am Not a Christian* (London: Allen & Unwin, 1957), p. 152: "I should say that the universe is just there, and that's all."

46 I use the somewhat awkward term 'secularist', rather than 'naturalist', since rejecters of the transcendent and the supernatural include those who would not class themselves as naturalists (for example, because they think that some things in the natural world have 'non-natural' properties).

47 G. K. Chesterton, "The Blue Cross", in *The Father Brown Stories* [1929], reprinted in *The Complete Father Brown Stories* (Harmondsworth: Penguin, 1981), p. 20.

48 Indeed, a subset of contemporary ethical objectivists, the so-called Cornell realists, would go so far as to construe ethical judgements as expressing necessary truths (albeit the necessity is taken to be of a synthetic *a posteriori* kind, and hence weaker than that envisaged in traditional theologically-based ethics). See, for example, R. Boyd, "How to Be a Moral Realist", in G. Sayre-McCord, *Essays on Moral Realism* (Ithaca, NY: Cornell University Press, 1988), pp. 181–228.

49 I defend the idea of moral truths as necessary eternal verities in Cottingham, *The Spiritual Dimension*, Chapter 3. For an attempt to accommodate such necessity within an entirely non-transcendent framework, see T. Metz, "God, Morality and the Meaning of Life", forthcoming in N. Athanassoulis and S. Vice (eds), *The Moral Life: Essays in Honour of John Cottingham* (London: Palgrave, 2008).

50 My argument here is, for reasons of space, highly compressed. It presupposes, in particular, the premise that a meaningful morality must be "more than a … fragile disposition possessed by a percentage (perhaps a minority) of a certain class of anthropoids" (Cottingham, *On the Meaning of Life*, p. 72).

51 "Laid down for us" may raise eyebrows. An important task for anyone wishing to defend the philosophical coherence of the notion of a transcendent source of value and meaning is to tackle the notorious Euthyphro dilemma; I say something about this in *The Spiritual Dimension*, Chapter 3, §4.

52 According to Pascal:

> What a chimera a human being is! What a novelty. What a monster, what a chaos, what a contradiction, what a prodigy! Judge of all things, imbecile worm of the earth; repository of truth, sink of uncertainty and error, the pride and refuse of the universe!
>
> (*Pensées*, no. 131)

3

DID WILLIAMS FIND THE TRUTH IN RELATIVISM?

Carol Rovane

Bernard Williams provided what must be the most distinctive and influential contribution to the topic of relativism in his lifetime, certainly in the English-speaking philosophical world. One thing that set his approach apart is the care he gave to formulating the doctrine of relativism before attempting to evaluate the various reasons that might be put forward in favor of it or against it. In this chapter, I aim to follow his example, likewise taking care to formulate the doctrine before I attempt to evaluate it. And throughout, I will be critically engaging the position he took in the article from which this one derives its title.[1]

We'll see in Section I that the task of formulating the doctrine of relativism is far less straightforward than one might have assumed. The most obvious first thoughts about how to formulate it either fail to capture its intuitive content, or they fail to be fully coherent. I will argue that it is not really feasible to try to capture its intuitive content without taking into account that it involves a commitment to the existence of what I will call "*alternatives*," by which I mean, *truths that cannot be embraced together*. Yet there is a difficulty that seems to stand in the way of formulating it in these terms, which takes the form of a dilemma. This *dilemma for alternativeness* assumes that any pair of truth-value-bearers must be either inconsistent or consistent, and then goes on to reason as follows: if they are inconsistent, then by the law of non-contradiction they cannot be equally true; but if they are consistent, then they may be logically conjoined and, hence, embraced together; in neither case do we have alternatives.

One sign that the idea of alternativeness is indeed central to the doctrine of relativism is that much of the instinctive opposition to relativism that emerges in informal philosophical discussions implicitly invokes the terms of this dilemma. Although the world "alternative" isn't always used, alleged examples of alternativeness are always discussed, such as Carnap's linguistic frameworks, Goodman's ways of world-making, Kuhn's scientific paradigms, or the anthropologists' cultural meanings. And the same challenge is always raised: how can such alleged alternatives be *competitors* that *exclude* one another unless they contradict one another? If they contradict one another, don't we just have an ordinary case of *disagreement* in which at most one party can be right? If they don't contradict one another, aren't they merely *different* in a way that permits us to embrace them together after all? And the same conclusion is always drawn: there simply isn't any logical room for whatever it is that relativists have in mind. Which is just to say, there isn't any logical room for alternatives in the sense I've specified, of truths that cannot be embraced together.

My guiding assumption, then, is that we cannot hope to formulate the doctrine of relativism in a satisfactory manner unless we find a way out of the dilemma for alternativeness. But Williams didn't agree. His strategy was to try to formulate the doctrine without appealing to the idea of alternativeness at all, looking instead to the *practical* dimensions of relativism, which he aimed to capture through his novel idea of a *merely notional confrontation*. Although there was something importantly right about his emphasis on the practical significance of the doctrine, we'll see that he couldn't really escape the force of the logic that drives the dilemma for alternativeness.

I will argue that there is only one feasible way out of the dilemma, and it lies in a third possibility that it overlooks – namely, that some truth-value-bearers might be neither inconsistent nor consistent. For when truth-value-bearers are not inconsistent, then nothing prevents them from being equally true; and when they are also not consistent, then they cannot be conjoined even if they are equally true; and this qualifies them as alternatives in the requisite sense. It should be easy to see that if alternatives are neither inconsistent nor consistent, then they do not stand in any logical relations at all. From here on I shall refer to the condition in which truth-value-bearers fail to stand in logical relations as *normative insularity*. And the core of my proposal about how to formulate the doctrine of relativism is that relativists affirm that there is such a thing as normative insularity – or, equivalently, they deny that logical relations run everywhere, among all truth-value-bearers.

Admittedly, it isn't immediately clear why truth-value-bearers would ever fail to stand in logical relations. But this doesn't mean that we should reject my proposal to construe alternativeness in terms of normative insularity. If we did, we would be confusing the two philosophical tasks that Williams so admirably kept apart: *formulating* the doctrine of relativism vs. *evaluating* it. My suggestion is that the best way to make sense of the relativists' idea of alternativeness is through the idea of normative insularity, because every other option falls prey to one or other horn of the dilemma for alternativeness. And if we have doubts about whether there is, or even can be, such a thing as normative insularity, we shouldn't see them as doubts about whether to formulate the doctrine of relativism along the lines I'm suggesting, but as doubts about whether relativism so formulated actually holds in any domain.

It might seem that the way I propose to formulate the doctrine reduces it to a purely logical thesis that doesn't carry any specifically metaphysical significance. But that isn't so. Consider the thesis that relativism so formulated requires us to reject, which is that logical relations run everywhere, among all truth-value-bearers. Although this too might appear to be a purely logical thesis, it has a definite metaphysical implication. If all truth-value-bearers stand in logical relations, then all of the true ones are consistent and conjoinable, and this yields a metaphysical picture of reality as consisting in a single, consistent and complete body of truths.[2] (This picture is very close to the one that Wittgenstein articulated at the beginning of the *Tractatus*, when he claimed that the world is all that is the case.) Now consider the contrasting metaphysical picture that follows from relativism when we formulate it in the way I'm proposing. Insofar as relativists deny that logical relations run everywhere, among all truth-value-bearers, they are denying that there is a single and complete body of truths and affirming instead that there are many incomplete bodies of truths that cannot be embraced together. This shows that what relativists most fundamentally deny is the *oneness* of reality. They are offering what I will call a *multimundial* metaphysical conception, that stands opposed to what I will call the *unimundial* conception of common sense.

Multimundialism has important implications for inquiry, and I will argue that this is where the distinctive practical significance of relativism really lies – in what it would mean for *inquiry* if we were ever actually to encounter normative insularity. As it happens, an encounter with normative insularity would aptly be describable with Williams' felicitious phrase, as a "merely notional confrontation." Yet it couldn't be said that this is what he had in mind when he introduced the phrase in his own effort to formulate the doctrine of relativism since, as I've already made clear, he aimed to formulate it without addressing the logical difficulty that the idea of normative insularity is supposed to solve – the dilemma for alternativeness. Nevertheless, he did aim to capture something *like* the idea of alternativeness with his account of merely notional confrontations. He aimed to capture a sense in which some systems of belief may be *profoundly unavailable* to some subjects. And it is certainly part of my suggestion that a system of beliefs that was normatively insulated from our own would indeed be profoundly unavailable to us. This means there is at least a family resemblance between merely notional confrontations, as Williams defined them, and encounters with what I have defined as normative insularity.

When I turn in Section II to the task of evaluating the doctrine of relativism, my ultimate aim will be to evaluate whether Williams provided us with compelling reasons for taking it seriously in the domain of ethics.

His non-dismissive attitude toward ethical relativism was informed by a set of familiar and, I daresay, rather standard and orthodox metaphysical and epistemological commitments. They included: (1) objective knowledge is possible in the scientific domain because realism holds there, and scientific methods are specifically designed to track mind-independent facts; (2) objective knowledge isn't possible in the ethical domain because there is no counterpart to scientific methods there, and that is because there aren't any mind-independent ethical facts for such methods to track; and (3) realism and relativism are mutually opposed doctrines. Taken together, these commitments entail that there is no scope for relativism in the domain of science while there is in the domain of ethics. But they don't suffice to secure a relativist conclusion in ethics. If they did, then every form of non-realism would be a form of relativism, and this clearly isn't so – Berkley's idealism is not a form of relativism, for example. Williams clearly saw the need for additional, positive grounds on which to affirm ethical relativism, beyond his arguments against ethical realism. And he claimed to find such grounds in the cultural and historical situatedness of ethical values – or, as I prefer to put it, their *locality*.

Even if we are not in the end convinced, I think we can nevertheless agree with Williams that this is a powerful consideration for taking ethical relativism seriously. However, there is no deep connection between it and the set of orthodox background commitments I just enumerated, that he brought to bear in his thinking about ethical relativism. Contrary to what he and many others assume, realism and relativism are not mutually opposed doctrines, and so, such serious considerations as there might be in favor of ethical relativism needn't begin by calling ethical realism into question. On my proposal, the metaphysical issue that really divides relativists and their opponents is the *oneness* of reality – whether there is a single, consistent and complete body of truths or whether there are many, incomplete bodies of truths. And we'll see that this metaphysical issue is wholly distinct from the issue that divides realists from their opponents, which concerns not the *oneness* of reality but its mind-independence.

I How should we formulate the doctrine of relativism?

In my introductory remarks, I claimed that the first, most obvious thoughts about how to formulate the doctrine of relativism either fail to capture our intuitions about its content, or they fail to capture anything coherent at all. But it is nevertheless worth exploring them, even if only to reject them. Doing so will help to ward off some natural confusions, and it will also provide a useful background against which to see the motivations both for Williams' proposal about how to formulate the doctrine and for my own.

Consider the slogan "truth is relative." On the most natural interpretation, it means that truth-value-bearers are not true or false *tout court*, but true or false relative to a context. *Prima facie*, this slogan doesn't capture any distinctively relativist thesis because it applies to truth-value-bearing sentences that contain indexical pronouns like "I," "here," "now," or "this." Such sentences are not true or false *tout court*, but true or false relative to context of utterance – to who is speaking, or where or when or with what in mind. Clearly, opponents of relativism have no stake in denying that indexical truth is relative in this way.

Perhaps the debate between relativists and their opponents concerns a universal claim, to the effect that *all* truth is relative. It has often been objected that when relativism is construed as a universal doctrine, it is incoherent. I'm not sure that this is so. But I do see that there is a problem about *stating* the doctrine as a universal one. For if all truth is relative, then any statement to that effect would only be relatively true and, in that case, the statement wouldn't rule out its negation since its negation might also be relatively true. This is closely related to another familiar objection, which assumes that whenever we assert something, we are asserting it to be absolutely true, and then proceeds to argue that if we ever were to assert that all truth is relative, we would be asserting *that* to be absolutely true, and the upshot would be a kind of implicit or pragmatic self-contradiction. Williams raised a more specific version of this latter objection against what he called *vulgar relativism*. His vulgar relativist claims that it is *always* wrong to criticize other ethical viewpoints, and he pointed out that this is something she cannot do without making her own relativist stance an exception. But he quickly dismissed this line of objection, and he was right to do so. Indeed, I think we should dismiss the whole family of objections that raise difficulties for construing relativism as a universal doctrine. For if such difficulties should prove to be insuperable, we can easily sidestep them by refusing to construe the doctrine as a universal one. We can construe it instead as a domain-specific doctrine that might hold in some domains, such as ethics or aesthetics, while not holding in other domains, such as mathematics or science. And there is no particular logical or pragmatic difficulty about asserting that it holds in one of these domains or another. (Though of course, there remains a difficulty for vulgar relativism, which can only be avoided by finding some other way to construe what the relativists' position would amount to in the ethical domain.)

Although it is a form of progress to construe relativism as a domain-specific doctrine, we are still left with the task of clarifying exactly what it is that relativists are supposed to be asserting when they assert that their doctrine holds in a given domain. And since indexical truth is relative, it isn't obvious that we can clarify this simply by invoking the slogan "truth is relative."

Perhaps we can do better by considering what relativists might be denying when they claim that truth is relative, with a view to finding something that isn't necessarily being denied by their opponents when they allow that indexical truth is relative. One such thing that relativists might be denying is that *truth is universal* in the following sense: when a claim is true, it is a truth that *everyone* can in principle embrace.[3] Certainly, opponents of relativism may regard the truths we express through our indexical utterances as universal in this sense, even though such utterances are not true or false *tout court* but true or false relative to context of utterance. Take, for example, the sentence "I am a woman." It is not true or false *tout court*, but true relative to contexts in which the speaker is a woman and false otherwise. Yet when I utter it, I am giving expression to a truth that *anyone* could in principle embrace. Of course, others cannot express the same truth in the same indexical way, for no one else can use the first person pronoun in order to say *of me* that I am a woman. But others can say that Carol Rovane is a woman. And, moreover, others can also articulate exactly how the truth of my indexical claim to that effect is relative to context, by employing the formal maneuver of semantic ascent and explicit relativization of truth to context. This formal maneuver makes it possible for us to understand, as well as articulate, how it is that indexical truth can be both relative and universal at the same time. For once we explicitly relativize the truth of indexical sentences to contexts of utterance, we put ourselves in a position from which it is possible to embrace any of the truths that anyone might express through them, no matter what relation we ourselves might bear to the contexts in which they are uttered. And if the same holds for everyone, then indexical truth is indeed universal.

When we construe relativism as involving a denial that truth is universal, we come very close to construing it as involving a commitment to alternativeness. Certainly, the latter commitment entails the former denial: if some truths cannot be embraced together, then not all truths can be truths for everyone. But whether the converse holds as well depends upon how we construe the idea of universality. Consider the fact that some subjects cannot embrace certain truths simply because they are too cognitively limited to apprehend those truths to begin with. If we were to count this as a failure of universality, then alternativeness wouldn't follow from such a failure. For it might be the case that the truths that such cognitively limited subjects can't apprehend could in principle be embraced together with the other truths that they can apprehend. Yet, intuitively, this doesn't seem to be a failure of universality at all. When we think of the truths that we embrace as truths for everyone, we are not aiming to rule out the possibility of *ignorance* of them, not even incorrigible ignorance. Our thought seems to be rather closer to what is being denied when we affirm alternativeness: that all of the truths can in principle be apprehended and embraced together. If that is our thought, then a failure of universality would imply alternativeness after all.[4] And it seems to me that if relativists do aim to deny universality, this is very much what they have in mind.

Before I attempt to formulate the doctrine of relativism along these lines, I want to continue to explore two other lines of thought, in order to bring out why they don't really lead us to a satisfactory formulation of the doctrine. According to one, the starting point for my own formulation – that relativists deny that truth is universal and, in so doing, affirm alternativeness – leads straight back to the formulation that I've rejected, according to which relativists claim that truth is relative. The other line of thought is Williams' proposal to formulate the doctrine without bringing in the idea of alternativeness at all.

I have suggested that if relativists claim that truth is relative, we ought not to take this literally, but see it as a way of denying that truth is universal. But it is hard to see what else could possibly undermine the universality of truth except some form of *contextuality*. In other words, it seems that some truths would have to be tied to contexts in a such a way that some subjects – namely, those who don't bear the right relation to the contexts in question – couldn't embrace them. This might happen in the ethical domain if the truth of ethical claims was a function of ethical standards that hold only locally, in a given social context. The same might hold in other domains involving value. And it might hold in domains where a strong version of anti-realism holds, and there is no more to the truth in that domain than meeting certain epistemic standards that hold only locally, in a given social context. In all of these cases, it is natural to think of truth as *relative* to the contexts in question. The trouble is that when we do, we are returned to the picture of relative truth that I sketched above in connection with indexicals, in which the relativity of truth turns out to be compatible with its universality. For the point I made about indexical truth generalizes to all cases of relative truth. Whenever we think of truth as relative to some contextual parameter or other, we can always make this explicit just as we do in the case of indexical truth, through semantic ascent and explicit relativization of the truth-predicate to whatever contextual parameters truth is supposed to be relative *to*. And then we can all embrace the same contextual truths, no matter what relation we might happen to bear to the contexts in question.[5] This leads me to conclude that it is a quite hopeless project to try to formulate the doctrine of relativism in terms of the slogan "truth is relative."

It is worth pausing to work through an example in order to drive this point home. Let's suppose for the sake of argument that ethical truth is a function of meeting ethical standards that hold only locally, within a given social context. And let's suppose that there is more than one social context and that different ethical standards hold in different social contexts. It would seem to follow that a given sentence and its negation could both be true. For example, "Suicide is wrong" might be true by the ethical standards that hold in my social context while "Suicide is not wrong" might be true by the lights of the ethical standards that hold in yours. It might seem to follow that ethical truth cannot be universal: all of the ethical truths could not be truths for everyone, because no one could embrace them all on pain of violating the law of non-contradiction. However, this wouldn't follow if we were prepared to portray ethical truth as relative to context. I would not contradict myself if I were to assert that the sentence "Suicide is wrong" is true relative to the ethical standards that hold in my social context, while also asserting that the sentence "Suicide is not wrong" is true relative to the different ethical standards that hold in your social context. One might still retain an intuitive sense that there is some form of relativism lurking here: if we don't all occupy the same social contexts, then we can't all live by the same ethical truths. This is an important point to which I'll return in Section II. But it doesn't undermine my point here, which is that the relativity of ethical truth to context is compatible with its being universal in the sense now under discussion. Even if different ethical standards prevail in different social contexts, and even if we therefore can't all live by the same ethical standards, we can still all be in complete ethical agreement – an agreement whose content would be roughly equivalent to the injunction, "When in Rome, do as the Romans do." It is certainly conceivable that we might not all agree on this. If you hold that suicide is wrong, you might infer that anyone who holds that suicide is not wrong must be mistaken, even if they occupy a different social context in which different ethical standards prevail. But if you were to infer this, then you would be denying that ethical truths are relative to social contexts. And this leaves my point about the universality of relative truth in place.

So if relativists want to deny that truth is universal, then they need to portray truth as bound to context *without* also portraying it as relative. *Prima facie*, it would seem that they can easily do this. They can claim that truth-value-bearers in some domains are true or false as a function of normative standards that hold only locally, within a given context; and they can claim at the same time that these truth-value-bearers are *not* true or false *relative* to those contexts, but true or false *tout court*.

This way of thinking about contextuality gives rise to what is currently the most common understanding of ethical relativism.[6] On this understanding, relativism arises with *irresoluble conflicts* among ethical truths. Thus, if I say "Suicide is wrong" and you say "Suicide is not wrong," there is a strong appearance of disagreement between us, and it is not to be removed by explicitly relativizing our claims to our different ethical standards, thereby rendering both as claims that both of us can embrace as true. And yet this isn't an ordinary case of disagreement. For in the ordinary case, we can't both be right, whereas, on this understanding of what makes ethical claims true, we *can* both be right. And, in that case, ethical truths are not universal. We cannot all embrace all of the ethical truths, because if we did we would be violating the law of non-contradiction.

Recall, however, the first horn of the dilemma for alternativeness, which insists that inconsistent claims cannot be equally true. I think we should agree. In other words, if this is the only way in which we can make sense of alternativeness – by allowing that there can be irresoluble conflicts in which both parties are right – then we should reject the doctrine of relativism as incoherent. And we should do this even if we endorse the underlying metaphysical picture that drives this common understanding of relativism. For if there are domains in which different local normative standards seem to yield conflicting judgements that are nevertheless equally true, we can always avoid violating the law of non-contradiction by explicitly relativizing the truth of those judgements to the different normative standards that yield them. That would clearly be the better thing to do if our only other choice is to allow violations of the law of non-contradiction.

Williams went some distance toward the common understanding of relativism that I just rejected, for he agreed that relativism arises with conflict. Yet he never went so far as to say that both parties to a conflict can be right. I infer that he didn't believe that they can both be right. For allowing such violations of the law of non-contradiction would have required an explanation and defense, and he never provided that. What he did say was that the first condition of the problem of relativism is that there are systems of belief that *exclude* one another. And he argued that there is only one way in which systems of belief can exclude one another, which is by conflicting with one another.[7] This argument was largely directed against Kuhn's picture of incommensurability, according to which theories that belong to different scientific paradigms don't share any meanings and, because they don't share meanings, there are no points of logical contact at which they can conflict. Kuhn thought that theories belonging to different paradigms nevertheless exclude one another. But Williams argued that they cannot, unless there are some points of logical contact, such as a common evidence base, at which they conflict.

Obviously, his first condition cannot by itself suffice to capture what is distinctive about the relativists' position. For no one could possibly deny that some systems of belief exclude one another because they conflict with one another. And it was a real innovation on his part to try to capture the particular kind of exclusivity that he thought relativists have in mind by turning to the practical aspects of their position. To this end he introduced his idea of a *merely notional confrontation*, which he defined as follows: the holders of one system cannot *go over* to another system without *losing their grip on reality*.

The terms of this definition are not typical terms for a philosopher to use, and they stand in need of further clarification. The first bit of clarification he provided was to contrast merely notional confrontations with *real* confrontations, which are marked by the fact that it is a *real option* for the holders of one system to go over to another. This contrast doesn't make everything suddenly clear. But it is clear enough to show that his first and second conditions taken together don't serve to isolate the right kind of exclusion – the kind that only relativists, but not their opponents, would want us to acknowledge. For as he himself noted, our confrontation with phlogiston theory meets both conditions: phlogiston theory conflicts with our current theories and, moreover, we couldn't go over to it without losing our grip on reality. But the reason why phlogiston theory is not a real option for us is that we regard it as seriously mistaken. And it isn't a particularly relativist suggestion that we would lose our grip on reality if we went over to a theory that, by our current lights, seriously misrepresents it.

This led him to introduce his third and final condition. Supposing that the first two conditions are in place – that we are confronted with a system of beliefs that conflicts with our own, and that the system is not a real option to which we could go over while retaining our grip on reality. He claimed that it would also have to be the case that any attempt on our part to rationally appraise it would be either inappropriate or pointless. The intuition here is that, according to relativists, some systems of belief may be profoundly unavailable to us, not because we view them as mistaken, but because we don't stand in any significant rational relation to them at all. I think this is *the* intuition about relativism that we ought to make central and develop, and I propose to do just that. But first I want to consider in detail how Williams aimed to incorporate this intuition with his third condition, for there are some minor problems of interpretation here.

One glaring problem is that his third condition appears to be ruled out by his first. For it is impossible to apprehend that another system of beliefs conflicts with our own without also acknowledging that the law of non-contradiction imposes the following normative constraints on us: either we must reject the conflicting system of beliefs as false, or we must revise our own standing system of beliefs so as to accommodate its truth, or we must suspend belief on all matters over which the two systems conflict. And no matter how we might choose to respond to these normative constraints – rejection, revision, suspense – we shall be engaged in a form of rational appraisal. This means that rational appraisal is never pointless in situations of conflict, but always appropriate. It must be appropriate, since it is unavoidable.

Since Williams couldn't have failed to see this, he must have had some other form of rational appraisal in mind. That is, he must have had in mind a form of rational appraisal that might be pointless or inappropriate even as we engage in the minimal form of rational appraisal that goes together with apprehending conflict. In most conflicts, many such other forms of rational appraisal are available. We can appraise whether one or the other side of a conflict is susceptible of a formal proof, or has some theoretical advantage (such as that it affords greater unity of explanation), or is better supported by empirical evidence. It is crucial that these further forms of rational appraisal usually are available in a conflict. For sometimes our current view is mistaken, and the only way to discover this is by finding a rational basis for going over to a conflicting view. Yet there is no general guarantee that we will always be able to find such a rational basis for taking sides in a conflict. And it seems plausible that this is what Williams had in mind when he raised the possibility that, in some cases of conflict, rational appraisal is either pointless or inappropriate – that there is no rational basis on which they could be navigated. Note that this would equip him with an explanation of how our confrontation with phlogiston theory can be merely notional without providing any support for relativism. As I observed earlier, one reason why we cannot go over to phlogiston theory without losing our grip on reality is that it is mistaken by our current best lights. But that is not all. Our view that it is mistaken is backed by *further* rational appraisal. We have determined that it doesn't meet the standards of scientific evidence and explanation that it would have to meet in order for us to deem it true (or highly probable). And I think Williams was on to something important here: when these forms of rational appraisal are appropriate, we are adopting a stance that is definitely quite unlike the stance of the relativist. The question is, did he manage to fully capture what is distinctive about the relativist's stance by raising the possibility of notional confrontations in which these forms of rational appraisal would not be appropriate?

The answer to this question depends in part on our attitude toward *conversion*. The occasion and need for conversion arise precisely when we are faced with a conflict and there is no rational basis on which we could navigate it. Williams certainly wouldn't have denied that conversion is sometimes a real option, and hence isn't always an occasion for a merely notional confrontation. In our own place and time, it is a real option to convert to Christianity or Islam, insofar as we wouldn't say that someone had lost their grip on reality by coming to faith in these religions. (If some narrow-minded atheists want to say this, they would be wrongheaded to do so. Religious conversion is a recognizable human phenomenon that has often been highly valued. In fact, it is part of the very content of the Christian and Muslim religious doctrines that the path to believing them may have to go via conversion.) Since conversion may be a real option, Williams owed us an account of the difference between those cases in which it is a real option and those cases in which it is not, so as to isolate the cases where we would have an instance of relativism as he was asking us to conceive it.

Some philosophers would seek to explain the difference between these cases by appealing to the issue of realism. Suppose we face a conflict that we believe we will never have a rational basis for settling, and this leads us to believe that we could never change our minds about what is at issue in the conflict without undergoing a conversion. And suppose we also believe that there are mind-independent facts in the light of which only one side in the conflict can be right. Then we might attach great importance to the idea that it is a real option to go over to the other side because, otherwise, we would be stuck with a dogmatic commitment to whatever view we happened to have arrived at first. One is reminded here of James's argument in "The Will to Believe."[8] But there is little sign that Williams would have exploited realism in this way, to support unforced decisions to believe. And more to the point here, it isn't obvious how he would have exploited realism in order to explain why conversion sometimes is and sometimes is not a real option. For the only realist arguments that impressed him were arguments for scientific realism, which emphasize that scientific methods enable us to track mind-independent facts and yield an accumulation of scientific knowledge through progressively better theories. This scientific realist story guarantees that his third condition is always satisfied in the domain of science – which means there would be no opportunity for conversion there (this is another part of his opposition to Kuhn's picture of science). So it isn't clear how he could have exploited his understanding of the issue of realism in order to explain why conversion sometimes is and sometimes isn't a real option, since all cases of conversion would in his view fall outside of the domain where he thought realism holds.

Richard Rorty wouldn't have seen any difficulty here. He would have thought it sufficed to point out that in some social contexts conversion is *regarded* as a real option and in other social contexts it is *not* so regarded.[9] But Williams clearly did not embrace Rorty's brand of relativism. Rorty's was an across-the-board relativism, that derived from a generally anti-metaphysical stance in philosophy. And what he substituted for metaphysics – his account of community and conversation – was supposed to apply in all domains, including science. In contrast, Williams' preoccupation with scientific realism as our main model for objectivity shows that his philosophical orientation was not thoroughgoingly anti-metaphysical. This needn't have prevented him from adopting Rorty's position in domains outside science, where he thought we don't have the sorts of grounds for realism that we have in the case of scientific realism. If that was his position, then perhaps he could have explained why conversion sometimes is and sometimes is not a real option in Rorty's way, by making it a matter of our attitudes, as they are dictated by our social conditions.

I'm not sure it would be right to attribute this Rorty-like view to Williams in domains like ethics, politics and aesthetics. But even if we did so, it couldn't be said that the result would be a satisfying formulation of the doctrine of relativism. For we simply cannot leave the issue of *truth* to the side in the way that Williams tried to do. (To Rorty's credit, he did not leave that issue to the side, but recognized that he needed to say something about it.) After all, his first condition for relativism was that there must be *conflict*. And this inevitably raises the question whether both parties in a conflict can be right. As I've indicated, he never came out and *said* that he thought this is possible, and for this reason it doesn't make sense to attribute to him the common understanding of relativism as arising with irresoluble conflicts in which both parties are (or can be) right. But if both parties to a conflict cannot be right, then it is completely unclear how *any* situation could be one that invites what we intuitively think of as a *relativist* stance. It doesn't matter whether a conflict gives rise to a real or a merely notional confrontation, and it doesn't matter whether it can be rationally navigated or not. In all cases of conflict, the law of non-contradiction requires us to suppose that someone must be wrong. And wherever we ourselves might stand in a given conflict, we must obey this law of logic, by granting that the following options are exhaustive: either we must conclude that the other party is wrong, or we must go over to their view, or we must suspend judgement. My point is, *this* attitude toward conflict is *not* the stance of the *relativist*.

My further point is that this shows us just how acute the difficulty is, which is raised by the dilemma for alternativeness. Each horn articulates an important aspect of the position that opponents of relativism advocate: inconsistent claims cannot be equally true, while consistent ones can always be conjoined. And each exploits what look to be undeniable truths of logic as given by the laws of non-contradiction and conjunction. Unfortunately, Williams' first condition for relativism – that there be conflicting systems of belief – immediately raises the first horn. And if he were right that this is the only form that exclusion can take, then there would be no scope for relativism.

But Williams wasn't right. There is a third possibility that the dilemma for alternativeness overlooks, which is that some truth-value-bearers are neither inconsistent nor consistent. When truth-value-bearers are neither inconsistent nor consistent, they do not stand in any logical relations at all, but are *normatively insulated* from one another. And when truth-value-bearers are normatively insulated from one another, they may qualify as alternatives in the sense that I've suggested is required by relativism: since they are not inconsistent, they can be equally true without violating the law of non-contradiction; but since they are not consistent, they cannot be embraced together.

In the introduction, I noted some immediate metaphysical implications of this way of formulating the doctrine of relativism, which I'll now quickly restate. When we suppose that logical relations do run everywhere, we are supposing that the world is *one* in the following sense: there is a single, consistent and complete body of truths, all of which can be embraced together. And it is this one-world thesis, or *unimundialism*, that relativists reject when they affirm alternativeness in the form of normative insularity. What they affirm instead is *multimundialism*, the view that there are many, distinct and incomplete bodies of truths that cannot be embraced together.

Although there are many issues to be worked out in connection with both of these metaphysical positions, I want to focus – as Williams did in his account of relativism – on their practical implications. Each of them brings in train a distinctive practical stance toward inquiry and interpersonal relations – the *unimundial stance* and the *multimundial stance*, respectively. And just as the metaphysical content of each position is a direct reflection of its logical commitments, the same is true of the practical stance that goes together with each. In fact, we'll see that none of these aspects of unimundialism and multimundialism can properly be appreciated independently of the others – logical, metaphysical or practical.

I'll start with the unimundial stance. According to the unimundial view, logical relations run everywhere, among all truth-value-bearers. As a result, we can never be indifferent to any truth-value-bearer that we might come across. For each and every one of them is guaranteed to stand in logical relations to what we already hold to be true, and these logical relations carry a normative force that we are never free to ignore. If a truth-value-bearer is consistent with what we already hold, then we may embrace it as true. But if it is inconsistent, then either we must reject it as false, or we must accommodate its truth by revising our prior beliefs so as to make them consistent with it, or we must suspend belief on it along with the prior beliefs that conflict with it. These same normative constraints carry over to our interpersonal relations. If others' beliefs are consistent with what we already hold to be true, then we may embrace them, but if they are inconsistent, then at most one of us can be right.

The normative constraints that unimundialism imposes on inquiry should not be confused with the goal of actually learning all of the truths. For one thing, we may not be interested in all of them. For another, it may lie beyond our power to learn them all. But this doesn't mean that there isn't a single, consistent and complete body of truths into which we might inquire, insofar as we are interested and insofar as it lies within our power to learn about at least some of them. And the sign that we think there is a single and complete body of truths in which to inquire, if we are interested and able to do so, is that we view the normative constraints I just described as holding *always*, without exception. There is a universal quantifier at work in this conception that signals a totality of all of the truth-value-bearers, of which the true ones form a single, consistent and complete body of truths. It may be the idea of such a totality of all of the truths is formally problematic.[10] But even if that is so, we can still think of our inquiries and interpersonal relations as governed by an idealized conception of it. In other words, we can embrace unimundialism as a regulative ideal – the *unimundial ideal*. And when we think of unimundialism in this idealized way, its metaphysical meaning collapses with its practical meaning, which in turn collapses with its logical meaning – consisting in its normative implications for inquiry and interpersonal relations.

Before going on to describe the multimundial stance, I want briefly to connect what I've just said about the unimundial stance with some points from the preceding discussion. When we adopt the unimundial stance, we recognize only the two possibilities that are identified by the dilemma for alternativeness: any pair of truth-value-bearers is either inconsistent or consistent. And the normative constraints that we are committed to respecting in inquiry and interpersonal relations are the very same constraints that the dilemma recognizes: inconsistent truth-value-bearers cannot be equally true, while consistent ones may be embraced together. So when I complained above that Williams failed to capture a distinctively *relativist* stance, what I really meant was that his first condition – the presence of conflict between systems of belief – imposes the unimundial stance; otherwise, he would have been forced to portray relativism as entailing violations of the law of non-contradiction.

There are three related ways to describe what the multimundial stance involves, and all of them have to do with recognizing normative insularity, along with its implication that truth is not universal. First, we must think of our inquiries as circumscribed by *boundaries* in such a way that logical relations hold only within them but not across them.[11] Second, when we come across such boundaries, we must be *epistemically indifferent* to what lies outside them. Such epistemic indifference is very unlike the more usual forms of indifference that we exhibit toward certain truths. Usually, indifference simply reflects a lack of interest. And usually, there is no bar to *becoming* interested, and commencing appropriate inquiries. But the case is different with truths that are normatively insulated from the ones that we embrace. Such truths do not stand in any logical relation to our beliefs and other attitudes. They cannot be conjoined with them, but nor can they be ruled out by them. They lie permanently outside the scope of our inquiries – which is why we are consigned to epistemic indifference toward them. The third way of describing what is involved in adopting the multimundial stance concerns the interpersonal counterpart to such epistemic indifference. If we were to come across subjects whose beliefs are normatively insulated from ours, they would be subjects from whom we cannot learn and with whom we cannot disagree. We would have to regard them as having *their* truths which are not for *us*, and this would result in a profound sense of *otherness*.

I said in the introduction that an encounter with a view that was normatively insulated from our own would aptly be described as a merely notional confrontation. Here is what I meant: it would be a view that we could not rationally appraise even in the minimal sense of apprehending whether it conflicts with our own, let alone in the more robust ways that go beyond logic; thus, the reason why we couldn't go over to it while retaining our grip on reality is that it would lie entirely beyond our normative reach.

It may seem doubtful that the dilemma for alternativeness can so easily be escaped. It will seem especially doubtful to those who are inclined to define *consistency* negatively, as *not* *in*consistent. They will see no way out of the dilemma and, so, no scope for alternativeness in the sense required by relativism. But as I said at the outset, we must take care not to confuse the two tasks that Williams rightly distinguished: formulating the doctrine of relativism vs. evaluating it. Those who are skeptical about whether there is, or even can be, such a thing as normative insularity are raising doubts about whether we have reason to *affirm* relativism; that is quite different from raising doubts about whether it ought to be formulated along these lines.

II Evaluating the doctrine of relativism

My ultimate aim in this section is to explore the extent to which Williams offered us reasons for taking relativism seriously in the ethical domain. But before proceeding to that task, I want to raise a methodological difficulty that arises once we formulate the doctrine of relativism as multi-mundialism. I suspect a similar difficulty would arise for any formulation, but I shall only concern myself with the way in which it arises for this one. The problem concerns what standard of justification we are required to meet when we attempt to settle the debate between unimundialists and multimundialists.

Whenever philosophers have an internally coherent philosophical position that they find satisfactory, they tend to presume that they are within their rights to retain it unless and until it is shown to be incoherent or otherwise untenable. It is generally assumed that unimundialism faces no such threat of incoherence. Certainly, if there is one, it is far less obvious than the threat which is posed for multimundialism by the dilemma for alternativeness. (As I observed in Section I, it may be that the unimundial conception of a single, consistent and complete body of truths is formally problematic, because it refers to a totality of truths. I proposed to get around any such problem by framing the conception as a regulative ideal that guides inquiry. But even if that is not an adequate response to the problem, I'm going to assume here for the sake of argument that it can be solved in one way or another. It seems especially likely that it can be solved when we construe unimundialism as a domain-specific doctrine rather than as a universal one.) So it shouldn't be surprising that unimundialists regard themselves as within their rights to retain their position unless and until it is demonstrated to them that it is incoherent or otherwise untenable in ways they hadn't noticed. This has the effect of shifting the entire burden of proof to relativists. What is more, it sets the standard of proof extra-ordinarily high, requiring nothing less of relativists than an actual *refutation* of unimundialism. And this is a standard that multimundialists have no chance of meeting, insofar as unimundialism is an internally coherent position.

But what if multimundialists likewise have an internally coherent position that they find satisfactory? (I gather from my colleagues who are logicians that there is no danger of logical incoherence; apparently, it is formally unproblematic to logically accommodate normative insularity by representing logical relations as being confined within boundaries.) Then they too may be within their rights to retain their position unless and until it is shown to be incoherent or otherwise untenable. And unimundialists who oppose them will never be able to demonstrate this to their satisfaction. For unimundialists assume that there isn't any such thing as normative insularity, and arguments proceeding from that assumption would beg the question against multimundialism in an unacceptable way.

Thus, a methodological difficulty arises in the debate between unimundialists and multimundialists, insofar as each side can reasonably expect that it will never be *refuted* by the other side. But I don't think we should conclude that there is no way to effectively settle the debate. What we should do is adjust our standards of justification so as to take due account of the difficulty we face. The first thing we must do is *minimize* the role that begging the question plays in our thinking about the respective merits of each side. This means that we shouldn't regard the fact that we *can* beg the question in favor of a given side as a sufficient reason to embrace it, but should seek other, more substantive considerations for favoring that side over the other, reasons that don't *merely* or *directly* beg the question. Optimally, these reasons would be *positive* reasons that speak for that side, but they may also be *negative* reasons that speak against the other side. In either case, they should be *substantive* reasons that go beyond merely begging the question.

Let me illustrate this methodological recommendation by gesturing at some possible reasons for taking a stand on relativism that do and don't meet this standard of justification. Then I'll turn, finally, to Williams' case for ethical relativism.

I noted in the introduction that when relativism is construed as multimundialism, realism and relativism are not mutually opposed doctrines, because the question whether reality is mind-independent is quite distinct from the question whether it is *one* in the sense that unimundialists affirm. This means that an argument in favor of realism doesn't necessarily amount to an argument against relativism. Of course, if there are mind-independent facts, we can conceive them as together constituting something unitary, namely, a *set* or *totality* that includes them all. But these conceptions of unity do not impose any normative constraint of consistency – the conjoinability of all truths. And so they don't directly deliver grounds for affirming unimundialism. This means that when realists invoke the sort of reasoning that drives the dilemma for alternativeness in order to take a stand against relativism, they usually fail to meet the justificatory standard I've set. For they usually smuggle in the unimundial stance as part and parcel of the realist attitude without providing any positive reasons for doing so – which means that they are merely begging the question on the issue of relativism even if they are not doing so with respect to realism.

Contrast the following pragmatic argument in favor of a unimundial stance in science, which has a better chance of meeting the standard I've set: sometimes special sciences can be pursued in a way that is completely autonomous from the rest of the sciences (in the spirit that Chomsky initially recommended in linguistics); whenever the autonomous pursuit of a special science is possible, this signals that the special science is, in effect, normatively insulated from the other sciences and it would make sense to adopt the relativists' multimundial stance; nevertheless it is always a scientific advance to achieve unity in science wherever it can be achieved; there is no *a priori* way of knowing whether or not such unity can be achieved; if we adopt a multimundial stance which assumes that some special sciences are normatively insulated from the rest of the sciences, we will have closed our minds about whether they can be unified with the rest; but if we adopt a unimundial stance, then we shall be open to achieving what unity in science can be achieved; therefore, we should adopt the unimundial stance in science.

I suspect that realists would not be satisfied with such a pragmatic argument. So it is worth reflecting further on whether the framework of realism might somehow afford substantive reasons that are more metaphysical in character for preferring one side in the debate about relativism – unimundialism or multimundialism. The defining commitment of realism is a conception of reality as mind-independent. In its most extreme form, the thesis of mind-independence implies a broad skepticism that leaves no basis for arguing one way or the other. But many realists think that we can know at least *some* of the facts in spite of their being mind-independent, because the mind itself is world-dependent – a mirror of nature, as it were. Such realists are usually prepared to allow that there are *other* facts that we cannot know, due to epistemic limitations imposed by our particular cognitive design. Chomsky finds this overwhelmingly plausible. And his way of understanding the significance of our cognitive limitations poses a difficulty for making sense of unimundialism within the framework of realism. In his view, abilities are *essentially limiting*, in the sense that if we have the ability to do one thing, say, jump, this makes it impossible for us to do something else, say, slither like a snake. And he sees no reason why the same shouldn't hold for cognitive abilities: if we are fit to know some things, then it is bound to be the case that we are unfit to know other things. The unimundial ideal requires us to suppose that all of the truths are consistent and co-tenable, and this presupposes the idea of a point of view from which all of the truths could in principle be apprehended and embraced together. This would have to be a *view from everywhere* – by which I mean, a view from which every truth that could be known by every kind of mind could in principle be embraced together. Such a view from everywhere would be quite different from Nagel's *view from nowhere*. The latter is meant to help capture the kind of objectivity to which realists aspire – their aspiration is to know the world as it is in itself, conceived apart from our own, and indeed any other, form of subjectivity. In contrast, those who aspire to a view from everywhere wouldn't try to transcend subjectivity in general, so much as incorporate every form of subjectivity together. But this looks to be impossible given Chomsky's conception of cognitive abilities as essentially limited. What I mean here isn't just that it would be impossible for *us human beings* to achieve a view from everywhere; I mean that it would be impossible for *any* kind of knower, because cognitive abilities typically can't be combined so as to function together any more than different motor abilities can be. If this reasoning is sound, then not only is it the case that realism doesn't directly entail unimundialism, it actually poses a significant problem for it – and insofar as it does, it tips the balance in favor of multimundialism where realism holds.[12]

To continue on the theme of how debates about realism might bear on debates about relativism. In the last section, I observed that one common understanding of relativism – as something that arises with irresoluble conflict – tends to draw its main support from anti-realism. And I allowed myself to fall into the usual terms of debate there, which don't quite harmonize with what I've been saying in this section about why realism doesn't suffice to establish unimundialism. On behalf of that common understanding, I said that in domains where anti-realism holds, it may be that there are no mind-independent facts in the light of which at least one party to a conflict must be wrong, with the apparent implication that both might be right. My words may have seemed to suggest that if there were such mind-independent facts, that would guarantee that the law of non-contradiction holds. But the real point is, realism is not what underwrites the law of non-contradiction and, so, arguments for anti-realism don't license us to give that law up.

However, although arguments for anti-realism don't speak against the law of non-contradiction, they might provide some support for multimundialism. If there is no more to the truth in domains where anti-realism holds than meeting normative standards that hold only locally, and if there is no basis on which we could comparatively evaluate the standards themselves, then it would be perfectly appropriate for those who are subject to one set of normative standards to adopt a multimundial stance toward those who are subject to other normative standards. I don't have the space here to fully elaborate this general argumentative strategy, which draws on features of anti-realism in order to defend the possibility of normative insularity.[13] All I can do is gesture at how it might work in connection with ethics, by drawing on aspects of Williams' ethical vision.

There are (at least) three aspects of his overall ethical vision that he deemed relevant to the issue of relativism. First, there was his negative assessment of the project of moral theorizing. Second, there was his negative assessment of the prospects for modeling objectivity in ethics on objectivity in science. And, finally, there was his positive vision of how ethical life is situated in culture and history.

Williams famously held that Morality is a failed project. I myself am completely convinced by his arguments. And anyone who is convinced by them should immediately see that he removed one of the major sources of support for unimundialism in ethics. For it is very much the aim of a moral theory in the sense he rejected to deliver a single, consistent and complete set of truths about what is morally right and wrong. The aim isn't usually presented in quite this way. The aim is more often put in terms of a practical requirement, which is that an adequate moral theory should always yield a determinate answer about whether a given action is morally right or wrong – to be done or not to be done. And it is a further aim of moral theory to portray these answers as following from moral principles that are universally binding. If these aims could be realized, then surely all of the moral truths – including both the principles and their applications – could all be embraced together.

Williams also offered convincing arguments to show that the scientific realists' model of objectivity cannot be carried over to the domain of ethics. Since he regarded scientific realism as our main current model of objectivity, he concluded that we cannot coherently aspire to objectivity in ethics. Many other philosophers would not accept this conclusion. Rationalists would not because, unlike Williams, they still think that the project of Morality is feasible. Likewise, pragmatists would not because, unlike him, they reject the metaphysical conception of reality that goes together with scientific realism. And John McDowell would not, because he thinks there is room for a kind of naturalism that doesn't reduce to what he calls the bald naturalism of science. But what concerns me is not the issue of objectivity in ethics *per se*. What concerns me is whether Williams' reasons for doubting whether we can achieve objectivity in ethics are also reasons to reject the unimundial ideal of a single, consistent and complete body of ethical truths. And it should be clear from my discussion of realism above that when the issue of objectivity is framed in terms of whether there are mind-independent facts, it is orthogonal to the issue of relativism as I'm proposing to construe it. So unlike his attack on the project of Morality, Williams' worries about ethical objectivity do not undermine any important source of support for unimundialism in ethics.

But let us suppose that his combined assault on the project of Morality and the aspiration to objectivity in ethics had left us without any positive reasons to embrace unimundialism in ethics. That would not automatically license us to adopt a multimundial stance in ethics. For then we would not be meeting the standard I've said, which requires that we go beyond merely begging the question, by finding substantive reasons to favor one view over the other. The question we are left with is, did Williams give us substantive reasons for adopting a multimundial stance in ethics, that go beyond merely begging the question?

Arguably, he did. The important point for him was that ethical values are unintentionally fashioned in response to fairly specific social conditions and, as a result, they do not always provide meaningful instructions about how to live in other social conditions. This point makes much more sense when we focus on what he called *thick* ethical values – the ones that reflect the specificity of the choices we actually face in our social conditions – as opposed to the *thin* values that figure in moral theory. If this point can really stick, it is because the thin values – good, bad, right, wrong, welfare, harm, respect, autonomy – can't really instruct us except in application to choice situations in which thick values are also in play. I'm inclined to think that this is so. What counts as a harm, or a form of due respect, for example, is typically a function of many other things that we value in an ethically thick sense as a result of our actual situations, with the effect that what does and doesn't count as a harm in one social condition may be quite different from what does and doesn't count as a harm in another social condition. For example, in a capitalist society, one thinks of oneself as harmed if one's property is harmed, and yet one doesn't think of oneself as harming others when one holds out for the best deal one can command in the market place; whereas, in another cultural setting there may not be the same institutions of property and commerce in the light of which the former counts as a harm and the latter does not. Similarly, in cultural conditions where honor codes prevail, one may be harmed by actions that wouldn't count as harms at all elsewhere, and when one's honor has been compromised, one may take retributive actions that would, in other settings, be viewed as causing impermissible harms. These reflections strongly suggest that ethical terms vary in meaning across social conditions – in this case, the term "harm" does not mean the same thing in different social conditions in which property and commerce, on the one hand, and honor, on the other, figure centrally. One may be reminded here of my earlier discussion in Section II of the common understanding of relativism, on which alternativeness arises with irresoluble conflict. I said there that we would do better to resolve those conflicts by explicitly relativizing truth to context, than to portray relativism as carrying a commitment to violating the law of non-contradiction. It might seem that all I have done here is find another way to remove the appearance of contradiction, by insisting that the terms involved don't carry the same meaning in the allegedly contradictory judgements. And then it might seem that the same lesson should emerge, which is that we can save unimundialism by portraying these ethical truths as consistent and co-tenable. But once we have the possibility of normative insularity in view, we ought not to infer directly from the fact that certain claims are not inconsistent, that they are consistent and co-tenable. To infer that directly would be to beg the question in favor of unimundialism. To repeat, what we want to do is investigate what substantive reasons there might be to prefer one view over the other – unimundialism and multimundialism.

So let us consider what it would be like to try to live the unimundial stance, on the assumption that different ethical standards prevail in different social conditions. The first thing we would have to do is try to assess whether the evaluative attitudes of others who occupy other social conditions are consistent or inconsistent with our own evaluative attitudes. Since the attitudes we'd be concerned with would incorporate *thick* ethical values, they'd presumably differ enough in content from our own that there wouldn't be any direct conflict between theirs and ours. By the lights of unimundialism, it would follow that they must be consistent and co-tenable with our own. And the upshot would be the sort of when-in-Rome-do-as-the-Romans-do morality that I've already discussed. However, when I first portrayed this as a kind of ethical agreement, I conceded that it seems to leave scope for some residual relativist intuitions. For it seems significant, somehow, that those who live in different social conditions cannot all live by the same ethical standards. This fact would not compromise the case for unimundialism if it could be shown that learning how others live in their social conditions might *teach* us something about how to live in our own. That was the old "Experiments in Living" model of ethical inquiry, which clearly would require us to adopt a unimundial stance (this model still lives on in some of our conceptions of a liberal arts education). But we would have to show that the learning in question would be *ethical* learning. Ethical knowledge isn't to be gained just by cataloguing all of the ethical standards by which people live in different social conditions. In order that something count as ethical knowledge it must be action-guiding, and having available a catalogue of how others live in other social conditions might not provide us with any guidance concerning how we should live where we actually are. Insofar as that is so, we lack positive reasons for adopting the unimundial stance in ethics and, moreover, we have far greater reason to adopt the multimundial stance of the relativist. For it would be entirely appropriate to see our own ethical inquiries as taking place within the boundaries of our own social conditions, and to see them as normatively insulated from what goes on outside them.

Thus, even if we aren't persuaded by Williams concerning whether scientific realism is the only available model for objectivity in ethics, we can nevertheless agree with him that there is an important contrast between ethics and science. And there is one further point that he made about this contrast that deserves to be emphasized. He insisted that if convergence ever did emerge in ethical life it wouldn't signify what he took convergence in science to signify. I think he got the latter wrong, because there are many ways in which we might explain convergence in the progress of science besides the hypothesis of scientific realism. But I also think he got the former right. All that convergence in ethics would signify is a tendency toward cultural homogenization. And although a condition of homogeneity would leave no opportunity to actually *live* the multimundial stance of the relativist, it would still leave metaphysical room for its possibility, insofar as it remains a human possibility *not* to converge in this way, but to retain the ethical diversity of our past traditions and even generate new forms of ethical diversity in the future. I don't mean to suggest that this is within our intentional control – as if we could decide to stop cultural homogenization and succeed. Nor do I mean to suggest that the relativist should passively value diversity of ethical outlook for its own sake, by feeling nostalgia for a past that was more diverse than the present, or hope for a future that turns out to be more culturally diverse than we presently expect it will be. Williams understood that cultural formation just happens, and it sets us practical possibilities not of our own making, and not always the same practical possibilities. It is because our ethical standards must help us navigate these possibilities, which are not all shared, that there is some scope for meaningful, lived ethical relativism.

There are lines of resistance to this case for ethical relativism that we might pursue, even if we accept Williams' overall ethical vision. It might be protested that I have underestimated the epistemic advantages of the unimundial stance – the possibility of learning from other social conditions and applying what we learn in our own conditions. Or it might be urged that the unimundial stance is ethically superior, because it would require us always to *ethically engage* others, by taking their views as something to either appropriate or contest. These lines of resistance are well worth pursuing, for they bring up important issues that need sorting out if we are to arrive at a fully considered position on relativism in ethics.[14]

However, it is striking that these lines of resistance to relativism can be formulated without bringing in the metaphysical issues that the prevailing orthodoxy deems relevant. Realism is the most obvious such issue, and I've already said a great deal about why it is less relevant than most would assume. There is another, not unrelated issue, that many would assume to be relevant, about which I've said very little, except to note Williams' own pessimism with respect to it – namely, the issue of objectivity in ethics. Not everyone agrees with Williams that science provides us with our main model of objectivity. Notably, John McDowell does not.[15] And, in closing, it is worth considering whether his account of ethical objectivity speaks against the serious consideration Williams offers in favor of ethical relativism, if for no other reason than to reiterate what is essential to it and what is dispensable.

McDowell actually accepts the aspect of Williams' ethical vision that I think provides the greatest support for relativism. He concurs that ethical values must guide us in the particular social conditions in which we find ourselves, and that they will therefore vary with time and place. But he still finds room for objectivity in the domain of ethics, by modeling value on secondary qualities such as red. In both cases, the phenomena at issue wouldn't exist were it not for our subjective ways of responding to the world – evaluation in the one case and color vision in the other. And yet there is still room for objectivity because there is still room for error.

Certainly, our believing that something is red doesn't suffice to make it so. And similarly, McDowell holds that our believing that a given action is ethically appropriate or required doesn't suffice to make it so either; the action would have to be a fitting response to the particular circumstance with which we are faced, and it may not be. Scientistically minded philosophers might be impressed by a remaining difference between the cases. We can aspire to give a scientific explanation of color vision that would allow us to view it as a *systematic* way of responding to various facts that we have learned about through the sciences.[16] And this contributes to our sense that color judgements may indeed be true or false: it is because they can be explained as systematic responses to, and hence as systematic ways of tracking, the sorts of facts that science studies. But it seems highly doubtful that we shall ever find a scientific explanation of our evaluative responses to the world, that would allow us to see them as tracking those sorts of facts. And this difference between the cases is exactly what drives Williams' reservations about objectivity in ethics. McDowell thinks we should not be overly impressed by this. According to him, even if there is no scientific explanation of what makes our ethical judgements true and false, we can still make sense of the possibility of error insofar as our judgements can still be fitting or not as ethical responses to the social reality around us. It seems to me that he's right about this and that, therefore, Williams' denial of ethical objectivity is dispensable to the consideration he offered for taking ethical relativism seriously. It also seems to me that we can draw further support for this picture of ethical objectivity from the fact that cultural formation is not directly intended by anyone, but simply happens. For although secondary qualities arise with our subjective responses, we can nevertheless retain our sense that there is something objective about them, precisely because they are responses to a world *not* of our own making. Similarly, we can retain our sense that there is something objective about ethical values in spite of the fact that they arise with our subjective responses, insofar as they too are responses to a world not of our own making.[17] And the crucial point is that this important insight is not compromised if there are *many* such worlds rather than one. There is still something to get right or wrong through our ethical judgements, even though this may vary with place and time. And precisely because social reality is variable and not fixed, McDowell's picture of ethical objectivity is compatible with the multimundial stance of the relativist. I say this even though McDowell's own instincts are entirely against relativism. This may just be because he has not considered carefully enough the sorts of considerations ("alternativeness," "normative insularity," "multimundialism" ...) that I have brought to bear on formulating what relativism is. At the very least, if he wants to rule out relativism, he cannot do so simply by arguing for objectivity in ethics in the way he does. Insofar as the truth in ethics is a *local* affair which is tied to particular social conditions, we ought to see our ethical inquiries as confined within boundaries, and view the ethical judge-ments that others might make in response to other social conditions as normatively insulated from our own. And this is the truth in relativism that Williams found.

It is a truth which may stand even if there is, as I am inclined to think, more objectivity in ethics than he thought.

Notes

1 "The Truth in Relativism," in Bernard Williams, *Moral Luck* (Cambridge: Cambridge University Press, 1981). I will also draw on some of the supporting arguments that he gave in *Ethics and the Limits of Philosophy* (Cambridge, MA: Harvard University Press, 1985).

2 Here I am not referring to completeness in the logicians' sense. For I am not at all concerned with the artificial languages that logicians have devised or what can be formally proved about them. What I mean to convey is the idea of a *totality*.

3 Just as I was not referring earlier to completeness in the logicians' sense, here I am not referring to the logical sense of universality that Kripke concerned him-self with in his "Outline of a Theory of Truth" (*The Journal of Philosophy* 72 (1975)) – the sense in which the truth predicate is a universal predicate that can apply to any sentence. I am concerned rather with universality in something more like the sense that moral philosophers are concerned with when they claim that moral reasons are reasons for everyone.

4 However, in spite of what I've just said here, we'll see in Section II that the existence of incorrigible ignorance *might* pose a threat to the universality of truth in this strong sense that stands opposed to alternativeness.

5 Perhaps this wouldn't follow if we formulated relativism as a universal doctrine which says that *all* truth is relative, since, in that case, each relativization of truth to context would land us with yet another claim that was only relatively true. Yet I have already made clear that there are good reasons *not* to accept the doctrine as a universal one. And these reasons go beyond the logical and pragmatic diffi-culties that I discussed above, that would attend any attempt to state such a universal doctrine. For there are widespread intuitions according to which we have much greater reason to take relativism seriously in domains involving value than in other domains such as mathematics and science. I don't see how we can make sense of such intuitions unless we construe relativism as a domain-specific doctrine rather than as a universal one. And as soon as we allow that there might be domains in which truth is not relative, then we have the means of conceiving relative truth in the way I'm suggesting here, as being compatible with universality.

6 I gather this from my general reading and, also, from numerous conversations that I've had with colleagues and students. The philosopher who I think has done the most to try to develop an adequate metaphysical basis for this common understanding of relativism is Crispin Wright. He set the stage for such an account in *Truth and Objectivity* (Cambridge, MA: Harvard University Press, 1992), though without mentioning relativism explicitly. There are several papers in which he did more to develop it, especially "Relativism and Classical Logic," and "Intuitionism, Realism, Relativism and Rhubarb," though in more recent work he takes quite a different line.

7 There is a minor qualification. He said they needn't actually conflict, so long as they have conflicting consequences. But I don't see any interesting distinction here. Systems of belief are distinguished by their *contents*, and if two systems of

belief have conflicting consequences, then their contents are such as to rule one another out – and I take this to suffice for *actual* conflict. However, this presupposes a somewhat controversial picture of content that absorbs, within the content of a given belief, its logical implications. Those who reject this controversial picture, should bear Williams' qualification in mind.

8 William James, *The Will to Believe and Other Popular Essays* (New York: Dover Publications, 1956).

9 See Richard Rorty, *Consequences of Pragmatism* (Minneapolis: University of Minnesota Press, 1982); and *Contingency, Irony and Solidarity* (Cambridge: Cambridge University Press, 1989).

10 If it is formally problematic, then the tables in the debate about relativism will be turned in a surprising way. For the presumption generally is that it is the relativists' position which is formally problematic, due to its commitment to alternativeness. Whereas, it turns out that when we try to formulate the opposed position in a way that fully articulates its opposition to alternativeness – by bringing in the idea of a single and consistent and complete body of truths – we cannot presume that there is no formal difficulty lurking there. The presumption seems especially questionable if we think of unimundialism as a universal doctrine rather than as a domain-specific doctrine, according to which *all truths in all domains* are consistent and conjoinable – for as I understand it, there are mathematical difficulties that beset trying to speak of *everything*. But as I go on to explain in the text, I propose to set aside this difficulty for the time being, by framing the positive metaphysical content of unimundialism as a regulative ideal.

11 Within boundaries the normative behavior of relativists looks unimundialist. It is only upon encountering a boundary, or perhaps acknowledging the possibility of one, that the distinctive character of the multimundial stance emerges – in the ways I next go on to describe.

12 This is what I was alluding to in note 4 when I said that incorrigible ignorance may pose a threat to the universality of truth. I've discussed this and related issues at greater length in "Why Realism May Not Refute Relativism," in M. DeCaro and D. MacArthur (eds), *Naturalism and Normativity* (New York: Columbia University Press, forthcoming).

13 See my "What Would Relativism Be if It Were True?" in Annalisa Coliva (ed.), *Language, Meaning and Mind: Themes from the Philosophy of Crispin Wright* (Oxford: Oxford University Press, forthcoming).

14 I pursued some of these lines of resistance to ethical relativism further in "Earning the Right to Realism and Relativism in Ethics," *Philosophical Issues* 12 (2002). (N.B. That article was written at the very earliest stages of my thinking about these issues. Although many of the basic ideas were already in place, I didn't express all of them in the ways I do now. Regrettably, I tried to use the word "realism" in order to refer to the doctrine that relativists oppose. I thought it appropriate to do so because it is generally assumed that realism and relativism are mutually opposed doctrines. And the only way in which I could make sense of this assumption is by using the term "realism" to refer to what I now call "unimundialism." However, although there surely are many varieties of realism, I have come to see that they all have in common a preoccupation with whether, and to what extent, reality is mind-independent. Since the issue of mind-independence is not the issue that divides relativists from their opponents, it was an ill-conceived move on my part to try to distinguish a particular variety of realism that relativists oppose, rather than simply introduce the new term "unimundialism.")

15 See his "Critical Notice of Bernard Williams: *Ethics and the Limits of Philosophy,*" *Mind* 95 (1986) and also, "Two Varieties of Naturalism," in his *Mind, Value and Reality* (Cambridge, MA: Harvard University Press, 1998).

16 Those who are impressed by the "hard problem of consciousness" will insist that such scientific explanations will necessarily fall short of explaining the subjective aspects of color vision, because the latter concern *what it is like* to see red, and this can only be known from a first-person point of view. If this line is to be taken seriously, it ought to be pushed to its natural skeptical conclusion, which is that none of us knows anything at all about what it is like for others to perceive what they perceive – or even whether there is anything it is like at all. Anyone who stops short of this skeptical conclusion will have no trouble seeing the point here, which is that we have good reason to believe that there is a systematic dependence of the phenomenological aspects of perception on other, natural facts.

17 Of course, social realities would not exist were it not for our intentional activities. Nevertheless, it cannot be said that we *make* them in the same sense that we make roads and buildings, and even corporations. Whether and how the latter come into existence is under our direct intentional control in the following sense: we can frame intentions to bring them into existence and, also, to change them, and then carry out those intentions. But our efforts at social engineering have shown that traditions are not susceptible to such direct intentional control, nor is the course of history that yields them.

Part II

HUMAN REASONS

4

WILLIAMS ON REASONS AND RATIONALITY

Joshua Gert

Given the bloom of responses, defenses, and clarifications touched off by Bernard Williams' seminal paper "Internal and External Reasons," it may seem silly to attempt to shed any new light on the views he expresses there.[1] However, it is surprising how little effort is typically made to fit this paper into the large and complex context of Williams' views. It is generally treated as if it were a one-off contribution by an anonymous philosopher who emerged from the mists and disappeared again, returning at intervals only to attempt to deliver virtually the same message. Another surprising fact, consistent with this myopic focus, is the following: no advocate of external reasons has attempted to answer the distinctive concern about external reasons that Williams presents in his oft-cited "Internal Reasons and the Obscurity of Blame." This concern is *not* that the external reasons theorist cannot deal with the phenomenon of blame at all (for example, by justifying it) but that she cannot account in particular for a certain *obscurity* in the point and appropriateness of blame. And there is another important reason to be hopeful about the possibility of bringing some increased clarity to the debate that Williams has touched off: a debate that is sometimes characterized as one between internalism and externalism. For, somewhat surprisingly, the view with which Williams' internalism is typically contrasted, and which goes by the misleading name of 'externalism,' is in fact a version of a view that has also been, appropriately, called 'internalism'. A more genuinely externalist view is available, but is hardly represented in the literature, and discussions of Williams have not benefited from an exploration of the contrast it can provide. This view is one that I have presented in a number of other places, and I hope I will be forgiven for giving those views another airing here. My excuse is that it will allow me to focus attention on a number of Williams' overlooked concerns. My aim will not be to offer new arguments for my own view, but only to show that it would allow Williams to say a great deal that he was concerned to say, while also allowing – contrary to what one might expect – for a more radical externalism about reasons than even critics of Williams have attempted to defend. The central claim that allows for this surprising conclusion is that Williams' internalism is not best interpreted as an internalism about reasons, but as an internalism about overall rational status. I will close with some remarks about another overlooked feature of Williams' initial paper: a list of nine questions and answers that appear in its final pages.

I Some groundclearing

First off, it will be necessary to present the view that I take Williams ultimately to have endorsed. Initially we can say that this is the view that there is a central and distinctive sense of 'reason' according to which one can only truly say of someone that he has reason to perform some action if there is what Williams calls "a sound deliberative route" from that person's existing set of desires, commitments, patterns of emotional response, and so on (what Williams calls the person's "subjective motivational set," or "S" for short), to that person's being motivated to perform that action. External reasons are simply reasons that are not internal in this sense. In his first paper on the topic his rhetoric against external reasons was very strong, and many commentators took away the idea that for Williams, any external interpretation of reasons-claims was simply incoherent.[2] Indeed, some commentators took away more than this: they were convinced by what they *took* William's argument to be, and ended up holding the view that external reasons really were impossible.[3] However, Williams' claim is actually more modest: it is that his account gives the only *distinctive* sense of 'reason.' What this means, and what Williams explicitly concedes, is that there are other senses in which one can legitimately say of someone that he has reason to perform some action, even when the internalist claim is false of that person – even when, that is, there is no sound deliberative route that could lead that person to perform that action. For example, we might legitimately use a claim couched in the language of reasons in order to express our belief that it would be desirable that the agent perform the action.[4] Perhaps because of the existence of this and other quite coherent senses of 'he has reason,' Williams only claims that his view is "roughly expressed" by the claim that there are only internal reasons for action.[5]

What is the "distinctive sense" of reasons-claims that Williams is attempting to capture? This is not absolutely clear, but one requirement Williams offers is that to say that A has a reason to φ is to say something distinctively about A: it should not merely be an instance of the general claim that anyone in A's position would have a reason to φ.[6] By itself, this way of expressing what we might call Williams' "distinctiveness requirement" is potentially misleading. In particular, it wrongly suggests that if there were some reasons that we all happened to share – perhaps in virtue of being human – they would not count as internal. But such a *necessary* exclusion of universally shared internal reasons goes strongly against what Williams says elsewhere. For example, he claims that "any rational deliberative agent has in his S a general interest in being factually and rationally correctly informed," and he even admits at least the theoretical possibility that the constraints of morality are part of everyone's subjective motivational set, so that everyone would have reasons to be moral.[7] I think that what Williams really wanted to say is hinted at in the following claim: "a statement about A's reasons is partly a statement about A's psychology."[8] The idea then is not that this reasons-statement is distinctively about A rather than about B. Instead, it is that it is a statement distinctively about A – an agent with an actual psychology – rather than merely about A's position in the world.

Williams moves back and forth with a remarkable – one might say shocking – lack of concern between expressing his view in terms of an agent's having *reason* to perform some action, and an agent's having *a reason* to do so. This minor grammatical difference conceals the very significant distinction between the idea of a wholesale practical judgement about what one ought to do, and the judgement that a certain consideration counts in favor of an action, though other considerations may count against it, even decisively.[9] In "Values, Reasons, and the Theory of Persuasion" Williams explicitly notes the simplification involved in using the phrase 'more reason to act than to do anything else,' and makes the rather bold claim that "additional qualifications would in fact enable one to drop this restriction."[10] Nowhere, however, does he even begin to make clear what these additional qualifications would be. This very surprising failure to come to grips with the importance of the distinction between having *a reason* to φ (a reason that can at least potentially conflict with reasons to do other things) and having *reason* to φ (which amounts to having *most reason* to φ, or to its being the case that one *ought* to φ) occurs most egregiously – and crucially – when Williams tries to motivate his internalist position.[11] The first of the "two fundamental motivations of the internalist account" is the following:

> It must be a mistake simply to separate explanatory and normative reasons. If it true that A has a reason to φ, then it must be possible that he should φ for that reason.[12]

But this second sentence is generally false in any case in which the agent appreciates that φ-ing is not such a good idea, overall. This also shows why one *must* separate explanatory and normative reasons: explanatory reasons paradigmatically serve to explain what actually did happen, whereas normative reasons quite often contribute nothing to the explanation of an action – *and not only in cases of akrasia or other forms of irrationality*. The normative reasons that favor an inferior option do not, at least typically, contribute to an explanation of what the agent does, even potentially. One might wish to dismiss this worry as a technical detail, and therefore amenable to some technical solution. I doubt that this is true, but even if one takes such a view, there is a deeper problem: Williams simply offers no argument for the claim that we must always – in each and every particular case – regard normative reasons as potentially explanatory. Surely it is true that a consideration cannot be regarded as a normative reason if it is not the sort of thing that *ever*, or, perhaps more strongly, *typically* or *commonly*, provides a motive to human beings. But Williams is making a much stronger claim.

A second motivation for internalism about reasons appeals to certain phenomena associated with what Williams calls "focused blame." This sort of blame implies that the person being blamed had reason to act otherwise than the way for which he or she is being blamed. Blame of this sort also seems to involve the attribution of some negative trait, though this trait need not have any particularly moral content. As Williams points out, one thief might blame another for a certain risky negligence in his preparations for a heist that has gone bad. In discussing the relevant phenomena Williams is again really appealing to the idea of having most reason. This should not be surprising, since we do not blame people for the simple failure to act on a reason that they have: after all, we may agree that they were right to act on certain countervailing reasons. If we are going to put the point in terms of reasons, the most that we can say is that when we blame people we assume that they had *sufficient reason* to have acted as we blame them for failing to have done.[13] Even this may not be enough, if we grant – as Williams surely would, given his views on tragic choices – that people can have sufficient reason for various incompatible choices. Granting this, blame seems to depend on the judgement that the agent ought, all-things-considered, to have acted in some other way.

Given the importance of the phenomena of explanation and blame to Williams' arguments, it would have been clearer and more convincing if he had described his view as an internalism about the wholesale rational status of an action, rather than as an internalism about reasons. And I think this is the most charitable way of interpreting his view. It is true that he sometimes expresses his position in terms of the presence of a relevant motivation providing a necessary condition on the existence of a reason. Indeed, this is the way he first formulated it.[14] Since we all have various conflicting motivations, this way of expressing his view is more apt if the target is the notion of a *pro tanto* reason. John Skorupski has argued that this more fine-grained, motivation-based *pro tanto* formulation allows us to resolve some obscurities that arise in attempts to apply the "sound deliberative route" formulation – a formulation that better lends itself to explanations of wholesale rational status.[15] Skorupski's primary worry is that there is a great deal of indeterminacy in what counts as a sound deliberative route, since for Williams the processes of sound deliberation will include much more than merely means/end reasoning. For instance, they will include processes of imagination, constitutive reasoning, and much more. Second, Skorupski points out that there is a difference between a question of the *existence* of a sound deliberative route, and the question of whether or not the agent could in fact follow that route, and that Williams leaves the relevance of the latter unexplored. But despite these perceived shortcomings, even Skorupski notes that Williams seems later to have explicitly preferred the "sound deliberative route" formulation of internalism. Moreover, while Skorupksi regards the relative indeterminacy of this formulation as a reason to give preference to the more fine-grained, motivation-based, *pro tanto* formulation, there are reasons to think that Williams took this indeterminacy to be a definite advantage. For example, he writes:

> It is sometimes held against the combination of the internalist view with this broad conception of deliberation that it leaves us with a vague concept of what an agent has a reason to do. But this is not a disadvantage of the position. It *is* often vague what one has a reason to do.[16]

As we will see later, Williams also saw this vagueness as useful in explaining why it is that the function and appropriateness of blame are often obscure.

Williams' position, then, making explicit the real target of analysis, should be taken to be the following

> W: It would be rational for A to φ only if there is a sound deliberative route from A's existing motivational set to the decision to φ.

What would validate a *pro tanto* reason claim, giving this internalist account of claims about what it is rational to do overall? It is tempting to think of the rationality claim as expressing the result of a resolution of the various rational forces – reasons – for and against the action. Reasons could then be identified with these forces. But Williams is very clear that he rejects this model, and that we cannot use the method of differences – the consideration of counterfactual cases – to isolate the normative force of any given consideration.[17] Another suggestion might be that for a consideration to count as a reason is for it to figure in some sound deliberative route to φ-ing, whether as a consideration that favors φ-ing, or as a consideration that disfavors it. The problem with this suggestion is that the relevant notions of favoring and disfavoring are no clearer than the notion of a reason for or against an action. My conclusion is that Williams has not provided us with much guidance as to how we should understand *pro tanto* reasons claims, so that W remains the best statement of his view.

II External reasons, internal rationality

In a supposed contrast to Williams' internalism, there are those who have suggested that there might be reasons that apply to agents quite independently of their contingent motivations. Paradigmatically, those who suggest this want moral reasons to figure among such external reasons. But, as noted above, Williams is happy to hold that some considerations – perhaps even moral considerations – might be reasons of this sort.[18] The question merely would be whether, given what it is to be a rational agent, all rational agents could be brought to the decision to act on that consideration via a sound deliberative route. Many attempts have been made, notably by Kantians, to show that this is a real possibility. Williams thinks that all these attempts fail, but there is nothing in his belief that all reasons are internal that entails that they *must* fail. And in fact in many places Williams seems to be committed not only to the idea that there are some universal reasons, but also to the idea that some of them have moral content. For example, in "The Idea of Equality" he writes that "It is a matter of logic that particular sorts of needs constitute a reason for receiving particular sorts of good."[19] And he also equates people's rights with "the reasons why they should be treated in a certain way."[20] This, together with his claim that "There are indeed clear cases of human rights, and we had better not forget it," certainly suggests that he holds that there are clear cases of reasons for action that do not depend on anything contingent.[21] There is a persistent temptation to try to argue for the possibility of external reasons by arguing for the possibility of non-contingent reasons shared by everyone in virtue of their rationality or humanity. Christine Korsgaard's "Skepticism about Practical Reason" is the paradigm example of such an attempt.[22] But Williams is quite happy to allow for the possibility of such reasons, and in places he seems to concede rather more than their mere possibility.[23]

What, then, would a genuinely external reason be? It would have to be one that an agent had, even though no sound deliberative route could bring that agent to act on that reason. This suggests that this understanding of the notion of a reason will not find its primary application in the first-personal perspective: what use would the concept of such a reason be, from that perspective? But that is fine. As Williams puts it, "The importance of an ethical concept need not lie in its being an element of first-personal deliberation."[24] Of course the concept of a reason is rather wider than that of the ethical, since there are reasons other than ethical reasons. But the point still stands. Whether or not a concept finds its primary application in first-personal deliberation is a matter to be decided on a case-by-case basis. Now, William clearly thinks that practical thought is radically first-personal.[25] And that may be true; if practical thought is simply thought that leads the formation of an intention, then it does seem essentially first-personal. I can no more form someone else's intentions than I can cast someone else's shadow. But all this says very little about the notions of reasons and rationality until we know more about how those notions are involved in practical thought. Relatedly, despite his analysis of reasons in terms of desires and values, Williams denies that we can deduce what we ought to do from any claims about our desires, or even from claims about what we regard as most important.[26] All of this very strongly suggests that the concept of a practical reason is largely useless from the first-person point of view. We do not deliberate from premises that describe our reasons *as reasons*: rather, we deliberate from our reasons – from premises such as "It will embarrass her."[27] Nor, plausibly, do we reason to conclusions such as "I should not reveal her secret." Rather, we reason, and our practical conclusion is simply to keep our mouths shut.[28] This is at odds, certainly, with some of what Williams has written about the deliberative or practical 'ought,' as that it expresses the agent's recognition of the appropriate course of action.[29] But it is simply a misrepresentation of ordinary deliberative practices to say that we express our deliberative conclusions to ourselves with ought-claims.

One way of arguing for the possibility of genuinely external reasons – reasons that an agent might have even if no sound deliberative route could lead the agent to act on that reason – appeals to the ideal of a well brought up person. This is John McDowell's suggestion.[30] An external reason for an agent A to φ would be a consideration that would move an *ideal* agent who found herself in A's circumstances. Since A might well not be ideal, A might be incapable of arguing himself or being argued into a position from which he might appreciate the external reason: this is precisely the fact that makes the reason count as genuinely external, rather than merely universal and internal. Still, if we grant the premise that there is a relatively determinate ideal of the well brought up person, we can see a point, and perhaps a measure of truth, in the claim that A has a reason to act in the way favored by the external reason. A concrete example might be the claim that a certain incorrigibly mean and insensitive person is blind to the reasons that he has to behave more kindly. Even if we grant that this person could not be argued into a kinder disposition, we need not hear this reason claim as ringing false.

Williams objects to this "ideal agent" account of external reasons on a number of grounds. Of primary concern to him is the fact that on this proposal the claim that A has a reason to φ is not a claim distinctively about A, in the sense explained above. Rather, on McDowell's proposal the reason that A has to φ in circumstances C is given by A's circumstances, and by facts about the psychology of *someone else*: the well brought up person. A second, more technical concern is that A's being rather far from an ideal agent can itself be the source of distinctive reasons for A to act in certain ways, and McDowell's proposal fails to allow for this. To borrow an example from Michael Smith: A might be the sort of person who becomes so angry when he loses at games that he has a reason, having just lost a game of squash, to leave the court immediately, rather than to try to congratulate his opponent. For if he tries to congratulate his opponent he may well get into a fight.[31] But the well brought up person would not have any reason to leave so quickly. Clearly Williams is trying to capture the distinctive sense of 'reason' that underwrites the following claim, which is distinctively about A: A has a reason to get out of the court right away.

I do not want to rehabilitate McDowell's attempt to argue for the existence of external reasons. But I want to take up one point that McDowell deploys in the course of his argument: a point that is very congenial both to Williams' general philosophical style, but that also provides a basis for a rather different argument for the existence of external reasons. The point is "the indubitable relevance of human psychology to what human beings have reason to do."[32] Williams' view may seem to make some concession to this point, at least to the degree that the processes that count as sound deliberation are human psychological processes, so that our cognitive limits place limits on what he is willing to say that an agent has reason to do. An angel endowed (*per impossible*) with precisely my motivations might well have different reasons than I do, simply because angels are so much smarter, more imaginative, and logical than I am. However, this admission does not grant McDowell's point in the spirit it is offered, for the point about the angel is simply an application of a point that also applies with regard to distinct human beings: the reasons one has depend not only on one's motivations, but also one's particular principles of deliberation, and one's capacities to apply those principles.[33] This makes the reasons that people have conceptually independent of the fact that they happen to be human beings. But this should strike us as strangely out of step with much of what Williams writes elsewhere. For it is a characteristic idea in Williams that we need to engage in a "genealogy" of our concepts if we are to understand them. That is, we need to ask why we have these concepts, and the 'why' here is broad enough to allow the answer to involve anthropological, historical, cultural, social and psychological elements.[34] Put in these terms, McDowell's point – a point that resonates with much of what Williams writes elsewhere – is that distinctive facts about human nature will figure in any acceptable genealogy.[35] Where McDowell goes wrong, I think, is in failing actually to provide a genealogy, and in thinking of human nature along perfectionist Aristotelian lines. For this has the unfortunate effect of suggesting that our reasons will always univocally point us in one direction: the direction in which the *phromimos* would move if situated in our position. And Williams is quite rightly skeptical that there is such a determinate human ideal.

There is, however, another sense of 'human ideal' that is not so determinate: it allows different people to meet the ideal even if they differ quite widely in their subjective motivations. Indeed, it allows different people to meet the ideal even if they differ in how well they have been brought up. For this reason it offers some hope that an account of external reasons for which it forms the basis will be able to avoid at least some of the worries Williams raises about McDowell's suggestion. It counts as an ideal not because it represents the pinnacle of human potential, but because it represents a kind of minimal standard implicit in our everyday notion of a grown-up person – a person capable of a minimal degree of deliberation and sustained control of her actions. Williams himself gives an account of such an ideal. He calls such people "subjects" and more or less equates them with the normal sorts of adults we encounter in our everyday lives. According to Williams, we get an idea of this ideal when we consider

> what is involved in a set of persons, not necessarily known to each other or specially important to one another, living under a common system of justice … They do have an interest in others' having powers of self-control and enough deliberative foresight to avoid unnecessary collisions with the law or with each other.[36]

Subjects need not share the same positive goals, but they must have goals that fit within certain limits: they will not have basic desires for saucers of mud, nor will their desires for another helping of dessert be strong enough to lead them to risk a fiery death.[37] Some subjects will pursue selfish pleasures, while others will seek to bring pleasure to others. Some will seek abstract knowledge, or the perfection of their own abilities, while others will seek to help other people develop in these ways. All subjects will be averse to certain things: that is what is implied by attributing to them "enough deliberative foresight to avoid unnecessary collisions with the law or with each other." The threat of legal sanctions gets a grip on subjects because of their aversion to the harms involved in punishment. Similar claims go for informal social rules and the informal sanctions that they involve. Given what it is to count as a subject, one description of an action that we can deduce to be the sort of action *any* subject will avoid (under the description) is the following:

> A: An action that risks bringing the agent some nontrivial harm (such as pain, death, or injury) without sufficient likelihood of bringing compensating benefits (such as pleasure, ability, freedom, or knowledge) to the agent or anyone else.

Of course, subjects will not always manage to avoid actions that meet the description given in A. They may quite reasonably be unaware that their actions meet that description. However, given their interest in avoiding actions that *do* meet the description, and the possibility of ignorance that their actions meet it, it will be useful to them to have a term in the language

81

that will allow one subject to inform another that his action does, in fact, meet that description. Note that the description essentially involves the idea of certain considerations counting against an action, without any counter-vailing considerations counting sufficiently in favor of the action. This talk of considerations counting in favor and against actions has the structure of reasons-talk: more, indeed, than does Williams' talk, which hardly ever makes any mention of countervailing considerations, or of considerations counting *against* action, or of the strength or weight of a reason, and which very often depends for its very intelligibility on the assumption that he is really talking about having *decisive* or *sufficient* reason to φ.[38] My suggestion is that the relevant considerations *are* reasons, and that the interest that subjects – that is, normal adults – have in knowing whether their actions meet the description given in A is part of a reasonable genealogy of the concept of a reason. Having such a concept allows for an easy discussion of whether and why an action meets the description. Because of this, I will call the actions that meet the description given in A "unjustified by reasons."[39] And my account of reasons will be the following:

> A reason is a consideration that makes a systematic contribution to the question of whether or not an action meets the description given in A. Sample reasons therefore include the fact that an action will bring the agent some substantive harm, such as pain or death, or some substantive benefit, such as pleasure, freedom or knowledge.

Now, the idea of a subject, on Williams' construal, is very closely related to the idea of responsibility for action. Indeed, Williams' claim is that we arrive at the idea of a subject from considering the idea of being "responsible for this action."[40] But clearly the fact that someone acts in a way that is unjustified by reasons need not say anything about whether or not that person is a normal grown-up person or not, or whether he is properly responsible for his action. This is because of the possibility, already noted, that one might perform such an action through completely reasonable ignorance of the fact that it was unjustified by reasons. What we need is something rather similar to the notion of an action unjustified by reasons, but that takes the agent's particular perspective into account. As we might put it, we need an account of the difference between an action's being *(un)justified by reasons* and its being *(ir)rational*. Williams is sensitive to precisely this sort of need. In "Internal and External Reasons," for example, he asks whether we should regard an agent as having a reason to drink from the glass in front of him given his reasonable belief that it is a gin and tonic and his desire for such a drink. Because the liquid in the glass is in fact toxic, Williams does not want to say that the agent has a reason to drink it. But, concerned to be able to say something about the agent's drinking it other than that there was a reason not to, Williams says that we can say that his action "displays him as, relative to his false belief, acting rationally."[41] For Williams, reasons are given by the facts, although the question of which facts are reasons is famously determined by the subjective motivations of the agent. But the rationality of an action is not determined solely by the facts: the beliefs of the agent are also relevant.

Williams' remark about the rationality of the agent who unknowingly drinks toxic fluid from a highball glass suggests a rather simple relation between what there is reason to do (which, coming from Williams, should always be taken to mean what there is *most* reason to do), and what is rational to do: what is rational is what, relative to the beliefs of the agent, there is reason to do. Elsewhere I have criticized this simple account of the relation between rationality and reasons.[42] The central problem is that an action can count as irrational if the agent *should have believed* something, but did not: the rationality of action is not completely separable from the rationality of belief. Recognition of this problem immediately suggests a simple modification to the first proposal: what is rational to do is what one would have reason to do if the world were as one *should* believe it to be, given one's evidence. The problem with this suggestion is that even if one *should* believe that a painful action will save one's life (for example), if one does *not actually* believe that it will produce that benefit, it is not rational to perform the action. That is, contrary to this second proposal, beliefs one does not actually have can never serve to render an action rational. Similar problems lie in store for any attempt to define rational action as action that would be justified by reasons, were the world as some class of propositions represents it.

How then should we conceive of the relation between what is justified by reasons and what is subjectively rational? Elsewhere I have argued for a reliablist account, along the following lines.[43]

> R: An action is irrational iff it proceeds from a state of the agent that (a) normally puts an agent at increased risk of performing actions that are unjustified by reasons, and (b) has its adverse effect by influencing the formation of intentions in the light of sensory evidence and beliefs. Otherwise it is rational.

For present purposes, the important thing to note about R is that it will make the rationality of an agent's action depend not only on the agent's beliefs, but also to a very great extent on the agent's subjective motivational set. And this is true despite the fact that the account acknowledges only external reasons. If this is right, then it avoids at least one of the problems that Williams had with McDowell's account. How is it that R makes the rationality of an action depend on the motivations of the agent? Consider two agents, A and B, each of whom is about to act in a way that will almost certainly entail a lot of pain, and each of whom is aware that his action is likely to have some very beneficial consequences for another person, C:

say, it will save C's life. Suppose A is motivated by these potential benefits to C, while B is indifferent to them. That is, A is motivated by the reasons that justify the action, but B is not. Because A is so motivated, his act of self-sacrifice does not count as irrational according to R. For it is no coincidence that his action is justified by reasons: he is performing it precisely because of the existence of the reasons that provide that justification. So his performance does not stem from any state that places him at increased risk of performing actions that are unjustified by reasons. B, on the other hand, would perform the painful action even if it were not likely to provide C with a benefit. That is what is implied by his indifference to those benefits. As a result, it is a matter of luck that it is justified by reasons, and his action therefore counts as irrational according to R.[44]

To call A's action irrational is therefore to make a distinctive claim about A – a claim about A's psychology – and not simply a claim about A's position or about the kind of action A is performing. For another agent in A's position might well not be irrational to perform the very same action. Similar claims obviously go for the statement that A's action is rational. Now, we have seen that Williams' claims about reasons are most charitably interpreted as claims about the overall rational status of an action. The present account of rationality of action is therefore a candidate account of the same notion that Williams is after. Reasons – real reasons, as we might say – figure, in this account, not as facts that find a corresponding motivation in agents who can be said to have them, but as the kinds of considerations that are relevant to the question of whether or not an action is justified by reasons. On this account many actions that are justified by reasons are nevertheless irrational, because the reasons that provide the justification are not the reasons for which the agent acted.

The above picture is very different from the one presented by Williams: so different that one might initially be excused for thinking that it is a picture of a different concept entirely. In some sense this is right. Williams has represented himself as offering an account of reasons. But almost nothing he says is consistent with this representation if we understand reasons as normal people do: as considerations that count in favor or against an action, and that can be combined with or opposed by other reasons. Some of the opposition to Williams' views may well have its source in his extremely misleading choice of terminology. My account of *reasons* is therefore admittedly not an account of the same thing Williams sometimes calls "a reason to φ," since he typically makes the simplifying assumption that the reason at issue is a decisive reason.[45] But I am trying to give an account of a distinctive concept with which we can say something distinctive about A when we say that, for A, it would be rational, or irrational, to φ. Williams' "A has a reason to φ" and my "A would be rational to φ" both can be understood as making the same sort of claim. But my way of explaining the content of this claim also allows us to say such things as: there are always sufficient reasons to behave morally. What this means is not that it would be irrational to act immorally, but that for people who are appropriately motivated, it will be rational to act morally, even when doing so involves a genuine sacrifice. This is not merely an instance of the vacuous claim that Williams' own account entails: that *any* sort of action – even insanely pointless self-destructive behavior – would be rational for someone with the appropriate motivations. Rather, it is true because morally required action that involves a personal sacrifice must bring with it some sort of benefit that provides a reason sufficient to justify the sacrifice.

III The obscurity of blame

As far as I know, no external reasons theorist has tried to address the central challenge that Williams presents in "Internal Reasons and the Obscurity of Blame." That challenge is to provide an account of external reasons that dovetails with the essential obscurity of the phenomena of blame. This is not a semantic obscurity in the concept of blame. Rather, it is an obscurity we often find when we seek to determine whether or not blame is appropriate in a given case, and what it is that blame, in such cases, might be effecting. As we have seen, on Williams' view there are many sources of vagueness in the notion of an agent's reasons (by which we should now understand him to mean: in the notion of what it is rational for the agent to do). Because of blame's link to the idea that the person being blamed had reason to act otherwise, vagueness with regard to an agent's reasons will help explain the obscurity of blame. As Williams puts it, "the inherent obscurity of focused blame and its operation are closely related to the vagueness ... of 'A has a reason to φ'."[46] One source of the relevant vagueness is the open-ended nature of the "sound deliberative route" that must be capable of yielding motivation to φ, if the agent can rightly be said to have a reason to φ. For there is no sharp line between paradigmatically deliberative activities, imagination, and conversion to a new point of view.[47] Nor is it fully determinate, much less transparent to those who offer blame, what precisely makes up the agent's subjective motivational set. Then too, when we blame an agent and offer him reasons why he should have acted differently we may be attempting, by that very act of blame, to provide reasons via a presupposed "disposition to do things that people he respects expect of him." Williams calls such uses of blame and their associated reasons-claims "proleptic," by which he means that the very expression of these claims is intended to bring about the changes that make them appropriate or true.[48] Because of all these sources of vagueness, including the question of whether prolepsis is a viable strategy, it can often be quite obscure whether blame is appropriate or not, even when someone has acted in a way that we regard as demonstrating a very significant ethical failure. For according to Williams, and also according to a reasonable view of blame, we cannot legitimately blame someone for a particular action if we admit that they could not rationally have performed any other.

In Williams' words, the problem for the externalist about reasons is that "the externalist account does not mirror the genuine obscurity of the phenomena."[49] This is a separate issue from the fact that in many cases in which it seems intuitively inappropriate to blame someone, the externalist account will still yield the claim that the person had quite powerful external reasons to act differently. This will happen not only in cases of ignorance, but also as the result of phobias or compulsions, or even a deep and abiding indifference to the relevant sorts of reasons.[50] But we can leave this issue to the side, both because it has nothing essentially to do with the *obscurity* with which Williams is concerned, and because Williams is best interpreted as linking the legitimacy of blame not to *reasons* – as reasons are commonly understood – but to an internal conception of *rationality*. The important question therefore is: how does the reliablist account of rationality (which involves an externalist account of reasons) fare in comparison with Williams' own view? First, notice that even for Williams, the appropriateness of blame is linked to external evaluative criteria. If blame is to be appropriate for an action, "there must be some generally reprehensible characteristic involved in [its] explanation."[51] These reprehensible characteristics are named by so-called "thick" ethical terms, though they need not be specifically moral. Williams offers 'careless' and 'lazy' as examples. What this means is that mere failure to act rationally, even on Williams' understanding of what that means, does not open one to the possibility of legitimate blame.

As we have seen, the externalist, reliablist account of rationality makes the rationality of action depend, in many cases, on the motivational set of the agent. One reason for this is that a reason cannot make an agent's action rational if the agent does not act at least partly *for* that reason. At the same time, however, it leaves open quite a wide range of potentially rational action, even for a given agent at a given time. For an action will count as irrational only if it proceeds from a state of the agent that places that agent at increased risk of performing actions that are unjustified by reasons: a self-destructive desire, for example, or a failure of instrumental reason, or a rage that blinds the agent to immediate dangers. If Williams is right that what counts as a sound deliberative route is an indeterminate matter, and if we grant that such deliberative routes are ones that do *not*, by themselves, place an agent at increased risk of performing actions unjustified by reasons, then the externalist reliablist will be able to mirror any resulting indeterminacies that Williams thinks he can find in the claim that it would be rational for A to φ in circumstances C. So far, then, the externalist can account for the same obscurity as can Williams.

The other important obscurity in the appropriateness of blame, for Williams, is an obscurity in the appropriateness of its proleptic deployment. In some cases such a use is not appropriate. This would be true of attempts to deploy blame against someone who not only remained unmoved by appeals to facts about, say, the well-being of other people, but who also had no particular interest in the respect of the sort of people who expect others to take such matters into account. Once we move far enough away from this "hard case," proleptic blame begins to get a grip. At the other end of the spectrum is someone who shares the concerns that lie behind our blame, and who failed to act only because of some lapse that could certainly have been overcome. This is someone who, it is quite likely, would blame herself. Let us call this the "easy case." Now, if proleptic blame gets at least some grip, or some point, in any case sufficiently short of the hard case, this cannot be because the blame will actually convince the person to perform a different action. After all, this is not possible even in the easy case. In *all* cases in which blame is even potentially appropriate, it is too late for this: the action has already been performed. This should strike us as significant, given that Williams thinks that restrictions on the appropriateness of blame parallel restrictions on the appropriateness of advice. How could the parallel be perfect, given that the potential for advice to affect matters is so different from the potential for blame to do so? Williams acknowledges that blame sometimes functions as an instrument of correction and disapproval.[52] Why not say, then, that this function plays a central role in the genealogy of blame? If we admit this independently plausible claim, then we need not hold that the path the agent is being blamed for having failed to take – a path that is now causally inaccessible – must have been rational for the agent to have taken at the time of his choice. Rather, the appropriateness of blame can at least sometimes have to do with the potential effects of disapproval and correction. Past action gives a good clue about what these potential effects may be, and this may partly explain why blame may seem inappropriate for the hard case. This partially consequentialist conception of blame also explains what Williams seems not to: our tendency not to blame people in the easy case either, at least people who are already full of remorse. Of course it is generally an obscure matter, whether or not blame will serve a corrective function. And, given that we are engaged in a genealogy of a *practice* of blame, it is also obscure to what degree the appropriateness of blame will depend on the likelihood of blame having a corrective effect in *each particular instance*. But these obscurities parallel the obscurity Williams appeals to in determining whether there is any point in deploying blame in a proleptic way. So again, the internal and external conceptions are on a par.

Where the external conception seems to have an advantage over Williams' own view is in the set of cases in which the externality of reasons is most manifest: when reasons involve harms to the agent. On the external conception, not only will the risk of harms always provide reasons, it will *always* be irrational to act in the face of such reasons, unless one also reasonably believes that there are other reasons sufficient to justify one's action. For Williams, this is not true: a sufficiently peculiar agent will, on his view, have no reason to get what he needs, or to avoid what he needs to avoid.[53] In cases in which this sort of irrationality plays a large role, we often do not blame the agent even for actions that cause a good deal of harm to other people. When this is so, it is partly *because* of the kind of irrationality involved. The agent is not blamed for a failure to have performed the action we would have preferred – an action that would have been rational – precisely because the failure was itself irrational in a certain way. Consider such a case: one in which the agent simply lacked, to any significant degree, the required self-concern to have avoided an action that ended up hurting both himself and a number of other people. Williams will have to say, given our stipulation, that this agent had no reason to act otherwise: that is, for such an agent, it would not have been rational to have acted in a less self-destructive manner. This strikingly implausible claim would, it is true, explain why we might not blame this agent. But it also makes unavailable the kind of excuse that seems natural to make. The externalist can offer a better explanation: given that blame is an instrument of correction, it relies partly on the fact that it is unpleasant to be the target of blame. Our irrational agent cannot be assumed to be averse to this sort of unpleasantness, or other pains or harms. So it is unclear whether blame here has any point.[54] And yet we can say, consistently with this, that the agent is acting irrationally. The question of when, precisely, an agent's irrationalities make blame lose its point, is an obscure matter, and an adequate account of blame would explain the scope and source of its obscurity. Understanding the practice of blame as at least partially a system of correction does this. Williams' account does not seem to give us similar resources, and actually suggests that the clearest cases of appropriate blame should be ones in which agents act irrationally – for in many such cases they clearly have reasons to have acted otherwise.

IV Nine questions and four more

At the end of "Internal and External Reasons" Williams asks, and answers, nine questions that help to make explicit the content and implications of his view. In this final short section, I would like to do something similar, first comparing the internalist and externalist answers to Williams' original questions, and then posing four more. The only one of Williams' original questions on which the external reasons account sketched above differs from Williams' account is the following:

> 3. Can we define a notion of rationality where the action rational for A is in no way relative to A's existing motivations?

To this question, Williams obviously gives a negative answer. The externalist about reasons can agree, but with one important qualification: in some exceptional cases there will only be one rational choice that an agent can make, because all other choices involve harms to the agent without compensating benefits to anyone. As for the rest of the nine questions, the externalist and Williams agree that (1) rationality is not purely egoistic and (2) that it is not purely means–end, but that (4) egoism is not necessarily irrational either. Both also agree that (5) egoistic reasons cannot always be offered to free-riders, but that (6) sometimes they can and that (7, 8) sometimes it is rational to decline to be a free-rider, even when one has no egoistic reason to do so, on account of altruistic motives. And, lastly, they agree that (9) it is rational for people in society to bring up other people to have the sort of altruistic motivations that discourage free-riding.

So far Williams and the externalist are in surprisingly comprehensive agreement. However, there are a number of additional questions on which Williams and the externalist will differ. Here they are.

10. Can we define a notion of rationality according to which an agent will count as irrational because he has an obviously insane and self-destructive motivational set?

Williams: No.
Externalist: Yes.

11. For such an insane self-destructive agent, can we call the self-destructive actions that flow from his mental illness irrational in virtue of the self-destructive aims they express?

Williams: No.
Externalist: Yes.

12. For a virtuous agent who reliably acts morally in the face of threats of harms such as pain and death, can we intelligibly say that those threats provided reasons against such action: reasons that the agent's virtuous character helps him to act against?

Williams: Not on the account in its present form, since it lacks an account of *pro tanto* reasons.
Externalist: Yes.

13. In the case of a selfish and immoral agent, can we say that the agent is insensitive to certain reasons, and that this is what it is to be selfish and immoral?

Williams: No, for such an agent, there are no such reasons to which he is insensitive.
Externalist: Yes.

Notes

1 Bernard Williams, "Internal and External Reasons," in *Moral Luck* (Cambridge: Cambridge University Press, 1981), pp. 101–13.
2 For example, see John McDowell, "Might There Be External Reasons?" in J. E. J. Altham and Ross Harrison (eds), *World, Mind, and Ethics: Essays on the Ethical Philosophy of Bernard Williams* (Cambridge: Cambridge University Press, 1995), pp. 68–85.
3 This seems to be the view, for example, of Timothy Chappell. See his "Bernard Williams," in Edward N. Zalta (ed.), *The Stanford Encyclopedia of Philosophy (Spring 2006 Edition)*, available at: http://plato.stanford.edu.proxy.lib.fsu.edu/archives/spr2006/entries/williams-bernard/
4 Bernard Williams, "Values, Reasons, and the Theory of Persuasion," in A. W. Moore (ed.), *Philosophy as a Humanistic Discipline* (Princeton, NJ: Princeton University Press, 2006), p. 109. See also Bernard Williams, "Postscript: Some Further Notes on Internal and External Reasons," in Elijah Millgram (ed.), *Varieties of Practical Reasoning* (Cambridge, MA: MIT Press, 2001), pp. 91–7, at p. 93.
5 Bernard Williams, "Internal Reasons and the Obscurity of Blame," in *Making Sense of Humanity* (Cambridge: Cambridge University Press, 1995), pp. 35–45, at p. 35.
6 See Williams, "Replies," in J. E. J. Altham and Ross Harrison (eds), *World, Mind, and Ethics: Essays on the Ethical Philosophy of Bernard Williams* (Cambridge: Cambridge University Press, 1995), pp. 192–4. See also "Internal Reasons and the Obscurity of Blame," p. 44.
7 Williams, "Internal Reasons and the Obscurity of Blame," p. 37. See also his "Values, Reasons, and the Theory of Persuasion," p. 111.
8 Williams, "Replies," p. 191.
9 In "Internal Reasons and the Obscurity of Blame," p. 35, Williams unfortunately explains the notion of having *a* reason by direct appeal to what wholesale conclusion the agent could reach as to what he should do. This is most charitably regarded as a lapse, since it eliminates the conceptual possibility of conflicting reasons, except perhaps in the odd case in which sound deliberation could issue both in the conclusion that one should φ and in the conclusion that one should not φ.
10 Williams, "Values, Reasons, and the Theory of Persuasion," p. 109. Williams is similarly blithe in his "Replies," p. 186.
11 The equation of having most reason to φ and its being the case that one ought to φ occurs at various places. See, for example, Bernard Williams, *Ethics and the Limits of Philosophy* (Cambridge, MA: Harvard University Press), p. 19; "The Primacy of Dispositions," in *Philosophy as a Humanistic Discipline*, pp. 67–75, at p. 68; "Values, Reasons, and the Theory of Persuasion," p. 113.
12 Williams, "Internal Reasons and the Obscurity of Blame," pp. 38–9.
13 In fact, the argument from the *possibility* of blame (as opposed to its obscurity) cannot bear very much weight. For in his "Practical Necessity," in *Moral Luck*, pp. 124–31, at p. 130, Williams makes it clear that genuine psychological incapacity "cannot turn away blame." As he puts it: "The incapacities we are considering here are ones that help to constitute character, and if one acknowledges responsibility for anything, one must acknowledge responsibility for decisions and action which are expressions of character." This means that if one's (bad) character makes it impossible to act in a morally acceptable way, one may nevertheless well be responsible for the failure, and an appropriate target of blame. Of course this position directly contradicts later claims in "Internal

Reasons and the Obscurity of Blame." But this calls those later claims into question as much as those later claims call the earlier into question. My conclusion is that Williams' intuitions about blame cannot do much to support his position on reasons. And even in his later discussion, he admits that "it may be that [with regard to blame] the connection with reasons is not as close as the parallelism [between blame and advice] makes it seem" ("Internal Reasons and the Obscurity of Blame," p. 41).

14 Williams, "Internal and External Reasons," p. 101.
15 John Skorupski, "Internal Reasons and the Scope of Blame," in Alan Thomas (ed.), *Bernard Williams* (Cambridge: Cambridge University Press, 2007).
16 Williams, "Internal Reasons and the Obscurity of Blame."
17 Bernard Williams, "Acts and Omissions, Doing and Not Doing," in *Making Sense of Humanity*, pp. 56–64, at p. 57. John McDowell expresses this very well in "Might There Be External Reasons?" p. 70.
18 Williams, "Internal Reasons and the Obscurity of Blame," p. 37; "Values, Reasons, and the Theory of Persuasion," p. 111.
19 Bernard Williams, "The Idea of Equality," in Geoffrey Hawthorn (ed.), *In the Beginning Was the Deed* (Princeton, NJ: Princeton University Press, 2006), pp. 97–114, at p. 108.
20 Ibid., p. 107.
21 Williams, "Human Rights and Relativism," in *In the Beginning Was the Deed*, pp. 62–74, at p. 65.
22 Christine Korsgaard, "Skepticism about Practical Reason," in *Creating the Kingdom of Ends* (Cambridge: Cambridge University Press, 1996), pp. 311–34. See also Rachel Cohon, "Are External Reasons Impossible?" *Ethics* 96(3) (1986), 545–56.
23 See, for example, Bernard Williams, "Consistency and Realism," in *Problems of the Self* (Cambridge: Cambridge University Press, 1973), pp. 187–206, at p. 200.
24 Williams, *Ethics and the Limits of Philosophy*, p. 11.
25 Ibid., pp. 21, 61.
26 As Williams has famously pointed out, practical thought need not involve any appeal to normative notions at all. In arguing against certain overly-intellectual views of moral decision-making, for example, he suggests that the thought that precedes the rescue of one's wife ought to be "It's my wife," as against "It's my wife, and it's being my wife provides me with a reason to act" (ibid., p. 126). These admissions seem to contradict Williams' rather breezy confidence that "it is obvious on the internalist view" how it is "that an agent's accepting the truth of 'There is reason for you to φ' could lead to his so acting" ("Internal Reasons and the Obscurity of Blame," p. 39).
27 Bernard Williams, "Acting as the Virtuous Person Acts," in Myles Burneat (ed.), *The Sense of the Past: Essays in the History of Philosophy* (Princeton, NJ: Princeton University Press, 2006), pp. 189–97, at p. 196.
28 Of course, we should not deny that in some exceptional cases – perhaps complicated ones – we do list our reasons for ourselves under the descriptions 'reasons in favor' and 'reasons against.' Nor should it be denied that we sometimes resolutely conclude "I should not," and, as a result, do not. But if these cases are sufficiently exceptional, they can be regarded as instances in which we take an external perspective on our own position – perhaps in order to avoid certain biases to which we know we are subject.
29 See especially Bernard Williams, "*Ought* and Moral Obligation," in *Moral Luck*, pp. 114–23. But, for a contrast, see Bernard Williams, "Egoism and Altruism," in *Problems of the Self*, pp. 250–65, at p. 253.

30 McDowell, "Might There Be External Reasons?"
31 Michael Smith, "Internal Reasons," *Philosophy and Phenomenological Research* 55 (1) (1995), 109–31, at p. 111.
32 McDowell, "Might There Be External Reasons?" p. 82.
33 Williams, "Values, Reasons, and the Theory of Persuasion," p. 110.
34 Bernard Williams, "Nietzsche's Minimalist Moral Psychology" and "Introduction to The Gay Science," in *The Sense of the Past*, pp. 299–310 and 311–24. Also see his "The Human Prejudice" and "Philosophy as a Humanistic Discipline," in *Philosophy as a Humanistic Discipline*, pp. 135–52 and 180–99.
35 Williams seems willing to appeal to a normative conception of human nature in giving an account of the *needs* of human beings. See his *Ethics and the Limits of Philosophy*, pp. 42–3.
36 Bernard Williams, "Voluntary Acts and Responsible Agents," in *Making Sense of Humanity*, pp. 22–34, at p. 29.
37 Compare Bernard Williams, "Saint-Just's Illusion," in *Making Sense of Humanity*, pp. 135–50, at p. 141, where Williams agrees with Susan Hurley's view that to ascribe beliefs and desires to a being – to interpret them as acting intentionally – we must ascribe some values, and "those values must make sense to us as values that human beings might have."
38 Williams' failure to address the issue of conflicts of reasons within his official theory of reasons is surprising, given his belief in the existence of tragic choice situations, value pluralism, and the general messiness and complication of human lives.
39 This sense of 'unjustified,' as opposed to that of 'not justified,' comes from Williams, and entails standing in need of justification, and not receiving it. See Bernard Williams, "Moral Luck," in *Moral Luck*, pp. 20–39 at 25–6.
40 Williams, "Voluntary Acts and Responsible Agents," p. 29.
41 Williams, "Internal and External Reasons," p. 103.
42 Joshua Gert, *Brute Rationality* (Cambridge: Cambridge University Press, 2004), Chapter 7.
43 Williams seems to favor such a reliablist account of knowledge, so he might be amenable to a similar suggestion here. See his "Knowledge and Reasons," in *Philosophy as a Humanistic Discipline*, pp. 47–56, at p. 51.
44 This dependence of what we might call 'the rationalizing power' of a reason of this sort on the motivations of agent explains a phenomenon that Skorupski notes: the apparent dependence of the strength of reasons that involve ideals on the values of the agent. See Skorupski, "Internal Reasons and the Scope of Blame," pp. 26–7. By not distinguishing the rationality of an action from its being justified by reasons, however, Skorupski's explanation makes the strength of a reason of this sort depend on the agent's view of its strength, and this threatens to involve a destructive sort of circularity. See also my "Internalism and Different Kinds of Reasons," *Philosophical Forum*, 34(1) (2003), 53–72.
45 Of course, he notes this simplifying assumption in a number of places: he is not blind to the existence of potential conflicts of reasons or to their *pro tanto* nature. But what he does not note is the impact that his simplifying assumption has on the arguments that it then makes sense to offer in favor of internalism. Arguments from blame and from explanation simply do not transfer easily from the simplified case to the general case.
46 Williams, "Internal Reasons and the Obscurity of Blame," p. 43.
47 Ibid., p. 38.
48 Ibid., pp. 41–2. Prolepsis, explained in this way, can only function as advertised in the case of advice. In the case of blame, even an unlimited power to change

someone's present subjective motivations cannot make it true that that agent *had* those altered motivations at the time of the action that has attracted our blame. And it is in the past that the presuppositions of blame lie.

49 Ibid., p. 43.

50 These sources of psychological impossibility do not have the same impact on the appropriateness of blame. Deep and abiding indifference to the suffering one's actions cause to others need not exempt one from blame. It seems to me an advantage of externalism that it allows blame in such cases to be backed up by reasons.

51 Ibid., p. 40.

52 Ibid., p. 43.

53 Williams, "Internal and External Reasons," p. 105.

54 It is true that we continue to blame people who are unresponsive to our criticisms, and the externalist explanation may seem inconsistent with our persistence. I do not have a full answer to this worry, raised by Dan Callcut. But it does seem to me that it is a worry that Williams himself cannot raise. The hard case – someone completely unresponsive to blame – *is* an inappropriate target for blame, according to Williams' view.

5

THICK CONCEPTS AND EMOTION

Peter Goldie

I will argue that thick concepts and emotions are made for each other. This was something very well seen by Bernard Williams, and explicitly discussed in his earlier work – in particular in his brilliant paper "Morality and the emotions".[1] However, although the relation between thick concepts and emotions is clearly important for moral philosophy and psychology, and clearly goes deep in the psychology of individual people, it is a relation that is not easily accounted for philosophically. I want to resist the temptation – one to which many philosophers have succumbed – of oversimplifying the relation by placing it at too general a level. Amongst the generalisers, Williams' target was emotivism. Mine will be neo-sentimentalism.

In place of these general accounts, I want to bring into the picture the role that emotional dispositions play in the psychology of individuals. These dispositions, properly understood, not only help to explain the connection between depth of feelings and sincere judgements involving thick concepts; they also help to explain, in ways that no general account can aspire to do, our individual inconsistencies.

First, though, I will need to begin with an outline of the notion of thick concepts, which I will take as an extension of what was Williams' main focus, thick ethical concepts. Then I will consider the very important idea of fully embracing, or being fully engaged with, a thick concept. It is at this point that the connection with emotion and the idea of depth of feeling and sincerity will emerge, and this will lead me to a discussion of what emotional dispositions are, and what their explanatory role is in this area.

I Thick concepts

The notion of a thick ethical concept, as introduced by Williams, will be familiar to most readers of this volume, especially from his *Ethics and the Limits of Philosophy (ELP)*, where it is discussed in a number of places.[2] Williams' examples include *treachery, promise, brutality, courage,* and *gratitude,* and these are in contrast to thinner concepts such as *good* and *right.*

The notion of a thick ethical concept can readily be extended beyond the domain of the ethical to include thick concepts of other kinds – an extension which Williams himself would surely be more than willing to make, particularly given his doubts about the possibility of any precise delineation of the ethical. With that extension in place, we will be able to encompass such concepts as *dangerous, crude, rude, inelegant,* and *embarrassing.* And outside the ethical we can find thinner notions too, such as *advisable, imprudent, beautiful,* and (perhaps the thinnest of all) *rational* and *irrational.*

In his "Morality", some twenty years before *ELP,* Williams also discusses thick and thin concepts, but without using that terminology: he mentions concepts such as *coward, destructive, mean, hateful, generous, contemptible, outrageous, appalling, disgusting,* and many more. And he explicitly contrasts these thicker concepts with the thin ones, to the advantage of the former. This is what he says, with the philosophical preoccupation with the fact-value distinction in mind:

> Since the preoccupation is one with fact and value as such, it has imposed on the linguistic enterprise a concentration on the most general features of moral language, or indeed, yet more widely, of evaluative language. Thus the attention goes to such very general linguistic activities as 'commendation', 'evaluation' and 'prescription', and to such very general terms as 'good', 'right' and 'ought', and the more specific notions in terms of which people a lot of the time think and speak about their own and others' conduct have, with the exception of one or two writers, largely gone by default.[3]

Thick and thin in all but name, we might say. Now, with these examples of thick and thin concepts before us, we can, at least roughly, characterise what are their distinguishing features. I will mention four.

First, thick concepts have more descriptive content than do thin ones. For example, to be told that an action was cruel is to be told more about that action than if you were told only that the action was wrong. Second, thick concepts have not only descriptive content, but they also have, as do thinner concepts, evaluative content. It is sometimes said that a judgement involving a thick concept has its evaluative content 'built into it', so that, for example, someone's judging that an action was cruel implies that that person thinks that action to be wrong. This further thought, however, will need significant qualification as we proceed. Third, thick concepts, as Williams puts it, "seem to express a union of fact and value", and this is often taken in the strong sense that the descriptive content of a judgement that an action was, for example, cruel, cannot be disentangled from its evaluative content. The details of these first three features of thick concepts are individually much discussed, but I do not think that these details matter much to what I am going to say.[4]

The fourth characteristic, though, is very important for what follows. The application of thick concepts is, as Williams puts it, "at the same time world-guided and action-guiding". That is to say, such concepts "may be rightly or wrongly applied" (this is world-guidedness); and their application is "characteristically related to reasons for action" (this is action-guidingness). For example, the thought that someone's action of beating his child for a minor wrong-doing was cruel will very likely be one that is, for observers of the action, "spontaneous", although in other cases there will be "room for judgement and comparison". And an observer's thought, that the action was cruel, will give him reason for action, "though that reason may not be a decisive one and may be outweighed by other reasons".[5] So, in this case his thought that he should intervene might be outweighed by prudential considerations – concern that the other man's brutality will be turned on the observer rather than the child.

These two aspects of thick concepts – world-guidedness and action-guidingness – are not necessarily found together in an individual's psychology: a person can be perfectly able to apply the concept accurately to features of the world, without its application being action-guiding in the way I have just outlined. As Williams puts it, "An insightful observer can indeed come to understand and anticipate the use of the concept without actually sharing the values of the people who use it."[6] Here I want to draw on a crucial notion introduced by Adrian Moore in a very insightful paper: the notion of fully embracing, or being fully engaged with, a thick concept. This is what Moore says:

> I need to provide a gloss on 'embracing' a concept. This is something of a term of art for me. To convey what I intend I need to draw a distinction. Thick ethical concepts can be grasped in two ways, an engaged way and a disengaged way. To grasp a thick ethical concept in the disengaged way is to be able to recognize when the concept would (correctly) be applied, to be able to understand others when they apply it, and so forth. To grasp a thick ethical concept in the engaged way is not only to be able to do these things, but also to feel sufficiently at home with the concept to be prepared to apply it oneself, where being prepared to apply it oneself means being prepared to apply it not only just in overt acts of communication but also in how one thinks about the world and in how one conducts one's affairs. What this requires, roughly, is sharing whatever beliefs, concerns, and values give application of the concept its point.[7]

Moore has a nice example, the concept of *the Sabbath*. This is a concept whose correct application is readily grasped by those who do not embrace the concept in an engaged way. "But only a Jewish person recognizing an obligation to keep the Sabbath can grasp the concept in an engaged way. We might say that such a person *lives by* the concept."[8] And we might add that we can readily see how someone finding their way into the Jewish faith, either as a young child or as an adult converting from a different faith, might come, by degrees, to live by such a concept.

There is one respect, though, in which the concept of the Sabbath is not typical of thick concepts in general. I will come to this later, but now I want to turn to the role of emotion in our use of thick concepts – a role which gets little or no recognition in what Moore has to say.

II Thick concepts and emotion

Consider the thick concept of *rude*. What would be involved in being fully engaged in this concept, in "sharing whatever beliefs, concerns, and values give application of the concept its point"?

This concept, like other thick concepts such as *brutal* and *respect*, has a wide range of application: all sorts of human behaviour – acts and omissions – can be rude: ways of talking, staring, shaking hands, gesturing, ignoring, arguing, writing, driving. Following Moore, we can say that someone who is fully engaged with the concept across this range of application will be able to recognize behaviour as being rude when it is, and to do so without falling into prudishness or over-sensitivity. In many cases, and in particular the central or paradigmatic cases, his application of the concept will be immediate and intuitive; he might, we can say, *see* that a certain action is rude – for example, the action of the person who engages in a long conversation on his mobile phone when dining in a restaurant with a friend.[9] More than just this, he will also find the application of the concept tied to reasons for action, for example, avoiding certain kinds of action himself, avoiding other people who engage in rude behaviour, and otherwise showing his disapproval of what they do. Of course, in his thinking and acting as he does, he need not actually be explicitly deploying the concept in conscious thought; for example, he might thank someone for paying for lunch without actually having the thought that it would be rude not to do so.

But is this enough? Is this enough to capture what is involved in being fully engaged with a concept such as *rude*, in "living by" it, in "sharing whatever beliefs, concerns, and values give application of the concept its point"? I think what is missing is reference to emotion. In ways which I hope now to show, it is our emotions that hold together the "beliefs, concerns, and values" that cluster around our use of the concept.

One of the central themes of "Morality" is that there is a complex relation in moral thought and discourse between sincerity and the emotions which is psychologically very important but which resists the making of any general connection between the two, linguistic or otherwise. Williams' main target in his paper was emotivism, the thesis that "the function and nature of moral judgements was to express the emotions of the speaker and to arouse similar emotions in his hearers."[10] But this was on the way to the larger project; as Williams puts it, "My aim will not be to reconstruct emotivism, but to steal from it; not to rebuild the pagan temple, but to put its ruins to a holier purpose."[11]

Williams begins at the simple end of our moral language, with sentences most amenable to the fact-value distinction: "He has broken his tricycle again, blast him." We have here assertion of the fact, that he has broken his tricycle again, and the evaluative expression of emotion, the expletive addition of "blast him". The use of a sentence such as this quite plainly *requires* that the speaker be expressing an emotion – irritation in this example.[12] Williams then goes on to consider sentences where difficulties begin to arise for the emotivist. These are sentences which incorporate thick concepts, such as: "Of course, he went back on his agreement when he got to the meeting, the little coward." The particular difficulty here is that the expression "the little coward" would seem to be both explanatory (he went back on the agreement out of fear), and emotional (revealing something like contempt for the man's lack of moral stature). Williams then asks if it possible to rephrase the sentence without the emotional element, without the "expletive addition". This is how he suggests it might go: "As might have been predicted, he went back on his agreement at the meeting through fear; which he ought not to have done (*or* this was a bad thing)." This may be the same moral judgement as in the original, Williams says, in the simple sense that both original and replacement reveal that the speaker is against – 'con' – what was done. But this is not enough if we are to take the notion of a moral judgement seriously. What matters, in addition to mere 'pro' and 'con' are the "moral overtones":

> in being interested in a person's moral judgement, so called, we are in fact not merely interested in whether he is pro this and con that, whether he grades these men in one order or another. We are interested in what moral view he takes of the situation, how those situations look to him in the light of his moral outlook.[13]

This will remind us of Moore's account of embracing a thick concept, given in terms of sharing beliefs, concerns, and values that give the application of the concept its point. But Williams goes on to show how the emotions are entangled in moral judgement itself. I hope I will be forgiven for citing this long passage, but it very well expresses what I take to be at the heart of Williams' view in this paper, and, in a less explicit form, in his later work:

> Does it [the replacement sentence cited above] lay before us the same moral view of the situation? Scarcely so. To agree to this

would commit us to saying that the contempt (or something like it) that the speaker of the first sentence felt and put into his words was not an integral part of his moral view of the situation; the contempt was an adventitious addition to his low rating of the man's behaviour at the committee, as my irritation is no doubt an adventitious reaction to my learning that Tommy has broken his tricycle. Something like this *could* be true; but very obviously, it need not be so. ... In the present case, the mode in which this man's behaviour appeared bad may precisely have been that of its being contemptible; and if the person who made the remark comes not to think of it in those terms, he will cease to take the same moral view as before of this man's behaviour. Where this is so, we may not be able to isolate the moral-judgement content of the utterances from what makes them expressive of emotion.[14]

So here we have an entanglement not just of fact and value, but also, in verbal expression, of emotion and judgement; these too cannot be put asunder. Williams gives an account of this kind of entanglement of emotion with moral judgement – those which involve the use of thick concepts – in terms of moral seriousness or sincerity, and that will be the topic to which I will turn shortly. But first, it might have occurred to many readers that we have before us today an account of the relation between thick concepts and emotion which is much more subtle than the emotivist's.[15] So I now want to look briefly at this account.

The account that I have in mind is what is sometimes called *neo-sentimentalism*. It comes in various formulations, but at its heart is the idea that, as Justin D'Arms and Dan Jacobson put it, "to make an evaluative judgement is not to *have* but to *endorse* a sentiment".[16] It is just here that the improvement on emotivism is to be found. Here is one formulation of the account from D'Arms and Jacobson: "to think that X has some evaluative property Φ is to think it appropriate to feel F in response to X."[17]

Neo-sentimentalism might seem to be quite amenable to Williams' overall purpose. It focuses in on evaluative concepts (albeit not only thick concepts), and it implicates the emotions, but without doing so in such a direct way as emotivism. So, for example, the fact that the man's behaviour at the meeting was contemptible is, according to neo-sentimentalism, such as to merit, or to make appropriate, contempt in someone who so judges. The idea, in principle, has considerable appeal: in particular, it does not fall foul of the emotivist idea that someone who judges the behaviour to be contemptible must be actually *expressing* contempt.[18] However, there are difficulties. The one I want to focus on is the *generality* of the account – its ambition of making a general, and, to my mind overly simple, connection between judgement and emotion of the kind that Williams was, rightly in my view, at pains to undermine.[19]

III The problem with generality

The real problem with general accounts of emotion and evaluative judgements (I will from now on limit my discussion to judgements involving *thick* evaluative concepts), is that there is a range of examples which have the following features: they are counterexamples to the general account; the general account does nothing to explain them or make sense of them; and yet these counterexamples can readily be explained and made sense of. I will consider three such examples.

First, let us consider a story made up by Allan Gibbard, of the Kumi tribe. This tribe has a thick concept of *gopa*, which is such as to make appropriate a pleasurable feeling of glory, and which arises, for example, on return from a successful headhunting expedition to a neighbouring tribe.[20] Visitors or anthropologists might reliably judge something to be *gopa*, and yet certainly not consider it a failing in themselves if they do not have a pleasurable feeling of glory when so judging; indeed, it would be entirely *inappropriate* for them to have that feeling.

Now, at this point, one might bring in Moore's notion of being fully engaged with a thick concept, and claim that a visitor's response to the returning headhunters, and his lack of appropriate emotionality, can be explained simply by the fact that he is not fully engaged with the concept of *gopa*: his use is world-guided but not action-guiding, or, as one might rather misleadingly put it, emotion-guiding. After all, as visitors, *gopa* is not *our* concept, and it is one that we would rightly shrink from sharing in a fully engaged way, even if we were capable of doing so.

This is surely right, so far as it goes, and it might be possible to fix the neo-sentimentalist account by borrowing from Moore to add a clause attempting to capture what it is to "make an evaluative judgement *in a fully engaged way*". But still, Moore's account is also general in a way that has a bearing on the examples that are to come. It is general, first, in the sense that the beliefs, concerns, and values which give application of the concept its point are ones which have to be *shared* with others; and second, it is general in the sense that, for someone fully engaged with the concept, these beliefs, concerns, and values – and, I would add, emotions – are ones that are presumably to be shared *across the board*, across all domains of application. In other words, there is no room here for a limited domain of fully engaged application of a thick concept.[21]

The next two examples bring out this difficulty. They come from R. M. Hare, who was, of course, opposed to accounts such as neo-sentimentalism, which claim that "the evaluative and descriptive meanings of some terms are inseparable, and that therefore the description brings with it an inescapable evaluation."[22] His first example is of an extreme kind of initiation ceremony for recruits to Sandhurst or West Point. "Some of the spectators are shocked by what has been done. Others just find it hilarious." He accepts that the amused perpetrators of this cruel deed might choose to withhold the concept *cruel* from any judgement about what they had done, because of its generally accepted evaluative implications. But Hare rightly insists that they need not withhold the concept in order to avoid these implications: "It may be that the *word* 'cruel' … carries with it an evaluative meaning which it does not readily give up (though it can: we can say 'Yes, cruel certainly, but that's just what made it such fun')."[23]

Hare's other example of the same phenomenon is borrowed from the developmental psychologist Lawrence Kohlberg and concerns a small boy's use of the word 'rude'. While a teacher is preoccupied at the back of the class, this happens:

> In the front row, a boy said something to his neighbor, who retaliated by quietly spitting in his face. The first boy equally quietly slugged the other without leaving his seat, by which time the teacher noted the disturbance. She said calmly, 'Stop that and get back to your workbooks.' The boy who had done the slugging said, 'Teacher, I hit him because he spit in my face.' The teacher replied, 'That wasn't polite; it was rude. Now get back to work, you're supposed to be doing your workbooks.' As they went back to work, the boy who had done the spitting said to his opponent with a grin, 'I will grant you that; it was rude.'[24]

The obvious response to these two examples is to say that the two individual users of the thick concepts concerned (*cruel* and *rude*) were not fully engaged with the concept. Agreed.[25] But what if they were fully engaged with the concept in other parts of their lives? For example, the man who imposed those cruel initiation ceremonies might fully embrace the concept when it has application to treatment of his own children. Such a person is by no means inconceivable or unimaginable; nor is such a person necessarily hypocritical, or confused as to "how one conducts one's affairs" as Moore puts it. The most I think we can say is that the man is inconsistent – not logically inconsistent, but inconsistent in the way that he treats people.[26]

We might find similar examples in the notion of *respect* (and its converse '*diss*') as deployed in certain gang cultures, where this thick concept has a fully engaged range of application for a member of a gang only when it concerns respect towards oneself and other members of one's gang, but not when it concerns one's parents or teachers or members of other gangs ("I will grant you that; I did diss them"). I oversimplify to make the point, which is just this: for any particular person, full engagement with a thick concept, and correlatively its action-guidingness in application by that person, need not apply across all domains. One can be fully engaged with a concept here but not there.

These features of the use of these thick concepts mark a contrast with the notion of the Sabbath and reveal a respect in which it is misleading as an example of its kind. The fully engaged range of application of the concept of the Sabbath is not likely to be restricted in the same kind of way. Someone who thought the Sabbath important when it came to one aspect of religious practice and not when it came to another might well be said not to be fully engaged with the concept at all. But this would not be the same, it seems, for *cruel*, *rude* and *respect*: here we are more inclined to say that the user is fully engaged in one domain and not in another. And the problem with generality is, first, that it is not able to accommodate this feature of our use of thick concepts; and, second, that if it were able to accommodate it (for example, by making the account one that applies generally or for the most part), it still would not be able to explain or make sense of the examples – of, for example, the fact that the man treats his children in one way and his recruits in another.[27] And yet, even with such sparse information as I have been providing, we can very readily see why they arise in individual cases – why someone could be fully engaged with a thick concept in one domain and not in another.

So what we now need is to see how this phenomenon of a limited engaged range of application of a concept can be a familiar and readily understandable aspect of human psychology. To do this we need a better appreciation of what is involved in "sharing whatever beliefs, concerns, and values give application of the concept its point". Williams looks to the notion of moral seriousness or sincerity, and it is to this that I will now turn.

IV Thick concepts, emotions, and sincerity

What is sincerity? Some kinds of speech act, Williams says, cannot be sincere or insincere: conventional greetings, for example, and orders. For others, such as promising, if we say that a promise is insincere, "the word 'insincere' is not what the scholastics called an *alienans* term, that is to say a qualification which weakens or removes the force of the term that it qualifies."[28] Thus an insincere expression of a promise is still the expression of a promise; that is why one can justifiably be held to it.

Things are different with the expression of belief, intention, and feeling or emotion, Williams says. An insincere expression of belief does seem to be *alienans*: an insincere expression of belief is not really an expression of belief. At least, as Williams nicely points out, it is not an expression of *his* belief:

> The 'his' is perhaps significant. His greetings, his orders, his commendations, his promises, are *his*, basically, just in that it is he who utters them; his expressions of intention or belief are *his* not only

in this way, but because they are expressions of *his* intentions or *his* beliefs, and these latter lie below the level of the speech act.[29]

Expressions of emotion are the same in this respect: to say that an expression of emotion is insincere is *alienans*. Thus, someone who says "Blast him!" must, to be sincere in his expression of emotion, actually be feeling irritation; and if he is not actually feeling irritation, then what he says is not really an expression of emotion. But is the same true of the relation between emotion and the sincere expression of moral judgements? Again, when it comes to the sincerity of moral judgements, what we are concerned with is "what lies below the level of the speech act."[30] But is it necessary that, below the level of the speech act, someone must actually be feeling an emotion if his expression of a moral judgement is to be sincere? Is the emotion necessary for sincerity in the same way as the belief is?

The answer, as Williams says, is no: "the facts stand firmly against any simple and general connexion of feelings and sincerity."[31] This was at the heart of the difficulties faced by emotivism. Occurrent strong feelings are neither necessary nor sufficient for sincere expression of moral belief (or of beliefs involving other kinds of thick concept). One might, for example, at a tribunal sincerely express the belief that someone's behaviour was contemptible without at the time actually having any feelings about it; one is too caught up in the procedural aspects of giving evidence. Conversely, one might have strong feelings about some topic without having particularly strong or sincere beliefs; for example, one might feel furious at the platitudes emerging from some politician without having strong or sincere beliefs in that particular direction – it's just the general grumpiness of old age, someone might say, which happens to have latched onto this particular public figure for no particular reason – other than that he happened to be on television at the time.

At this point, one might be tempted to move in the other direction, to reject the idea that having strong feelings is *in any way* connected to sincere beliefs and judgements, moral and otherwise, involving thick concepts. But this is surely a mistake. Can we really conceive of a person who, as Moore puts it, shares "whatever beliefs, concerns, and values give application of the concept its point" and yet who has no emotions in connection to those beliefs, concerns, and values? The examples just discussed may illustrate how strong occurrent feelings are neither necessary nor sufficient for sincere expression of moral beliefs, but, as Williams says, such cases "exist against a background in which there is some connexion taken for granted between strength of feeling displayed on moral issues, and the strength of the moral view taken."[32] He continues:

> The connexion appears to me to be basic enough for the strength
> of feeling to be called *a* criterion of taking a strong moral view,

rather than saying that there is a mere empirical correlation between them. If it were a mere empirical correlation, we could imagine a world in which people had strong moral views, and strong emotions, and their emotions were not the least engaged in their morality. Some moral theories certainly involve the conclusion that such a world is conceivable; but I do not think it is.[33]

If it is right that we should not give up on our search for a connection, the question now facing us is where to look for that connection. The answer that Williams gives, and the answer I too want to put forward, is that we should look not just below the level of the speech act, but also below the level of occurrent thought and feeling, to emotional dispositions.

V Sincerity and emotional dispositions

To begin with, we should observe that the notion of someone's *having strong feelings* does not require that those feelings be occurrent. For example, one can truthfully and sincerely say "I have strong feelings about the war in Iraq", while at the time feeling calm and unemotional. We might reasonably question this man's truthfulness and sincerity if he had *never* occurrently had strong feelings towards the target of his remarks, but that, of course, is another matter. So when Williams says, in respect of those moral utterances that are expressed "in strong terms", that it will be a condition of sincerity of utterance that it be "expressive of emotions or feelings that the speaker has",[34] he means that the utterance could be expressive of an emotional disposition and not (or not only) of an occurrent emotion. We have seen, for example, that for the utterance of "I find his action contemptible" to be sincere, it is not necessary that the speaker feels contempt, where this last phrase implies that the speaker is *actually and at the time* strongly feeling that emotion. Williams here refers to

> [a] general doctrine in the philosophy of mind, that the truth-conditions of the claim that a man was sincere in what he said on a particular occasion are not in general to be found in features of that particular occasion (for instance, in some internal psychological state of the man on that occasion), but to be found rather in some broader pattern into which this occasion fits.[35]

I now turn to this broader pattern, and to emotional dispositions in particular.

Let me briefly summarise where we have got to so far. We started with thick concepts, and Moore's idea, that fully engaging with a thick ethical concept requires "sharing whatever beliefs, concerns, and values give application of the concept its point". We can now add that, if someone is fully engaged with a thick concept, 'lives by' it, then this person's expression of his moral views, when related to this concept, will be sincere just so long as he also shares (subject to the above qualifications) the feelings and emotions that give application of the concept its point. And if he is sincere in his moral views, he will (also subject to the above qualifications) be motivated to appropriate action.[36]

Now, the idea is that all these psychological states, verbal expressions, actions, and action-tendencies are, in some sense, held together by the emotional dispositions that underlie them. What is an emotional disposition? An emotional disposition involves a *focus* and a *stance*.[37] The stance of an emotional disposition is the kind of emotional 'attitude' held towards the focus. And the focus is that towards which the stance is held. For example, if we say that Mary is compassionate towards vagrants, then the stance is compassion, and the focus is vagrants. If James loves Jane, then Jane is the focus and love is the stance. If Peter is envious of Paul, then Paul is the focus and envy is the stance.

The focus of an emotional disposition is to be contrasted with the object of an emotional experience, although the two are closely related. For example, James' emotional disposition of love, with Jane as its focus, can be expressed in emotional and other experiences towards a diverse range of objects, although these objects will all have Jane as a common focus. Moreover, the emotions experienced as expressive of a disposition will typically be more diverse than the description of the stance might at first suggest. For example, James' love for Mary, in the dispositional sense, might be expressed not only in feelings of love, but also in feelings of joy when her plans work out well, in anger if another person says something rude to her, in fear and worry if she has what might turn out to be a serious illness, and so forth. Thus, a single emotional disposition – love in this example – can be expressed in thought, feeling, and verbal utterances with a wide range of thick concepts.

With these remarks in mind, we can now see why it is so important to add the requirement to have strong feelings, understood now as an emotional disposition and not (not necessarily that is) occurrent emotional feelings, if one is to be sincere in one's behaviour and verbal utterances, and if one is to be correctly judged to be fully engaged in the related thick concepts in that domain of application. Emotional dispositions provide the deep explanation and unity; being fully engaged with a thick concept in this domain is just one manifestation or expression of this. And it is this feature of providing psychological and behavioural unity that enables us to see someone's thoughts, feelings, and actions as genuinely expressive of an underlying emotional disposition, and not as a mere syndrome, a mere collection of disparate states, ways of seeing the world in a certain light, actions, action-tendencies, gestures, feelings, bodily changes, and so forth. The emotional disposition is what holds all these things together in a single explanatory framework. Here is my final citation from Williams to bring the point home:

> My suggestion is that, in some cases, the relevant unity in a man's behaviour, the pattern into which his judgements and actions together fit, must be understood in terms of an emotional structure underlying them, and that understanding of this kind may be essential. Thus we may understand a man's particular moral remark as being, if sincere, an expression of compassion. This may then be seen as part of a general current in his behaviour which, taken together, reveals his quality of being a compassionate man; and it may be that it is only in the light of seeing him as a com-passionate man that *those* actions, judgements, even gestures, will be naturally taken together at all. It is understanding this set of things as expressive of a certain emotional structure of behaviour that constitutes our understanding them as a set.[38]

Williams in this passage is referring in part to compassion as a state of character, and I want to distinguish this from the emotional disposition. Both state of character and emotional disposition are indeed dispositions, and they will both characteristically be expressed in a variety of ways along the lines that I have been discussing. But a state of character does not have a focus in the same way as an emotional disposition. A compassionate person, one with the character trait, will be compassionate towards all sorts of things; his disposition does not have a particular focus. Whereas a person who is compassionate towards vagrants does have a focus, namely vagrants, and this person might not be disposed to express compassion towards other kinds of things.

With this contrast in mind, we can now return to a question which I left outstanding earlier on: the question of why a person's fully engaged range of application of a thick concept may not extend to all aspects of his life. The answer lies, again, in his emotional dispositions. The man who behaves cruelly towards his recruits and who abhors such behaviour towards his children is thus revealed and understood as expressing his love and concern for his children, and his lack of concern for his recruits (other than as potential objects of amusement). This is precisely why his domain of fully engaged application of the concept *cruel* is restricted in the way that it is. A person's emotional dispositions, and the thick concepts which can be involved in their sincere, fully engaged, expression in thought and speech, are often in these ways restricted in their domain of application, so that we rightly withhold the attribution of a general character trait – a virtue or a vice – to that person: he is a man who is kind and compassionate to his children, cruel, brutal and lacking in compassion to his recruits, and his use of thick ethical concepts tracks, and is explained by, these emotional dispositions, or by the lack of them ('Yes, cruel certainly, but that's just what made it such fun').

Many of us are inconsistent in the way that we treat people – some we care about, others we do not – and the reasons for this are often to be found in the contingencies of our personal history rather than as a result of our deep reflection on the principles and demands of morality. Acts of kindness and generosity need not spring from a virtue which has a wide and general range of application, but rather from a more particular, person-specific emotional disposition. We all know this, but it is Williams who helps us to see it, and to see the importance of emotions, not only in morality and the thick concepts that are involved in ethical thought and speech, but more widely too, extending to cover our whole lives. I cannot resist one final citation from Williams' wonderful paper. He asks this question, with Kant very much in mind, of course:

> [I]s it certain that one who receives good treatment from another more appreciates it, thinks the better of the giver, if he knows it to be the result of the application of principle, rather than the product of an emotional response? He may have needed, not the benefit of universal law, but some human gesture ... we can reasonably entertain the proposal that we should not seek to produce moral men, or very many of them, but rather those, whatever their inconsistencies, who make the human gesture.[39]

Bernard Williams, in word and deed, never failed to make the human gesture. For this, as well as for so much else, he was loved and admired.

Acknowledgements

Earlier versions of this chapter were presented at talks at The Institute of Philosophy in London, and in Basel and in Fribourg. I am very grateful for the many comments and suggestions made on those hospitable occasions. I would also like to thank Dan Callcut, Christine Clavien, and Neil Dillon for their very helpful comments and suggestions.

Notes

1 Hereafter "Morality". This was Williams' inaugural lecture at Bedford College, London, in 1965; it is in his *Problems of the Self* (Cambridge: Cambridge University Press, 1973), pp. 207–29. The connections between thick concepts and emotions are somewhat less explicit in his later writings.
2 *Ethics and the Limits of Philosophy* (London: Fontana Press, 1985), pp. 129–30, 140–2 (henceforth *ELP*).
3 "Morality," p. 208.
4 The idea of thick ethical concepts has been discussed in more places than I can name here. See, for example, Simon Blackburn, "Morality and thick ethical

concepts", *Proceedings of the Aristotelian Society*, suppl. vol. 66 (1992), 285–99; Alan Gibbard, "Morality and thick ethical concepts", *Proceedings of the Aristotelian Society*, suppl. vol. 66 (1992), 267–83; Kevin Mulligan, "From appropriate emotions to values", *The Monist* 81 (1998), 161–88; Samuel Scheffler, "Morality through thick and thin: A critical notice of *Ethics and the Limits of Philosophy*", *The Philosophical Review* 46 (1987), 411–34; Christine Tappolet, "Through thick and thin: *good* and its determinables", *dialectica* 58 (2004), 207–21. Tappolet argues that the relation between thick and thin is as determinate to determinable. For my purposes, all I need is the idea that thick concepts are, as Williams puts it, more 'substantive' or more 'specific', in the sense that they have more descriptive content that thinner concepts. (Perhaps controversially, I take the distinction between thick and thin to be one of degree; and in this I believe I am following Williams. Cf. Scheffler's critical notice of *ELP*, where he questions whether the distinction between thick and thin can be clearly made out.)

5 *ELP*, pp. 129, 140, 141.

6 Ibid., pp. 141–2.

7 "Maxims and thick ethical concepts", *Ratio (new series)* 19 (2006), 129–47, at p. 137.

8 Ibid.

9 I discuss how we can literally see that certain kinds of thing have thick properties in my "Seeing what is the kind thing to do: Perception and emotion in morality", *dialectica* 61 (2007), 347–61.

10 "Morality", p. 208.

11 Ibid.

12 Williams shows, with a very neat use of the Frege–Geach argument, borrowed from John Searle, that whilst such simple sentences can bear an emotivist analysis in embedded contexts, it is not a general feature of our evaluative talk. I will not discuss this in any detail here, as it has been the focus of so much attention since Williams' paper. His essential idea, though, is to undermine the semantic version of emotivism, according to which it is essential to the correct use of sentences used to make moral judgements that they express the speaker's emotion. He does so by considering their use when embedded in conditional contexts, and in negation. Thus, Williams says, whereas the sentence "If he has broken his tricycle again, blast him, he'll go without his pocket money" can only be used appropriately by someone who is *already* irritated, the sentence "If he did wrong in not going to the appointment, I shall have something to say to him" does not (necessarily) express indignation on behalf of the speaker ("Morality", 211). Resistance to losing their force in these contexts, Williams says, "may well be a mark of sentences which *semantically incorporate* the expression of emotion" ("Morality", p. 212).

13 "Morality", p. 213.

14 Ibid., p. 214.

15 I do not have the space here to consider those accounts that see themselves as being more direct successors of emotivism – accounts such as Simon Blackburn's quasi-realism, and Alan Gibbard's account of norm endorsement. See, for example, Blackburn's *Essays in Quasi-Realism* (Oxford: Oxford University Press, 1993); and Gibbard's *Wise Choices, Apt Feelings: A Normative Theory of Judgment* (Oxford: Clarendon Press, 1990).

16 "Sentiment and value", *Ethics* 110 (2000), 722–48, at p. 729.

17 Ibid.

18 This formulation of emotivism is intended to capture both the semantic thesis which I have been discussing above, and the *speech-act* thesis, which is, as

Williams puts it, "that a speaker's expressing emotions should be regarded as a necessary condition of his utterance's counting as the making of a moral judgement" ("Morality", p. 214).

19 Other objections to the neo-sentimentalist project are that it is analytic, circular, and uninformative (see, for example, Simon Blackburn, "Circles, Finks, Smells and Biconditionals", *Philosophical Perspectives* 7, *Language and Logic* (1993), 259–79); that it fails to make a distinction between moral appropriateness and other kinds of appropriateness (see, for example, Justin D'Arms and Daniel Jacobson, "The Moralistic Fallacy: On the 'Appropriateness' of Emotion", *Philosophy and Phenomenological Research* 61 (2000), 65–90); and that it results in an unacceptable kind of intuitionism (see, for example, Simon Blackburn, "Errors and the Phenomenology of Value", reprinted in his *Essays in Quasi-Realism*); and others too.

20 In his "Morality and thick ethical concepts". I discuss this example in my *The Emotions: A Philosophical Exploration* (Oxford: Clarendon Press, 2000).

21 Having said that, so far as I can see, there is nothing to prevent this addition. Moore emphasises that the notion of being engaged admits of degrees, and there is no reason why the degree of engagement might not vary across domains. These remarks will become clearer as I progress.

22 R. M. Hare, *Moral Thinking: Its Levels, Methods, and Point* (Oxford: Oxford University Press, 1981), p. 74.

23 Ibid., p. 73.

24 Ibid., p. 74.

25 There is a saying that it is a mark of an English gentleman that he is only ever rude intentionally. The small boy might also be rude by mistake. But Hare's point about the boy would also apply to the gentleman: we have no reason to insist that, as a matter of meaning, he cannot understand intentional rudeness as, in fact, falling under the concept *rude*.

26 These remarks would, of course, be disputed by Kant. I will return to Kant and the notion of inconsistency in behaviour at the end of this chapter.

27 D'Arms and Jacobson suggest that an emotion is appropriate only "in certain contexts". They add, "To think the tiger fearsome is to think fear at it appropriate, but only when the tiger is nearby and on the loose – not for instance while you sit reading this article. Similarly, some act of lying may be wrong, but it is appropriate to feel guilty about it only if it was your lie (or you were otherwise responsible for it). We will assume these qualifications throughout" ("Sentiment and value", p. 729). To my mind, these qualifications will ramify to such an extent that the general account of the relation between judgement and emotion will collapse under their weight.

28 "Morality", p. 216.

29 Ibid., p. 216.

30 Ibid., p. 217.

31 Ibid., p. 218.

32 Ibid., p. 220.

33 Ibid., p. 220.

34 Ibid., p. 218.

35 Ibid., p. 221.

36 Ibid., pp. 221–2; cf. Moore's "Maxims and thick ethical concepts".

37 In what follows, I am much indebted to Bennett Helm's *Emotional Reason: Deliberation, Motivation, and the Nature of Value* (Cambridge: Cambridge University Press, 2001).

38 "Morality", p. 222.

39 Ibid., p. 227.

6

THE ARCHITECTURE OF INTEGRITY

Daniel Markovits

I Two approaches to ethics

Impartiality—the idea that everyone's life is as important as everyone else's and, in particular, that each person is equally a source of independent, authoritative moral claims on others—is modern morality's characteristic ideal and also its greatest achievement. But a second and older set of ideas about ethics endures even in the face of modernity's advances. These ideas approach ethical justification from the agent's own point of view, in what I shall call the *first person*. This more intimate approach to ethics elaborates the thought that ethically justified acts should promote the actor's success (writ large and not just his narrow self-interest)—that is, his efforts to live according to his own suitable life plan and to achieve his own admirable ends. This theme recalls the venerable Aristotelian tradition according to which morality is not just about the claims that others make against a person but instead serves, as Bernard Williams once helpfully put it, "as an enabling device for the agent's own life,"[1] so that virtue promotes the general well-being or flourishing (in Aristotelian terms, *eudaimonia*) of the virtuous.[2]

The modern view of ethics in many respects represents a substantial advance over earlier conceptions. But the modern emphasis on impartiality causes modern ethical thought to neglect that a person's ambitions and the actions by which she pursues them do not just fix her treatment of others but also determine, and indeed constitute, the kind of person that she will be. Even with equality and impartiality in place, each person therefore continues to identify specifically with his own actions, to see them as contributing to his peculiar ethical ambitions in light of the fact that he occupies a special position of intimacy and concern—of authorship—with respect to his own actions and life plan. Moral persons form and carry out ambitions and plans with an eye not just to their effects but to the ambitions and plans in themselves—they seek ambitions and plans that leave them reflectively satisfied not just with what they have done to others, but also with what they have made of themselves.[3] And, having adopted such ambitions and plans, moral persons seek to live in a way that is true to them, to live lives, one might say, of moral *integrity*.

The modern hegemony of impartialist moral ideas neglects and even suppresses this feature of moral life. This suppression has given rise to a new and distinctive form of subjugation, associated with understanding morality solely in terms of sacrificing oneself to satisfy burdensome duties owed to others—so that morality is no longer experienced as a form of self-expression but instead as an external force in one's life, to which one must *submit*. It has also engendered a distinctive form of alienation, associated with identifying guilt as the principal moral motive. Both difficulties are dramatically articulated in existentialist calls for making integrity—or, as it is more commonly said, authenticity—the prime virtue of action.

II Jim and the Innocents

It is possible, moreover, to develop a philosophically precise conception of personal integrity and to defend this ideal against the insistent encroachment of impartial duty, and Williams himself initiated one important approach to this task.

The argument begins with a thought experiment.[4] Imagine that Jim is confronted by a dictator who has captured twenty political prisoners and offers Jim the following choice: either Jim must kill one of the prisoners or the dictator will kill all twenty.[5] What should Jim do? Jim's situation has been constructed so that his killing an innocent will minimize the total number of innocents killed. Moreover, Jim's refusing to kill the one is better for *nobody*. (The dictator, after all, has not told Jim "You kill that one or I will kill these twenty" but has instead presented Jim with a circumstance in which even the one Jim might kill will be killed in any case.) Indeed, there is a sense in which all the innocents are *benefited* by Jim's killing—one might even imagine that the innocents ask Jim to join them in adopting a (fair) procedure for choosing which innocent he will kill and that the chosen innocent accepts being killed by Jim's hand. An impartial concern for the innocents therefore recommends that Jim kill.

Nevertheless, Jim may have a good first-personal ethical reason for refusing to kill the one. The ambition not to kill innocents is likely foundational, or at least comes very early, among Jim's first-personal ethical ambitions, in the sense that honoring this ambition is central to being the person that Jim aspires to be. If Jim refuses to kill, then he will be true to this ambition. As Williams has observed, the result will not be simply that twenty innocents are dead or even that Jim has caused twenty innocents to die, but rather that the dictator (and not Jim), pursuing her projects (and not Jim's) has killed twenty innocents.[6] If Jim declines the dictator's offer

111

and refuses to kill, then he is, in some measure at least, enforcing the distinction between his projects and the dictator's and insisting on the moral significance of this distinction, in particular with respect to the intimacy of each of their connections to whatever killings are committed.

On the other hand, if Jim accepts the dictator's offer and kills the one, then he allows himself to become a partner in the dictator's active malevolence. If Jim kills, then he must abandon, or at least betray, his own benevolent projects and, as Thomas Nagel observed, come himself to aim at part of the dictator's evil—the death of the one—making this evil into his own end. If his chosen method of killing the one fails, for example, Jim must adjust his actions to correct the failure and accomplish the killing. Accepting the dictator's offer therefore requires Jim to "push ... directly and essentially against the intrinsic normative force" of his ordinary ends.[7] In accepting the dictator's offer, Jim allows his projects to be determined by—and, indeed, to adopt—her evil ends.

Now because of the numbers involved in this case, Jim may reasonably decide that he should in the end kill the one. Jim may conclude that the badness of becoming implicated in the dictator's malevolence is simply outweighed by the nineteen lives that his doing so will save. But even if it is right, when the numbers are large enough, for Jim to think in this way, the numbers may not always be large enough, and the moral relevance of his having killed the one will in any case not be *erased* by these observations.

Changing the terms of the example slightly makes this side of the question stronger still. In Williams' example, Jim's confrontation with the dictator involved a single action that remained isolated from the rest of his moral life (Williams even made Jim a tourist on a foreign vacation). But imagine that the dictator tells Jim that she intends to kill the prisoners by some involved method, say, a slow and deliberate torture, and that to save the remaining prisoners, Jim must kill one by this same method—a method whose execution will command Jim's protracted effort and attention, requiring him to pursue debased skills and master dark arts that further conflict with his own benevolent ideals and ends. Moreover, imagine that the dictator's offer applies not just to one set of prisoners but as an ongoing arrangement, so that the dictator is in effect offering to moderate her evil going forward if Jim will become her henchman.

Although it remains impartially best for Jim to accept the dictator's offer even in these modified circumstances (indeed, the impartial case for accepting may be thought stronger still), the first-personal arguments for rejecting the offer become even more robust than they were before. Indeed, looking ahead somewhat, one might say that if it is self-indulgent for Jim to refuse to kill when the numbers get large enough, accepting the dictator's offer can involve Jim in self-indulgence of another kind—the self-indulgence of believing that he can so signally betray his own ideals and yet somehow remain faithful to them. Certainly it would be grotesque for Jim to ignore this betrayal entirely—to deny that he has cooperated with the dictator or killed at all, and instead to congratulate himself on cooperating with the innocents in saving (some of) their lives. Jim *will* help the innocents and save lives by accepting the dictator's offer, but that is not *all* he will do.

Jim's case illustrates broader ideas about the moral importance of the special relation, which I am calling the relation of authorship, that a person has to his own projects and actions. Someone who thinks it *straightforward* that Jim should kill the one (that Jim has *no* good reason for refusing) in effect insists that there is never a morally relevant distinction between pursuing a project oneself and failing to prevent someone else from pursuing the same project and so denies the moral importance of authorship. Such a person— who takes whatever actions and pursues whatever projects will produce the best consequences overall—therefore places his own decisions at the mercy of other people's projects and thereby attacks his own moral personality. Such a person sees himself as merely a cog in a causal machine or, using Williams' metaphor, as nothing more than a "channel between the input of everyone's projects, including his own, and an output of optimific decision."[8]

This makes it unclear how someone who understands himself in this way retains a well-defined moral self—a sense of his own distinctive moral agency—at all. Such a person's projects are so completely determined by other people's ideals—he adopts new interim projects so capriciously—that he measures his moral ideals and agency as the weather measures the wind and cannot recognize any projects and ideals as, finally and properly, his own. And he therefore suffers, as Williams says, "in the most literal sense, an attack on his integrity."[9] Jim's integrity seems, therefore, to depend on his resisting (at least in some measure) the demands of impartial morality and at least sometimes refusing to kill the one even when it would be impartially best for him to kill.[10]

III An impartialist rejoinder?

Williams introduced the Jim example and developed the arguments that I have just rehearsed as part of an extended polemic against utilitarianism— which Williams took, metonymically, to represent what I shall call a *third-personal* conception of impartiality. This conception insists that value inheres fundamentally in states of affairs and that an action is morally justified if and only if taking it maximizes the value in the world, which is to say, produces the state of affairs that is overall best.[11] This is a conception of impartiality because it weights all persons equally in determining the value of a state of affairs and therefore insists that in order to act rightly a person must give all others equal concern and respect, as under Bentham's dictum: "everybody to count for one, nobody for more than one." It is third-personal because it focuses morality on the "they" who collectively constitute the world whose value is to be promoted.

Third-personal impartiality instructs Jim to decide whether or not to kill the one on the basis of an utterly mechanical reasoning process: first, Jim must recognize that killings are *ceteris paribus* bad and that more killings are *ceteris paribus* worse than fewer killings; second, Jim must conclude that impartial morality requires him, *ceteris paribus*, to adopt the course of action, of those available to him, that minimizes the number of killings the world contains; and third, Jim must recognize that causes and effects (including in particular the dictator's evil plans) have arranged themselves in such a way that his killing one will minimize the number of killings overall.

These features of the third-personal approach to impartiality make it natural to elaborate the threat to integrity that impartial morality poses in terms of maximizing and causal metaphors. Moreover, this is no mere accident of language, but instead reflects structural inadequacies in the third-personal approach to impartiality. On the third-personal view, the fact that Jim minimizes overall killings only by *committing a killing himself* appears only as an afterthought, if it appears at all. Indeed, once the causal levers that exist in the world arrange themselves, as they have in Jim's case, so that an ordinarily value-decreasing action becomes inexorably connected to an increase in total value, then the action's wrong-making properties are, from the third-personal point of view, simply *erased*.

The third-personal conception of impartiality is therefore committed, as Christine Korsgaard has said, "to the view that it is *obvious* that Jim should kill," whereas in fact "few people can imagine themselves in Jim's position without some sense of dilemma."[12] Indeed, third-personal impartiality is structurally committed to the view of Jim's circumstance that I earlier characterized as grotesque, namely that, having killed the one, Jim might congratulate himself on saving nineteen lives.

All of this makes the third-personal account of impartial morality an especially easy target for arguments about integrity. In particular, there is a connection between the threat that third-personal impartial morality poses to integrity, on the one hand and, on the other, its peculiarly wooden insistence that once Jim can save nineteen by killing one, he has no remaining moral obligation to those whom he might kill. This obtuse refusal to recognize a moral remainder in such cases makes the mechanistic metaphors through which Williams accuses third-personal impartial morality particularly apt and the threat to integrity that those metaphors expose particularly vivid, by rendering more particular personal projects—like not killing—ultimately contentless, at least as anything other than contingent summaries of more basic moral calculations. As Barbara Herman has observed, the third-personal conception requires that a person "not only be prepared to interrupt his projects whenever utility calls, but … also [that he] pursue his projects without the sense that what makes them worth pursuing is connected to the fact that they are his."[13]

The third-personal approach is not, however, the only possible account of impartialist morality. And it may be that the argument concerning integrity does not display the limitations of impartial morality generally but instead makes only a narrower point about the limitations of the peculiar utilitarian account of impartiality that Williams was, as a historical matter, addressing. Perhaps if this crude, third-personal conception of impartiality is replaced with another more sophisticated conception, impartial morality will no longer pose any threat to integrity.

IV The second person

The third-personal approach to impartiality can insist that Jim's killing poses no moral dilemmas only because it denies that individual persons underwrite separate bilateral moral claims on others even apart from any contributions that they make to overall value. As John Rawls has said in a related context, "[u]tilitarianism does not take seriously the distinction between persons."[14] Furthermore, the threat to integrity that third-personal impartial morality poses may perhaps be traced back to this purely impartialist error: The inadequacy of the third-personal analysis of Jim's case— the failure to recognize the case's complex and conflicted quality—may perhaps be explained in terms of the third-personal failure to credit that Jim must justify killing not only based on aggregate effects but also in terms that fully respect the separate demands for moral justification directed at him by the individual persons against whom he acts. Perhaps, then, reconstructing impartiality to reflect the distinction between persons will enable impartialist morality to explain the full moral complexity of cases like Jim's and to protect the integrity of persons who act impartially in the face of such complexity.

The most prominent impartialist effort in this direction seeks to cure the mistake in the third-personal conception of impartiality by abandoning the theory of value on which this conception is founded. According to this argument, it is the fact that value is supposed to inhere, fundamentally, in states of affairs that makes it so difficult for the third-personal approach to impartiality to credit that there could possibly be a reason against produc-ing a state of affairs that is not founded in its badness and is therefore equally a reason to prevent that same state of affairs from being produced by someone else or in some other way.[15] It is this difficulty that leads third-personal impartiality to ignore the moral differences between Jim's killing and the dictator's and so to conclude (contrary to all common sense) that Jim must *of course* kill the one. And that is why third-personal impartiality threatens individual integrity in such stark terms.

Observations like these appear prominently in the work of philosophers (such as Korsgaard) who reject the third-personal idea that value inheres exclusively or primarily in states of affairs and emphatically insist that "[t]he subject matter of morality is not what we should bring about, but how we should relate to one another."[16] Similarly, these views insist that the content of morality is not that we should maximize aggregate well-being (or some other similarly-structured value including, incidentally, morally good relations among persons), but rather that we should relate to other persons always as ends and never as mere means. This requires, as Korsgaard says, that we treat persons only in ways to which they can consent,[17] or expressed a little differently (this time by T.M. Scanlon), that we act only in ways that no person could reasonably reject.[18]

This is a conception of impartiality because it insists that each person's entitlement to justification is equally compelling and therefore that each person be given equal concern and respect. But this conception of impartiality elaborates equal concern and respect in a new way and departs fundamentally—indeed, in its natural grammar—from the third-personal view. Whereas the third-personal approach to impartiality insists that moral justification must take others into account, this approach to impartiality insists that moral justification must be acceptable to them. It insists that moral justification must not *count* others so much as *address* them, so that one may say, speaking loosely, that it requires impartial morality to proceed not in the *third-* but rather in the *second-person*.

Proponents of the second-personal approach to impartiality—which, engaging in another metonymy, I shall sometimes call the Kantian approach—have suggested that it can account for the complex ethical intuitions that cases like Jim's generate, and preserve integrity in these cases, entirely from within impartial morality. This suggestion is most vigorously pursued by Korsgaard, who begins by observing, as I have done, the tinniness of the utilitarian failure to see a dilemma in Jim's circumstances and the sense that even though Jim is in a position to save nineteen lives, he is not being offered "a happy opportunity for doing some good."[19] Instead, Jim is being asked to stand, *vis-à-vis* his innocent potential victim, in the relation of intentional, and indeed deliberate, killer. The fact that Jim's killing the one will also save the other nineteen does not undo or eliminate impartial morality's concern with this relationship including, in particular, morality's insistence that this relationship be justified *to that one*. The Kantian principle that Jim must treat each person (one-at-a-time) with respect and as an end rather than a means comprehends that Jim's obligations to the one whom he might kill are not simply extinguished by the fact that this killing will save nineteen others. It therefore recognizes that Jim retains a special obligation to justify his killing (but not the dictator's killings) to this victim.

But even as it recognizes moral complexities in Jim's circumstance that the third-personal approach to impartiality ignores, the second-personal conception of impartiality nevertheless recommends that Jim sometimes kill. In Jim's case, the demands of second-personal impartial morality turn on what the innocents themselves, and especially his potential victim, want him to do. Thus Korsgaard asks us to imagine that one of the innocents "steps forward and says, 'Please go ahead, shoot *me*, and I forgive you in advance.'"[20] Adding this feature to the example makes a substantial difference to the impartial moral case for Jim's killing the one,[21] at least on the Kantian conception of impartiality, because it includes that innocent in Jim's deliberations and addresses him—his individual point of view—in a way in which no utilitarian counting of total lives saved could ever hope to do. "*Very* roughly speaking," suggests Korsgaard, "[Jim is] not treating him as a mere means if he consents to what [Jim is] doing."[22] This is especially so given that the innocent, who will be killed in any case and regardless of what he says and of what Jim decides, is made no worse off by consenting to Jim's killing. This feature of the situation, the Pareto superiority of Jim's killing one innocent, makes it possible to say that even though it is not reasonable for the innocents to consent to being killed *absolutely*, it is reasonable to consent to being killed *by Jim*.

V No solution

The question now arises whether the increased sophistication of the second-personal approach to impartial morality can accommodate the demands of integrity. Kantian arguments, after all, recognize moral complexity—and indeed a moral dilemma—in Jim's circumstance that the third-personal approach to impartiality obscures: even as the Kantian argument concludes that, under certain conditions at least, Jim should kill, it narrows these circumstances and denies that these choices are in any sense *obvious* or *easy*. The second-personal account of impartiality appears, therefore, to correct many of the inadequacies in third-personal impartial morality while remaining purely within the impartialist moral tradition.

The problem of integrity, however, endures. Even after the appropriately full subtlety and complexity of second-personal impartial moral analysis are brought to bear on Jim's ethical circumstances, an ineliminable component of the dilemma that he faces remains unaddressed. And the Kantian advance does not eliminate the threat to integrity that impartiality poses or diminish the attractions of alternative, more personal approaches to ethics.

The second-personal approach to impartial morality calls on Jim to betray his personal ideals and ambitions less often and less completely than third-personal impartiality would do. But in appropriate circumstances, second-personal impartial morality still requires Jim to kill and, moreover, imposes this requirement without reference to Jim's personal ideals and ambitions. Accordingly, the second-personal reconstruction of impartial morality still requires persons who face such circumstances to betray their native ambitions in ways that blur the distinction between their own projects and other people's and therefore to alienate themselves from their personal projects and ambitions in ways that threaten their integrity.

Indeed, in spite of the Kantian's advance, she risks committing an error that is similar to the grotesque error that (I have suggested) is committed by the utilitarian who insists that Jim should kill and congratulate himself on saving nineteen lives. The character of this error is revealed in something Korsgaard says in the course of explaining why Jim might kill an innocent without violating the Kantian principle of respecting all persons, one-by-one, as ends in themselves. After admitting that any innocent Jim kills has been wronged absolutely—or, as she puts it, in the "larger moral world"—Korsgaard says that Jim and the innocents are forced by their circumstances to regard the dictator and their powerlessness before him as natural phenomena, and that there arises, therefore, a "smaller moral world within which the issue is between [Jim and the innocents]."[23] And when an innocent agrees to be the one Jim kills, then, says Korsgaard, "in that world this [innocent] consents."[24]

In adopting this "smaller world" metaphor (and particularly in applying the metaphor in connection with characterizing the dictator), the Kantian treats Jim as of necessity engaged in a noble cooperative project with the innocents, whose purpose is to respect persons' lives given the injustice imposed by the dictator's evil motives and their own inability simply to defeat him. (These noble purposes are achieved by the collective adoption of a fair procedure for selecting the innocent who will die, a procedure that requires Jim to kill.) But this treatment is merely the Kantian analog to the utilitarian claim that Jim has a happy opportunity to save lives. Like the utilitarian, the Kantian attempts to domesticate ordinarily immoral conduct by colonizing these activities for impartial morality, this time casting the argument not in the utilitarian calculus of beneficence but rather in the Kantian frame of respectful relations.

Moreover, Kantian ideas are no more persuasive on this point than their utilitarian counterparts. Even though second-personal impartial considerations concerning Jim's circumstances are exhausted by describing the smaller world in which Jim pursues a cooperative venture with the innocent whom he kills, these impartialist accounts again incompletely characterize Jim's activities in killing. When Jim kills (even if Jim's victim consents), then he is *also* engaged in a second, debased collective project *with the dictator*. The goal of this project, which arises in the larger moral world, is to kill an innocent, whose death remains, from the point of view of this larger world, not necessary and not consensual. Accordingly, adopting it requires Jim to betray personal ambitions (against killing) in precisely the manner that threatens his integrity.

The dilemmas that these cases involve arise because Jim's circumstances make it impossible to adopt one cooperative project without becoming implicated in the other, making it necessary to choose between participating in neither project or participating in both. And just as the utilitarian's exclusive focus on the lives that Jim saves grotesquely ignores the fact that

Jim is also intimately involved in killing, so the Kantian's exclusive focus on Jim's noble collaboration with the innocents grotesquely ignores the fact that Jim is also involved in a debased collaboration with the dictator. Even if Korsgaard's analysis is right, Jim's decision will determine how intimately he is connected to the debased project; that is, will fix the authorship of this project. The "smaller world" that second-personal impartial analysis invokes in such cases is therefore inadequate to the moral content of the cases, and this reflects a substantial limitation of second-personal impartial morality and not just a careless metaphor. Like the utilitarian, the Kantian in the end just ignores or even suppresses the fact that impartial morality requires Jim, betraying his personal ideals and ambitions, to sacrifice his integrity.[25]

To be sure, the shape of the problem is rendered slightly different under the second- than under the third-personal conception of impartiality, and the metaphor through which the problem is developed has changed accordingly. Thus, the Kantian's emphasis on individualized, intersubjective justification allows her to recognize that there can sometimes be a difference between a person's doing an act herself and failing to prevent someone else from doing the same thing. And this, relatedly, allows her to resist the unattractive, overtly mechanical characterization that Williams successfully imposed on utilitarianism, namely that it requires persons to see themselves as nothing more than "channel[s] between the input of everyone's projects, including [their] own, and an output of optimific decision."[26]

But although, unlike the utilitarian, the Kantian can recognize that (because of the dictator's supervening responsibility) Jim's refusing to kill the one is not *equivalent* to murdering nineteen, she cannot adequately recognize that the difference between these two—the degree of intimacy of Jim's connection to his course of action—*may properly matter more to Jim than to third parties*. And although, unlike the utilitarian, the Kantian can (because she recognizes the separate importance of all moral creatures and relationships) avoid the mechanistic cog-like account of individual agency of which Williams accused utilitarianism, she cannot adequately recognize the degree of independence each moral agent may properly claim from all others. For both these reasons, the person whose practical reasoning follows, exclusively, the Kantian conception of second-personal impartial morality once again displays an insufficiently secure relationship to his own moral ideals and ambitions. He may not quite measure his ideals and agency as the weather measures the wind, but he nevertheless suffers, once again, "in the most literal sense, an attack on his integrity."[27]

Perhaps Jim can, in the shadow of the dictator's threat and offer, justify his killing either in utilitarian terms, as minimizing aggregate killings, or in Kantian terms, including to the one whom he would kill. But while it may be that, in the shadow of the wrong that confronts him, Jim is impartially justified in killing, he is not simply *subsumed* in the shadow of this wrong.

Moreover, such an impartial justification cannot resolve, and must make room for, the separate question of how far and how fully Jim should enter into the shadow of the wrong that he confronts. And this is necessarily a more intimate, more personal question, because it involves considering whether to retreat (for the moment) from his own benevolent ideals and instead to implicate himself in the wrongful projects of another, at least in the sense of making one of these projects—killing the one—into his own.

The dilemma that Jim faces is not dissolved by impartial moral analysis because the problems of the intimacy of Jim's connection to the killing— the problems of authorship—that the dilemma poses are not dissolved, or indeed even addressed, by impartial moral analysis in either its utilitarian or Kantian forms. Nor, on reflection, could they be. Impartial moral analysis necessarily proceeds from the points of view of others, and the Kantian innovation was to focus this moral inquiry not on the third-person-plural point of view of aggregate value, but rather on the independent, second-personal points of view of individual agents, taken one at a time. The problems of authorship and integrity that lie at the core of these dilemmas, on the other hand, are *first-personal*. They must be addressed not from the points of view of others, but from the point of view of the agent herself— that is, from *Jim's point of view*.

Finally, the importance of Jim's point of view for his ethical circumstances may be given an intuitive illustration by changing the example slightly to imagine that the dictator offers Jane the same choice she earlier offered Jim—that she brings twenty more innocents into the prison courtyard and tells Jane: "You kill one or I will kill twenty." Furthermore, imagine that Jane (unbeknownst to the dictator) is not a stranger to the situation but is instead the leader of an organized and cohesive underground opposition to the dictator's rule. Although Jane despises killing innocents and aspires never to do so, her ethical circumstances do not place "never kill innocents" so centrally among her ethical projects. Instead, Jane's ambitions are much more hard-hearted than this and favor the executory virtues. They include securing freedom for her people and overthrowing the dictator by any reasonable means necessary. And, more specifically, they include maintaining the ruthlessness and self-control needed for making difficult and unpleasant choices, including the choice to sacrifice innocents, in pursuit of these goals.

Unlike Jim, Jane could accept the dictator's offer and kill the one and nevertheless develop an account of her actions that made them consistent with the most important of her first-personal ambitions and that did not require her to see herself as abandoning her own ideals in favor of the dictator's simply because impartial morality required it. Although she would, regrettably, be killing an innocent, Jane would also be pursuing political liberation with the courage and self-command she admires and aspires to display. She could therefore recast the dead innocent as a casualty of a guerilla war to which she is committed, and recast her part in the killing as a battlefield decision that displayed the steely virtues of effective command. Although killing the one would represent a *defeat* for Jane, the killing would not represent a *betrayal* of Jane's first-personal ideals, and her integrity would remain intact.

VI An insubstantial ideal?

The idea of integrity suggests that living an ethical life involves more than responding impartially to the claims of others, whether these arise in the third person (through the contributions they make to overall value) or in the second person (through the demands they make for individuated justification). Instead, persons also have a deep and distinctively ethical interest in living a life that can be seen, from the inside, as an appealing whole and, moreover, a whole that is authored by the person who lives it. Insofar as integrity is ethically important, therefore, a person who forms ambitions and plans—who undertakes to author her own moral life—thereby (in a way) creates ethical reasons for herself. As I have been saying, integrity and the plans and ambitions through whose recognition and pursuit integrity arises involve not third- or even second- but rather *first-personal* ethical ideals.[28]

The argument has so far said nothing, however, about the weight or importance that persons may reasonably attribute to their integrity, and it certainly has not defeated the plausible suggestion that it is simply self-indulgent for a person to insist on her integrity even to the point of persisting in first-personal ambitions that can no longer be impartially justified. In particular, it is not obvious that the burdens associated with lost integrity are *ethical*, rather than merely *emotional*. Indeed, it is tempting to doubt integrity's ethical appeal—to say that although integrity would be a nice thing in a perfect world, it should not be sought in our imperfect world, at least not when integrity comes at a cost to impartial morality.

The very example through which I have introduced integrity contributes to this doubt about integrity's ethical *bona fides*. No matter how noble or benign his motives, Jim would act *unjustly* in refusing to kill. This is a serious matter, and I have accepted from the beginning that when the injustice becomes great enough (or, as I put it, when the numbers get big enough) then it seems self-indulgent for a person to insist on his integrity and refuse to do what impartialist morality requires. Moreover, it is unclear why the sense of self-indulgence depends on the extent of the injustice—even smaller injustices involve failing to satisfy obligations to others, after all. Accordingly, a person who insists on his integrity at the cost of doing injustice, no matter how trivial, seems to display an unappealing interest in his own moral purity.[29] At the very least, he appears utopian, which is to say not quite morally serious. Insisting on integrity in Jim's case seems to

121

wish away evil rather than to confront it. Integrity, it seems, is nothing much to vaunt of, being unsuited to moral life in the world as it actually is.

These suggestions express a more basic idea, namely of the ethical hegemony of impartiality. This idea acknowledges that personal moral ambitions may conflict with impartiality and that insisting on impartiality in the face of such conflicts may threaten integrity. But the hegemonic view of impartiality insists that personal moral ambitions, and the ideal of integrity that frames them, are categorically less substantial than impartial values, so that the conflicts must, in every case, be resolved in favor of impartiality. Alternatively, bringing the hegemony of impartiality within the agent's personal ambitions, as it were, one might say that a good person will look to impartiality in constructing his personal ambitions, and will in particular make it his ambition always to comply with the demands of impartial morality. Integrity may, of course, be emotionally important; but it is not, on either view, an ethically substantial value, since considerations concerning integrity carry vanishingly little free-standing weight in all-things-considered ethical deliberations. Rather than indulging integrity, as I propose to do, ethical thought ought to overrule it.

I shall argue, against this view, that insisting on integrity is not self-indulgent or frivolous. The argument proposes that the first-personal ideals and ambitions that establish the architecture of integrity are essential to the ethical personalities of creatures like us. Moreover, always complying with impartiality is not a first-personal ambition that it is reasonable for creatures like us to have. If first-personal ambitions are not respected, and sometimes even held to outweigh impartial morality in all-things-considered practical deliberations, this attacks the very features of persons to which impartial morality latches on (and in particular their individual agency). Integrity and its associated first-personal ambitions are therefore not optional for ethics—not optional from the point of view of the agent who insists on them and also not optional for ethical theory, either, which cannot go about placing demands on persons that attack the personality in whose name it arises.

VII Hegemonic impartiality

The pathologies of purely third-personal impartial ethics are already familiar from the initial treatment of the problem of integrity. The third-personal construction of impartial morality does not just occasionally oppose particular ambitions—as these ambitions come into conflict with the common good—but instead always opposes *every* personal ambition, and indeed runs roughshod over the *very idea* of a personal ambition.

To see why, recall Herman's observation that even when utilitarianism allows a person to pursue a personal project, "the utilitarian agent must accept as the justifying reason for his action that it turned out to be the impartially preferred path."[30] Utilitarianism insists, in other words, that the agent "must not only be prepared to interrupt his projects when utility calls, but he must also pursue his projects without the sense that what makes them worth pursuing is connected to the fact that they are his."[31] Utilitarianism, once again, fails to "take seriously the distinction between persons,"[32] and not just in the familiar sense of denying that persons, as patients, are free-standing sources of individual demands on others, but also in a second sense. It also denies that persons, as agents, may possess individual projects that are peculiarly theirs and for which they bear special responsibility.

The practical personality of an agent who attempts perfectly to satisfy the third-personal conception of impartial morality thus falls apart, so that the third-personal view quite literally deprives morality of its subjects and reduces persons to being morality's many objects. (Third-personal morality represents, in this respect, an abstract generalization of the view expressed by Arthur Koestler's old Communist Rubashov, that "honor is to be useful without fuss,"[33] which similarly deprives honor of any persons who might display it.) Accordingly, it is neither self-indulgent nor utopian to resist the hegemony of third-personal impartial morality, because it cannot be morally self-indulgent for a moral agent to insist that she is, simply, a moral agent, even if this comes at some cost to the common good. It cannot be self-indulgent because the alternative—which is to abandon any sense of her individual and distinctive moral personality—leaves morality with no one to whom to apply, and so renders morality itself obsolete.

Moreover, even second-personal impartiality can override an agent's first-personal ambitions. Second-personal impartiality is famously no cakewalk: Kantians admit that it "does involve a requirement that one be prepared to set aside one's deepest projects if they require [impartially] impermissible actions."[34] Kantians celebrate this feature of impartial morality. They insist that impartial morality should play a special role in practical life—that whereas all other ambitions must yield in the face of conflicts with impartial morality, "the attachment to morality," as Herman says, "*is* supposed to be unconditional."[35] Put slightly differently, "[t]he Kantian argument is that at the limit, where the conflict with morality is serious and unavoidable, morality must win."[36]

But Kantians also claim that the second-personal elaboration of impartiality is nevertheless more modest, in respect of first-personal ambitions, than the third. Impartiality, on the second-personal view, does not attack the very idea of a first-personal ambition, but instead functions only to set the limits within which first-personal ambitions may flourish.[37] Instead of insisting that impartiality must subsume all of an agent's projects, the second-personal approach to impartial morality merely subjects these projects to a kind of appellate review based on an impartial standard.[38] Accordingly, second-personal impartial ethics allows persons to pursue their projects and plans in many cases, including even for the reasons that these are their projects and plans, and cuts a person off from her ambitions only when these ambitions come into conflict with the requirements of second-personal impartial justification.

Kantians claim that this modesty makes second-personal impartiality consistent with integrity. They observe that not every constraint on first-personal ambitions attacks integrity and propose that the discrete (rather than pervasive and continuous) sacrifices of first-personal ambitions that second-personal impartial morality requires merely limit the expression of an individual moral personality whose underlying endurance the second-personal view recognizes and even values. Thus although Herman recognizes that, "[f]or morality to respect the conditions of character (one's integrity as a person), it must respect the agent's attachments to his projects in a way that permits his actions to be the expression of those attachments," she insists that it need not "honor *unconditional attachments*."[39]

Indeed, Kantians go even further and propose that because second-personal impartiality allows agents to retain and promote a broad range of first-personal projects and ambitions, respecting the commands of second-personal impartiality might *itself* become a first-personal ambition, whose adoption *promotes* integrity—that "an attachment to impartial morality can itself be a project that gives a life meaning."[40] Kantian morality proposes, along these lines, to sustain in persons "an idea of the whole: a project whose point is to shape and limit other projects so that they are compatible with an ideal sense of how a person ought to live."[41] For the Kantian, second-personal impartial morality "can be (and is meant to be taken as) defining of a sense of self" so that "in having a moral character, a person will not have given up something in the way of integrity that standing aside from impartial morality would allow."[42] And accordingly, the Kantian concludes that although it might not be self-indulgent or utopian to resist the (complete) sacrifice of integrity that the totalizing demands of third-personal impartiality impose, it is self-indulgent to resist the more modest restrictions on first-personal ambitions that second-personal impartiality requires.

The Kantian development of second-personal impartial morality therefore accepts that integrity is important and squarely poses the right question, namely what limits on first-personal ambitions, and what sacrifices of integrity, it is reasonable for impartiality to require. Moreover, the Kantian position is surely right to insist that no first-personal ambition may be held *unconditionally*, so that when impartial considerations become important enough, they override *every* first-personal ambition. As I have said from the beginning, as the numbers get larger, it eventually does become simply self-indulgent for Jim to insist on his personal ambition to benevolence and to refuse to kill the one. But there is a large gap between the irresistible and indeed banal idea that every first-personal ambition must be sometimes

124

overridable, including by impartial considerations, on the one hand, and, on the other, the much stronger and less obviously appealing claim that impartiality should *itself* be the limiting principle of first-personal ambitions, so that boundaries of integrity are *precisely* established by the delicate balance of second-order impartial moral reasons. And this is the claim that Kantians who promote the hegemonic reconstruction of second-personal impartial morality assert.

VIII The architecture of integrity

Although persons should of course be attuned to impartiality and make it an important consideration in their practical lives, an unconditional attachment to impartiality, even in the limiting sense associated with the second-personal approach, is not appropriate for creatures like us. As Jim's case illustrates, *every* first-personal project will sometimes conflict with impartiality in a way that can place integrity under threat, so that second-personal impartial morality is too broad-reaching in its concerns and consequently too fluid in its requirements for narrow and imperfect creatures like us to take it hegemonically as our own. Moreover, the problem of integrity cannot be resolved simply by making impartiality itself into a first-personal ambition, just as people cannot avoid developing inconsistent beliefs by abandoning all particular beliefs and adopting only a generic belief in "the truth."

On this view, forming first-personal ambitions that sometimes outweigh impartial morality all-things-considered is constitutive of the kinds of creatures that we are, and indeed of our capacity to engage morality (including impartial morality) at all. Put slightly differently, our interest in integrity is not just an ordinary ethical failing (like petty selfishness), which we would do better to suppress (insofar as we can). Instead, if we lacked this interest we would be not better but rather so different that the ethical ideals we find familiar (including the ideals associated with impartiality) would no longer properly apply to us in the familiar way. (Our interest in status perhaps serves as a useful analogy in this respect. We could not lose this interest without totally transforming ideals concerning non-subordination that are central to ethical life as, being creatures concerned with status, we now know it.)

This suggestion again develops a line of thought introduced by Williams, who also sought to resist the hegemony not only of utilitarian but also of Kantian impartial morality. Williams did not quite succeed at sustaining the necessary resistance, because his arguments never quite escaped merely psychological reflection and so never quite set aside the emotional structure of our first-personal ambitions in favor of their practical structure. But Williams' approach nevertheless provides a useful introduction to the practical argument that I ultimately prefer.

125

Williams' argument seeks to enlist the psychological structure of first-personal ambitions in resisting the hegemony of impartialist morality. His argument develops along two lines. First, Williams observes that certain projects—Williams calls them *ground projects*—are so central to a person's ambitions overall that "the loss of all or most of [these] would remove meaning [from that person's life]"[43] and therefore leave him "unclear why [he] should go on at all."[44] These projects—which in Jim's case presumably include benevolence or even gentleness—therefore set the limits of persons' engagements with morality in any form.[45] Williams proposes that the hegemonic claims of impartial morality should be rejected because they make no adequate room for these limits.

That is plain on the third-personal approach, which subjects a person's attachment to her ground project (just at it subjects all her attachments) to the vicissitudes and contingencies of the causal connections that she confronts, which as Williams observes, "is a quite absurd requirement."[46] Moreover, even the second-personal approach, even as it makes room for personal ambitions and attachments, cannot make the space for ground projects that the special character of the attachments they involve demands. If the hegemonic idea that only impartiality is unconditional means anything, it means that persons must abandon even their ground projects whenever these transgress the limits that impartiality establishes. Indeed, it must mean that an ambition's status as a ground project *does not figure* in deliberations about how to proceed when circumstances bring the ambition into conflict with impartiality.[47] (There is no room, in the Kantian approach to Jim's dilemma, for consideration of the depth or centrality of Jim's first-personal attachment to not killing innocents, something that is strikingly reflected in Korsgaard's analysis: although Korsgaard asks how the *innocents'* possible pacifism might affect the Kantian analysis of the situation—by causing them to withhold their consent that one of their number should be killed—she gives, revealingly, no consideration to the question of *Jim's* possible pacifism or how this might affect the analysis of what Jim should, all-things-considered, do.[48]) And although this approach is less sensationally absurd than its utilitarian counterpart, it remains, Williams thinks, unacceptable: "[t]here can come a point," he says, "at which it is quite unreasonable for a man to give up, in the name of the impartial good ordering of the world of moral agents, something which is a condition of his having any interest in being around in that world at all."[49]

Williams argues, moreover, that this tension—between the conditions of a person's continued moral engagement, *überhaupt*, and the demands of impartiality—cannot be resolved simply by having persons adopt appropriate (ground) projects. In particular, it cannot be resolved by insisting that persons put doing what is impartially best at the center of their first-personal projects or, as Williams puts it, that they acquire the (overriding) disposition to promote the conclusions of casuistical argument.[50] This suggestion, he says, is inconsistent with "the psychological form in which ethical considerations have to be embodied"[51] in practical deliberations, namely that they can be effective only if they are incorporated—or, to revert to more familiar language, *integrated*—into an agent's *character*.

Williams insists that the problem of character imposes a bound on people's responsiveness to the conclusions of impartial moral argument, including even in the merely limiting role proposed by the second-personal reconstruction of impartiality. The ethical dispositions that make up a person's character display, Williams says, "resistance or (to change the metaphor) momentum" and this is one reason why "we can have, and we need, more than the one [or, I add, the overriding] ethical disposition of asking the question 'what ought [impartially] to be done?' and abiding by the answers to it."[52]

This dual effort to resist the hegemony of impartiality, even in its second-personal incarnation, has some intuitive appeal. But it is less than entirely satisfactory even on its own terms. Moreover, and more importantly, it is ultimately let down by its psychological nature.

Certainly one might object to the details of Williams' moral psychology. The idea of a ground project, for example, is artificial in ways that threaten to undermine the conclusions Williams draws by employing it, or at least to force Williams' argument to be recast in more complex terms. For one thing, a person's ambitions are not generally arranged in such a way as to produce a neatly, or even only roughly, distinguishable ground project. Instead, most people adopt and develop a large set of messily overlapping ambitions, no subset of which is necessary, and many subsets of which are sufficient, for producing meaning in their lives. Accordingly, most people will have no special subset of projects that can be sensibly distinguished and isolated from their other projects, so that threats to this subset display the qualitatively distinctive features that Williams attributes to threats to ground projects, namely calling into doubt a person's reasons for proceeding at all.

Furthermore, the scope of our intuitive concern for integrity is not limited to cases that involve the psychological intensity conjured up by Jim's example and rendered articulate by the idea of betraying a ground project. Instead, integrity seems equally clearly at issue even in cases of less dramatic and instantaneously intense conflicts between impartiality and first-personal ambitions. A person's integrity, and her motivation to continue to engage the world, may be ground away by a life of small betrayals just as surely as by a single great one—just think of the idealistic do-gooder who joins the establishment in order to change the system from within but makes so many compromises that she is in the end changed herself—and it is just as unreasonable for impartiality to insist on the slow surrender as on the quick one.

Accordingly, although it remains intuitively plausible that hegemonic impartiality will sometimes demand discrete sacrifices that have the existential quality Williams describes and that this demand is unreasonable, backing up this intuition and connecting it to the broader concern for integrity is a more complex matter than Williams supposes. Indeed, it is difficult to imagine how the complexities I have just described might be rendered tractable—how Williams might elaborate the psychological and indeed almost emotional architecture of integrity—within the frame that Williams has set, because the psychological and emotional mechanisms through which persons engage the world are too intricate and too fluid for the techniques of moral philosophy to latch on to them.

Moreover, and much more importantly, Williams' psychologism undermines his conclusion that it is *unreasonable* for impartial morality to take a hegemonic turn, or at least confines this conclusion to giving "unreasonable" a philosophically less interesting meaning than the circumstances require. Although Williams' argument might establish that persons have only a fragile moral resolve and only a limited moral flexibility, it does not establish that these limitations are anything more than ordinary moral weaknesses, like greed or cruelty, which should be suppressed insofar as possible, although they will inevitably resurface. And although it may be unreasonable, in the sense of being unrealistically optimistic, for morality to ignore that we are, in respect of our integrity, flawed creatures, it is surely not unreasonable, in the sense of ignoring a form of value, for morality to seek to correct and constrain our integrity insofar as this is possible and to lament that we are flawed insofar as it is not. I have proposed to argue that integrity, far from being self-indulgent, is a positive value and that ethics should adjust itself in recognition of this value, and in particular should abandon the hegemony of impartial morality and accept the free-standing authority of first-personal ambitions. But Williams' psychological argument supports only the much weaker conclusion that integrity expresses one of the ways in which persons are irredeemably self-indulgent and that, in this connection as in others, ethics cannot realistically hold them to too high a standard.

To sustain the view that our interest in integrity, far from being self-indulgent or reflecting moral weakness, defeats the hegemonic ambitions of impartialist morality requires developing a *practical* and not just a psychological elaboration of the idea that integrity gives ethical ambitions an inertial force capable of overpowering the shifting demands of impartialist morality (including even in its second-personal development). To this end, I borrow some of the intuitions that Williams' argument pursued but reconstruct these intuitions using ideas from the theory of bounded rationality rather than from moral psychology. Our practical rationality is bounded in ways that make it reasonable for us sometimes to insist on our integrity and to pursue first-personal ambitions even when this is not impartially best and that make it unreasonable for us to accept an unconditional attachment to impartialist morality.

The most familiar sense in which persons are only boundedly rational is that they possess limited deliberative capacities. Persons are not "frictionless deliberators,"[53] as Michael Bratman says, but instead "have limited resources for use in attending to problems, deliberating about options, determining likely consequences, performing relevant calculations, and so on."[54] These limits render persons open to the values of repose. The outcomes of persons' practical deliberations—the intentions or plans that these deliberations generate—must "resist ... reconsideration,"[55] so that they have "a characteristic of *stability* or *inertia*,"[56] which is, Bratman proposes, "appropriate for guiding the education and development of agents like us over the long run."[57] If they did not, persons would revisit their intentions in response to new reasons (or even just a new appreciation of old reasons) even when the increased accuracy of the conclusions that the additional deliberation generated could not justify its deliberative costs. In the extreme case, which is never far off, persons would be made practically impotent—literally paralyzed—by endlessly revisionary deliberation, being bankrupted (as it were) by the costs that such deliberation involves. Given the costs of deliberation, "the partiality of [our] plans is," as Bratman says, "essential to their usefulness to us."[58]

The inertia of intentions necessarily has effects on practical reasoning going forward—"prior intentions not up for reconsideration *constrain* further intentions"[59]—so that a boundedly rational person who appropriately does not reconsider one of her intentions may depart from what, in a sense, she has all-things-considered most reason to do. Indeed, insofar as the friction associated with deliberation about whether or not to reconsider an intention makes it reasonable for an agent to apply the same dispositions of non-reconsideration across many cases, it can be reasonable for the agent to fail to reconsider even when the improvement in the accuracy of her intentions that reconsideration would have produced exceeds the frictional costs that the reconsideration would have involved specifically in the case at hand. Moreover, it can be unreasonable, even from a point of view outside the agent and not subject to the inertial constraints associated with the agent's intentions, to criticize the agent in such a case. The criticism is unreasonable insofar as (because of the friction that deliberation necessarily involves) the habits and dispositions of non-reconsideration that the agent applies are reasonable for the agent to have, because they tend, over the long run and given the costs of deliberation, to promote the effectiveness and accuracy of the agent's practical deliberations.[60]

This analysis of bounded rationality suggests a practical reconstruction of first-personal morality that resists the hegemony of impartial morality while avoiding the psychologism that undermined Williams' account. Insofar as it is reasonable for an agent not to reconsider his intentions, it can be reasonable from the agent's own point of view sometimes to persist in pursuing her first-personal ambitions—which are simply grandiose and highly general intentions—even when, as circumstances have developed, these ambitions have become inconsistent with impartial morality. An agent who persists in this way is not giving in to her shortcomings or being self-indulgent but, to the contrary, managing her unavoidable limitations as best she can. Indeed, it is unreasonable for others to criticize such an agent even though they perceive, as she does not, that she is in a sense departing from what impartiality requires—unreasonable because such criticism ignores the costs of the friction that unavoidably accompanies the reconsideration necessary for her to track impartial morality more perfectly in the case at hand.

This friction (and the unreasonableness of ignoring it) will of course be greater if impartial morality is given a third- than if it is given a second-personal interpretation, because the maximizing conception of impartiality that the third-personal view elaborates is much more fickle in the face of changed circumstances than the limiting conception associated with the second-personal view. But even the second-personal approach to impartiality is sensitive to circumstance (as Jim's case illustrates), so that the deliberative costs of tracking even second-personal impartiality cannot be ignored and sometimes underwrite retaining first-personal ambitions that transgress the limits that second-personal impartiality would impose under conditions of perfect rationality. Integrity, rather than being self-indulgent, is revealed by this argument to be an expression of the necessarily inertial character of the intentions of boundedly rational creatures.

But even as these observations explain why it is in many situations unreasonable for a person always to sacrifice her ambitions to the demands of impartial morality and unreasonable for others to criticize her for not doing so, they do not quite apply to circumstances like Jim's. The resistance to impartial morality that the argument so far supports depends on the reasonableness of not even reconsidering the first-personal ambitions under whose banner this resistance arises. But the one fixed fact about situations like Jim's, the fact to which the argument has returned again and again, is that these situations involve moral dilemmas. The impartial principles and the first-personal ambitions at stake in these cases are both so weighty, and the tensions between them are so great, that any reasonable person facing Jim's circumstances will experience an almost irresistible impulse to deliberate intensively about what she should do. And so the account of integrity developed in the previous paragraphs does not, by its very nature, quite apply in the cases at hand.

Nevertheless, it is possible to adapt this argument to explain why it is unreasonable hegemonically to make impartial morality into the limiting condition of first-personal ambitions, even in dilemmas in which reconsideration is clearly appropriate. The necessary adaptation proposes to give a practical reconstruction to the intuitions concerning the limits of human motivation that Williams gave a merely psychological expression.

The deliberative frictions that the argument so far has emphasized do not exhaust the ways in which our practical rationality is bounded. Instead, we remain boundedly rational even after our deliberations have been concluded. Even after we have determined what we have most reason to do, it takes energy to *intend* to do what we have identified as best, and even once we have formed an intention, it takes further energy to *endeavor* to do as we have intended. We may therefore trip over the bounds of our rationality not just during deliberations but also in the subsequent stages of our practical engagements: even when we have concluded our deliberations and decided, we may fail to intend; and even when we have intended, we may fail to endeavor.[61] Both phenomena are familiar from ordinary experience: we know that we have most reason to make generous charitable donations and yet never even intend to give; we intend to diet and yet never seriously endeavor to lose weight, instead abandoning our intention when we pass the first bakery.

Moreover, just as our deliberations are costly, so the subsequent stages of our practical engagements, in which we intend to do as we have decided and endeavor to do as we have intended, are also not frictionless. In order to act as we have decided rather than giving in to contrary temptations that subsequently confront us, we must shepherd our practical energies so that they stand behind the course of action that we have decided upon, to produce intentions and endeavors that conform to our conclusions. This process of marshalling our inclinations—which I shall call, adopting a usage that is only slightly unusual, by the name *motivation*—is the structural analog to deliberation's marshalling of reasons. Motivation employs what Richard Holton has called *will-power*, that is, the faculty that allows us actually to endeavor to do what we have concluded is best.[62]

Like deliberation, motivation is costly, and we must often struggle to motivate ourselves to remain true to the conclusions of our deliberations in the face of temptations to depart from them, even going so far as to engage others—trainers, for example, or inspirational leaders—to help us to realize our conclusions. Indeed, one of the costs of motivation is paid in will-power itself, which is diminished when it is redirected from one undertaking to another (especially when the alterations and reversals come too frequently or too suddenly for whatever natural process of replenishing will-power we possess to keep pace). This is again familiar from our practical experience of the world. Donors, for example, become fatigued when confronted with a succession of humanitarian crises, so that they give progressively less even as they acknowledge that they have more rather than less reason to give; and soldiers become progressively less careful to avoid risks as a war continues, even though they acknowledge that the new risks that they ignore are as serious as the risks that they once evaded. Indeed, we are all susceptible to fatalism, which is just the state in which, perhaps because of the friction associated with repeated motivational efforts and perhaps for some other reason, our will-power has been completely depleted, so that we feel quite simply no longer able to direct our own lives.

DANIEL MARKOVITS

Moreover, these costs of motivation have also been demonstrated in the laboratory. Experimental subjects given the opportunity to donate money to anonymous others increase their giving less than proportionally as the number of others increases.[63] And other experiments directly demonstrate that, as Holton puts it, "will-power comes in limited amounts that can be used up."[64] For example, exercising will-power to resist one petty temptation makes experimental subjects less likely to resist a second temptation than their fresher counterparts.[65] Indeed, Holton, in summarizing the experimental literature, goes so far as to suggest that will-power "works very much like a muscle" in that it "takes effort to employ" and "tires."[66] This is of course just a biological alternative to the economic metaphor that I prefer.

Even if deliberation itself were frictionless, we could not continually translate the revisions brought on by reconsideration into action, because incessant revision would increase the costs of motivation and eventually cause us to run out of the will-power that we would need to resist temptation and act as we had concluded. The economy of motivation therefore elaborates another source of inertia in the practical reason of boundedly rational persons—another way in which the intentions and endeavors of such persons constrain their future intentions and endeavors—which answers the costs of marshalling persons' inclinations (of motivating them) so that they intend and endeavor to do the acts that their deliberations recommend. This inertia survives reconsideration and therefore applies even when reconsideration would otherwise appropriately trigger revisions in an agent's beliefs about what she had most reason to do.

Thus it is possible to say that even a person who has (following reconsideration) discovered that his old intentions and endeavors are flawed, perhaps because they are no longer impartially best, may yet reasonably decline to change his intentions and endeavors in light of his economy of motivation. Moreover, it may be unreasonable, in light of the economy of motivation, for someone else to criticize the agent in such a case. This will happen insofar as the inertial force that the agent gives his intentions and endeavors even in the face of revisionary reconsideration tends, over the long run and in light of his economy of motivation, to help the agent to motivate himself to intend to do that which he identifies he has reason to do and to endeavor to do that which he intends.

Moreover, the practical effects of motivational friction will naturally grow as an intention and endeavor comes to occupy an increasingly central place in an agent's practical personality, and in particular as it matures into what I have been calling a first-personal ambition or project. Ambitions and projects, in their place in the economy of motivation and therefore also in their inertial properties, resemble what Jed Rubenfeld has called *commitments*. They are cases in which "the self permits itself to be *thrown* into its own engagements,"[67] making "investments and attachments ... deliberatively and motivationally."[68] The physical metaphor is again helpful here, because, like Bratman's metaphor of friction, it emphasizes the energy that motivation requires and the possibility that changing course involves loss.

The motivational loss people experience after shifting away from basic and important ambitions is again familiar from ordinary experience, for example, in the tendency (which people often describe as being at loose ends) to drift aimlessly from temptation to temptation that commonly follows the breakup of a marriage, the abandonment of a career, or even the sacrifice that inevitably accompanies action in the face of a moral dilemma. Indeed, Williams' idea of a ground project, and his insistence that a person cannot effectively shift away from his ground project, may now be recast (setting aside its psychological roots) as the most extreme case of the marshalling of inclination that motivation involves. A ground project arises when so much of a person's will-power is thrown into an ambition that shifting from the ambition to another would involve such friction that the person would have too little will-power left over reliably to pursue a new project, which is why he literally could not (at least for the moment, until the reservoir of will-power is replenished) carry on.

Finally, although first-personal ambitions, being path-dependent products of an agent's deliberative and motivational history, are in a way self-given, they are neither fundamentally self-regarding nor purely private (in the sense of being absolutely inaccessible to persons other than the agent whose ambitions they are). After all, the reasonableness of first-personal ambitions (including in respect of their departures from impartial morality) may be judged by others as well as by those who have them, in both cases attending to the same ideas concerning the economies of deliberation and motivation. The idiosyncrasy of first-personal ambitions and the reasons that they generate come, on my account, not from some fundamentally self-regarding or private domain of normativity but rather from the ways in which boundedly rational persons incorporate the public reasons to which they all have access into forms that can sustain actual practical engagements: the economies of deliberation and motivation that govern persons' practical lives require them to organize the public normative realm that they all share into personal (first-personal) ambitions, which are only imperfectly revisable, including in response to changes in the public norms out of which they were formed. Instead of involving an unappealing (and perhaps incoherent) inward-looking retreat from the idea that normativity is fundamentally public and impartial, concerns for integrity and first-personal morality reflect a clear-eyed appreciation of the limits, as well as the possibilities, for ethical action in persons who are only boundedly rational and therefore cannot always attend to impartial morality directly but must instead marshal moral reasons through their own deliberative and motivational processes, to produce ambitions that have free-standing influence over them and are distinctively theirs.

If persons were perfectly rational—if they enjoyed frictionless delibera-tion, so that to consider was to conclude, and frictionless motivation, so that to conclude was to intend and to endeavor—then their integrity might not clash with impartial morality.[69] They would have no need to throw themselves inertially into their ambitions or indeed to have any sense that these ambitions were distinctive to them, as opposed simply to tracking impartiality, at all. In this case, morality would be a much simpler thing for persons: much of the skill involved in living morally would become unne-cessary, and being fair-minded—which is to say, adopting the deliberative stance that proponents of impartiality champion—would be enough to secure living a good life.

But persons are only boundedly rational, so that it is reasonable, in light of their economies of deliberation and motivation, for them to endow their ambitions with inertia and, moreover, unreasonable for others to criticize such inertia, including even in circumstances in which it causes persons' actions to depart from what impartiality would ideally require. In parti-cular, it is unreasonable to insist that persons form the overriding ambition to conform to the demands of impartial morality, because these demands (even on the second-personal approach to impartiality) shift too capri-ciously for it to be efficient for persons to track them, either in their beliefs (given the economy of deliberation) or even (given the economy of motiva-tion) in their intentions and endeavors.

The ideal of integrity is the natural consequence of these features of per-sons' practical rationality, stated in terms of the boundaries of their moral personalities. Integrity expresses, practically, and not just psychologically, the inertial qualities of persons' ambitions—the fact that persons can understand and engage the world most effectively in terms of beliefs and through intentions and endeavors that are distinctively theirs, both in the sense of being holdovers of their prior deliberations, intentions, and endeavors and also in the sense of themselves introducing an idiosyncratic path-dependency into their future practical lives. Far from being self-indulgent, the interest in integrity, and the related idea that first-personal ambitions might sometimes resist the hegemonic claims of impartial morality, reflects deep features of human nature—features that are intimately involved in ways in which morality applies to human persons, *tout court*, from the practical stance to which human persons, as they are, should aspire. One might say, simply, that integrity reflects that fact that persons are *examples* only and not *representatives* of the moral point of view.

Notes

1 Bernard Williams, "History, Morality, and the Test of Reflection," in Christine M. Korsgaard, *The Sources of Normativity* (New York: Cambridge University Press, 1996), pp. 210–11.

2 See Aristotle, *The Nichomachean Ethics*, Book I, Chapters. 4–12, trans. W.D. Ross, in *The Basic Works of Aristotle*, ed. Richard McKean (New York: Random House, 1941).
3 This paragraph borrows loosely from Thomas Hill's similar expressions of related ideas, see Thomas E. Hill Jr., *Autonomy and Self-Respect* (New York: Cambridge University Press, 1991), pp. 176–7, although my development of these ideas will ultimately depart from Hill's.
4 See Bernard Williams, "A Critique of Utilitarianism," in J.J.C. Smart and Bernard Williams (eds), *Utilitarianism: For and Against* (New York: Cambridge University Press, 1973), pp. 76, 98.
5 Williams' thought-experiment is a philosopher's fancy of course. But it is not hard to identify real circumstances that display an analogous moral structure. One such case, which I develop in detail elsewhere, is that of the lawyer in an adversary legal system. See Daniel Markovits, *A Modern Legal Ethics: Adversary Advocacy in a Democratic Age* (Princeton, NJ: Princeton University Press, forthcoming).
6 Williams, "A Critique of Utilitarianism," p. 108.
7 Thomas Nagel, *The View from Nowhere* (New York: Oxford University Press, 1986), p. 182. Nagel adds that this will produce "an acute sense of moral dislocation." Ibid.
8 Williams, "A Critique of Utilitarianism," p. 116, n.18.
9 Ibid., p. 117.
10 Notice that this argument does not involve the suggestion that killing the one is in itself burdensome for Jim and thus involves a greater self-sacrifice than morality can require Jim to bear. The argument's theme is not that Jim cannot be required to sacrifice his *interests* to the common good but rather that Jim cannot be required to sacrifice his *ideals* to the common good. Rather than emphasizing the distinctness of persons as *patients*—the idea that people have a special relationship to their own well-being—the argument developed in the main text emphasizes the distinctness of persons as *agents*—the idea that people have a special relationship to their own actions and to the ideals that guide them.
11 The third-personal approach to impartiality is more commonly called *consequentialism*.
12 Christine Korsgaard, "The Reasons We Can Share: An Attack on the Distinction between Agent-Relative and Agent-Neutral Values," in Christine Korsgaard (ed.), *Creating the Kingdom of Ends* (New York: Cambridge University Press, 1996), pp. 275, 292.
13 Barbara Herman, *The Practice of Moral Judgment* (Cambridge, MA: Harvard University Press, 1993), p. 39.
14 John Rawls, *A Theory of Justice* (Cambridge, MA: Harvard University Press, 1971), p. 27.
15 This way of putting the point paraphrases remarks of T.M. Scanlon and Thomas Nagel. See T.M. Scanlon, *What We Owe to Each Other* (Cambridge, MA: Harvard University Press, 1998), p. 82; Nagel, *The View from Nowhere,* p. 178.
16 Korsgaard, "The Reasons We Can Share: An Attack on the Distinction between Agent-Relative and Agent-Neutral Values," p. 275.
17 Here Korsgaard, ibid., p. 295, cites, unsurprisingly, Kant's "Groundwork," in *Immanuel Kant, Foundations of the Metaphysics of Morals*, trans. Lewis White Beck (Indianapolis, IN: Bobbs-Merrill Press, 1969), p. 430.
18 See Scanlon, *What We Owe to Each Other*, p. 153; T.M. Scanlon, "Contractualism and Utilitarianism," in Amartya Sen and Bernard Williams (eds), *Utilitarianism and Beyond* (New York: Cambridge University Press, 1982).

19 Korsgaard, "The Reasons We Can Share: An Attack on the Distinction between Agent-Relative and Agent-Neutral Values," p. 292.
20 Ibid., p. 296 (emphasis in original).
21 The consent of the victim was, as Korsgaard acknowledges, present in Williams' statement of the original example. See ibid., p. 292. It did not, however, figure prominently in Williams' discussion.
22 Korsgaard, "The Reasons We Can Share: An Attack on the Distinction between Agent-Relative and Agent-Neutral Values," p. 296.
23 Ibid.
24 Ibid.
25 The Kantian might try to avoid this result by observing that although Jim must *intend* for his debased projects to succeed, he is not principally *motivated* by the considerations underlying the debased project. The Kantian may argue that this creates a protective distance from the project that helps preserve integrity.
    But while the distinction between intent and motive may be helpful in other contexts, it cannot usefully be employed here. The ordinary first-personal ambitions that the debased project betrays include the ambition to avoid intentional (indeed, probably even negligent) and not just ill-motivated killing. Moreover, and probably more importantly, the ambition to avoid only ill-motivated killings cannot properly be formulated as a personal ambition at all, at least not where ill-motivated is understood merely to mean inconsistent with the demands of impartial morality. As I shall argue, integrity requires forming ambitions at a greater level of particularity than the generic ambition to do what is impartially required.
26 Williams, "A Critique of Utilitarianism," p. 116.
27 Ibid., p. 117.
28 Note that first-personal ideals may be just as other-regarding, and therefore have as much claim to being called "ethical," as impartial ideals. Agape, after all, is a first-personal ideal, as are any number of the traditional virtues.
29 The reference to moral purity borrows from Thomas Hill. See Hill, *Autonomy and Self-Respect*, p. 68.
30 Herman, *The Practice of Moral Judgment*, p. 39.
31 Ibid.
32 Rawls, *A Theory of Justice*, p. 27.
33 Arthur Koestler, *Darkness at Noon* (New York: Bantam Books, 1941).
34 Herman, *The Practice of Moral Judgment*, p. 39.
35 Ibid., p. 40 (emphasis in original).
36 Ibid.
37 I borrow the idea of impartiality as a limiting condition from Herman, *The Practice of Moral Judgment*, pp. 31, 39.
38 I borrow the metaphor of appellate review from Thomas Nagel, who proposes to "take the conflict between [first-personal] and [impartial ethics] back to the [impartial] standpoint on appeal." Nagel, *The View from Nowhere*, p. 202.
39 Herman, *The Practice of Moral Judgment*, p. 39.
40 Ibid., p. 38.
41 Ibid., p. 40.
42 Ibid.
43 Bernard Williams, "Persons, Character and Morality," in *Moral Luck* (New York: Cambridge University Press, 1981), pp. 1, 13.
44 Ibid., p. 12.
45 Note that whatever else they may be, ground projects are not mere symptoms of petulant self-absorption. Persons do not act in accordance with ground projects

for the sake of having a reason to continue (just as persons do not act in accordance with their ambitions more generally for the sake of preserving integrity). Instead, they act because of that which would make them have no reason to continue (which would make them lose their integrity) were they to act otherwise.

46 Williams, *Moral Luck*, p. 14 (citation omitted).

47 To be sure, an ambition's status as a ground project may figure in her practical deliberations in one way, by increasing the suffering that she will experience if required to give it up, and this may lead the Kantian (and indeed even the utilitarian) to conclude that she should not give it up. But this suggestion cannot explain why the person's suffering should not be thought to express morally unjustifiable attitudes and therefore viewed as the person's own fault. Moreover, the suggestion also fails to capture the concerns reflected in the argument about integrity. It treats the person whose ground project is under threat as a patient and asks how much he may fairly be required to suffer, so that the dilemma faced by Jim becomes an exercise in the limits of self-sacrifice. The argument about integrity, by contrast, approaches the problem from an altogether different angle and is concerned with ground projects not in order to protect their authors' interests as patients, but rather to preserve their integrity as agents.

48 Korsgaard, "The Reasons We Can Share: An Attack on the Distinction between Agent-Relative and Agent-Neutral Values," p. 296.

49 Williams, "Persons, Character and Morality," p. 14.

50 See Bernard Williams, "Professional Morality and Its Dispositions," in David Luban (ed.), *The Good Lawyer: Lawyers' Roles and Lawyers' Ethics* (Totowa, NJ: Rowman & Littlefield, 1983), pp. 259, 267.

51 Ibid.

52 Ibid.

53 Michael Bratman, *Intention, Plans, and Practical Reason* (Chicago, IL: University of Chicago Center for the Study of Language and Information, 1987), p. 28.

54 Ibid., p. 10.

55 Ibid., p. 16.

56 Ibid.

57 Ibid., p. 70.

58 Ibid., p. 30.

59 Ibid., p. 32.

60 Ibid., pp. 65–6.

61 This distinction is not always appreciated in the philosophical literature, which has a tendency to lump together all cases in which a person fails to do what she judges best. A notable exception is Richard Holton, who distinguishes between *akrasia*, which he uses (unconventionally) to refer to the state of intending to do other than what one judges best and weakness of will, by which he means (again unconventionally) the state of too readily reconsidering (and abandoning) one's intentions in the face of inclinations that the intentions were designed to defeat. See Richard Holton, "How Is Strength of Will Possible?" in S. Stroud and C. Tappolet (eds), *Weakness of Will and Practical Irrationality* (Oxford: Clarendon Press, 2003), p. 39.

62 See ibid., pp. 40–1. This account of will-power is not quite true to Holton's own views, because it treats will-power as both enabling intentions to track decisions about what is best and enabling endeavors to track intentions. Holton, by contrast, (following the distinction between *akrasia* and weakness of will reported in note 61 supra) limits will-power to the second function.

63 See Ray Fisman, Shachar Kariv, and Daniel Markovits, "Individual Preferences for Giving," *American Economic Review* 97 (2007), 1858–76.

64 See Holton, "How Is Strength of Will Possible?" p. 56.

65 See ibid., pp. 56–7.

66 See ibid., p. 49.

67 Jed Rubenfeld, *Freedom and Time: A Theory of Constitutional Self-Government* (New Haven, CT: Yale University Press, 2001), pp. 95–7.

68 Ibid., p. 97. I am not quite using *commitment* as Rubenfeld does, because I am proposing that all intentions and endeavors possess motivational inertia and that commitments (or ambitions) merely possess greater inertia than usual. Rubenfeld, by contrast, treats commitments as qualitatively (and not just quantitatively) different from ordinary intentions, which, by implication, possess no motivational inertia (or at least nothing like the inertia possessed by commitments).

69 I say "might" here rather than "would" because it remains possible that something besides the necessarily inertial character of persons' practical engagements with the world might generate conflicts between the conditions of their integrity and the requirements of impartial morality. One candidate for this source of conflict is the existence of a sphere of non-moral values, which generate practical reasons independent of (impartial) morality that can properly compete with morality in persons' all-things-considered practical deliberations. Williams himself would likely have endorsed a suggestion like this. He famously opposed the view that practical reason should be organized according to a coherent and hierarchical scheme of values, with impartialist morality at the top – an idea he sometimes referred to, derisively, as the "morality system." See, generally, Bernard Williams, *Ethics and the Limits of Philosophy* (Cambridge, MA: Harvard University Press, 1985), pp. 174–96. It is certainly plausible that thoughts such as this contributed to Williams' own belief that personal integrity requires resisting the hegemony of impartialist morality, in all its forms. In this connection, see, for example, Susan Wolf, "Meaning and Morality," *Proceedings of the Aristotelian Society* 97 (1997), p. 299. Nevertheless, Williams' express development of the idea of integrity emphasizes the ways in which hegemonic impartiality might threaten integrity even from within morality, and this is the line of argument that I have chosen to address. I would like to thank Daniel Callcut for enlightening commentary on this point.

Part III

STORIES AND SELF-CONCEPTIONS

7

D'OÙ VENONS-NOUS ... QUE SOMMES NOUS ... OÙ ALLONS-NOUS?[1]

Elijah Millgram

In retrospect, Bernard Williams was, during the second half of the twentieth century, perhaps our most refined philosopher of common sense. He spent his life exploring a handful of ideas current either among philosophers or the general public, and typically both. The one that will anchor our discussion is that there is a deep difference between matters of fact and evaluations or decisions. A closely related thought, which we will also take up, is that there is an important distinction between science, which is fully objective, and ethics, which is only subjective. A further and connected idea, which will serve as our entry point into the discussion, is that your reasons for action bottom out in whatever it is you happen to care about.

The theses on which Williams concentrated his intellect count, if anything does, as the collective default view about their respective topics, but they have also proved surprisingly hard to formulate satisfactorily. Thus although they have been much criticized over the course of their run of popularity, it has been hard to tell whether the criticism sticks to the ideas themselves, or rather to the clumsy ways they were put. But Williams returned to them repeatedly, carefully recasting those thoughts, and the reasons for them, in ever more nuanced, ever more stripped down form.[2] With a good philosopher's concern for the consistency of his intellectual commitments, he worked insistently at tracing the connections between them, and both negotiating and sharpening the tensions among them.

Philosophy of the analytic variety is evidently at a turning point. If we are to determine where it is to go next, we must first take stock of where we are, and for such stocktaking, we cannot do better than to turn to Williams. His views are the most intelligent and articulate expression of what someone who is reasonably mainstream and reasonably hardheaded can be presumed to think. So we may be fairly sure that when larger criticisms stick to Williams' mature view, they are registering real objections to ideas that philosophers and the public tend to take for granted, rather than superficial difficulties with inept renderings of them.

I am going to recapitulate the evolution of Williams' understanding of a few of these ideas, and sketch a constellation into which his mature thought assembled them. The path through the material will be just a bit complicated: because much of our interest is in the distinctions Williams worked to articulate, we will be shuttling back and forth between the subject areas on the contrasting sides of one or another such distinction. For expository purposes, I will organize the first part of the presentation around his criticism of what he called the "morality system," but bear in mind throughout that my interest is not in the relatively familiar arguments against morality: they are sketched merely to display some of the intellectual machinery at work in them. These arguments have generated a large literature which I will not engage here, and where there are differences of opinion between myself and other readers of Williams as to how the arguments are supposed to run, I will not now take up the controversy.

Once the pieces have been put on the table, I will turn to assessment and diagnosis. Those pieces amount, I will suggest, to a rendering of what it is to be a human being, and what sort of world it is that humans are suited to inhabit. I will ask what presuppositions would have to be in place for the creatures Williams has implicitly described to make sense as a design decision. And I will conclude that the unintended lesson of Williams' work is that we have made an astonishing mistake about who we are. The philosophical common sense of the past half-century has been suitable for impossibly simple-minded creatures, creatures competent to live only in impossibly simple environments. Consequently, the descriptive metaphysics and ethics that have been spun out of it are useless to us.

I

Williams' early critique of utilitarianism shows why it pays to unload the excess baggage from a vehicle of philosophical thought. Doing so allowed him to elicit an incoherence in the most straightforward way of spelling out and accommodating one of the widespread ideas that preoccupied him.

One's reasons for action, Williams believed, are a matter of what one cares about. Philosophers have for the most part rendered this thought as instrumentalism: roughly, that one has a reason for action only when the action would be a means to the object of a desire one has. (Slightly more colloquially: the only reason to do something is that it will get you what you want.) Williams put a great deal of thought into streamlining this awkward and rather blunt theory.[3] Especially generous about what could do the work foisted by instrumentalists on narrowly conceived desires, he introduced a generic label for the more broadly conceived class: your 'subjective motivational set.' Williams habitually and indifferently referred to its elements as 'desires' or 'projects,' but an indication of how much more flexible and inclusive he meant to be was counting emotions and loyalties among them, and we will shortly encounter a further variety of subjective motivation, not normally regarded as desire-like at all, namely, the disposition to apply a certain sort of concept. Williams was equally generous about how, formally, reasons invoking one's motivations could work. They would not have to be what many philosophers think of as means-end reasoning in its strict sense, that is, finding a cause for an object of desire and adopting the intention to bring it about, and he allowed for much more freedom of movement in addressing one's motivations and concerns.[4] The resulting view, which came to be called 'internalism,' retains the requirement that reasons for action be capable of jointly explaining and justifying the actions in connection with which they are adduced; the substantive but pared-down claim which Williams endorsed was that you could neither explain nor justify if your subjective motivational set did not contain suitable elements.[5]

If one's projects and desires are what underwrite all of one's practical reasons, then they must be very important indeed. We ought—and this is another widespread idea which Williams explored, and which, to get ahead of our story, he eventually rejected—to be able to capture and represent their importance to us in a suitable theory. Utilitarianism, the moral theory whose slogan ran, *The greatest good for the greatest number*, is perhaps the most straightforward way of doing so. Williams decomposed utilitarianism into its consequentialist structure, on which actions are chosen to produce the highest-ranked globally-assessed outcomes, and a substantive view as to what it is in virtue of which outcomes are to be ranked: happiness, subjectively construed, that is, the extent to which the objects of one's subjective motivations are realized.[6]

Williams pointed out that in even-handedly taking everyone's subjective motivations into account, utilitarian agents could easily be put into the position of having to surrender their own projects and desires. Worse, because this eventuality is bound to be anticipated, intelligent utilitarians will come to hedge their emotional investments in their projects long before they are actually required to replace them, in something like the way that employees who are liable to be fired on twenty minutes notice avoid becoming overinvolved in their jobs. Utilitarians end up lacking 'integrity,' meaning that they do not act for the reasons they have, but for reasons that they have been bamboozled into thinking they have. When such agents disinvest in their projects, the subjective commitment to them which was evidently the source of their importance is washed away. A world of self-consciously utilitarian agents would be a world in which projects and desires lacked the vigor needed to support the seriousness with which utilitarian theory proposes to attend to them.

Still worse, such agents are unable to acknowledge the peculiarly personal importance of their projects and concerns to themselves. Desires and projects are at the bottom of—for present purposes, pretty much *are*—all of one's practical reasons. So one's reasons to go on living must be projects or desires. Williams noticed that some projects or desires are conditional in content: an old man in a retirement home may want to play golf, but only as long as he's alive anyway; it is not as though he would choose to live longer in order to play more golf. By contrast, he might also want to see his granddaughter graduate, and will do his very best to stay alive until she does. Desires or projects that are not conditional on one's being alive anyway (like that desire to attend the graduation) are, in Williams' lexicon, *categorical desires* or *ground projects*. These would be no less vulnerable to being overridden in a utilitarian decision than any other desires or projects; internalism casts them as indispensable ingredients of one's reasons to stay alive; thus, utilitarian moral theory is likely to demand that one give up one's very reasons to go on. Moral theories are, logically, advice, in the sense that they purport to tell you what to do. A good touchstone for the acceptability of advice is whether it undercuts one's stake in one's life: generally, one shouldn't take advice if, were one to take it, one would have no reason to go on living. So utilitarianism gives advice that one should be entirely willing to ignore, which is just to say that it fails as a moral theory.[7]

II

The incoherence of utilitarianism has to do with the attempt to capture the person-by-person importance of desires and projects (consisting or expressed in being the source of a person's own reasons for action) in an impersonal theory of what would be on the whole best. This first-pass diagnosis invites the response that if utilitarianism is trying to have its cake and eat it too, some other moral theory will do better: say, a Kantian (or, as the terminology went, back when Williams was starting out, a 'deontological') theory. But Williams' characteristic practice of revisiting earlier attempts on a problem led him to broaden his earlier claim: the mistake was moral theory itself, not just the utilitarian flavor of it.[8] His progress toward his eventual understanding of that conclusion started off with attempts to think through another widely accepted idea, that there is a difference between—as some of the usual ways of marking the hard-to-put contrast have it—values and facts, or 'ought' and 'is,' or practical reasoning and theoretical reasoning (that is, thinking about what to do vs. thinking about what the facts are). Williams first took up the question as it was framed by the metaethics of the period, that is, as asking what distinguishes, on the one hand, desires, commands, or statements about what ought to be done (I'll say 'oughts' from here on out) from, on the other, beliefs, assertions (exclusive of those oughts), or evidence for belief. Williams' developing view of that distinction passed through three stages.

Among the many formal contrasts he found in his sensitive exploration of it, *agglomeration* came to the forefront early on.[9] Beliefs agglomerate: if the belief that *p* is in order, and the belief that *q* is in order, then the belief that *p* and *q* must be in order—though we'll have to qualify this claim shortly. Desires do not agglomerate: I want to go to Palo Alto today, and I want to go to Berkeley today, but I do not want to go to Palo Alto and to Berkeley today. Imperatives do not agglomerate: when you are instructed by one authority to close the door, and by another to leave it open, each command may be perfectly in order, yet their conjunction is an incoherent and impossible-to-execute proposal for action. In a paper on ethical consistency that became something of an instant classic, Williams argued that oughts do not agglomerate. Although he allowed that this last conclusion was unobvious and his argument for it less than knock-down, a theory of tragedy seemed to follow from it: tragedy consists in having obligations that are jointly unsatisfiable.[10] Williams was impatient with the tendency of analytic ethics to keep "all the important issues ... off the page, and [the] great caution and little imagination ... used in letting tiny corners of them appear";[11] that taking failure of agglomeration to be a central formal feature of the practical allowed him to broach an ambitious theory of tragedy would have been, in his eyes, one of the more powerful attractions of his analysis.

The view that seemed to be emerging at this point was that considerations about matters of fact are to be formally distinguished from practical reasons and their relatives in that the former agglomerate, and the latter do not.[12] Theory is responsible to facts—to what is really out there—and so must come out the same from any point of view.[13] Decision and evaluation, and now Williams could invoke his internalism in an explanatory role, are driven by subjective motivation, which comes in packets associated with persons, and which allows for a great deal of not-very-coordinated variation among the packets.

Williams' understanding of the distinction went through a next round of modification and complication when he served on the Committee on Obscenity and Film Censorship.[14] In proposing legislation, it is hard to avoid attempting to define its key terms, and in doing so, he observed that concepts such as 'pornographic' and 'offensive' function as guides for action, and that full control of such concepts requires already occupying an appropriate evaluative stance. This seemed to place them squarely on the practical side of the distinction he had been honing. Nevertheless, such concepts figure into beliefs and assertions, and are responsible to matters of fact; this seemed to place them on the theoretical side of the distinction. And, indeed, their applications *behave* like beliefs, in that they agglomerate: if I believe that it's adult material, and I believe that it's offensive, I'd better believe that it's offensive adult material. Williams argued that the mix of features exhibited by *thick ethical concepts* could not be accounted for by supposing there to be distinct theoretical and practical thoughts in play: the application of a thick ethical concept does not factor into factual and eva- luative components, and so seems to straddle the fact-value distinction.[15]

The obstacles which thick ethical concepts posed for the agglomeration- based distinction directed Williams back to a further contrast which had long been of interest to him. That our subjective motivations figure into our applications of our concepts is a special case of those contributions to concepts which make them more local, more subjective and more tied to the idiosyncrasies of our constitutions. Think of how our color concepts reflect the idiosyncrasies of the human visual apparatus, and are therefore local to human beings; if birds and bees could speak, they would have dif- ferent color vocabularies; if mole rats could speak, they would have no color vocabulary at all. The disposition to apply a thick ethical concept is a special case of such contributions; it can be counted as an element of one's subjective motivational set; such concepts are typically shared within cul- tures, which is why beliefs that embed them agglomerate, but within single cultures, and not, generally, across different cultures.

Now, our local and constitution-laden descriptions differ among them- selves as to whether they are amenable to a certain sort of reformulation. In certain cases, we can, Williams supposes, "form a conception of the world which *contains* [ourselves and our] representations," and which will then permit the indirect agglomeration of what were formerly only locally agglomerable applications of concepts.[16] For instance, I may start out with the belief that litmus paper turns red in acid, and space aliens might start out with a belief that I am not in a position to so much as state, because it contains vocabulary tied to the deliverances of the aliens' peculiar sensory organs; these cannot be conjoined into a claim in our vocabulary or in theirs. Once our account of pH has become that of contemporary chem- istry, we can describe what happens to litmus paper without having to deploy our secondary-quality vocabulary for color; once our color science is good enough, we can explain the response of our visual system; our transformed account could thus in principle be understood by intelligent space aliens, creatures who do not share our secondary-quality vocabulary. Our chromatic and other descriptions can thus be transformed so as to render them (and now we are giving content to the hazy words that figured in one of our popular *ur*-thoughts) more objective and less subjective. We introduce the Absolute Conception of Reality (or, as Williams sometimes also put it, when he was raising his eyebrows at the moral version of the ambition, the Point of View of the Universe) as the limit in which all knowledge amenable to such transformation has been rendered *completely* objective. Knowledge inflected by our constitutions need not agglomerate with the knowledge of alien communities, but knowledge so transformed as to constitute part of the Absolute Conception *does* agglomerate with any other knowledge so transformed: when we encounter the space aliens, our theoretical physics will join with theirs—again, this is Williams' under-standing of science, and not one I am endorsing myself—to form a single body of doctrine.

It is a guiding aim of the scientific enterprise to produce knowledge that forms part of the Absolute Conception, and Williams takes it that this is not an unrealistic or misguided aspiration. But ethical knowledge—to a first approximation, knowledge in which the application of thick ethical con-cepts centrally figures—does not survive the reformulation we have descri-bed. When our subjective contribution to the application of a thick ethical concept (that is, in the first place, the role of our subjective motivational set) is made explicit, our ability to deploy the concept is undercut, and knowledge evaporates, in something like the way that the funniness evapo-rates when you explain the joke: reflection, Williams summarized his claim, destroys ethical knowledge.[17]

The deep distinction, then, that had been initially supposed to run between what to believe and what to do, or between fact and value, seemed instead to be the distinction between science and ethics. Scientific knowl-edge agglomerates, once suitably transformed; ethical knowledge does not. The enterprise of moral theory is defective in that it treats ethics as though it were science; that is, as though ethical considerations and conclusions could be gotten to agglomerate, whether they were anchored to different cultural backgrounds, or to different persons, or to different commitments copresent in a single person (recall Williams' explanation of tragedy), or to different times in a single person's life (the case exploited by Williams' famous discussion of moral luck).[18] The morality system's distinctive com-mitment is to this very idea, roughly that there is available in principle a point of view of the universe on what it is right (permitted, and so on) to do. That is why morality is a mistake.

The problem with utilitarianism had at the outset been narrowly con-strued as an internal tension: that of trying to capture the importance to persons of their reasons for action, from the standpoint of no person at all. There were thus two ways of resolving the conflict. Having explored and rejected the attempt to retain moral theory by deemphasizing the impor-tance of subjective motivation, Williams found that the fatal objection to utilitarianism was just that our thought about—to put it as neutrally as possible—what one should do, or how one should live, cannot be config-ured as anything like a scientific theory. Here we are seeing the benefits of paring the ideas in play down to their most skeletal form.

Williams was, again, our most refined philosopher, in that his *modus operandi* and signature style was progressive refinement. Opting for the alternative resolution, he began to revise and reformulate what had been traveling under the heading of "morality," sloughing off its unsustainable commitments to agglomeration and systematic theory. "Ethics" came to be Williams' term of art for what he hoped would come of that reformulation, and if you are wondering what it would look like, *Shame and Necessity* is almost certainly meant as his demonstration of ethical thought cleansed of moral theory. But I am going to leapfrog it, and proceed directly to Williams' final investigation of the factual materials for which, he was convinced, theory remains an appropriate medium.

III

When distinctions like those between fact and value, or science and ethics, crop up, philosophers are all too often tempted to explain them metaphysically: in this case, by appealing to the notion that science is about the facts, and ethics isn't. Williams' early essays had flirted with such metaphysical explanations, and later discussions made much of the Point of View of the Universe, or the Absolute Conception of Reality. Critical responses have unsurprisingly tended to focus on the merits of this sort of explanation.[19]

However, the complications which thick ethical concepts forced on Williams' rendering of the distinction made it clear that what is demanded is not (or, not just) a metaphysical explanation of it. The principled difference between science and ethics appears only when the attempt is made to reformulate knowledge as part of the Absolute Conception. Those attempts are expensive (a point we will return to shortly). So the pressing question is practical: why, of all the metaphysically available distinctions we could draw and emphasize, is *this* the one (or, *a* one) we would prefer to use? Accordingly, when bouts of multiple myeloma forced him to choose the one project he would finish, Williams settled on *Truth and Truthfulness*: a book devoted to explaining, in terms of basic structures of human social life rather than those of metaphysics, the role and importance of truth.[20] The choice was well motivated; the account of truth is meant to serve as the keystone of his lifelong reconstruction of common sense.

Several years previously, Edward Craig had developed some of Williams' early remarks into an account of knowledge.[21] Craig proposed sidestepping the exercises in conceptual analysis that still dominate epistemology by asking what function ascriptions of knowledge serve; he addressed his question by imagining a society that lacked the concept (a society in an epistemological 'state of nature'), and considering whether and why they would want to introduce it. The need he identified was a generic and transmissible certificate for information. To say "I know that *p*" conveys roughly that *p* is good enough to go on; that I can tell you so without having to ask precisely to what use you are going to put *p*; and that you can tell the next person to come along what I have just told you. (Of course, the first-person use of such a certificate is not necessarily the primary one.) Any society lacking such a certificate would have to invent one, and when they did, it would have roughly the contours familiar from our concept of knowledge.[22]

Now, Craig's treatment perhaps inadvertently highlights a choice that epistemologists have made, for the most part unawares: to provide a theory of the most generic epistemic certificate, rather than the many other more specialized certificates in circulation. Some examples of the latter: not all knowledge is *news* (which implies recent provenance and salience); publication in academic journals provides a very large variety of different sorts of epistemic certification; degree-granting institutions provide a very large number of distinct forms of epistemic certification to individuals (rather than to packets of information); labels on products may inform you that they contain chemicals "known to the State of California to cause cancer, birth defects, or other reproductive harm." The choice historically made by epistemology as a field is reasonable if the generic certification is especially important, but not otherwise.

Williams self-consciously modeled his treatment of truth on Craig's account of knowledge. The function of the concept of truth was to be elicited from a state-of-nature argument, one that showed why, if we did not already possess and use the concept, we would have to invent or adopt it.[23] Human beings are social creatures that pool information.[24] Williams focused his discussion on the virtues that need to be in place if information is to serve as a shared resource: sincerity, the disposition not to withhold information from the pool, and not to intentionally add fraudulent information, and accuracy, the disposition not to add to the pool sloppy or shoddy information. What those virtues are meant to assure is the quality and the range of the contents of the common pool. Quality control of this sort requires an appropriate assessment concept. Truth is the feature of (and 'true' the label for) suitable contributions to the pool.

'True' is the *generic* label for information appropriately added to the pool. There are perhaps fewer standardized nonepistemic certifications that stand to 'true' as the more specialized epistemic certifications stand to knowledge. (Call these *specialized alethic concepts*.) That is because, in actual use, epistemic certificates tend to shoulder the real communicative work, and so end up doing duty for the alethic ones. (Here's the sort of thing I mean. When you tell someone that something is true, normally you mean to assure him that it is: that is, to give him the generic certification that says he can go with it, on your say-so. But then you might as well just tell him that you know it.) There are, however, exceptions: the censor's *nihil obstat* confines itself to matters of concern to the Church. And *ad hoc* alethic certificates, with variable content, are common, as when you tell someone that an approximation is true enough (accompanied by an implicit or explicit gesture at the circumstances in which it is), or that a claim is true for present purposes, or that it's good enough for government work. Choosing to focus on the generic certification will be reasonable if the generic certification is especially important, but not otherwise. To anticipate, its centrality or otherwise will be determined by the use made of the contents of the pool: how people go about withdrawing or accessing the information in it.

A few observations about this third stage of Williams' thinking about the distinction he meant to be refining, before we move on to the next round of argument. It had looked as though Williams was committed to there being just *one* deep distinction after which both philosophers and ordinary speakers were groping, and the real question was exactly what content it had. At this point, however, the earlier version of the distinction is back in play, side by side with what had looked like its successor. I am not now going to pursue the question of how that happened, and so we have, on the one hand, the earlier contrast between beliefs and assertions and, variously, imperatives, oughts, desires, and the like; the generic label, 'true,' accompanies the use of this contrast. On the other, we have the contrast between truths that can be rendered fully objective, and those which can't, typically because they involve applications of thick ethical concepts. (And possibly the latter category should be understood to include as well those other expressions of motivation that aren't so much as true at all.) Let's think of the pool of more impressive information on one side of *this* contrast as marked by another label, 'objectively true.' Because the points I mean to make about them are analogous, I will consider the distinctions in parallel. We have just seen a social explanation advanced for using the former; such an explanation would be equally in place for using the distinction between objective and merely subjective truth (whether or not Williams himself ever got around to giving it).

There is a delicate point here: To say that 'true' is the (or a) generic alethic certificate is to say that we do not, in using it, have to specify which pool of information is in question, or who the certificate is meant for, or what its ranges of acceptable use are. However, that we do not specify which pool of information the certificate is for does not entail that there is only one such pool, but only that the work of picking out the relevant pool is done tacitly. For example, and this was one of the prompts to cultural relativism, different cultures may employ different ethical vocabularies. The different languages may effectively segregate their ethical observations into distinct, nonagglomerating pools, even though both cultures nonetheless use the generic tag, 'true' (or rather, the words for 'true' in the respective languages).

Now, putting a generic certificate into circulation implies that you can just go ahead and use it, without knowing anything *else*. Philosophers nowadays are much enamored of contextualist approaches to one problem or another, so notice that a generic certificate does not give you what you need to apply an item of information in a context-sensitive manner. The certificate's failing to tell you whether its use is restricted to particular contexts is equivalent to its not telling you when it is and isn't permissible to agglomerate that information with other items of information: restrictions can be represented as restrictions on agglomeration. And notice that it doesn't tell you whether *you* have, as it were, the right security clearance for the information. When agglomeration is restricted, additional detail is required, to enable more nuanced data management. So a presumption built into use of a generic alethic certificate is that any items in the pool of information can be agglomerated.

Much information starts out its life with many restrictions on its use. Trivially, statements containing indexicals like 'now' or 'I' or 'here' must be processed into a different form if they are to be used later on, or by someone else, or elsewhere. More importantly, much information is generated as approximations, idealizations and their less-than-accurate kin, and whether these are usable or not depends on what aims or concerns one has. (There is no such thing as an approximation's being good enough, plain and simple; to use an approximation competently, one must be able to answer the question, good enough *for what?*) Typically they are explicitly or implicitly accompanied by more specialized alethic certificates, such as 'true enough, when $v \ll c$,' or 'acceptable when the volume is far enough away from the vessel wall.' Since what I mean by calling an alethic certificate 'generic' is that it does not specify conditions of use, both 'true' and 'objectively true' will count for present purposes as generic alethic certificates. So, perhaps counterintuitively, we are thinking about more than one generic certificate.

If expiration dates, owners, and framing concerns are not specified on a generic certificate, that must mean that they are not needed (as a general rule, anyway). So the exclusive (or almost-exclusive) use of a generic alethic certificate implies that available information is being *transformed* into a nonrestrictedly or indiscriminately agglomerating form, as it is being contributed to the pool. Thus exclusive focus on generic alethic certificates presupposes that the costs of making information indiscriminately agglomerable are being paid up front. How high those costs are depends, of course, on which pool the information is being added to: the merely true, or the objectively true.[25] Either way, they're generally quite high—a point that seems to have escaped Williams' attention because he was preoccupied by the dangers of wishful thinking and self-deception.

A policy of assuming high costs up front had better come with decent reasons, amounting to an argument that a pay-as-you-go policy would not be more efficient. Why not use specialized alethic certificates instead, and perform context-to-context conversions on a demand-driven basis? Why wouldn't it be more cost-effective to partition the contents of the pool of information into ranges on which a single user might plausibly draw (where the partitions are chosen to minimize the costs of conversion while enabling

151

agglomeration within each range)? The alternative to a pay-as-you-go system is one in which indiscriminate usage is made of the information in the pool. So near-exclusive use of a generic alethic certificate practically presupposes widespread and indiscriminate use of the information in the pool.

Drawing distinctions around one or the other of these generic alethic certificates, and treating them as deep and important, makes sense if there is exclusive (or near-exclusive) use of those certificates. The overhead is perhaps more daunting in converting information into the format demanded by the Absolute Conception. However, the costs incurred in making information belonging to either pool indiscriminately usable is reasonably assumed only if information resources really are held in common: only if (pretty much) anyone could realistically help himself to any of the items in the pool.

Williams takes the significant contrasts to be: information vs. motivation, and motivation-inflected information vs. fully objective information. Information agglomerates (within the local generic pool, or within the more ambitious generic body of information sharable among scientists of all species). Motivation fails to agglomerate (even when motivations are shared by groups, as when a culture shares the use of a thick ethical concept; such motivation-inflected information will not generally agglomerate across group boundaries). Indeed, it is this variation in motivation that make the virtues of accuracy and sincerity into the urgent issues that Williams saw them to be: in human social life, individuals and groups are often at odds with each other, and thus our use of the distinctions marked by the generic alethic certificates is being explained as a consequence of our belonging to a species whose members compete uneasily with one another, but who nonetheless pool information.

V

The time has come to consider what design justification there might be for creatures of which Williams' account would be satisfactory.[26]

The elements of a subjective motivational set function as inputs to choice and decision, that is, as something on the order of guidelines or priorities. These do not generally agglomerate, and in fact the distinctive *logical* features of the different sides of Williams' contrasts are accounted for by the care taken to assure agglomerability on one side of the contrast, and not on the other.[27] Agglomeration and the possibility of correction are procedurally tied to one another: if A and B don't agglomerate, pressures for consistency (and so, what consistency amounts to) come to something very different than if they do. Formally, even if A is inconsistent with B, in that it wouldn't make sense to advance 'A and B,' that fails to show that there is anything wrong with either A on its own or B on its own (or with the reasons for them).

Thus the incorrigibility of elements of a subjective motivational set is equivalent to their not being subject to an agglomeration principle. That motivations fail to agglomerate is exhibited in the most striking logical feature of internalism (and of its cruder relative, instrumentalism), that one's bottom-line desires and projects are incorrigible. You want what you want, and someone who insists that you are wrong to do so, when mistakes about such things as how to get what you want are not at issue, is just *bluffing*.

Subjective motivations can change, in all manner of ways, but they cannot be corrected, and this means that nothing could count as the rational investigation, on the part of such a creature, as to whether its bottom-line guidelines and priorities were correct.[28] Since the creatures do not correct their own motivations, the design strategy is reasonable only if they do not need to; in other words, only if, for the most part, the designer can equip them with motivations (or ensure that they pick up motivations from their surroundings) that will not need correction. That in turn is feasible only if the designer can anticipate the practical problems his creatures will face, and only if the guidelines his creature would need to negotiate them are sufficiently compact to be stored and accessed. Given plausible cognitive constraints on processing, memory, and so on, that in turn requires that the environment the creature is anticipated to face be both stable and simple.

Coloring in the line drawing, we see that Williams' alethic state of nature is something on the order of a tourist-brochure version of a village in the hills of Provence, where life goes on as it has since time immemorial. The villagers work their plots of land, growing the same grains and vegetables they always have; they herd their sheep and goats; they bake rustic bread and knit rustic clothes; they hunt rabbits and deer; they build houses out of the local stone; they marry and raise children; when they get old, they sit outside the village pub and drink pastis; they play boules in the park; eventually, they die, and are buried in the cemetery behind the church.

The internalist design solution is satisfactory for this form of life. The designer knows that his peasants will have to work the fields, so when it comes time to own a field and work it, they come to have a desire to do so. They need to be made to reproduce, and thus are built so that, when they get old enough, they will want to have children, or anyway want to do things that as a predictable side-effect produce children. Not all of a subjective motivational set need be hardwired, of course; a disposition to mimic others, and to learn and adopt one's elders' thick ethical concepts, will keep the games of boule going and the pastis flowing. Because life in the mythical village never changes, there is no need to delegate to the peasants themselves the task of investigating what their motivations ought to be, and no need to equip them to correct their motivations; thus, there is no need to complicate their cognitive or normative systems with the gadgetry that would take. A Dinah Shore song called "Doin' What Comes Natur'lly" nicely captures the internalist's implicit faith in such programming.[29]

We live in a complicated world. Because it is complex and unstable, it repeatedly confronts us with practical choices that we cannot (and that an imaginary designer could not) anticipate; no set of preformulated guidelines could carry us successfully through the challenges we face. Even if an omniscient designer were somehow able to foresee all of the vicissitudes into which we might be thrust, their number and variety are too great to allow the case-by-case advice he might want to bequeath to us to be compressed into small enough packages: that is, packages capable of being stored and accessed by our small–finite cognitive systems. (Data compression formats of the sort I have in mind include utility functions and Aristotelian virtues.) Internalism could not be a satisfactory design for creatures that have to live in *our* world.[30]

VI

Creatures that pool their information (whether all of it or just the high-value part they allocate to their science), and pay the costs of converting it into a form that makes it generically agglomerable, are a sensible design decision if, realistically, each of them can withdraw and deploy arbitrary items of information from the shared pool. That requires, among other things, that all (or almost all) information in the pool be comprehensible by any (or almost any) of the creatures that might use it. And that in turn requires an environment simple enough to keep the representation of information uniform enough to allow across-the-board comprehension, given the cognitive limitations of the creatures in question.

Although there may be difficulties in getting the suspicious, lazy and quarreling villagers to contribute accurate information to their shared body of knowledge, the obstacles to deploying and to agglomerating arbitrary information retrieved from the pool are temporary and surmountable; as far as the model goes, they are noise and can be ignored. While it may be, for instance, too late for a villager to use a bit of gossip he has heard, there are no obstacles on the order of: in principle he could not understand it. And that is true even though there is division of labor, and thus division of intellectual labor, within the village; the farmers tend to know things that the housewives do not, and vice versa, but each can understand what he or she is told by the other. In such an environment, assuming the up front costs involved in a generic pool of information is a good strategy.

But, once again, our own circumstances are nothing like those of the peasants in Williams' state of nature; our forms of life are consequently nothing like theirs; consequently, the design solution that made sense for our mythical peasants would not be workable for us. And consequently, just as the practical rationality and ethics or morality that come with that design solution could not be, for us, a correct ethics or rationality, the descriptive metaphysics that comes with it could not be a correct metaphysics for our species.

A good way to get a sense of how complex our environment actually is would be to survey the strategies we are forced to use in representing and navigating it. I won't undertake that sort of survey here, but as a stopgap, consider how we academics and intellectuals divide up the task of understanding, defining subject matters small enough to be mastered by individuals, or by groups of individuals with shared training. We develop discipline-specific forms of representation: not just specialized vocabulary and notation, but distinctive representational techniques, tailored to discipline-specific modes of reasoning and argumentation. In order to avoid being swamped by the complexity of maps even of particular subject matters, we deploy approximations, idealizations and many other related devices.

If the world is complicated enough for these coping strategies to be necessary, then we have what we need to say why the image of humanity that Williams uses to explain the formal features of truth and science cannot be an image of us. Because we are intellectually specialized, the information we store is not in fact generically accessible: if you are not a specialist yourself, you cannot read the journal articles.

If we cannot expect across-the-board preprocessing that would permit the extensive use of one or the other of our generic alethic certificates, we might imagine that information is agglomerated *within* the narrow confines of a specialized subject matter. But once we have parcelled out the information to smaller groups of users, what we in fact find within scientific and other disciplines is only sporadic agglomeration of information, due to the already-remarked widespread use of approximation and idealization. As we have seen, approximations and idealizations must be tagged with conditions of use, and typically with goals or other concerns, and cannot be assumed to agglomerate. Notice further that representations of these sorts can be used only when one has sufficient control of thick ethical concepts proprietary to a specialization, and of the goals that are internal to the disciplinary enterprise. Within a small group of specialists, the local skills and additional training required to manage the more complicated certificates and the hedged representations they accompany turn out to be affordable.

Now, if this is what science is really like, something has gone wrong in Williams' rendering of the science-ethics distinction. Recall that Williams marked the distinction by claiming that science, but not ethics, supports (anyhow, postprocessing) agglomeration: that is, that the results of science can eventually be shared with just anyone. But the idea that we can share information with just anyone is most plausible precisely when we are not considering science.[31]

VII

If I am right, the generic alethic certificates on which Williams lavished his attention could not have the near-monopoly on usage that his account presupposes. But then, what allowed Williams (and has allowed others) to imagine that they did? I'm going to sketch a candidate explanation, one which will have the added bonus of explaining the scientism that worried Williams, but to which—if I am hearing his emphasis on the Absolute Conception of Reality rightly—he fell prey himself.[32] The mark of scientism, as I will construe the disposition, is that of placing at the center of one's philosophy an emphatic insistence on what scientific theory and practice are like, but one that doesn't have much to do with the activities or products of actual science. (A crude but familiar representative might be physicalist metaphysics, with its confidence that everything supervenes on, for instance, the values of fundamental physical quantities at space–time points.)

Consider how information exported from within a discipline to outside users must be formatted. Elaborate qualifications on when it can be applied, and with what it may be agglomerated, must be for the most part stripped off: nonspecialists will not have the training necessary for this sort of information management. That is, the sort of information passed across disciplinary boundaries is, almost always, a watered-down version meant for popular consumption, and not the complexly qualified formulation that carries the most authority *within* the discipline. The impression that we operate largely with generic alethic certificates is, I am hypothesizing, a byproduct of the fact that, outside one's own specialization, one operates with *exported* information, which does bear simplified alethic certificates. (And because we do not see past the border of an exporting discipline, we do not see how vastly greater are the number of occasions on which less-simplified certificates are being relied upon.) But these simplified certificates do not have the force of the generic 'true.' Rather, they mark the exported information as 'true-enough-for-*you*.'[33]

Allow that we are (these days, anyway) as intellectually specialized as I have claimed. What would be an appropriate cross-disciplinary information management strategy? In general, those who are equipped to criticize the results within a specialized field are those who are also in the field; critical attitudes are appropriate on their part. For those outside the field, the correct attitude is simply to accept the pronouncements of respectable representatives of the field as authoritative. Philosophers, standing outside of one scientific enterprise or another, are the consumers of the information such enterprises export, and we have seen that it is normally presented as much more cut-and-dried than it is, and as much simpler than it is. It is often enough presented imagistically, and it is all too natural for such consumers to turn an image of science into a metaphysics.

That is to misapprehend the point of what is after all a correct information-management strategy. The scientistic philosophers' mistake is two-fold. First, they are misinterpreting the authority they correctly accord to a foreign discipline as warranted by the secure status of its results.[34] The justification for the deference towards authority required by the strategy is not the high quality of the information, but the incompetence of its consumers. If you are on the outside, such and such is authoritative, but if you are on the inside, it's the dubious and likely-to-be-superseded opinion of someone else's research group. Second, information tagged for export generally is massaged into a form which just about anyone can consume. So it looks (from the outside) like a science is delivering generically sharable information: information that you can agglomerate with any other information (or anyhow, any other information like *it*). But whether or not scientists are after the Absolute Conception of Reality, those aspirations are not what explain the exported information being in this way shareable.

Scientism in philosophy is a predictable side-effect of failing to recognize how creatures like ourselves compartmentalize their information pool. Most of the alethic certificates in circulation do not come with elaborate warnings about their circumstances of use; that gives us the impression that we are deploying a generic certificate that merely marks items belonging to a generic (or to a generic scientific) information pool. But when it does, we are failing to appreciate how our information management handles specialization.

VIII

We cannot conduct ourselves in the simple-minded manner of our imaginary peasants. Instead, we partition our environment into what we might as well think of as niches. We specialize, and indeed we *hyper*specialize to the different niches we occupy. And it is a remarkable feature of human beings that our first specialization is not necessarily our last: an individual may over the course of his life move from niche to niche, respecializing to each of them. A good description of the strategy might be this: human beings are serial hyperspecializers. If that is the strategy we implement, the observations we have made fall into place as its consequences.[35]

Because we cannot know up front what the guidelines and priorities suitable for navigating a particular niche might be, when we enter a novel niche, we have to *learn*, in a very demanding sense of the notion, what the appropriate action-guiding standards are. That means that the cognitive elements that guide action in creatures like ourselves must be correctable, and that we can ourselves attempt to correct them, which in turn means that internalism must be false for our species.

Because we construct specialized representational systems for the different niches we occupy, and because reasoning and inference within a niche tend to rely heavily on approximation, idealization, and related techniques, information cannot be relied upon to agglomerate—neither across niches, nor within a niche.

Finally, although philosophers tend to argue about distinctions as though they were arguing about matters of truth and falsity, a distinction is neither true nor false. Quine famously argued that the analytic/synthetic distinction was impossible to draw, and Williams attempted much the same with the fact/value distinction. But the point of arguing that a distinction is hard or even impossible to draw is that it is, as a *practical* matter, badly chosen. If a distinction is well- or badly-chosen, it can be so for a variety of other reasons as well. The real question is normally not whether the distinction is, metaphysically, *there*, but how much attention it should get. If we are serial hyperspecializers, the distinctions which will help us understand our lives and practices are not those that Williams spent so much time and effort articulating. And so I have been arguing that Williams' error was to devote his attention almost exclusively to the wrong distinctions, distinctions that matter to us scarcely at all.

IX

University presses do not like to pay for four-color cover art. I suspect that Williams made the case for using a Gauguin on the jacket of *Moral Luck* because the title of that painting—which I have taken as the title for this paper—asked the questions that Williams found he was trying to answer: Where do we come from? What are we? Where are we going?

The questions were well-chosen; as the title of his next collection put it, what philosophy is in the business of is making sense of humanity. But if my argument to this point has been on target, Williams' answers were deeply mistaken, and, I have been claiming, the answers were not his alone: one more time, Williams was our most refined philosopher of common sense. Analytic philosophy has done something that is quite peculiar: instead of making sense of humanity, we have been philosophizing for the inhabitants of a romantic fantasy of traditional peasant life—or, bearing in mind Williams' choice of illustration, a European fantasy of life on a South Pacific Island—and not for the sort of creatures any of us are, with the lives any of us have. (And when I say 'any of us,' I mean, not real peasants, either: farmers are not simple-minded in the way that the presuppositions of common sense require.) It would not be overstated to say that we professional philosophers have misidentified the very species for which we have been philosophizing.

In being critical of what I am claiming are central theses of contemporary philosophical common sense, and in recapitulating where that criticism has brought us, let us not forget that we are standing on the shoulders of a giant. It is easy enough to object to the picture of humanity implicit in internalism, in the preoccupation with the fact/value and science/ethics distinctions, and in other ideas belonging to the closely connected cluster of theses that Williams explored over the course of his career. But it is easy only because his ever more refined reformulations of them are so clear that we can finally see what it is that they really express.

Analytic philosophy is visibly in a high-entropy condition; it needs a new agenda. Thinking through Williams has presented us with one. At its top are a descriptive metaphysics and an ethics—not necessarily theories, but rather a careful and uncluttered rendering of a number of interconnected ideas, of just the sort that Williams hoped to provide—suitable for *us*: not for impossibly simple-minded almost-people capable of living only in an impossibly simple world, but metaphysics, ethics, and an understanding of rationality for serial hyperspecializers.

Acknowledgments

For helpful conversation, I'm grateful to Amy Johnson and Gloria Park, and for comments on earlier drafts, to Chrisoula Andreou, Sarah Buss, Dan Callcut, Alice Crary, Heather Douglas, Sam Fleischacker, Mark LeBar, Alasdair MacIntyre, Toni Nicoletti, Valerie Tiberius and an audience at the University of California, San Diego.

Notes

1 I have regularized Gauguin's orthography.
2 Take Williams' engagement with cultural relativism, the thesis that there are claims which are true for, or inside, a culture, but not for members of, or within, other cultures. It appears as early as his first book, *Morality* (2nd edn: Cambridge: Cambridge University Press, 1993), pp. 20–5, which refutes a "vulgar" version of it. He subsequently returns to the topic in his piece on "The Truth in Relativism" (in *Moral Luck* [Cambridge: Cambridge University Press, 1981], Chapter 11); as its title suggests, it is an attempt to articulate the important thought of which vulgar relativism is a failed expression. Relativism is taken up once again by *Ethics and the Limits of Philosophy* (Cambridge, MA: Harvard University Press, 1985), Chapter 9, and is a subtext of *Shame and Necessity* (Berkeley, CA: University of California Press, 1993), especially Chapter 5, in which the questions of how deep cultural divides realistically turn out to be, and whether and how cross-cultural ethical assessments are possible, occupy much of Williams' attention. Finally, the topic comes up in *Truth and Truthfulness* (Princeton, NJ: Princeton University Press, 2002), pp. 52, 258ff. Cultural relativism will appear now and again at the fringes of our discussion.
3 See Williams, *Moral Luck*, Chapter 8; *Making Sense of Humanity* (Cambridge: Cambridge University Press, 1995), Chapter 3; "Some Further Notes on Internal and External Reasons," in Elijah Millgram (ed.), *Varieties of Practical Reasoning* (Cambridge, MA: MIT Press, 2001), pp. 91–7. He has not been alone in thinking that there is something at the core of instrumentalism that escapes the numerous refutations of it; for a very different attempt of this sort, one which follows Anscombe in seeking to depsychologize means-end rationality, see Candace Vogler, *Reasonably Vicious* (Cambridge, MA: Harvard University Press, 2002).
4 There is a well-known short list at *Moral Luck*, on p. 104f, which mentions scheduling, coordinating, adjudicating conflicts between ends, being imaginative, and finding 'constitutive solutions,' i.e., what now is called specificationist deliberation.

5 Elijah Millgram, "Williams' Argument Against External Reasons," *Nous* 30(2) (1996), 197–220, explores the connections between instrumentalism and internalism, and argues that they are substantially congruent views—which, if Williams was trying to express the thought at the bottom of instrumentalism, is just as it should be.

However, now that I have praised Williams for his deft reformulations of familiar notions and questions, let me gesture at one of those exceptions which prove the rule, and a reminder that Williams, too, could make mistakes. Notice an asymmetry in the dichotomy between internal reasons (reasons that depend on the presence of a suitable element in your subjective motivational set) and putative external reasons (those that do not). If the reason depends on a motivation (any motivation at all), it counts as internal; all reasons for action, Williams argues, involve *some* subjective motivation; therefore, all reasons are internal. But why wouldn't it be more helpful to allow for a mixed category of reason in one's taxonomy? Even when there is some tie to a motivation, why can't some of the force of a practical reason nevertheless come from elsewhere? And if there are such cases, why assimilate them to those in which all the force is derived from subjective motivation?

Compare Williams' taxonomic set-up and its upshots to the ways we find it useful to think about theoretical rationality. Call an *internal conviction* one that is in any way derived from convictions you already have. An *external conviction* will be one derived entirely from elsewhere—perhaps, one might expect, from observations. However, if you don't believe your observations are any good, you can observe anything you like, and it won't change what you believe. So *theoretical internalism* (analogously, the view that all of your reasons for belief depend on convictions you already have) is true of theoretical reasoning.

But now, isn't the interesting thing about observation, and its effect on belief, that the observations come from outside? Even if this is only possible against a suitable background of already-present conviction, surely much of the force of reasons for changing one's beliefs comes from something other than one's already-present convictions. A set of terms that makes this truism invisible, by making theoretical internalism almost trivially true, is certainly a mistake. Why shouldn't reasons for action likewise derive their force *both* from one's subjective motivations *and* from further sources, e.g., from a practical analog of observation? Given the questions Williams means to address by taking up the question of internalism, it must be an error to settle the outcome of the debate by choice of terminology.

6 Williams, "A Critique of Utilitarianism," in J. J. C. Smart and Bernard Williams, *Utilitarianism: For and Against* (Cambridge: Cambridge University Press, 1973); it is worth keeping in mind how much of Williams' discussion is conducted in the shadow of Henry Sidgwick's *Methods of Ethics* (7th edition; Indianapolis: Hackett, 1981).

7 In Williams' usage, ground projects are categorical desires writ large; they're either more important such desires, or enterprises or pursuits driven by and involving categorical desires. Thus, a categorical desire is a little ground project, and a ground project is, or is built around, a big categorical desire; thus there is no deep difference between them, as far as Williams is concerned; and accordingly we can move back and forth between the terms casually.

The argument we just saw renders the observation that utilitarianism can run roughshod over one's stake in one's life this way: one's most weighty or important concerns are what give one reason to go on living. But I doubt that the identification can be sustained, and so I doubt that the rendering has been done correctly. The Stoics believed in caring only about what one can control; they took it that one can control whether one is virtuous, but not the length of one's life; so history records Stoics whose deep commitment to their virtue is none-theless conditional on their being alive anyway. A more modern version of such a personality might care most deeply about taking life as it comes; might think of death as part of life; and so would *not* make a point of living longer, in addressing his deepest concern. The worry here is that the construction which Williams provides is—like similar constructions in the work of Frankfurt, Velleman and others—a surrogate for an important idea we are trying to use, and one which can be at best extensionally adequate, rather than an explication of the idea itself.

8 Williams provided a straightforward extension of the argument against utilitarianism to Kantian and, incidentally, other consequentialist theories, which the interested reader can find in *Moral Luck*, Chapter 1. Here the individual agent's stake in his desires and projects is treated as an independent premise, rather than a commitment of the theory under attack.

9 *Problems of the Self* (Cambridge: Cambridge University Press, 1973), Chapters 10–12.

10 For the reservations, see *Problems*, 182.

11 *Morality*, p. xviii.

12 Intentions have come in for much discussion since Williams wrote these early essays (e.g., Michael Bratman, "Taking Plans Seriously," in Millgram, *Varieties*, Chapter 9) and might seem to be an obvious counterexample: they are evidently practical, but the intentions of a single person are required to agglomerate. Notice, however, that intentions do not agglomerate across persons.

Williams' claim in any case requires reasons for action to undergo fairly drastic regimentation. Suppose that one's reason for going to a café is that they have a manually controlled espresso machine; Robert Brandom ("Actions, Norms, and Practical Reasoning," in Millgram (ed.), *Varieties*, Chapter 20), takes after Anscombe in holding the reason to be just that, and not also that one has a desire for coffee made with such a machine. On such an understanding of practical reasons, one would not find failure to agglomerate to be a likely marker of them.

13 Williams, *Problems*, pp. 202–5.

14 It was "appointed ... to review the laws concerning obscenity, indecency and violence in publications, displays and entertainment in England and Wales" (Bernard Williams (ed.), *Obscenity and Film Censorship: An Abridgement of the Williams Report* [Cambridge: Cambridge University Press, 1981], p. 1.)

15 The term was adapted from Clifford Geertz, *The Interpretation of Cultures* (New York: Basic Books, 1973). I once complained that Williams had not supported this last claim with satisfactory argumentation (in "Inhaltsreiche ethische Begriffe und die Unterscheidung zwischen Tatsachen und Werten," in Christoph Fehige and Georg Meggle (eds.), *Zum moralischen Denken* [Frankfurt: Suhrkamp, 1995]). However, I had overlooked the sometimes quite amusing arguments at Williams, *Obscenity*, pp. 119–23. Williams' exercise in applied ethics should be read more frequently by philosophers than it is, both because it nicely exhibits methodological differences between applied and theoretical ethics, and because it identifies the concrete instance used by Williams to think through the topic of thick ethical concepts. The thin and moralistic-sounding list he gives at *Ethics*, p. 140, is quite misleading; it becomes much clearer why Williams arrived at the conclusions he did when one redirects one's attention to concepts like 'obscene.'

16 Williams, *Descartes: The Project of Pure Enquiry* (New York: Penguin, 1978), p. 64f; Jenann Ismael, *The Situated Self* (Oxford: Oxford University Press, 2007) provides useful discussion both of what this process realistically looks like, and what, realistically, are the benefits to be had from it.

17 For Williams' supporting argument, see *The Sense of the Past*, ed. Myles Burnyeat (Princeton, NJ: Princeton University Press, 2006), pp. 289, 294. That famous slogan has been taken to mean that nihilism is inevitable in a reflective culture such as our own: pretty soon, all our thick ethical concepts, and so all our ethical knowledge, will be destroyed. (In a later paper on "Truth in Ethics," *Ratio* 8 (3) (1995), 227–42, at p. 238, Williams hedged, insisting that he had meant that our ethical knowledge *can* be destroyed, but not that it *must* be.) But, and here I mean (hedge notwithstanding) to correct Williams, that does not quite follow. Even though ongoing reflection is busily whittling away at our ethical knowledge, we need not run out of workable thick ethical concepts if they are being introduced faster than they are being destroyed. That is evidently our own situation; think of such recent accretions to our repertoire as 'eggshell plaintiff,' 'big organic,' 'unputdownable' ... or slightly less recent but still undissolved instances as 'kitsch,' 'camp,' 'politically correct' ... Still, such concepts are unlikely to serve in adjudicating disagreement as effectively as their vanished predecessors; since they come and go, they are much less likely to be widely shared.

18 This was a further argument against the "morality system," and I will briefly sketch it so as to bring out the role played in it by the ideas we have introduced. The distinctive formal commitment of the morality system, reflected in its requirement that what we are bound to do can be systematized into something like a scientific theory, is that its oughts and its assessments more generally must agglomerate, in something like the modified sense we have just seen: like knowledge deploying our color vocabulary, they can be recast into a form that is conjoinable and consistent. Williams worked up thought experiments meant to elicit from his readers pairs of vicarious moral judgements, one in anticipation of a course of action, and the other, in retrospect and with the advantage of hindsight. The standards of assessment invoked in those judgements differ deeply. To take Williams' famous discussion of Gauguin as an instance, it was Gauguin's body of work that created the artistic standards by which it could be judged successful enough to justify, perhaps, the step of leaving his family for the sake of his art; obviously those standards could not have been appealed to before the course of action had been embarked upon. The cases are chosen with the intent of forestalling transformations, analogous to those that turn theoretical knowledge into components of the Absolute Conception, that make them out to express what is at bottom a single, consistent set of standards. If that intent succeeds, then (and this is the point of his argument) moral judgements that we find intelligible and compelling turn out to violate the agglomeration requirement to which the morality system is committed.

19 For example, Hilary Putnam, *The Collapse of the Fact/Value Dichotomy* (Cambridge, MA: Harvard University Press, 2002), pp. 40–5; Putnam, "Objectivity and the Science/Ethics Distinction," in James Conant (ed.), *Realism with a Human Face* (Cambridge, MA: Harvard University Press, 1990). For a brief reply, see Williams, *Philosophy as a Humanistic Discipline* (Princeton, NJ: Princeton University Press, 2006), pp. 184–7.

20 For Williams' gloss on this bit of shorthand, see *Truth*, pp. 6–7. For a survey of themes in the book that I'm here leaving to one side, see Sam Fleischacker's review, in *Ethics* 114(2), (2004), 380–5.

21 *Problems*, pp. 145–7; around the time that Craig's book (*Knowledge and the State of Nature* [Oxford: Oxford University Press, 1999]) was published, Williams was known to begin lectures on unrelated subjects by urging his audiences to read it.

22 Many devices could serve while varying a great deal in the details, and this is why, on Craig's account, an exact conceptual analysis of 'knowledge' is an

unpromising project. That implicit prediction is confirmed by Jonathan Weinberg, Shaun Nichols and Stephen Stich, "Normativity and Epistemic Intuitions," *Philosophical Topics* 29(1 and 2), (2001), 429–59; the Chinese version of the certificate differs from the Western with respect to Gettier intutions. (For a review of the Gettier literature, see Robert Shope, *The Analysis of Knowing* [Princeton, NJ: Princeton University Press, 1983].) Here is another way to see the consequences of Craig's account. Philosophers have been exercised by the question of what challenges we must be able to meet if we correctly claim to know something; they have tended to set the bar very high indeed. The standards a certification with a real social function must meet are negotiable, and normally the certificate is useless if they are set unrealistically high.

23 Its function, not its definition: Williams followed his sometime colleague Donald Davidson in holding that truth neither needed nor bore definition (*Truth*, p. 61). Williams invokes Craig very early in his discussion (ibid., p. 21), and again later on implicitly (ibid., p. 79); in doing so he runs together—ill-advisedly, in my view—state-of-nature arguments and the rather different exercise of Nietzschean genealogy.

24 This a statement to be heard in roughly the register of: bees are hive creatures that store honey. But only roughly; Williams devoted a great deal of worry to what he called the Representation Problem (*Making Sense*, p. 102), that is, the problem of how to talk about the phenotypic traits of a species that is essentially cultural.

I should emphasize that 'information' is every bit as problematic a concept as 'truth' and 'knowledge,' and is unlikely to be independently intelligible. That is, the train of thought we are following is not one of those attempts to explicate a difficult concept by substituting an easy one for it.

25 The Absolute Conception of Reality was a limit concept introduced as, roughly, the body of information we obtain by converting all information amenable to such conversion into a form that renders it maximally agglomerable with any other similarly processed information. Our second distinction thus presupposes or aspires to a pool of information that can be shared by absolutely anyone, including intelligent space aliens. It is obvious that science directed towards this goal will require a very large "investigative investment"—a phrase Williams uses at *Truth*, p. 124.

This observation tells us that we really do need an explanation of very much the sort we are edging up on for generic truth: under what social circumstances will the distinction between fully objective truth and everything else be one for which we have a real use?

26 The heuristic has a precedent in Paul Grice, "Method in Philosophical Psychology (From the Banal to the Bizarre)", *Proceedings and Addresses of the American Philosophical Association* 48 (1975): 23–53, especially at pp. 37ff; he calls it "creature construction." At this stage in our collective intellectual history I should not have to provide the following disclaimer, but here it is anyway: The thought experiment we are about to undertake does not require or imply that we are the products of a design exercise. A further disclaimer: neither does it purport to provide the elements of an adaptationist evolutionary explanation.

27 In accepting the labels 'information' and 'motivation' for the contrasting classes, we are allowing them whatever features enable the differing uses made of them; I am leaving whatever metaphysical questions these may raise for other occasions, and in particular, whether and why agglomeration can be assured on one side, but not on the other.

28 That 'bottom-line' requires reiterated emphasis: internalists attempt to accommodate what look like practices of correction by expanding the range of

corrigible but derivative desires. Or again, they typically insist that you may be mistaken about what your desires are; here the correction is not of your bottom-line desires, but of your opinions about them. A further but related issue: some self-declared internalists have taken pressures for motivational coherence to allow for correction proper of bottom-line desires; because Williams thought otherwise, I won't consider this possibility further just now.

29 Dinah Shore, *16 Most Requested Songs* (Sony, 1991).

30 This brief account should not on its own persuade an internalist, who will wonder why a course of action, or a life, should count as a failure if it is not a failure by the lights of one's own desires. He will also wonder why a designer cannot equip his creature with suitably generic ends: social status, perhaps, or even just plain happiness. For one way of filling in the argument, see Millgram, *Practical Induction* (Cambridge, MA: Harvard University Press, 1997), Chapters 3–5, and Section 6.7.

We can now redescribe the contrast between morality and ethics. The internalist solution presupposes an environment stable enough to permit programming agents up front, with reasonable performance in the field assured. Unfortunately, it is obvious that the subjective motivations required to make societies run smoothly are not programmed into us. The "morality system" appears when the conclusion is drawn that the built in motivations must be overridden by a set of rules. Such systems of rules are generally formulated to satisfy an agglomerability constraint; normally, they can be represented by a moral theory. What the morality theorist (or moral legislator) shares with the internalist is the assumption that the environment is stable, and that we can know enough about it up front to design a satisfactory system of rules. That those who produce moral theories do not expect their rules to need subsequent correction is clear enough from the history and practice of moral theory: neither Kantians nor utilitarians nor Aristotelians allocate theoretical resources to anticipating the circumstances in which—and the cognitive mechanisms by which—their own theories will be shown to have been superseded.

31 That is of course not to deny that there is a distinction, and no doubt a very interesting one, between the two; if there were not, we wouldn't be able to discriminate them. But Williams has made what is, by his own lights, a mistake in how he tries to say where the line is. 'Scientific,' is, formally, a thick ethical concept; to deploy it correctly, one must occupy the appropriate evaluative standpoint, one amounting to a nuanced appreciation for science done right. (The point is made—if not quite in those words—by Hilary Putnam, *Reason, Truth and History* [Cambridge: Cambridge University Press, 1981], pp. 132–6.) Williams was, if you think about it, attempting to factor 'scientific' into its factual and evaluative components, and to give a value-free definition of the free-standing cognitive or factual component—the very factoring and definition he had elsewhere insisted was not possible.

32 Williams, *Philosophy as a Humanistic Discipline*, p. 182ff.

33 See Jerome Ravetz, *Scientific Knowledge and Its Social Problems* (New York: Oxford University Press, 1979), pp. 13, 103–4, 200–1, for some descriptions of information that has been watered down for export.

We now have a way to say how cultural relativism misses the boat, namely, in its preoccupation with the first- and third-personal 'true-for-us' and 'true-for-them' that are its bread and butter. The second-personal form we have just introduced is far more important in the lives of members of a species like our own.

Confusion about the workings of 'true-enough-for-*you*' certificates frequently plays out as confusion in public policy debates. For example, when creationists insist that the theory of evolution is only a *theory*, that is their way of expressing the observation that the results exported from various scientific specialties are accompanied, within those specialties, by complicated, qualified and nuanced alethic and epistemic certificates. They take this to be a matter for complaint, because they assume that the uncomplicated certificates are and ought to be routine inside a scientific specialty, and because they assume that the unqualified certificates are of higher quality than the qualified ones. Or again, work on climate change is, among the specialists, managed using sophisticated and not-at-all-generic alethic certificates: there are many different models, each with its own management issues. Politicians who would like to disregard the prospect of climate change talk as though this meant that the scientists are not sure about what they are doing, or about their results, and we should not be, either. The politicians understand that the nongeneric alethic certificates are what underwrite the simpler certificates accompanying results exported to the general public; they mistakenly take the qualified certificates to be shakier currency than properly issued unqualified certificates; thus they take the unqualified certificates accompanying predictions of global warming to be thereby discredited.

34 This is what gives discussion of the so-called Pessimistic Meta-Induction its nervous edge. The cause of the misinterpretation is nicely rendered by Ravetz, *Scientific Knowledge*:

> informal knowledge of the higher elements of the craft of scientific inquiry ... is so different in character from that embodied in the published results, and is transmitted through a different channel, [that] it is not capable of the same universality of diffusion, nor of the same closeness of control of quality.
>
> (ibid., p. 103; I have reversed the order of parts of the quotation)

35 This is a good occasion to attempt to forestall a handful of misunderstandings. First, my occasional choice of vocabulary notwithstanding, the claims I am making about human beings are not to be mistaken for the exports of some scientific subspecialty; I hope to avoid the solecisms of scientism myself. Second, my descriptions of the surrounding novelty and complexity that account for our information management strategies should be understood as true enough for present purposes, but not as a fully accurate rendition of how matters are backstage, when viewed from what Williams called the Point of View of the Universe. Third, my claims should not be expected to agglomerate indiscriminately with further and similar claims, and here's a way to see why. There have been many characterizations of 'man' that are true as far as they go, for example, that man is the rational animal, and that man is the animal that laughs; but people laugh a great deal when they are being silly rather than rational. My description of humans as serial hyperspecializers is, like these other descriptions, partial and idealized.

8

WILLIAMS AND THE PHENOMENOLOGICAL TRADITION

Charles Guignon

I Introduction

At first blush, it would seem that nothing could be more inimical to Bernard Williams' own aims than connecting his thought to any philosophical schools, movements or "-isms." In his view, subscribing to a movement means letting one's thoughts and observations be forced into the grids of the school's official doctrines and outlook, with the result that over-simplification and doctrinaire pronouncements come to replace careful and truthful examination of the issues. So I doubt he would be pleased with what I hope to accomplish in this essay. For my goal here is to see how Williams' thought has affinities to some of the best thought of the phe-nomenological tradition, a tradition that comes down from us from Martin Heidegger and has been developed by such continental thinkers as Maurice Merleau-Ponty, Hans-Georg Gadamer and Paul Ricoeur and by Anglophone philosophers such as Charles Taylor, Bert Dreyfus and Harry Frankfurt. My hope is that comparing Williams' work with the phenomenological tradition will give us a wider framework for understanding what Williams has to say while at the same time sharpening and filling in some of the wide-ranging generalizations and occasionally oracular sayings emerging from that tradition.

When I talk about phenomenology in what follows, I will be using the term in a very loose and broad sense. It is the sense in which Aristotle talks about our need to be true to the phenomena, where that means describing the things we do and the way our lives show up as accurately as possible, without forcing the phenomena into prior assumptions drawn from high-level theoretical considerations. Aristotle's aim, in Martha Nussbaum's words, is to describe "the world *as it appears to*, as it is experienced by, members of our kind."[1]

Heidegger, who claimed that he had derived his conception of phenomen-ology more from Aristotle than from the founder of modern phenomenology,

Edmund Husserl,[2] expresses his own "formal" (roughly, most open-ended) definition of phenomenology as "letting that which shows itself be seen from itself in the very way in which it shows itself from itself."[3] In this formal sense, the idea of phenomenology is encapsulated in Husserl's slogan, "To the things themselves!" What Heidegger adds to fill out this definition is the recognition that very often what is most important about what shows up for us is something that for the most part tends to be overlooked or concealed. Some crucial dimensions of our lives are missed because they are so all-pervasive that we never notice them – like the spectacles on our noses, we see everything through them and so we never see them themselves. Other important aspects of our existence are distorted or covered over as a result of theoretical constructions or religious doctrines that have emerged over the course of history. What "appears," then, is often a distortion or cover-up of what is really crucial to us.

Because concealment haunts our understanding of our lives, Heidegger holds that phenomenology must be coupled with a *hermeneutics* (interpretation) that tries to bring to light the deeper meanings of our average everyday sense of things. As these meanings often characterized earlier ways of understanding things in our historical culture, the investigation also has a historical dimension. As hermeneutic phenomenology requires a "de-structuring" of the hardened layers of the philosophical "tradition" in order to get a fresh view of what is actually going on in our concrete lives. Such a project of "destruction" is what Paul Ricouer calls a "hermeneutics as the recollection of meaning."[4] De-construction of this sort is always in the name of an anticipated reconstruction of what Heidegger calls our "primordial" understanding of things, the understanding that first set us on our course in Western civilization and continues to sustain our practices to this day.[5]

In trying to point out some connections between Williams' thought and phenomenology, I will have in mind the sort of "hermeneutic phenomenology" that stems from Heidegger's reading of Aristotle and comes down to us through Gadamer, Taylor and others. In many ways, Williams' thought is quite conducive to a conversation with this phenomenological tradition. First, Williams was not always averse to continental thought, noting mainly that analytic philosophy is often clearer and more careful than continental writings. Second, in speaking of his own work, he speaks favorably of a "phenomenology of the ethical life",[6] a label that suits his own approach of describing our pre-reflective, pre-theoretical understanding of the ethical (what are called *intuitions* in analytic philosophy) while bracketing or holding in abeyance the presuppositions of traditional systematic philosophizing. Third, like Heidegger, he is interested in uncovering the overlooked, tacit background of understanding that inhabits our ordinary experience of things. In these and other respects, Williams' approach and thought seem to be in accord with phenomenology in the broad sense of that term I employ.

But noting similarities should not make us overlook profound differences. Williams does indeed employ a kind of hermeneutics, but his interpretative method is not so much the "hermeneutics of recollection" found in the phenomenological tradition as it is an example of what Ricouer calls "hermeneutics as the exercise of suspicion," the interpretive orientation adopted by Nietzsche, Marx and Freud.[7] The outcome of Williams' interrogations of the everyday understanding of ethical life is not a disclosure of a stable background of meaning, but is instead the acknowledgment of deep and irreconcilable tensions in our everyday ways of speaking and thinking about such things as blame, responsibility, voluntariness and other moral ideas. In this respect, Williams sees his thought as more in line with Nietzschean genealogy than with phenomenology. Moreover, Williams' commitment to naturalism, with its tendency to countenance only that which can be discerned in familiar empirical ways, puts him at odds with most representatives of the phenomenological tradition.

My approach first will be to explore some similarities between Williams and phenomenology in their general views concerning the limitations of method and theory. The next section will try to show a convergence in their views concerning the nature of human agency, and the concluding section will consider some of the deep differences that divide Williams from phenomenological thinkers.

II Against method

Williams and phenomenologists have both raised questions about the applicability of the theoretical attitude and traditional conceptions of method to understanding human life as it is at the ground level of daily practices and ordinary thought. They agree in supposing that method and theorizing may be useful in the natural sciences, where abstraction from particular cases is needed in order to arrive at universally true generalization. But they are dubious about attempts to employ the same sorts of method and theory in trying to understand the human lifeworld. The question they ask, in questioning the role of method, is not so much "Does method lead to the correct results?" as "What sort of life would a person have who actually handled his or her affairs using such methods?" The issue, posed in this way, is whether applying methods of the sort posited by philosophy generally and moral philosophy in particular could be part of a viable way of life.

The belief in the importance of method is central to the conception of the theoretical attitude that arose in Europe in the seventeenth and eighteenth centuries. The theoretical attitude assumes that the best way to achieve knowledge is to detach ourselves from our ordinary involvements in the world and to adopt a cool, impartial, objective point of view on the subject matter we wish to know. The ideal stance for a knowing subject is one in which all presuppositions, passions and day-to-day concerns are set aside so that one can view the world *sub specie aeternitatis*, that is, from a God's-eye perspective or from nowhere in particular. Its goal, in Williams' terms, is to get a view of reality as it is *anyway*, what he calls an "absolute conception of reality."

Phenomenologists have often noted that adopting such a theoretical standpoint has important consequences for the way the world shows up for us. In the form it takes in modern science, the theoretical attitude tends to objectify what it studies: by abstracting out the meanings and values that normally show up in our dealings with things, it portrays reality as an aggregate of brute objects, interacting according to law-governed causal processes, with no "real" properties other than those that are quantifiable. The familiar sense of holistic interconnectedness and rich significance that characterizes our everyday experience of things is removed from the world-picture and in its place is found an atomistic and mechanistic view of the universe. Phenomenologists suggest that when things are seen in terms of such an objectifying point of view, the world seems to "go dead" for us: the thick texture of meaning and values that presents itself in our everyday lives is bleached out, covered over, with the consequence that the bases of our ordinary motivation are concealed.

The theoretical attitude goes hand in hand with a faith in method that has come to be called *methodologism*. Methodologism is the assumption that rational belief-formation and decision-making must be guided by a step-by-step procedure that needs to be laid out in advance of inquiry and deliberation. In a broader sense, the term "methodologism" is used to refer to the tendency in the modern period to read the picture of ideal method formulated by the early scientists into the conception of human beings as they are when practically engaged in the world. There is an ontologization of method in the sense that human beings come to be thought of as, at the deepest level, basically disengaged subjects, centers of experience and will, who process information received through the senses and then form beliefs and make decisions. The decisions they make therefore manifest inter-subjectively specifiable, rational procedures that can be used in public discourse to justify the decisions. The reifying of method leads to the view that we are only fully rational when we act according to statable, justified principles. Thus, methodologism lends itself to the adoption of what Williams calls a *"rationalistic conception of rationality,"* a conception of rationality requiring "that in principle every decision [be] based on grounds that can be discursively explained."[8]

Methodologism assumes not just that humans *ought* to arrive at their beliefs and decisions in this way, but that, when they are functioning properly, humans *do* in fact act in this way, so that any failure to do so indicates some defect in an individual's humanity. Understood in the light of this conception of method, we can see why hermeneutically inclined social scientists such as Brent Slife and Richard Williams write, "method itself is a theory – a philosophy. Similar to any other theory or philosophy, it makes assumptions about the world, and important implications arise from those assumptions."[9] According to hermeneutic phenomenologists, then, the theoretical attitude with its faith in method can act as a distorting lens that gives us a constricted and one-sided view of life. This is why phenomenologists are content simply to describe the background of meanings, practices and patterns of life that make possible our familiar ways of dealing with the world. In their view, theoretical activity is understood as just one way of dealing with things among others, a way of construing things with possible advantages for prediction and control, but lacking any privileged insight into human phenomena.

A vivid example of how phenomenology undercuts methodologism is found in Heidegger's description of "average everydayness." According to this description, the standard conception of our epistemic predicament presupposed by methodologism and the theoretical attitude is unable to make sense of how we actually encounter entities in the course of our ordinary dealings with familiar situations. In Heidegger's account of the everyday, our being as humans is always a *being-in-the-world* in which we find ourselves initially and most basically enmeshed in situations, engaged with contexts of equipment, and underway in doing things. The world at the most basic level of life is experienced as a familiar *dwelling* where we are from the outset and for the most part quite at home. Our activities in such contexts of significance are characterized by the kind of *know-how* that inhabits our skilled coping with equipmental totalities, not by the propositional *knowing-that* presupposed by theoretical accounts of awareness.

Our ordinary competence in handling things is in turn made possible by our initiation into and participation in the forms of life of the public world in which we find ourselves, what Heidegger calls "the they" or "the anyone" (*das Man*). In growing up into the public world, we come to respond to situations in roughly the way "anyone" would respond. Even the more mature and more self-possessed way of life described as "authentic" is grounded in and made possible by this shared mastery of public ways of interpreting and acting. In Charles Taylor's phrase, "we are aware of the world through a 'we' before we are through an 'I'."[10]

Heidegger argues that the standpoint of detached theorizing, which is characterized by explicit propositional beliefs and methodical procedure, can arise only when there is a *breakdown* of the original seamless flow of engaged agency. When normal contexts of activity break down – when, for example, a tool breaks or some component of the situation ceases functioning – we can first encounter the worldly context as a collection of objects in a spatio-temporal coordinate system. With this transition to the sense of reality as an aggregate of objects comes the tendency to think of ourselves as *subjects* – that is, as self-encapsulated minds or centers of inner activity – with no real or defining connections to anything outside ourselves. The result of such a breakdown is the emergence of the subject/object picture of our condition as human beings. But it should be clear that the subject/object picture of our human condition is derivative from and always dependent upon our prior involvement in contexts of agency. On Heidegger's view, *theoria* is made possible by the background of *praxis* that typifies the vast majority of our lives. From this standpoint, the world we live in is the meaning-filled, smooth-functioning field of practical involvements into which we are immersed in everydayness, whereas the world revealed by the breakdown to theorizing is a construction resulting from abstraction and contraction.[11]

Though Williams is mainly concerned with examining the ethical dimension of life, many of his observations have general implications for the privileging of theory and method characteristic of most mainstream philosophy. His descriptions of everyday life show that theories succeed neither in capturing what actually goes on in everyday life nor in providing agents with a framework of intelligibility for making meaningful decisions in actual situations of choice.

Many of Williams' writings point out the distortion and concealment that result from thinking of agents as self-encapsulated centers of thought and decision acting in particular contexts of choice. In his study of Greek literature and culture, *Shame and Necessity*, for example, Williams shows how the modern portrayal of agency in terms of the notions of voluntary action and responsibility makes unintelligible such dimensions of life, central to Greek experience, as luck, tragedy and regret. In *Ethics and the Limits of Philosophy*, he points out how moral theory's picture of action as springing from an act of will of a subject conceals the relevance of such fundamental dimensions of agency as character formation and background. Williams' writings also show how the picture of agency derived from methodologism covers over other crucial dimensions of life, dimensions such as meaningfulness, importance, supererogation, the place of care, the role of dispositions, the possibilities of nobility and the heroic, and questions about what we ought to *be*.[12] Looking for an alternative to pictures of the agent as a center of will following a decision-procedure, Williams turns to Hegel's account of *Sittlichkeit* and its role in showing the social background of agency.[13]

The theoretical attitude requires the ability to abstract out all human-relative qualities of things (including meanings and values) in order to see things as brute objects with primary qualities. Such an abstraction naturally leads to a sharp dichotomy between fact and value in thinking about the basic make-up of reality. Williams agrees with Gadamer that such a distinction between facts and evaluations may have a useful role in the natural sciences.[14] But, like Gadamer, he holds that this distinction has no applicability to attempts to understand the specifically human dimension of reality.

In response to the tendency in theorizing to separate fact and value, Williams points out that our everyday understanding of ourselves often employs language that undercuts this distinction. Our characterizations of ourselves and others make use of what Williams calls "thick ethical concepts," concepts that contain both descriptive and prescriptive components. Words such as *courage, treachery, lie, brutality, shame,* and *honesty,* for example, contain both an empirical component, one that is guided by the way things are in the world, and a normative or action-guiding component, one with implications for the way things ought to be.[15] These two dimensions are so intricately interwoven that, as used in normal life, they cannot be disentangled. To understand such concepts – to "know how to go on" using them in different contexts – it is necessary to share with other speakers of the language "the evaluative perspective in which this kind of concept has its point."[16] Mastering the word requires grasping "the kind of interest that the concept represents," the kind of role it has in the life of a community. And that in turn means that one can grasp such a concept only if one is, to some extent at least, an *insider* in a shared form of life. As Williams says, an outsider – an observer who is not in on this way of life – could never "pick up the concept simply as a device for dividing up … certain neutral features of the world."[17] The idea that understanding requires being a participant in a particular type of a community undercuts the picture, built into the theoretical model, of the self as a neutral spectator encountering a world of intrinsically meaningless objects.

The fact that one needs to be an insider in a way of life in order to grasp thick concepts points to a wider observation about the inadequacy of the theoretical attitude's conception of the knowing subject. Williams points out a number of ways in which an outsider's view of our agency would be quite different from our own insider's, first-person viewpoint. For instance, from an outsider's position – from the standpoint, say, of a sociologist looking on at the practices of a particular cultural group – what is most important about the group's activities is that they have internalized dispositions that support whatever types of action are socially acceptable. But if we, as insiders in the form of life, regarded this as what is most important about our own practices, adopting such a viewpoint would tend to undermine those very practices. This is so because such an outsider' point of view would encourage the belief that those actions are merely patterns of behavior conditioned by "the they," and so would tempt us to see them as culturally conditioned responses with no real ethical ground. From inside the insider's point of view, in contrast, we see the real value of things as inseparably tied up with our being the people we are.[18] In Williams' view, the theoretical model's ideal of the disengaged subject who stands outside of the practical world of human affairs is incoherent. Trying to adopt an impartial standpoint toward our own lives would dry up the bases of motivation that make it possible for us to live such lives, and, in doing so, would distort our sense of what those lives consist in. The impartial self of pure theorizing could never act, because it would be robbed of all the interests that motivate it to act.

Williams also tries to imagine what it would be like to try to live life in such a way that one could periodically shift from everyday involvements in practical affairs to a theoretical standpoint in order to make decisions about what to do, and then, equipped with insights drawn from the theoretical stance, switch back to practice again. Such an image of life seems to be presupposed by accounts of ethical existence that assume we ought to adopt a theoretical, methodical point of view when we need to decide what is right, and then return to the insider's standpoint once we have made a rational decision. In Williams' view, such a picture of life is incoherent, for "any actual process of theorizing ... would have to be a part of life, itself a particular kind of practice. One cannot separate ... the theorist in oneself from the self whose dispositions are being theorized."[19] Any attempt to adopt an outsider's stance in relation to our own lives relies on the "assumption that the reflective agent as theorist can make himself independent from the life and character he is examining." It is not clear, however, that this is possible:

> The belief that you can look at all your dispositions from the out-side, from the point of view of the universe, assumes that you could understand your own and other people's dispositions with-out tacitly taking for granted a picture of the world more locally familiar than any that would be available from there.[20]

But there is no reason to think that "the theoretical reasonings of the cool hour can do without a sense of the moral shape of the world, of the kind given in the everyday dispositions."[21] The bifurcated intrapsychic life pre-supposed by methodologism gives us an incoherent view of what it is to be human.

III Moral ontology

Considerations about the view of humans put forward by the theoretical model lead to more general questions about the being of the human in general. So it is not surprising that one of the central concerns of herme-neutic phenomenology is addressing "the question of Being," that is, the question that asks about the fundamental make-up of things in general and of human beings in particular. "Phenomenology is the science of the Being of entities – ontology," Heidegger says.[22] Given his disdain for "-isms," it might seem odd to suggest that Williams has affinities with philosophers who label themselves "ontologists." But I believe there are good reasons to think of Williams as an ontologist in the sense Heidegger had in mind. His

173

criticisms of ethical theory and morality are often based on the claim that the picture of human existence underlying such theories and programs are completely out of touch with the realities of human life. And such a claim presupposes some view of what human life is actually like at the ground level. Much of what Williams says about our everyday ways of being is of an ontological nature. His interest in addressing the question, "What is it to be a moral agent?" brings his thought into alignment with the concerns of phenomenologists.

Williams shares with hermeneutic phenomenologists the belief that there is no pregiven human nature – no "Form of Humanity or "proper function of humans" – that determines in advance what all humans are like or ought to be like. He agrees with phenomenologists in holding that physiologically or genetically determined traits can be taken up and manifested in widely different ways in different cultures and times. But, again like phenomenologists, Williams seems to believe that even though there is no human essence, there is a *human condition* shared by all humans. As Hannah Arendt observes, "the conditions of human existence – life itself, natality and mortality, worldliness, plurality, and the earth – can never 'explain' what we are or answer the question of who we are for the simple reason that they never condition us absolutely."[23] But even though these features of the human condition are not unequivocal determinants of our nature, they provide insight into certain structural characteristics that underlie and make possible a wide variety of ways of being.

One of the principal tenets of phenomenology is the claim that any attempt to understand the human must start out from the way things appear in concrete, particular situations of life, that is, from the here and now of lived experience. Using the term "facticity" to refer to what shows up in concrete contexts, Heidegger called his method a "hermeneutics of facticity."[24] Its goal is to characterize human existence (*Dasein*) as it is in the midst of ordinary affairs. In his words, "Existence is here and now, in its specific role at this moment [*Jeweiligkeit*] it is *factical*. The *facticity* is not a concrete instance of some universal, but [is] instead the primordial determination of its specific being qua existence."[25] Heidegger uses the German word for existence, *Dasein*, exclusively to refer to the existence of human beings, and he places a special emphasis on the stems of the word: *Da* ("here" or "there") and *sein* ("being"). What is important for phenomenology about the human is the way it is *there* (or *here*), solidly planted among things, already in play in the dramas being enacted in the world.

We have already seen that Heidegger (along with Sartre and Merleau-Ponty) starts from the idea that humans are at a basic level *being-in-the-world*. We are beings who are first and foremost grounded in concrete lived situations, "always already" involved with contexts of equipment, bodying forth into meaningful situations of activity, and up to our elbows in dealing with the demands of a shared life-world. What makes it possible for us to be enmeshed in the world in these ways, according to Heidegger, are certain "essential structures" that characterize any human existence whatsoever.[26] Unlike traditional ideas about a "human essence," these structures provide the scaffolding, so to speak, on which individuals configure their own personal lives by "existing."[27]

First among the essential structures is what Heidegger calls "thrownness" or "finding [oneself] situated" (*Befindlichkeit*). To be human is to find yourself already thrown into the midst of a public life-world, a world that is itself embedded in a history and so is redolent with the meanings, commitments and ideals that have formed over time. This dimension of thrownness provides us with a shared intelligibility concerning what things are, what is worth doing, and who we are. Yet this background of understanding for the most part remains tacit and inchoate, explicable only with respect to particular aspects and for particular purposes. Our access to the pervasive facticity or situatedness of our lives is achieved mainly through affective experiences that Heidegger calls "moods" (*Stimmungen*, suggesting "ways of being tuned in"). In feeling fearful or ashamed – or even in the "pallid, evenly balanced lack of mood" of everydayness – we get a sense of how things *count* in our world and an insight into who we are in the scheme of things.[28] On this view, emotions and feelings play a fundamental role in disclosing what things are all about.

A second essential structure characterizing the human condition is called "projection." At any given time, human beings have undertaken certain ways of being that constitute their identity, certain "possibilities" (as Heidegger calls them), including roles, commitments, personality traits, propensities to respond in certain ways, habits, inclinations and so forth. These acquired possibilities of being make up the *stand* a person has taken on his or her life, and they provide guide rails for the concrete choices and directions a person will follow out in living his or her life. The "futural" aspect of projection provides us with the standing characteristics or dispositions that make us people of a specific sort.

The third essential structure Heidegger identifies pertains to our mode of being in relation to the present. In its everyday agency, a human being articulates things according to the patterns of interpretation made accessible in the public language he or she has mastered in growing up into a community. This dimension of "discursiveness" or linguistic articulation ensures that we are in tune with the community or the "they" into which we are thrown.

For Heidegger, these three essential structures taken together form the unity of a life course, a unity characterized by what he calls *care*. We are beings who care about what we are in the sense that we find our lives to be in question for us. And this "being in question" means that we do not just act on every impulse or whim, but we typically assess our immediate, *de facto* desires and motivations in the light of higher, second-order concerns about the kinds of life-story we are realizing in our lives as a whole, right up to the end.[29] The care structure – the structure of being "ahead-of-itself-Being-already-in-(the-world) as Being-among (entities discovered within-the-world)" – makes up the "ontological structural whole" of a human life as a temporally unfolding life course.[30]

Hermeneutic phenomenologists have pointed out that human existence has a circular structure that mirrors what is called the "hermeneutic circle." The hermeneutic circle, familiar from the experience of reading and understanding texts, refers to the fact that understanding any particular passage in a text requires some anticipation of where the train of thought of the text is going as a whole. This means that, at every moment in understanding, we are operating with anticipations and expectations rooted in our overall understanding of the text. Yet, at the same time, we are also revising that overall understanding in the light of the particular passages before us at the moment. Phenomenological ontologists hold that a similar circularity characterizes life itself. At every moment of our lives we are interpreting the particular situation in which we find ourselves in the light of a larger sense of what life as a whole is all about. But, at the same time, we are constantly revising our sense of what life is all about in terms of the concrete demands that the current situation makes on us. Life therefore has a circular structure: it is an unending process of interpretation and reinterpretation, a constant quest for understanding that ends only with death.

Although Williams would have little patience with the heavy-handed architectonic Heidegger imposes on his characterization of the human condition, many passages in his writings suggest he would be sympathetic with key ideas in this account of what humans are. Throughout his writings, Williams paints a picture of human existence according to which we live situated lives, located in a specific place and time – lives lived by agents for whom things are meaningful because of concrete projects that give life its shape and directedness. The self portrayed by Williams is, in Sandel's familiar phrase, an encumbered self, "always already" committed in certain ways and shaped by events that have unfolded in the past and point toward the future. This conception of the situatedness of life leads Williams to see that we can only fully understand the ethical dimension of life if we see it in terms of what is genuinely important to people, of how people experience ethical conundrums in terms of their goals, ideals and commitments, and of how particular situations are experienced as hanging together with a person's (and community's) overall sense of life.

It is because of this concern with the whole person in real situations that Williams is so sensitive to the role of emotions and feelings in giving us access to what genuinely matters to us in life. One of the major failings of the moral system, as he sees it, is its tendency to think that right actions must be guided solely by reason (however that is construed). The disdain shown toward emotions has led moral theorists to suppose that an agent's moral convictions must result from decisions made in the relatively cool atmosphere of rational deliberation. Williams notes, however, that genuine convictions seem to come from somewhere deeper than decision-making: a phenomenology of our experience as ethical agents shows that convictions result not from decisions, but rather seem to come from outside us, as if we are *called* to act in certain ways. But Williams thinks that this impression is also misleading, and that what *seems* to come from outside in fact comes from deep inside the individual: what "he – that is, the deciding 'he' – may see as coming from outside him," we see as coming from deeper in him. And he immediately adds, "So it is with the emotions,"[31] suggesting that what people see as something with respect to which they are passive (*passio*), the "passions," are in fact produced by deep inner sources within the person. The larger point here is that convictions arise in the whole person – the thinking, willing, feeling person. Any attempt to do away with emotions would make us not more ethical, but less capable of being ethical agents.

Moral theories that call for the agent to override his personal emotions or treat them as only one case among many – theories such as utilitarianism and Kantianism – alienate the individual from his own feelings and thereby undermine the bases for being a moral agent at all. Insofar as "our moral relation to the world is partly given by such feelings," Williams says, betraying those feelings will lead to a loss of one's moral identity.[32] It is important to see that emotions are not just extra items added to one's psychic kit, items we can excise at will. For emotions have complex ties to all dimensions of our lives. An emotion such as shame ties together an agent's appreciation of the situation with his or her self-understanding, and these together are bound up with the social expectations and cultural attitudes that typical participants in the community have internalized. To imagine that the emotion can be extruded without tearing apart the fabric of self that makes us who we are is simply out of touch with lived reality.

Williams emphasizes the importance of dispositions in living an ethically good life. As he says, "The characteristics that people acquire and exercise in ethical life … are not best understood on the model of cognitive or perceptual capacities, but rather on the model of dispositions of character."[33] Dispositions are settled, habitual patterns of response that have become deeply ingrained in an individual, either through upbringing or through self-cultivation, in such a way that they become part of a person's "second nature." Moral dispositions make up the subset of dispositions that manifest what we would consider proper or exemplary behavior in ethical situations, for example, traits of character that incline us to help someone in dire need or prevent us from stealing someone else's money. In this respect, Williams' dispositions seem similar to what Heidegger calls "possibilities." They are traits of character that are built into our "know-how" in coping with the world, and they give us an orientation toward the future in the sense that they determine, to a great extent, our propensities and proclivities in dealing with situations.

Insofar as dispositions define our identity as agents of a particular sort, they cannot be thought of merely as means to ends. And that implies that they cannot be grasped properly in ethical theories that picture human behavior on the model of a set of mechanisms designed to attain certain goals. It also implies that there is no way for an agent to step back from his or her dispositions in order to determine whether they are doing their job. In Williams' words,

> Moral dispositions, and indeed other loyalties and commitments, have a certain depth of thickness: they cannot be regarded, least of all by their possessor, just as devices for generating actions or states of affairs. Such dispositions and commitments will characteristically be what gives one's life some meaning, and gives one some reason for living it ... There is simply no conceivable exercise that consists in stepping completely outside myself and from that point of view evaluating *in toto* the dispositions, projects, and affections that constitute the substance of my own life.[34]

A human being just *is* his or her dispositions; the "substance" of human life consists in the loyalties, projects and commitments that define the overarching trajectory of a life. As for Heidegger, so for Williams, there is no "self-thing" distinct from projects and dispositions that can step back from those traits in order to reflect on their value.

Williams' criticism of attempts to treat the self as essentially split into "self-thing" and "attributes" is in agreement with the conception of the *wholeness of the self* characteristic of hermeneutic phenomenologists. A well-formed self has a coherence and cohesiveness that ensures that it has an orientation toward the world and a way of grasping things in all the rich and varied ways they can *matter* or *count* in life. This wholeness makes possible the *integrity* of the self, its having a life that is its own and therefore being motivated to act in meaningful ways. As Williams says, "Unless [one is] propelled forward by the conatus of desire, project and interest, it is unclear why [one] should go on at all."[35] The whole constituted by emotions and dispositions as they unfold over time make up a person's *motivational set*. One of Williams' chief concerns is to criticize any moral theory that relies on the idea that we can bracket off or abstract out the motivations definitive of a person's identity in order to isolate a "true self," where that is understood as a self that can rationally and dispassionately act according to moral principles. Such a maneuver of abstraction would alienate a person from herself, putting her at odds with the springs of motivation that make it possible for her to act at all.

The holistic picture of life as a cohesive, unfolding life story bound together by specific commitments is in agreement with the thought of the contemporary hermeneutic phenomenologist, Charles Taylor. In his essay "Self-Interpreting Animals," Taylor argues that our peculiarly human emotions, our deepest aspirations and our sense of the ideals of the surrounding community "form a skein of mutual referrals from which there is no escape" into an objectified picture of a self-thing methodically manipulating objects.[36] For the same reason, there can be no escape to the standpoint of a detached, punctual subject who makes use of evaluations and character traits in order to attain morally defined goals.

As we have seen, a fundamental claim of phenomenology is that attempts to understand life must start out from the way things show up within concrete, specific situations of life. Williams also has a strong sense of this importance of *Jeweiligkeit* (the situation of the one who is occupying a local position in the world at a particular moment and place). One of Williams' best-known views, the account of "internal reasons," holds that the only real reasons for action are those that figure into an agent's actual motivational set in such a way as to be seen by the agent as applying to himself as he finds himself in a particular situation. This view is grounded in the idea that we must always start from where we are, that we can't step out of our own skin in order to attain a purely objective view from nowhere. In this respect, Williams' views again agree with those of Hans-Georg Gadamer, whose *Truth and Method* argues that all attempts at understanding must start out from where we find ourselves, from our thrownness into a specific time and place, with all the assumptions and expectations such a local context contains. But Williams would also agree with Gadamer that our situatedness in a particular context does not act as a door that closes us off to other possibilities of understanding. For life has a circular structure: it involves a constant back-and-forth movement between immediate interpretations and the bigger picture in which those interpretations are nested. Because of this circular structure, we can always expand our horizons of understanding beyond the limited and the local, though such an expansion is achieved not by a "leap," but by an ongoing dialogue that has the "logic of question and answer."[37]

Williams' picture of human existence transforms our understanding of what it is to be an ethical agent. Moral philosophy has tended to assume that morality covers a specific sphere of life that is well known to us all from our ordinary dealings with things. The moral agent, on this view, is one who can spot moral conundrums when they arise and can set aside personal feelings and inclinations in order to be responsive to obligations of the sort that moral philosophy is concerned to specify. Seen from this standpoint, being a moral agent requires the ability to set aside all other concerns in order to do the right thing. In other words, moral philosophy assumes that moral obligations must trump all other motivating considerations. Moral precepts and principles have the last word: to be a moral agent is to hearken to the unconditional demand of morality.

Williams, in contrast, holds that moral considerations "make sense only if they are related to other reasons for action that human beings use, and generally to their desires, needs and projects."[38] When morality is seen as inextricably enmeshed within the whole of life, many of the claims of moral theorizing come to be seen as an impoverishment and distortion of the resources for ethical life already embedded in life itself. In Williams' view, a moral agent is a person whose life is a complex and rich tapestry of ideals, rules of thumb, inclinations, dispositions and feelings, a person who experiences her indebtedness to the wider historical community that opens her onto the world. A person of this sort will be constantly revising her motivational set in the light of experience and reflection. It is because such a person has been attuned to the shared patterns of life of a larger community that in most cases she does best just to let go and act, without bringing into play any confusing and superfluous thoughts about moral imperatives. In most situations in life, we can simply let ourselves go and do what needs to be done, with no special reflection at all. In fact, the very tendency to think that one is facing a moral conundrum in certain situations (e.g., considering whether to help a child who has been hit by a car or whether to steal money left on a table) raises questions about one's being a moral agent at all. So Williams speaks of the "significance of the immediate," of directly doing what is set before you as something to be done:

> The significance of the immediate should not be underestimated. Philosophers ... repeatedly urge one to view the world *sub specie aeternitatis*, but for most human purposes that is not a good *species* to view it under. If we are not agents of the universal satisfaction system [posited by utilitarianism], we are not primarily janitors of any system of values, even our own; very often, we just act, as a possibly confused result of the situation in which we are engaged. That, I suspect, is very often an exceedingly good thing.[39]

This conception of agency as involving what might be called "releasement," a "letting-be" that is as free as possible of methodological baggage, is a far cry from the preoccupation with self-control and principled, self-aware action that has dominated the tradition of moral philosophy.

IV Phenomenology contra Williams

Noting affinities between Williams and the phenomenological tradition should not make us overlook the important differences between them.[40] It seems to me that these differences might be brought out by focusing on one particular disagreement between the two outlooks. Phenomenology from its very inception has opposed philosophical naturalism, the dominant philosophical movement of the past century or so. Husserl devotes the majority of his 1911 manifesto, *Philosophy as a Rigorous Science*, to attacking naturalism, especially in the form of psychologism.[41] And Charles Taylor, in the Introduction to his 1985 *Philosophical Papers*, describes himself as a "monomaniac" single-mindedly concerned to argue against naturalism, defined as "the ambition to model the study of man on the natural sciences."[42]

Of course, there is widespread disagreement about the definition of "naturalism." Taylor explicitly takes his definition of naturalism from Williams' own account of the ideal of achieving an "absolute conception" of reality, the seventeenth-century scientists' attempt to provide a complete account of reality solely in terms of physical substance and primary qualities.[43] Though Williams himself thinks that such an ideal makes sense for the natural sciences, he clearly recognizes that it has little to offer for the project of "making sense of humanity" (to use the title of one of his later books). It is true that he calls his own method "naturalism," but he sees this approach in a more tempered way than what Husserl or Taylor attack.[44] Williams' mild form of naturalism seems to claim that, in trying to make sense of the human, one should refuse to countenance entities or connections that are not empirically discernible in some straightforward way by ordinary people. Using a criterion of this sort, Williams eschews notions such as God and the sacred. But he is also careful to avoid positing such things as "goods" *per se*, "higher purposes," "social agency," and "meanings" that are assumed to exist independent of the thoughts or feelings of agents. His naturalism seems to be grounded on the sort of physicalism taken by common consent to be the "default setting" of contemporary philosophy. But he is amenable to talk about beliefs, feelings and desires so long as these play a role in actual experience.[45]

So Williams fastidiously avoids any reference to entities that cannot be cashed in in terms of the most widely agreed-upon notion of what is empirically discernible in concrete experience. For this reason, he rejects Aristotle's teleological biology, with its claim that a proper understanding of the essence of humanity will show what is the best possible life for humans. This is a case where there is no valid inference from fact to value. And he would reject any supposition to the effect that humans might have some deep obligation that no one has ever heard of or thought about, so that our lives are all morally deficient in some way unbeknownst to us. Moral obligation, such as it is, is inseparable from the actual motivations, commitments, feelings and aspirations of actual people. Values and obligations, like goods and higher ideals, are not part of the furniture of the world; they are projections of our culturally conditioned commitments and dispositions onto an intrinsically meaningless world, and must be understood as such.

Williams' mild naturalism has consequences for a number of positions he takes on issues in the humanistic studies. First, this commitment leads him to develop a nuanced but nevertheless hardheaded individualism in thinking about humanity. All reasons and motivations must be attributable to what goes on in the minds of individuals; the idea of social goods must be unpacked in terms of individual concerns.[46] Second, Williams holds fast to what Charles Taylor has called the "inner/outer model" of our comportment toward the world.[47] According to this inner/outer model, all phenomena must be thought of as either "out there" in the world – primarily physical objects and their properties – or "in here," inside the individual – including such psychic phenomena as sensations, emotions, value-judgements, likes and dislikes. The idea that there might be entities that fall into neither the inner nor the outer category is, on this view, untenable. Third, as already suggested, Williams will reject any view of reality that holds that meanings, values, and functions such as usefulness are actually components of the world. Such things, if they exist in any sense, are projections of the human mind. The fourth view implied by Williams' naturalism, and a consequence of the third claim, is an attenuated form of relativism. This relativism is attenuated because it allows for objective considerations about value claims (e.g., a tyrant is properly called "bad" if he slaughters thousands of people), but this objectivity itself must be interpreted in terms of a widespread consensus together with certain factual information about individual experiences of pain, the nature of the dictator's motives, the innocence of the victims, and so forth.

It is not possible to discuss any of these issues in even moderate detail in this space. But it is important to see that most phenomenologists adopt an anti-naturalist stance on these issues. In their view, the positions that philosophers such as Williams take on these issues result more from an uncritical acceptance of the tenets of mainstream naturalism than from any reasoned reflection on the question of the truth of naturalism. It is, in the phenomenologists' view, an obsessive fastidiousness rather than rational consideration that leads naturalist philosophers to adopt the positions they take.

Let me take a quick look at each of these four issues, making some quick and broad remarks about what phenomenologists might say on each. With respect to the first, the idea of what Robert Bellah and his colleagues have called "ontological individualism," it should be noted that hermeneutically inclined social philosophers have criticized this notion ever since de Tocqueville introduced it in the nineteenth century.[48] In opposition to the idea of individualism, Heidegger has made a good case for thinking that much of everyday agency arises from motivations that are intrinsically and irreducibly social, namely, the conformist tendencies of the "they." Charles Taylor's essay "Irreducibly Social Goods" provides compelling reasons to think that the aims that motivate communities to act are in some cases not explicable in terms of aggregations of individual decisions and interests.[49] This is a complex issue and it is not easy to see how it might be resolved. But it seems at the outset that any attempt to show that group dynamics can always be understood in terms of what goes on in the heads of each individual in the group has little to contribute to making sense of a group's behavior. My hunch is that the desire to see all behavior as rooted in the minds of individuals is more a symptom of a prejudice than it is the result of a reasoned position about an important issue.

The commitment to individualism has traditionally gone hand in hand with the inner/outer model of reality. If all that exists is the physical world and the individuals who inhabit it, and if those individuals consist of an outer and an inner component (e.g., body and mind), then for anything that counts as real, it must be possible to locate that real thing either inside some individual or individuals or "out there" in the physical realm. But the inner/outer model creates some puzzles for Williams. We have already seen that, in discussing strong convictions, he says that though our deepest feelings *seem* to come from outside ourselves, they must in fact come from deep *inside* ourselves. This "either/or" shows that in the end Williams is unable to provide a phenomenology of a *calling*. Failing to acknowledge the force of social meanings that provide the medium in which we live, he is unable to see how feelings can arise not quite inside or outside of us, but rather *between* or *among* us.

Charles Taylor, in contrast, follows in the footsteps of Heidegger and Merleau-Ponty, who have shown us how to escape from the prejudice of the inner/outer model. In their view, our embodied agency always involves a back-and-forth, interactive relationship between the worldly affordances that solicit our responses (e.g., handles and hand-holds) and the responsiveness of antecedently oriented humans to familiar contexts of purposeful activity. Seen from the standpoint of these accounts of being-in-the-world, an enforced restriction of ontological commitments to what is either inner or outer seems unduly constraining and unable to make sense of many of the most important features of our actual ways of being. From the phenomenological perspective, it is a prejudice engendered by naturalism and enshrined in our technical vocabulary, not an open-minded approach to making sense of the human condition.

Williams seems to be wary of talking about significance, salience, relevance, importance and meaning as existing in the world, and tends to assume that such things first and foremost exist in our heads. His refusal to countenance entities of this sort is based not on a mechanistic reductionism, he notes, but on a "suspiciousness" concerning explanations that rely on abstract ethical notions where plain, non-ethical explanations will do just as well.[50] This exercise of suspicion leads him to reject Taylor's notion of a higher form of "importance" that corresponds to what he calls "strong evaluations," where such evaluations are supposed to contrast with ordinary desire. It is worth noting here that Williams makes no attempt to justify this "rule of suspiciousness" other than to cite some masters of suspicion he takes as models for his own work (Nietzsche and Stendhal among others).[51]

At this point, however, it appears that the only basis for Williams' view is a preference for one style of thinking over another. But phenomenologists have good reasons for saying that meanings and importance ought to be considered part of the furniture of the world. In the essay referred to earlier, "Self-Interpreting Animals," Taylor argues that there is no way to regard the import things have for us as mere projections of human desires and feelings onto things, because people can be wrong about the import things have and can change their emotions in the light of their discoveries about the "fact of the matter" of import. That people can be wrong about such feelings shows that imports have a reality independent of how anyone feels at any time.[52]

It might seem that in the current intellectual environment, where naturalism has such an iron grip on the minds of academics, that the burden of proof falls on phenomenologists to provide evidence for their non-naturalistic ontology. But it should be noted that even a mild naturalism of the sort Williams presupposes leads to severe tensions in his thought. We have seen this in his uncritical acceptance of the inner/outer model. It is evident as well in his insistence that, although ordinary agents may need to go on projecting meanings and values in order to be able to function as ethical agents, philosophers must deny all such projections. It should be obvious, I would think, that this invidious distinction between ordinary folks trying to live well and philosophers with a superior viewpoint tends to duplicate the very split between plain life and the theoretical standpoint Williams has so brilliantly critiqued.

Finally, Williams has always been quite frank about the tendency of his thought to lead to some version of relativism. With his usual carefulness and attention to detail, he has put forward a palatable form of relativism, one that can be distinguished from the sort of "vulgar relativism" all philosophers despise.[53] But many phenomenologists would not be content with embracing even this attenuated form of relativism. In their view, to say that the sentence "Love is better than hate" is not exactly a factual belief, that it is more the expression of emotional preferences of a particular (albeit very large) group, seems to be out of touch with what presents itself to us in our concrete experience. In a similar way, to think that such practices as slavery, genital mutilation or cutting off children's arms to prevent them from becoming fighters are not wrong as such, but are rather wrong only in the minds of members of some group, fails to capture phenomenological insights that are very deep in us. Such conclusions seem to be products of a theoretical commitment rather than of a realistic characterization of ethical life as it is actually experienced and lived.

Williams' use of a Nietzchean "hermeneutics of suspicion" can be seen as representative of a debunking tradition that goes back at least as far as the Radical Enlightenment of the early nineteenth century. It has had a tremendous impact in dispelling illusions and freeing people from prejudices and superstitions. Foucault summarizes Nietzsche's version of this strategy using a quote from *Dawn*: "In what ... do we find the original basis (*Ursprung*) of morality, a foundation sought after since Plato? 'In detestable, narrow-minded conclusions. *Pudenda origo*.'"[54] Needless to say, Williams does not go as far as Nietzsche goes in his attempts at disillusionment, nor does he show Nietzsche's *Schadenfreude* in tearing down moral structures to reveal the rot at their core. But his professed "realism" about morality can have the effect of leaving us bewildered about how we can go on thinking of ourselves as ethical agents, as the final pages of *Ethics and the Limits of Philosophy* attest. In reflecting on the work of masters of suspicion, thinkers such as Marx, Freud, Nietzche and B. F. Skinner, it is important to see that much of the force of their debunking operations comes from the assumption that the natural sciences have shown us the truth about reality, so that moral philosophy can only pick through the debris to find what might still be serviceable after the collapse of the old world picture. In contrast to the hermeneutics of suspicion, the hermeneutics of recovery refuses to give the last word to science and instead tries to reconstruct a viable image of the ethical life from the deepest insights embodied in our current practices and ways of thinking. Described in this way, the difference between Williams and phenomenology seems to hang on one's final assessment of the impact of the scientific worldview for our practical lives. The project of reaching such an assessment is already underway in the phenomenological tradition.[55]

Acknowledgments

My thanks to Daniel Callcut, Michael Gibbons, Frank Richardson and Brook Sadler for useful comments on an earlier version of this chapter.

Notes

1 Martha Nussbaum, *The Fragility of Goodness: Luck and Ethics in Greek Tragedy and Philosophy* (Cambridge: Cambridge University Press, 1986), p. 245.
2 See the references in Thomas Sheehan's "Heidegger, Aristotle and Phenomenology," in *Philosophy Today* 19 (Summer, 1975), 87–94.
3 Martin Heidegger, *Being and Time*, trans. J. Macquarrie and E. Robinson (New York: Harper & Row, 1962), p. 58.
4 Paul Ricoeur, *Freud and Philosophy: An Essay on Interpretation*, trans. D. Savage (New Haven, CT: Yale University Press, 1970), pp. 37–56.
5 *Being and Time*, Section 6, especially pp. 42–4.
6 Bernard Williams, *Ethics and the Limits of Philosophy* (Cambridge: Cambridge University Press, 1985), p. 93.
7 Ricoeur, *Freud*, op. cit.
8 Williams, *Ethics and the Limits of Philosophy*, p. 18.
9 B. Slife and R. Williams, "Toward a Theoretical Psychology: Should a Subdiscipline Be Formally Recognized?" *American Psychologist*, 52 (1997), 117–29.

10 Charles Taylor, "Interpretation and the Sciences of Man," *Philosophy and the Human Sciences, Philosophical Papers*, vol. 2 (Cambridge: Cambridge University Press, 1985), p. 40.

11 For a full account of Heidegger's conception of being-in-the-world and its breakdown, see C. Guignon, *Heidegger and the Problem of Knowledge* (Indianapolis: Hackett Publishing, 1983), Chapter 3, and H. L. Dreyfus, *Being-in-the-World: A Commentary on Heidegger's "Being and Time," Division I* (Cambridge, MA: The MIT Press, 1991), Chapters 3 – 6.

12 Charles Taylor gives a full account of these occlusions in his essay, "A Most Peculiar Institution," in J. E. J. Altham and R. Harrison (eds), *World, Mind, and Ethics: Essays on the Ethical Philosophy of Bernard Williams* (Cambridge: Cambridge University Press, 1995), pp. 132–55.

13 Williams, *Ethics and the Limits of Philosophy*, p. 104.

14 Gadamer holds in *Truth and Method*, trans. J. Weinsheimer and D. G. Marshall (New York: Crossroads, 1989), that

> Whereas the object of the natural sciences can be described idealiter as what would be known in the perfect knowledge of nature, it is senseless to speak of the perfect knowledge of history, and for this reason it is not possible to speak of an "object in itself" toward which its research is directed.
>
> (Ibid.: p. 285)

It is "senseless" because what counts as the historical depends on ever-changing interpretations. (It should not be assumed that Williams would agree with this very strong claim.)

15 Williams, *Ethics and the Limits of Philosophy*, p. 141.

16 Ibid.

17 Ibid., p. 142.

18 Ibid., p. 51.

19 Ibid., p. 110.

20 Ibid.

21 Ibid.

22 Heidegger, *Being and Time*, p. 61.

23 Hannah Arendt, *The Human Condition* (Garden City, NY: Doubleday, 1959), p. 13.

24 Martin Heidegger, *Ontology – The Hermeneutics of Facticity*, trans. from Heidegger's 1923 lectures by J. van Buren (Bloomington, IN: Indiana University Press, 1999).

25 Martin Heidegger, *Introduction to Phenomenological Research*, trans. from Heidegger's 1923/24 lectures by D. O. Dahlstrom (Bloomington, IN: Indiana University Press, 2005), p. 221.

26 Heidegger, *Being and Time*, p. 38.

27 Heidegger writes that each "particular Dasein decides its existence [who or what it is] … The question of existence never gets straightened out except through existing itself" (*Being and Time*, p. 33). But existing is always carried out within certain parameters, for example, that life has a temporal dimension or is lived in a world.

28 Ibid., p. 173.

29 Heidegger's claim that human beings are the beings for whom their Being is *in question* or is *at issue*, that human existence is a "relation" (*dass es in seinem Sein zu seinem Sein ein Seinsverhältnis hat*) (*Being and Time*, p. 32) has been echoed in Harry Frankfurt's essays in *The Importance of What We Care About: Philosophical Essays* (Cambridge: Cambridge University Press, 1988) and in Charles Taylor's

Human Agency and Language (Cambridge: Cambridge University Press, 1985), especially Chapters 1, 2 and 4, and in his *Sources of the Self: The Making of the Modern Identity* (Cambridge, MA: Harvard University Press, 1989), Section 2. The idea goes back to Kierkegaard and Hegel – see my Introduction to *Existentialism: Basic Writings*, ed. C. Guignon and D. Pereboom (Indianapolis: Hackett Publishing, 2001), pp. xvii–xxi.

30 Heidegger, *Being and Time*, p. 237.
31 Bernard Williams, *Problems of the Self* (Cambridge: Cambridge University Press, 1973), p. 227.
32 Bernard Williams, "A Critique of Utilitarianism," in J.J.C. Smart and Bernard Williams (eds), *Utilitarianism For and Against* (Cambridge: Cambridge University Press, 1973), pp. 103–4.
33 Bernard Williams, *Philosophy as a Humanistic Discipline*, ed. A. W. Moore (Princeton, NJ: Princeton University Press, 2006), p. 74.
34 Bernard Williams, *Making Sense of Humanity* (Cambridge: Cambridge University Press, 1995).
35 Bernard Williams, *Moral Luck* (Cambridge: Cambridge University Press, 1981), p. 12.
36 Charles Taylor, "Self-Interpreting Animals," in *Human Agency and Language, Philosophical Papers*, vol. 1 (Cambridge: Cambridge University Press), p. 57.
37 Gadamer, *Truth and Method*, pp. 369–80.
38 "Preface to the Canto Edition of *Morality: An Introduction to Ethics*" (Cambridge: Cambridge University Press, 1993), p. xiii, quoted in Mark P. Jenkins, *Bernard Williams* (Montreal: McGill-Queen's University Press, 2006), p. 51.
39 Williams, "A Critique of Utilitarianism," p. 118.
40 Many of these differences have been brought out by Charles Taylor in his "A Most Particular Institution," in Altham and Harrison (eds), *World, Mind, and Ethics*, pp. 132–69. I rely heavily on this essay. See also Williams' reply to Taylor in the same volume, pp. 202–5.
41 Translated by Quentin Lauer in Edmund Husserl, *Phenomenology and the Crisis of Philosophy* (New York: Harper Torchbooks, 1965).
42 Taylor, *Human Agency and Language*, p. 1.
43 Ibid., pp. 2 and 79. The reference is to Bernard Williams, *Descartes: The Project of Pure Inquiry* (Harmondsworth: Penguin, 1978).
44 For example, Williams uses the term in his reply to Taylor in the Altham and Harrison collection, *World, Mind, and Ethics*, where he admits that the notion of naturalism is not very perspicuous and doubts that it can be defined (ibid.: p. 203).
45 A complete account of Williams' view, one that acknowledged his Nietzschean "hermeneutics of suspicion," would note that he treats as illusory a number of things that many people *think* they have direct access to, things such as free will and eternally valid moral truths.
46 This, stated in bald terms, seems to be the upshot of "Formal and Substantial Individualism," in *Making Sense of Humanity*, pp. 123–34.
47 Taylor has described this view in various essays. See, for example, his "Rorty and Philosophy," in C. Guignon and D. Hiley (eds), *Richard Rorty* (Cambridge: Cambridge University Press, 2003), pp. 158–80.
48 Robert N. Bellah, Richard Madsen, William M. Sullivan, Ann Swidler, and Steen Tipton, *Habits of the Heart: Individualism and Commitment in American Life* (Berkeley, CA: University of California Press, 1985). The term "ontological individualism" is defined in the "Glossary," (p. 334), and throughout the book.
49 Charles Taylor, "Irreducibly Social Goods," in Taylor's *Philosophical Arguments* (Cambridge, MA: Harvard University Press, 1995), pp. 127–45.

50 "Replies," in Altham and Harrison (eds), *World, Mind, and Ethics*, p. 204.
51 Williams, "A Critique of Utilitarianism," p. 118.
52 Taylor, *Human Agency and Language*, pp. 48–9. See also the explication of Taylor in Frank C. Richardson, Blaine Fowers and Charles Guignon, *Re-envisioning Psychology: Moral Dimensions of Theory and Practice* (San Francisco: Jossey-Bass, 1999), pp. 213–21. Taylor's example is Malcolm X's feelings of shame about his kinky hair, whereas what is truly shameful is such shame itself.
53 Mark Jenkins gives a clear account of Williams' views on relativism in his *Bernard Williams*, especially pp. 140–6.
54 Michel Foucault, "Nietzsche, Genealogy, History," in P. Rabinow (ed.), *The Foucault Reader* (New York: Pantheon Books, 1984), p. 77.
55 Hans-Georg Gadamer writes:

> the central question of the modern age … is the question of how our natural view of the world – the experience of the world that we have as we simply live out our lives – is related to the unassailable and anonymous authority that confronts us in the pronouncements of science.
> (*Philosophical Hermeneutics*, trans. D. E. Linge (Berkeley, CA: University of California Press, 1976), p. 3)

9

BERNARD WILLIAMS AND THE IMPORTANCE OF BEING LITERARILY EARNEST

Frances Ferguson

> If you could decide on characters' destinies it would be like going to the desk of a travel agent who says: 'So where do you want to find the whale, in Samoa or in the Aleutian Islands? And when? And do you want to be the one who kills it or let Queequeg do it?' Whereas the real lesson of *Moby-Dick* is that the whale goes wherever it wants.
>
> (Umberto Eco, "On Some Functions of Literature")

The essay that follows proceeds with a certain indirection.[1] Although I mean to present the view that Bernard Williams—rightly—found literature to exemplify insights that were crucial to his philosophical views, my discussion of his philosophical uses of literature does not become prominent until the midpoint of the essay. In pursuing this indirect course, I am trying to honor the track of Williams' own development. My sense is that Williams developed certain key positions with fairly limited direct reliance on literature:

1 This distinction between morality, conceived as a separate field of activity that continually aimed to become systematic, principled, generalized, progressive, and ethics, conceived as a range of activity that embraced the moral and the amoral, the things that one had seriously undertaken in the intention of doing good and the things that one discovered, almost after the fact, that one was involved in, whether with maximal or minimal fault of one's own.
2 The view, obviously related to the first, that morality is sometimes most fully expressed in what Williams calls "an agent's regret," in which moral capacity shows itself not in the form of the ability to make a morally admirable decision but rather as the willingness to recognize one's link to an action even when one had not intended it and even in its defeat (in having issued in unsuccessful or even catastrophic consequences).[2]

3   The view that our feeling connections with other persons are crucially at stake not merely in our extension of sympathy to those who suffer but also in negative moral judgements that, in expressing horror of the actions of certain persons, extend to them a recognition of their humanity.

4   The view, related to the preceding one, that the motive of avoiding shame similarly expresses a sense of the importance we attach to other persons (and that it, rather than an injunction that we should all accord respect directly and universally, is a moral emotion).

5   The view that moral positions that stress equality and uniformity crucially fail to capture the ways in which persons are not interchangeable or substitutable for one another, which, stated differently, resolves itself into the view that perspectivism rather than what Williams called "world-guidedness" was inevitable in ethical thinking and that the notion of universalized "moral obligation" retarded this insight rather than advancing it.[3]

Part of what the distinctiveness of persons means—for Bernard Williams, as for the rest of us—is that we tend to perceive similarities or unities across a field that appears wildly variegated—not to say, completely miscellaneous—to others. So I do not mean to suggest that Williams did not see the affinities between his philosophical views and various literary works throughout his career. The argument I want to advance here is not that he increasingly during the course of his life saw literature and opera as an expression of his philosophical views. Literature was not, I think, time off from work for him; it was not an expression of a dissatisfaction with the philosophical enterprise. Rather, literature (and here I'm thinking not of all things that could be called literature by anyone but rather of all things that Williams would have been particularly compelled by) provided him a language for tracking some of his most central thinking. Increasingly, he moved from using literary examples to illustrate a particular point (as he did with *Anna Karenina* in "Moral Luck") to an emphasis on character and plot (in *Shame and Necessity* and in *In the Beginning was the Deed*) that expressed a thought he had offered in discussing obligation—namely, "that each person has a life to lead."[4] He found examples from literature preferable to "examples from life," because literature presented itself as an alternative to the self-reflection and self-consciousness that he thought moral philosophy frequently put on offer.[5] He said that our responses to Greek tragedies "can tell us not just who we are, but who we are not: they can denounce the falsity or partiality or the limitations of our images of ourselves."[6] And he thought that the fact that "tragedy is formed round ideas it does not expound"[7] suited it particularly well to the task of identifying such things as the sense of responsibility and connectedness that might attend a completed action. Literature, as he described it, was particularly effective in registering how in the story of "one's life there is an authority exercised by what one has done, and not merely by what one has intentionally done."[8] Moreover, he argued that literature achieved an especially definitive account of persons by creating "such a chain of significance as to kill speculation about alternatives" and thus creating a heightened sense of necessity that put individual characters in a relation to their actions that was more intense than any that might be achieved merely by self-examination or an account of life unshaped by narrative.[9]

I

In *Shame and Necessity*, Bernard Williams described what classical Greek literature—and particularly tragedy—might have to say to us about the ethical picture of the ancient Greeks and, through a ricochet effect, about our own conceptions of ethics and morality. Although his project was historical, in that he was using the words that Homer and Sophocles, Aeschylus and Thucydides had chosen to describe the worlds that they knew and imagined, it was also very much directed at the present. For Williams was testing to see what Greek literature could teach us—not by giving us a set of positive maxims or a series of role models but rather by helping us to examine our reactions and ask whether we really need and want the kinds of extensions and developments that modern moral thinking has sought to provide. His central target—in both *Shame and Necessity* and throughout his career, though he did not frequently use the word outside of this particular book—was moral "progressivism," the conviction that moral problems do not simply have different guises and urgencies in different historical eras but that modern thinking has made progress in tackling moral problems.[10] The Greeks, from the perspective of such modern progressivism, are mere children, and only modernity—sometimes seen to have begun with the advent of Christianity, and sometimes seen as having waited on Kantianism and utilitarianism—showed itself capable of mature and sophisticated moral thinking.[11] It was against such a progressivist account that Williams sought to defend the ancient Greeks along lines that Nietzsche had broached when he praised the Greeks for their superficiality and said, as Williams notes with the approval of repeated quotation, that they were "superficial out of profundity."[12]

Over the course of his career, Williams introduced and developed a contrast between ethics and morality. Ethics, on his account, represented a very wide range of activities, but perhaps the crucial feature of his notion of ethics was that it enabled him to reject the project of establishing a line of division between the moral and the amoral. Ethics was not for Williams a distinct domain, as Kant had suggested in representation of practical reason. Williams used the term "ethics" to designate the situations in which one suddenly came to realize that an action that had begun without any clear moral implications—driving a car, say—might end in accruing them—with accident and injury.

Williams' insight about the difficulty of cordoning off moral deliberations, decisions, and reactions enabled him to dispute both the notion that we were doing something more than usually weighty when we acted morally and the sense that the recognition of the importance of morality involved an advance for civilization. We might imagine that someone might object to morality on the grounds of its being commonplace in the most conformist way imaginable—in retailing the wisdom of village gossips and advice books and those whom Williams refers to as "the neighbours"—but his objections did not begin or end there. We might imagine, as well, that someone might object to morality on the grounds that it failed to register the force of the imaginative power of evil—in dismissing any idea that one might have sympathy for the devil—but Williams' objections did not revolve around any desire to recommend ingenious reversals in which the courage of the villainous was seen as a form of moral accomplishment.[13] Rather, for him, morality was "a peculiar institution" in that it represented a kind of collusion between some impulses of Christianity—taking the state of one's individual will to be particularly important, imagining that one ought only to think of one's own commitments insofar as they might be applied to other people and their commitments, minimizing the claims of negative judgement—and some of the ways in which Kant and utilitarians like Jeremy Bentham and John Stuart Mill had posed questions of the relationship between individuals and the collective world—in various adaptations of Kant's notion of an obligation to legislate to oneself as if on behalf of the world and Bentham's notion of the artificial identity of interests that a society adopts in developing laws and the legislative capacity to change them. In particular, Williams objected to the way in which the individual quickly ceased to be discernible in Kantianism and utilitarianism.

Because Kant vigorously stressed the importance of individual autonomy in moral judgement, Williams' observations about the disappearance of the individual from a scheme that seems to be centered on nothing except the individual may sound paradoxical. Yet even as Kant depicts moral judgement as so thoroughly lodged with the individual will that one might, on the basis of one's solitary judgement alone, take a position that was wildly at odds with that of everyone around one, the Kantian move, in Williams' view, so far defines the moral activity of the individual in terms of duty that the individual is merely free to be under obligation. The she or he that staffs the categorical imperative owes her soul or his to a company store so large as to include the world. Moreover, in a process that Williams tracked in his *Truth and Truthfulness*, Kant and Kantianism made the project of purifying the will ever more central. It became important to scan one's will for ambiguous or malign motivations, and one could not rest content with doing good but must also be able to assure oneself that one had, in addition, meant well.[14] Indeed, one of Williams' most strenuous objections to John Rawls's account of justice as fairness was what he took to be its aim to stress rational deliberation so strongly as to claim that the effort at fore-sightfulness might eliminate regret. All the deliberation in the world could not, he thought, eradicate the possibility that one would decide worse—and regret more—for having deliberated more: if an agent

> deliberates well, and things go wrong; particularly if, as sometimes happens, they would have gone better if he had deliberated worse; what is the consciousness that he was "justified" supposed to do for the disposition of his undoubted regret about how things actually turned out?[15]

As is clear from an essay like "Pagan Justice and Christian Love" in which Williams addressed the work of Gregory Vlastos, Williams recognized that what he saw as ethical progressivism and that he increasingly termed "moralism" can be seen to have begun its career with Socrates, in the moment in which Socrates sought, as Vlastos claimed, to argue that one's treatment of one's enemies "should be guided not by the matter of their being friends or enemies, but by moral considerations."[16] And as Williams acknowledges the longevity of the argument, he also poses the question that he regularly puts to its modern versions:

> How far could it [the Socratic outlook] go on the path it had chosen without running into a problem familiar to Christianity and unknown to earlier paganism, that the value of an individual human being, by becoming morally infinite, runs the risk of becoming effectively zero?[17]

The Kantian individual who can only respect herself when she properly respects others thus exemplifies for him a view that he keeps returning to and that he memorably characterizes (in "Moral Luck") as "only super-ficially repugnant."[18] On the other side of the repugnance, he suggests, lies the appeal of justice and the dream of being able to do right by others or, failing that, to make one's efforts to do right by others look as though they were justified. What Williams called moral progressivism and what we might call moral ambition did not, as he knew, wait on an historical process of development. It might appear in Socrates, but it might equally well appear in such moments as those that George Eliot creates in which she depicts it as somehow selfish for a central character to be central and moves with ironic apologies from Dorothea Brooke in *Middlemarch* to the other characters in her novel. The impulse to make care for oneself look as though it were a moral failing or limitation was one of Williams' principal targets, and he repeatedly observed the strangeness of our difficulty accepting the fact that we have only ourselves to work with.[19] Thus, his ethical defense of what might by others be characterized as egoism—that if it is wrong to injure the being of other people, morality deeply compromises itself when it depicts individuals as needing to sacrifice their integrity, their convictions about who they are, for the sake of their obligations to others. A morality that enjoined people not to murder by forcing them to commit what would effectively be psychological suicide was, he thought, intolerable. Moreover, he saw the desire to get past the bounds of oneself in moral projects as a strange variety of moral leveraging in which it makes no more sense for me to "hinder my future projects from the perspective of my present values" than to try to accomplish the impossible and "to inhibit my present projects from the perspective of my future values."[20]

Thomas Nagel suggested that Williams himself held out the prospect of moral wagering in his account in "Moral Luck" of how a significant life choice—Paul Gauguin's decision to leave his family and to go to Tahiti to paint, Anna Karenina's decision to leave her family to spend her life with Vronsky—might be judged by the success of the outcome. But, for Williams, I think, the point of the examples was just the reverse. For although Rawls used the device of the "veil of ignorance" to identify an artificial modeling of society in which it is crucial to the parties deliberating about the fairness of the society that no one should be able to identify his own position and seek to forward it, Williams saw the veil of ignorance in a form closest to its Rousseauvean sense—as an image of what we cannot know about our own futures as individuals—whether we will live to a ripe old age or be struck down by disease or accident tomorrow. He thought that, however things might turn out, we could only act as the persons we are now. Thus, we might well deliberate and come to decisions that we would later endorse or regret, but he affirmed that there was no escaping our limitations as agents who, by virtue of existing in the present as who we are, cannot occupy a future perspective or exchange our views for those of other persons. And he thought as well that even the model of insurance provided cold comfort for a person who knew himself to have committed an action about which he felt an agent's regret. The lorry driver of Williams' "Moral Luck"

> who, through no fault of his, runs over a child, will feel differently from any spectator, even a spectator next to him in the cab, except perhaps to the extent that the spectator takes on the thought that he himself might have prevented it, an agent's thought.[21]

And that there might be insurance—an impersonal compensation paid to the victim of his action—becomes a kind of test of agency. For Williams, being able to relegate the costs of "the unintentional aspects of our actions" to, "so to speak, the insurance fund" takes a toll on "our identity and character as agents."[22] And in this Williams' conception of ethical agency differs—from the utilitarian view as he presents it, which would be perfectly content to employ the insurance fund to make any reparations that might be made and to eliminate regret altogether, and the Kantian view as he sees it, which treats the agent as clinging to his conviction of his good will toward others in the face of its inefficacy. By overstating Williams' position only slightly, we can see that his chief target is the notion that life (and literature as well) may offer us a moral education, that there is something to be learned from one episode of agential regret that we can apply in another. Such a scheme can be followed only if we mistakenly imagine that the workings of ethical agency can be treated as if they followed the regularities of science. And while Williams thought that there might well be changes in scientific norms, he vigorously maintained both that the claims of science must be understood as universal and that they exposed, by contrast, the limitations of a universal perspective in ethics.[23]

Williams' critique of relativistic accounts of science—as of relativistic accounts of ethics—at bottom involved an insistence on clarifying situations in which one might feel regret and might feel it as first-person regret, an agent's regret. In that sense, the universality of science represents a kind of foil to the regret of an ethical agent. Science, in offering the possibility of observation and experiment equally to everyone, can be plausibly talked about in terms of a progress, whether individual or collective, as soon as one can establish that consistent experiments produce consistent results. Williams' stress on luck in ethics, by contrast, absolutely revolves around the perceptions, first, that life projects such as Gauguin's and Anna Karenina's will sometimes succeed and sometimes fail and, second, that those life projects will only be justified by life itself—so that it would be foolish past all imagining to say to Anna that she should have rallied herself with either the thought that it's merely an accident of fate when one's life project doesn't work out or the thought that there is a moral doctrine by which her life has really worked out better than she realizes. The differences of character that "give substance to the idea that individuals are not inter-substitutable," along with the judgements that luck so randomly passes on individual project, suggest why ethics cannot be reduced to a science as Jeremy Bentham aimed to do in his *Introduction to the Principles of Morals and Legislation*. Whereas science can work with notions of typicality and causation, ethics remains a collection of individual projects for Williams.

The two claims—that one does feel regret when one, even unintentionally, causes harm to another person and that one justifies one's life decisions not by appealing to a set of moral doctrines but by pointing to more of one's life—go a long way toward explaining why Williams saw moral progressivism as problematic. First, he suggested the unreasonableness of expecting every individual to become the bearer of moral progress. While Bentham had insisted that the law had an obligation to announce itself to individuals if they were to follow it, Williams saw the dangers in the utilitarian heritage—in the form of what he called "Government House utilitarianism" that allows for the creation of an ethical elite, experts who are in a position to make the kinds of judgements about ethics that highly knowledgeable scientists can more plausibly make about the objects of their knowledge.[24] For him, it was entirely unclear what it would mean to be able to make moral progress when one might—and frequently knew oneself to—fail despite one's most earnest deliberations and one's settled intentions. Moreover, there remained a question about how ethical agency might relate one to other people—not merely the persons whom one had done well or ill by but the larger audience to whom one might hope to justify oneself. The Kantian might be able to insist that the internal promptings of individual conscience might put one at odds with the opinions of virtually everyone else in one's world and enable one to say something like "They might criticize me but they would be wrong to do so." The utilitarian might be able to insist that everyone else ought to be able to arrive at the same calculation that one has oneself. Williams saw, however, the limitations of both positions—the former in imagining justification that might dispense with and ignore all the norms of one's society, the second in imagining that justification could command general agreement.

Indeed, when Williams criticized the attempts to make moral philosophy systematic he was largely indicting them as a kind of pseudo-science, in that they claimed to be able, as one could in making statements about scientific facts, to identify a situation in which someone could be said to be right—even when, and especially when, others said that they were wrong in their decisions. Williams, by contrast, repeatedly finds his ethical actors on the same side of a decision as popular opinion. Thus, when the hapless lorry driver of his "Moral Luck" unintentionally runs over a child, Williams will say,

> Doubtless, and rightly, people will try, in comforting him, to move the driver from this state of feeling [that he himself might have prevented it], move him indeed from where he is to something more like the place of a spectator, but it is important that this is seen as something that should need to be done, and indeed some doubt would be felt about a driver who too blandly or readily moved to that position.[25]

He will observe, even more strongly, of Nausikaa that she does not pit her own judgement against the opinions she imagines that other people will have: when she contemplates the scandal that will attach to her being seen with the handsome stranger, Williams points out that she adds "And I myself would think badly of a girl who acted so."[26] Moreover, in the even more striking example that Williams instances just before he speaks of Nausikaa,

Telemachus, complaining to the Ithacan assembly about the behaviour of the suitors, tells them that they must both be outraged
themselves and feel shame in the face of other men who live
around them, and he is not saying the same thing twice.[27]

Williams' notable formulation is quietly emphatic: it is "not saying the
same thing twice" for Telemachus to say that the members of the Ithacan
assembly must themselves react with outrage at the suitors' behavior and
must also feel shame in seeing the other members of their community, in
the grip of the conviction that they must themselves be feeling outrage.
Here Williams sets up a position rather different from those of a host of
thinkers—from the eighteenth century through the present—for whom the
capacity to engage with fiction involves sympathetic identification in which
readers enter into the positions of a host of characters and thus can, in their
own persons, enact in reading the accommodation of differences among
persons that liberalism calls for. (Keats's description of the "negative cap-
ability" that enabled Shakespeare to enter into personalities as different as
those of Iago and Imogen is only one among the many resonant statements
of this general position.)[28] Moreover, the liberal aspiration to understand
what Jean Renoir identified as "the hell of it," namely, "that everyone has
their reasons" meets a strikingly different treatment in Williams' account of
the *Odyssey*—and elsewhere in his work. From Williams' perspective, even
Richard Rorty's feeling account of how the Nazis deployed humiliation as a
weapon against prisoners in the camps involves casting shame as a structural abstraction that is abstract precisely because it omits mentioning the
ways in which the participants in any act of shaming are linked by "the
bonding, interactive effects of shame."[29] Williams, alert to the ways in
which someone might experience shame even in the first person by imagining himself observed, is eager to distinguish his account of shame from
one that simply treats it as a negative internalization of "an other who is a
representative of the neighbours."[30] More important even than his account
of the role of internal imagining is his attention to the reciprocal evaluations involved in shame: "people can," he says, "be ashamed of being
admired by the wrong audience in the wrong way. Equally, they need not
be ashamed of being poorly viewed, if the view is that of an observer for
whom they feel contempt."[31]

In refusing to describe a general dynamic of shame—that might center
not just on the greater power of one party but also on that party's calling
attention to its own greater power and the toll it can take on the weaker
party's usual ways of persisting as a self-respecting person—Williams here
suggests how shame, though a negative emotion, might establish a relationship among persons that is both comparative and particular. Shame, in its
uneven distribution, indicates the force of regard and the dissatisfaction of
thinking that one has lost or is losing it, and it focuses an awareness of

exactly whose regard an agent values. Yet even as Williams anatomizes the negative emotion of shame so that it might serve the purpose of a sociologist who wanted to identify different social groups, he drives toward a further thought. While one can be unashamed when belittled by the wrong people and ashamed when praised by still other wrong people, Hector, Williams observes, "was indeed afraid that someone inferior to him would be able to criticize him, but that was because he thought the criticism would be true, and the fact that such a person could make it would only make things worse."[32] What Williams imagines Hector's having felt is that the particular criticism could rightly be made by anyone who was human. The judgement that he feared was a judgement he thought so truthful that he imagined that its truth communicated itself to everyone, whether they were social inferiors or equals. And Hector's thinking presents a case that is a kind of companion piece to Williams' example of the limits of cultural relativism, in which he treats the Spaniards' having been horrified by the Aztecs' practice of human sacrifice as an example not of the Spaniards' ethnocentric commitment to their own European values but instead of the Spaniards' recognition that the Aztecs were human. The negative judgement on the Aztecs was, for Williams, a sign of a larger bond, a recognition of their humanity that made their killing of humans shocking in a way that neither animal attacks nor natural disasters could be.[33]

Williams recurrently appeals to examples of the kind I have just mentioned, and he recurrently analyzes them along similar lines (which are not dissimilar even when they sometimes move in different directions). He regularly examines the kinds of reactions that persons (and characters in literature) have, and he just as regularly sifts them to see exactly how many thoughts they involve and when those thoughts may seem either superfluous or necessary. Just as he can describe Telemachus as "not saying the same thing twice" when he says that the members of the Ithacan assembly "must be outraged themselves and feel shame in the face of other men who live around,"[34] so he can say of the difference between infanticide and abortion that, in the personal arena, our recognition of the child as a human may powerfully disambiguate the difference between a child and a foetus. No Supreme Court judge would be able to do without an explanation of the difference between infanticide and abortion, but Williams brings into view the sufficiency of saying, by way of preemptive reaction to a threatened infanticide, "You can't kill that. It's a child."[35] He expressed his principle of ethical parsimony particularly forcefully in his criticism of "one thought too many" in relation to debates about specific actions. For writers like William Godwin and Charles Fried, saving one's wife, child, or friend rather than a social inferior or a stranger looked like a decision that required further moral justification—a demonstration that one's decision conformed to the doctrine of fairness. For Williams, the ability to perform such a calculation in the face of the emergency is itself a symptom of disregarding the force of the personal attachments and projects that "compel ... allegiance to life itself" by treating impartial moral decisions as better, higher, and nobler than decisions that were made when an agent was wearing her or his street clothes.[36]

Although the thought may at first be improbable, it was, I suspect, Williams' honoring of his own principle of ethical parsimony that led him to devote as much attention to literature as he did. He wrote of the limitations of philosophical examples, of how their lack of detail contributes to the starkness of the choices they pose, so that it comes to look as though no ethical decision could arise directly out of one's circumstances and as though "*only an obligation*," as he put it, "*can beat an obligation*."[37] He takes "an everyday obligation—to visit a friend, let us say (a textbook example), because you have promised to," and says parenthetically, "To make the example realistic, one should put in more detail; and, as often in moral philosophy, if one puts in the detail the example may begin to dissolve."[38]

What Williams saw about the force of literary examples, I believe, was something like the power that literary examples have to show what feels like retrospective inevitability, the sense that the actions and the characters who perform them could only have been what they had been. Moreover, that inevitability—however formulaic it may be in its basic situation—must have been arrived at in a way that, on his account, moves as far from the exemplary as possible in the course of arriving at the sense that the audience confronts a character confronting herself in the face of inescapable circumstances and in the consciousness of herself as a social being, someone who is capable of supposing herself as not merely guilty but also shamed in the presence of others.

And here the link between Williams' conception of necessity and his account of shame becomes clearer. While a narratologist like Propp was able to provide an outline of the necessities of the development of plot and to identify the opening of a tale with a disequilibrium that calls for resolution by—and at—the end of the tale, Williams would, I think, have found such an account inadequate to account for the power of the felt necessity of the cases he considers. Propp, in depicting folk tales with characterizations so general as to be plausibly applied to pots and pans as well as to guileless humans who are lucky or unlucky enough to be chosen by the particular plots that govern them, can provide good examples of the logical necessity of action in narrative as such. But what Williams adds to the basic sense that a certain set of circumstances must appear as a state (as both Proppian narratology and Benthamite utilitarianism would have it) is the sense that one cannot simply chart the movement from one state to another (for Proppian analysis, from the initial disequilibrium—with absentation or the establishment of a lack—to the restoration of order; for Benthamite utilitarianism, from this state to the better or worse that succeeds it). For literature enables Williams to make a point that he has made about actual persons in "Persons, Character and Morality"—that the notion of character militates against the notion of the interchangeability of persons. The aggregative impulses that govern Benthamite utilitarianism and Proppian narrative theory alike cannot depict individual character. They can only assign a proper name to a representative of a collection of persons.

Literature, as Williams presents it, coordinates plot and character so as to reveal the actions that one has performed and the outcomes they have yielded, and so as to drive home the idea that one's actions are one's character (along the lines that Freud had in mind in saying that character was destiny). I shall have more to say shortly about Williams' conception of the character-defining nature of action. First, however, I would like to address his sense of the inadequacy of the analyses we have of classical Greek literature and its treatment of character.

For it is not simply philosophers who have tried to promulgate an account of action and the understanding of it that both extends the same view to everyone of an era and suggests that it can plausibly be related to the present as the primitive ancestor of our more highly developed moral understanding. One standard story about the ancient Greeks—told in slightly different ways by Bruno Snell and Christian Voigt—is that they had no conceptions of such things as deliberate action (because, as Snell puts it, "Homer's man does not yet regard himself as the source of his own decisions";[39] because, as Voigt puts it, "man still possesses no concept of deciding for himself"[40]) and a unified or integrated self (because, as Snell claims, they saw even their bodies as collections of parts[41]). And the progressivist story about morals gets launched as soon as the iteration of all that the Greeks lacked starts seeming like a list of positive accomplishments for civilization. We, progressivists say, have a conception of individual autonomy and internal coherence. We moderns honor the importance of the freely operating will in morality; and our legal systems incorporate the fruits of our having learned about the importance of the autonomous will. We have learned not just to judge bad actions as bad but also to develop a special legal vocabulary of blame in which we sort the voluntary from the involuntary crime and urge the authors of acts with catastrophic consequences to feel remorse only about the evils that they meant to accomplish.

To all of this, Williams replies that even the examples that Snell and Voigt draw from the *Iliad* would simply have no point if the ancient Greeks had not had the "concept of deciding for oneself." If the Greeks had thought that the gods were simply directing their actions in the way that puppet-masters might, then Homer's depiction of moments of deliberation would have seemed like a kind of science fiction. Instead, Williams affirms, "Homer's characters are constantly wondering what to do, coming to some conclusion, and acting."[42] If the Greeks had thought that there was no such thing as a unified body, then Priam's concern with recovering Hector's body from Achilles and his pleasure in learning that it was intact would have seemed nonsensical. And Williams rebuts the mechanical view of Greek action simply by attending to the text when he says:

> In wanting Hector's body to be whole, Priam wanted Hector to be as he was when he was alive. The wholeness of the corpse, the wholeness that Priam wanted, was not something acquired only in death: it was the wholeness of Hector.[43]

Here it would not be accurate to say that Williams is offering one interpretation that asks to be taken as seriously as Snell's and Voigt's. Rather, he is contradicting their accounts in crucial ways and showing that their positions simply do not adequately capture the kinds of things that Homeric characters say. When characters debate with themselves and consider their courses of action, it follows from their behavior that they are not imagining their fates to be entirely in the hands of the gods. (To talk to oneself rather than to a deity becomes, for him, an indubitable symptom of moral capacity and not just empty muttering.) When characters have a sensibility expressive of "the thought that this thing that will die, which unless it is properly buried will be eaten by dogs and birds, is exactly the thing that one is," they manifest a conception of personhood. It is from such insights that Williams derives the authority to say that Snell "overlooked the whole that they, and we, and all human beings have recognised, the living person himself."[44] Snell has, that is, set himself up as a schoolmaster who says that a particular usage is not supported by a dictionary entry when one ought to be using the texts to develop the dictionary.

Williams will go on to speak of Snell's fondness for "saying, for instance, that if the Homeric Greeks did not recognize a certain item, then that item 'did not exist for them'" and thus for asserting, for example, "Of course the Homeric man had a body exactly like the later Greeks ... but he did not know it *qua* body, but merely as the sum total of his limbs."[45] And he will identify the element that Snell found lacking in Greek thought that marks the primitivism of the Greeks—a Platonic and Christian conception of the soul as distinct from the body that seems to Snell essential for selfhood as such. But, in addition to making the point that Snell presents a misleading conception of Homer's depiction of individuals and their decisions, Williams calls attention to a distinct difference between Snell and Voigt's focus and his own: "I said 'Homer's characters'; Snell and Voigt said 'Homer's man.'"[46] Williams, in the first place, calls attention to the way in which looking at "the world view of Homer's man," the members of the Homeric audience, Snell and Voigt stack the deck; they free themselves to override plausible inferences about the agents in Homer's poems by shifting the discussion to the world view that the audience would bring to those poems. On his account, the best evidence for the views of the audience is the poems themselves, and the comprehension and response of the

audience that have provided the main support for their continued pre-
servation make a claim that should not be overridden. What, Williams all
but asks, were people attending when they heard epic poems that animated
a concern for bodily integrity if they had no such concept, or when they
saw tragedies that showed characters deliberating if they understood persons
as only the puppets of the gods.

Williams, in insisting on the distinction between Snell and Voigt's
"Homer's man" (or "Homeric man") and his own "Homer's characters,"
does not merely identify the centrality of a Christianized soul to Snell and
Voigt's accounts and the irrelevance of such a figure to his own. He also, in
framing the distinction between "Homer's man" and "Homer's characters,"
enables us to see how bizarre it is to perform the gesture of collecting
"Homer's man" into a single image that one might generalize in much the
way that one might generalize about various hominids. "Homer's man," in
sounding a bit like the "Java man," or "Neanderthal man," or "Cro-magnon
man" of evolutionary development, already points toward an implicitly
progressivist story of moral development. Snell and Voigt, as Williams
suggests, don't merely do literary history; they provide literary history with
the trappings of evolutionary development.

There is, moreover, an important aspect to Williams' insistence on
"Homer's characters" that he does not address directly at this point in his
text, and I want to call attention to it because I think it defines his particular
sensitivity to the way in which literature addresses philosophical problems.
At various points in his earlier writing, he referred to the way in which
philosophical examples might fall apart once one began to elaborate them.
And, as I have observed before, he called attention to the difficulties of
relating individuals to a Kantian categorical imperative that applied to all
individuals equally and of seeing how an individual might see her actions as
both necessary and her own in the utilitarian picture. When Williams uses
the words "Homer's characters," he thus quietly notes that there are many
of them, and that they are all distinct from one another.

For him the idea that character militates against the idea of the interchangeability of persons has many resonances. In this, he is by no means
alone. Indeed, John Rawls, whom Williams would put on the side of a
generalizing perspective, identifies ineliminable differences between persons
as a basic element with which philosophy must deal. Yet literature provides
an argument on behalf of the significance of the person as a distinctive
individual that is easy to overlook—namely, that it is impossible to imagine
a literature without characters, distinct and distinctive characters who are
recognizably themselves and not interchangeable with other characters.
That version of a notion of non-substitutability looms large in the ways in
which Williams discusses classical Greek literature and helps him to see
how it is that literature relates to life. For the realism of literature scarcely
derives from its fidelity to the facts. Moreover, it is not embarrassed by

differences in perspective (the various tellings of a story by different characters) or the sense that there is nothing really there except the story (that the story does not bear relation to actual persons and actual events). This is to say that there may be one reason too many to one's explanation of why one saved one's wife, but that stories do not try to recruit their characters to unanimity or precedence-guidedness, or even general agreement about decisions and outcomes. Literature, that is, presents life as having many voices, and treats it as a matter of course that we will not mistake Othello's voice for Imogen's, Hamlet's for Polonius's.

For stories—even in the stark forms in which the folk tale presents them—depict differentiated characters. And in depicting characters' differences from one another and the consequences of those differences that precipitate themselves as plot, stories are not so much imitating world views or specific sets of beliefs and ways of going about things as they are testifying to a sense of the inevitability of the differences among persons. The literature that assembles characters thus is, for Williams, the native language of our recognition of the primacy of the personal and its positive value. For literature does not need to make an argument for itself that suggests that it involves an essentially liberal politics in asking us to enter into a variety of different perspectives. Indeed, it does not even require that one enter into the consciousness of characters whom one would otherwise judge harshly. Rather, the differences among characters are so crucial to literature that they pass unnoticed, with all the inobviousness of the absolutely central.

Moreover, we can see the importance of the distinctiveness or ineliminability of character in every aspect of Williams' discussion of the *Iliad* itself. The basic situation of the poem involves conflict and participation in disputes that are swallowed up in the larger collective dispute between Achaians and the Trojans; it is thus designed in all its parts to emphasize differentiation of character in the stark contrast between friends and foes. But even in milder and more harmonious situations, it is essential to the progress of the narrative as a narrative that the characters should not collapse into one another, that their actions and their words do not look as though they might be indiscriminately assigned to any one of them. (Interestingly, the tragic chorus of communal and undifferentiated speakers does not absorb Williams' interest as does the series of individual and differentiated characters whom the chorus behold.) Williams thus describes a character like Agamemnon who "is not dissociating himself from his action ... but, so to speak, dissociating the action from himself,"[47] and he evokes the state of mind of a character like Ajax, who, after having killed the army's flock of sheep and cattle under the illusion that he is killing the leaders of the army, "knows that after what he has done, this grotesque humiliation, he cannot live the only kind of life his ethos demands."[48] In doing so, he operates with an implicit definition of literature here that sharply distinguishes it from allegories in which persons are asked to represent types—and thus to be so much themselves that they become unalterable—or Don Quixotes whose relation to the world is so thoroughly dictated by imagination that they are unaffected by experience.

Indeed, on Williams' account, the importance of literature is not that, as in many accounts of the novel and its ability to make us sympathize with a variety of different kinds of character, literature teaches us how to enter many consciousnesses—as if to treat them even-handedly or to discount their actions by understanding them so thoroughly that we try to adjust our reactions and imagine that we can adapt our receptions to allow for their mania or their depression. Rather, he focuses on the way in which characters in literature provide a model for seeing how the variousness of character is ineliminable—and how mistaken it is to try to adjust our sets so as to try to imagine Achilles without his anger or Hamlet without his melancholy (or, alternatively, to imagine that psychoanalysis will be able to perform surgical extraction of particular undesirable traits while leaving the desirable aspects of a person untouched).

While Williams does not try to depict characters without their distinctive psyches, neither does he attempt to imagine that what they happen to do is fully detachable from them. Indeed, acting and the ability to connect oneself with one's actions and their consequences are not merely ethical occasions; they are more deeply definitive of the self than the kinds of policy statements that people can make about their dispositions, treating their own particular virtues as if they were position papers issued by types, and even damaging the rather more general notion of personal integrity by acting as if they needed to stand on ceremony about whether a project should come about through them, concerning themselves more with reflection on themselves performing an action than with performing the action. We frequently have "real-life stories" to recount about persons who connect themselves with their own past actions, but Williams (particularly in *Shame and Necessity, In the Beginning was the Deed*, and *On Opera*) treats literature as if it sharpened our understanding of the varieties of noble and contemptible ways in which persons take up—or attempt to avoid—their connection to their own actions. Literature shows us what it is for a variety of particular characters to acknowledge the weight of their connection to their own actions. Williams captures just such a point when he delivers a description of the play that encapsulates his view that its power resides in its being a "dreadful machine" moving "to the discovery of just one thing, that *he did it*."[49] In that formulation he eliminates all of the content that allowed Oedipus' story to be turned into a generalizable complex and renders the story in its most minimal, telegraphic lines of connection between the "he" and the "it," the agent and the action.

Williams uses pronouns perhaps as effectively as anyone has ever done. And it would be a mistake to see his heavy reliance on the "he" and the "it" in the partial sentence I've just quoted as an example of his simply speaking of the isolation of Oedipus in the face of his mounting realization of his own past action or as an example of the generalizability of Oedipus's situation to an Oedipus complex that everyone faces in the normal course of human maturation. Instead, that "he" and that "it" mark the ways in which the sequelae of an action pick out particular characters with a necessity born of narrative conceived as a series of continuous present moments—rather than the kind of attempt that a structuralist anthropologist like Claude Lévi-Strauss makes in offering individuality as a simple epiphenomenon or product of generic and species terms.

And it is that attention to the sequential ordering of the words on the page, the sequence of events in literature, and the sequence of events in an individual's experience that prompts Williams to observe with elusive clarity the importance of refusing to define who the "we" of his *Shame and Necessity* might be.

> More than one friend, reading this book in an earlier version, has asked who this ubiquitous "we" represents. It refers to people in a certain cultural situation, but who is in that situation? Obviously it cannot mean everybody in the world, or everybody in the West. I hope it does not mean only people who already think as I do. The best I can say is that "we" operates not through a previously fixed designation, but through invitation. (The same is true, I believe, of "we" in much philosophy, and particularly in ethics.) It is not a matter of "I" telling "you" what I and others think, but of my asking you to consider to what extent you and I think some things and perhaps need to think others.[50]

The moment in which he wrote those words was probably the golden age for a challenge to any use of the first-person plural that wasn't well armed with a full iteration of the extent of one's presumption in identifying with and speaking for other people. And since I have been arguing that Williams consistently maintained great skepticism about universalizing perspectives in morality, it might seem surprising that he didn't simply revise his text to bring the "we" into greater proximity to "I." My guess is that he didn't restrict his first-person plural more decisively because he was genuinely interested in seeing how literature might push us beyond statements about norms and how they should be taken up or rejected simply on account of being norms. For his claim on behalf of classical literature was not that it was classic, not that it constituted a significant part of our history that we needed to retrace in order to participate in our culture. Rather, he argued, more directly, that it is important because we already recognize it as speaking to us. Whether we are individual readers who think that we are closer to Homer than Snell and Voigt were, whether we describe ourselves as of our moment, literature—Williams all but says—continually engages us in an experiment of seeing what we find to be conversable with us.

But here I don't mean simply to trumpet the flexibility and resilience of literary examples as simultaneous tokens of individual distinctiveness, ways of registering the inevitability of our claim that persons see certain outcomes as having their names on them, and the development of a relationship between readers and characters. Rather, I mean to suggest a deep connection between the impatience that Williams expressed in various essays about discussions of the Wittgensteinian notion of "forms of life" and Williams' own conception of a plural composed through the act of reading. Williams wittily observes the way in which the notion of "forms of life" is treated as weighty because vague. I'd like to think that Williams sees literature as important not because it mimics or resembles life but rather because it enables us to consider life from an insistently non-generalized perspective. And I'd like to think as well that his way of conceiving this project implies a consequential new translation of phrases like *die Lebensformen* and *die Formen unseren Lebens*. Not "forms of life" but "ways of life." Literature not as representations of worlds that are completely different from any world we know (as we are knuckle-rappingly told by High Church historicists like Snell and Voigt) but literature as the occasion for recognizing that we are not Ajax or Oedipus or Nausikaa but that we participate in the non-doctrinal version of their ways of life by recognizing them less as actors on a theatrical stage than as ethical agents—who, like Melville's whale, go wherever they want.

Notes

1 See Vogler, "The Moral of the Story," *Critical Inquiry* 34 (Autumn 2007), 5–35. I am grateful to Lauren Berlant for having alerted me to Vogler's essay while Berlant was preparing a special issue of *Critical Inquiry*, and to Vogler for having permitted me to see an earlier version of this essay as she was readying it for publication. I am grateful also to Richard Strier for having shown me a copy of his "Shakespeare against Morality," in which he relates Williams' distinction between "morality" and "ethics" and his argument "that the second identifies a much larger domain than the first, and that the first identifies a very limited and peculiar realm indeed" to a claim that Shakespeare participated in a similar view. Strier's essay appears in Marshall Berman (ed.), *Reading Renaissance Ethics* (London: Routledge, 2007). In the concluding pages of a serious overview of Williams' work, Mark P. Jenkins discusses Williams' suggestions about how "the defective consciousness of moral philosophy can be extended by appeal to fiction," and I have found that discussion—and many others in this careful consideration—helpful (*Bernard Williams* [Montreal: McGill University Press, 2006], pp. 177–81). I have also profited from the insightful readings that Daniel Callcut and Thomas Laqueur generously offered.

2 For "agent-regret," see "Moral Luck," in *Moral Luck: Philosophical Papers, 1973–1980* (Cambridge: Cambridge University Press, 1986), p. 27.

3 Bernard Williams, "Morality, the Peculiar Institution," in *Ethics and the Limits of Philosophy* (Cambridge: Cambridge University Press, 1985), p. 186.

4 Ibid.

5 *Shame and Necessity*, p. 13.

6 Ibid., p. 20.

7 Ibid., p. 15.

8 Ibid., p. 69.

9 Ibid., p. 146.

10 In *Shame and Necessity*, Williams apologizes for using the term out of his felt sense of its ugliness. He also, however, felt compelled to use it in "The Elusiveness of Pessimism: Responding to the *Ring*," in which he spoke of Wagner's responsiveness to Schopenhauer's rejection of "progressivist readings of history." See *On Opera*, ed. Patricia Williams (New Haven, CT: Yale University Press, 2006), p. 67.

11 "Morality, the Peculiar Institution," *Ethics and the Limits of Philosophy*, p. 186.

12 Williams applauds Nietzsche's account of the superficiality of the Greeks in *Shame and Necessity* (Berkeley, CA: University of California Press, 1993), pp. 9–11.

13 I think specifically of the kind of reversal that Norman Mailer saw as a Nietzschean courage to violate obvious norms. Martha Nussbaum offers a less riotous version of such a position in her discussion of James's *The Golden Bowl* when she produces an account of moral courage as the courage to undertake morally questionable courses of action in a somewhat Kantian vein, as in Kant's claim that moral conduct needs to be disambiguated from good actions that stem from an unreflectively sunny disposition. Martha Nussbaum, "Flawed Crystals: James's *The Golden Bowl* and Literature as Moral Philosophy," in *Love's Knowledge: Essays on Philosophy and Literature* (Oxford: Oxford University Press, 1990), pp. 125–47.

14 Williams has illuminating things to say about Rousseau's self-consciousness in the *Confessions* and *Reveries* in a book he published late in his career, *Truth and Truthfulness: An Essay in Genealogy* (Princeton, NJ: Princeton University Press, 2002), but his extending the general picture of self-consciousness among a series of writers does nothing to undermine the force of his attributing the model of internalized, self-reflective, and self-punishing consciousness particularly to Kant.

15 *Moral Luck: Philosophical Papers 1973–1980* (Cambridge: Cambridge University Press, 1986), p. 32.

16 *The Sense of the Past: Essays in the History of Philosophy*, ed. Myles Burnyeat (Princeton, NJ: Princeton University Press, 2006), p. 71.

17 Ibid., p. 72.

18 "Moral Luck," in *Moral Luck*, p. 21.

19 Although Williams does not dwell on the work of Foucault, Williams spoke respectfully of Foucault's work in a fashion that, I think, reflects their shared appreciation for Nietzsche and for an account of ethics that does not involve self-abnegation but rather self-cultivation.

20 "Persons, Character and Morality," in *Moral Luck*, p. 10.

21 *Moral Luck*, p. 28.

22 Ibid., p. 29.

23 See Nicholas Jardine, "Science, Ethics, and Objectivity," in J. E. J. Altham and Ross Harrison (eds), *World, Mind, and Ethics: Essays on the Ethical Philosophy of Bernard Williams* (Cambridge: Cambridge University Press, 1995), pp. 32–45. Jardine is principally concerned in this essay to qualify a universalist claim on behalf of science and to offer in its stead an account of "precedent-guided convergence," which he sees as a more accurate, because more elastic, notion. He

concludes, however, with a general endorsement of Williams' position on the limited usefulness even of agreement in ethical thought, saying that in ethics "the historical record manifests little enough convergence, let alone of the precedence-guided sort" (ibid.: p. 42) and that "the insights about objectivity that Williams uses to underwrite his world-guidedness standard are satisfied by my precedence-guided standard" (ibid.: 43).

24 Williams, *Making Sense of Humanity and Other Philosophical Papers, 1982–1993* (Cambridge: Cambridge University Press, 1995), pp. 166–7. He speaks in a similar vein of "an elite of utilitarian thinkers who possessed an esoteric doctrine unknown to others" in "Utilitarianism and Moral Self-indulgence," in *Moral Luck*, p. 52.

25 Ibid., p. 28.

26 *Shame and Necessity*, p. 83.

27 Ibid., p. 83.

28 See Steven Knapp, "Literary Value," in *Literary Interest: The Limits of Anti-Formalism* (Cambridge, MA: Harvard University Press, 1993), pp. 88–105.

29 See also Williams' discussion in *Shame and Necessity*, p. 81.

30 Ibid., p. 83.

31 Ibid., p. 82.

32 Ibid., p. 82.

33 Williams, in providing the example, gives something like character sketches of the Spaniards:

> The morally unpretentious collection of bravos was genuinely horrified by the Aztec practices. It would surely be absurd to regard this reaction as merely parochial or self-righteous. It rather indicated something which their conduct did not indicate, that they regarded the Indians as men rather than as wild animals.
> (*Morality: An Introduction to Ethics* (New York: Harper & Row, 1972), p. 25)

34 *Shame and Necessity*, p. 83.

35 Williams is discussing the question of "imperfect rationalization," the situation in which some distinction, not further reasoned, can ground agreement in private and less impersonal connections, but may not serve, or may not continue to serve, where a public order demands a public answer. To take an example which has been recently discussed a distinction between abortion, which is permitted, and infanticide, which is not, is one which can probably be naturally sustained in a certain context of shared moral sentiment without further reason being needed. The fact that further reason is not needed does not mean that that distinction is *irrational*. It means only that the basic distinction is more directly convincing than any reason that might be advanced for it: another way of putting it is that 'You can't kill that, it's a child' is more convincing as a reason than any reason which might be advanced for its being a reason. In his discussion of deliberation and deliberative priority, he similarly defends a less rather than more effortful mode:

> An effective way for actions to be ruled out is that they never come into thought at all, and this is often the best way. One does not feel easy with the man who in the course of a discussion of how to deal with political or business rivals says, "Of course, we could have them killed, but we should lay that aside right from the beginning." It should never have come into his hands to be laid aside.
> ("Morality, the Peculiar Institution," in *Ethics and the Limits of Philosophy*, p. 185)

While Williams certainly thinks at various points about the question of public and political reason, my main concern is with his interest in noticing how much work may not need to be done. See his "Conflicts of Values," in *Moral Luck*, p. 81.

36 See, in particular, "Persons, Character and Morality," in *Moral Luck*, pp. 1–19.

37 *Ethics and the Limits of Philosophy*, p. 180.

38 Candace Vogler launches her essay "The Moral of the Story" by quoting some of the same words I have quoted here. Williams' work is not a principal focus of her essay, because she is chiefly concerned to call attention to the limitations of imagining that literature can provide something like a laboratory in which actions can be tested in conditions of safety. Her view, as I understand it, is that precisely such conditions of experimental safety debar literature from providing adequate moral examples, because the lives of characters are known completely (in that there is nothing about them to know past what their author has said of them, in that we often see either the full circuit of the life of a character or the full circuit of a particular episode in a character's life). With actual persons, however, the consciousness of the limitations of our knowledge of other persons does—or ought to—complicate our interactions with them. My guess is that Vogler would find Williams' treatment of literary characters to verge on a discussion of actual persons, and it is certainly the case that Williams provides powerful accounts of the acts of individual characters that seem to call forth a sense of them as equivalents of actual humans. But I also suspect that she does not take issue with his position because she recognizes that Williams is not simply analogizing actual persons and literary characters. See Vogler, "The Moral of the Story," *Critical Inquiry* 34 (2007), 5–35.

39 *Shame and Necessity*, p. 22.

40 Ibid., p. 22.

41 Ibid., p. 24.

42 Ibid., p. 22.

43 Ibid., p. 24.

44 Ibid.

45 Ibid., p. 25.

46 Ibid., p. 22.

47 Ibid., p. 54.

48 Ibid., pp. 72–3.

49 Ibid., p. 69.

50 Ibid., p. 171.

Part IV

POLITICAL REALISM

10

BERNARD WILLIAMS

Tragedies, hope, justice

Martha C. Nussbaum[1]

I Williams and the Greeks

Bernard Williams made a large demand on behalf of philosophy: that it
come to terms with, and contain, the difficulty and complexity of human
life. He believed that much philosophy of the past had represented a flight
from reality, a rationalistic defense against complexity, emotion, and tragedy. Utilitarianism and Kantianism, particularly, had simplified the moral
life in ways that he found egregious, failing to understand, or even actively
denying, the heterogeneity of values, the sometimes tragic collisions
between one thing we care for and another. These theories also underestimated the importance of personal attachments and projects in the ethical life, and, in a related way, neglected the valuable role emotions play in
good choice. Finally, they failed to come to grips with the many ways in
which sheer luck affects not only happiness, but also the ethical life itself,
shaping our possibilities for choice and the ethical import of our choices. A
lover of both literature and opera, he asked philosophy to come up to the
higher standards of human insight these other forms of expression exem-
plified. What was the point in it, if it didn't? Clear obtuseness does not
contribute anything to human life. "Writing about moral philosophy
should be a hazardous business," he wrote in the opening sentence of
Morality – both because one reveals "the limitations and inadequacies of
one's own perceptions" more clearly than in other parts of philosophy and
because one runs the risk of "misleading people about matters of importance."[2] Most writers on the subject, he continued, avoid the second
danger by "refusing to write about anything of importance."[3] Williams
never refused.

At the heart of Williams' attempt to turn philosophy back to questions
of fundamental importance was a lifelong engagement with ancient Greek
literature. From his early essay "Ethical Consistency"[4] to the discussion of
Thucydides in *Truth and Truthfulness*,[5] the Greek poets and historians

commanded his respect; he thought, along with Nietzsche, that they were more truthful about our condition than most philosophers. In "Ethical Consistency," he argued powerfully that modern moral philosophy had incorrectly characterized conflicts of obligations by holding that in all such cases there is at most one genuine obligation; no claim that conflicts with a genuine obligation exerts any legitimate residual ethical pull. Using the example of Agamemnon's dilemma at Aulis, Williams argued that Aeschylus knew better. When Agamemnon says, "Which of these is without evils?" he correctly records the fact that the world is more powerful than such ethical theories allow: bad luck may cause two genuine obligations to collide. Even if one makes the best choice available in such a situation, some genuine obligation will be violated, and it will be correct for the agent to feel and express remorse, and to make reparations. This insight, of profound importance for the political as well as the moral life, was announced in a characteristically low-key way, without fanfare. It leaves simplistic approaches to public choice in tatters. Its implications have not yet been fully taken on board, for example, by the practitioners and theoreticians of cost-benefit analysis, who proceed, still, as if there is only *one* question before us, namely, what is the best choice, with the best balance of benefit over cost.[6] Williams showed that there are really two questions – the obvious question, and a further question, namely, whether any of the alternatives before one is free of serious wrongdoing. The latter question has major consequences not only for subsequent reparative conduct, but also for future attempts to create a world in which such conflicts will assail agents less frequently.

Over the years, Williams' engagement with Greek tragedy continued – in an elegant historical piece for Moses Finley's *The Legacy of Greece*;[7] in the nature of the questions he confronted in *Moral Luck*, a book in which Greek tragedy, if not often mentioned, is a constant presence;[8] and in his direct confrontation with the Greeks in *Shame and Necessity*, which makes an admirably lucid argument against various condescending progressivist interpretations of Greek culture, putting to rest, once for all, the tired allegation that the early Greeks had no concept of deliberation and choice and a primitive notion of agency.[9] The book also returns to the concerns of "Ethical Consistency" and generalizes them, arguing that the Greek poets show us a view of the world that we would do well to ponder: a world in which the things that matter most are not under the control of reason, or indeed under human control at all, and we are exposed to luck on a grand scale.

As time went on, Williams pushed his interest in the Greeks in a Nietzschean anti-Enlightenment direction – though whether it was a change in his view or a revelation of elements that had always been there is difficult to say. Certainly the Nietzschean turn involved a displacement, at least temporary, of the constructive political side of his work that had been in evidence earlier. This anti-Enlightenment direction perhaps shows up most clearly in an essay he wrote later than *Shame and Necessity*: "*The Women of Trachis*: Fictions, Pessimism, Ethics."[10] This essay is so important for Williams' thought that I shall focus on it alone in this chapter. After giving an account of the essay's argument, I shall suggest that Williams greatly underestimates the Greek tragedians' interest in calamities of human origin and in the capacity of human beings for addressing constructively the bad things in their world. I shall suggest that one of the valuable contributions of Greek tragedy to ethical thought is in fact a subtle process of deliberation about luck and bad human behavior, as we are again and again led to ask ourselves, "What, in the terrible events we witness, is sheer luck and necessity, and could not have been otherwise? What, by contrast, is human folly, rapacity, and negligence, and could possibly have been otherwise?" In this way, I shall try to bring back into Williams' picture of the Greeks a feature that seems indubitably central to the tragedies in their historical setting, namely their contribution to the process of democratic deliberation, and, perhaps, to the envisaging and constructing of a world that is at least a bit better than the one we currently know.

II "Stark fictions" and "the horrors"

Williams begins by announcing that moral philosophy "is still deeply attached to giving us good news."[11] No longer, on the whole, do philosophers seek a Leibnizian theodicy, in which "the horrors" are seen as necessary for a world that is better than any other possible world. No longer do they even seek Hegel's type of "good news," in which the unfolding of the Geist within history turns suffering into achievement. Williams suggests that we might reject Hegel for Kant's reasons – because we see morality as radically outside of history – or for other reasons, for example, because we do not believe that the sufferings could possibly be redeemed by any good result to which they might lead.

Williams is so elegant and brusque in his dismissal of Hegel that he does not pause to consider more modest views that incorporate a notion of historical progress. There is, for example, the view to which Kant seems inclined, namely that we understand morality better over time, and do learn by slow degrees to avoid some especially heinous types of moral error.[12] With Kant, I think that Williams should not so quickly dismiss the idea of moral progress within history.[13] Anyone who is a feminist has to think that there is at least something to it. Certain forms of bad behavior can be exposed and criticized in a manner that makes it impossible to return to them, at least in the old way. Just as, in Kant's example, the ferment surrounding the French Revolution made it impossible to return to feudalism and monarchical absolutism in the old way, just so in this case. Men used to dominate women heedlessly, thoughtlessly, because that was simply the way things were. Now there are still many cases in which men dominate women (just as there are still many cases of political tyranny). But the exposure of their behavior as what it is, the sheer naming of it as oppression, and the existence of widespread public argument about it, change things in a lasting way – are, as Kant said, "already a form of improvement in itself." In today's world, such male behavior has to be conscious, malicious, disdainful. It cannot be just routine or tradition. I think this is enormous progress. The only way one can imagine this progress being reversed is to imagine a political cataclysm that would eclipse free speech over much of the globe, something that modern media make very unlikely. Much the same can be said of slavery, of the cruel treatment of people with disabilities. Some insights about human dignity cannot be thrown away once they are attained, short of repression on a large scale. So, I believe that Williams dismisses Hegel – or at least the part of Hegel that Kant prospectively endorsed – far too quickly. If Hegel was overambitious about the totality and unity of the progress of the Geist, there is still something in the world that we can recognize as the progress of the Geist unfolding itself. I raise this objection only as an aside, however. This part of Williams' argument is not my primary concern.

Williams quickly moves on from Hegel to impugn even Kant's insistence on the dignity of the good will under pressure of adverse fortune. The Kantian idea that no absolutely bad news can be found within history is, he says, "its own type of good news."[14] What texts, then, might promote an adequate and honest confrontation with "the horrors"? Certainly not, in Williams' view, the texts of modern moral philosophy, which simply pretend that the gravest issues, the issues posed by our subjection to chance and necessity, are not there. "[I]n addressing what it claims to be our most serious concerns, it would do better if it did not make them disappear. Yet this is what in almost all its modern forms moral philosophy effectively does."[15]

Williams now turns to literature, suggesting that it can "significantly help" moral philosophy, and also that a test of adequacy for moral philosophy might be its ability "to learn from compelling fictions."[16] Williams briefly considers what he calls "dense fictions," fictions concerned with the details of character and social life, of which nineteenth-century English novels are our prototypes. Such fictions can investigate our relationship to chance and necessity, but they have their limitations: sometimes the representation of necessity in such novels brings them close to farce or comedy.[17]

Of special interest to moral philosophy, Williams argues, is a different type of fiction that can better approach our relationship to the ungovernable in our lives. These fictions are called by Williams "stark fictions."[18] Greek tragedies, especially those of Sophocles, are paradigmatic examples. Stark fictions are different in style from dense fictions: they have less of the incidental and the anecdotal;[19] they proceed, we might say, on a higher level of generality. They are also different in content and structure: their "resources are typically directed in a concentrated way to displaying the operations of chance and necessity."[20] Such works honestly confront us with "the horrors,"[21] with "undeserved and uncompensated suffering."[22] A tragedy, however, "lays its fictional horrors before us in a way that elicits attitudes we cannot take toward real horrors."[23] With real horrors, we usually ignore them, are "necessarily, and ... healthily, inattentive."[24] If they are imminent and cannot be ignored, our practical engagement with them prevents us from contemplating them. With tragedy, however, we can approach "some understanding of the real horrors,"[25] as the dramas "revea[l] their metaphysical structure, their relation or lack of it, to the universe."[26] In addition to this specific understanding, the works, by directing our attention to "the horrors," offer "a necessary supplement and a suitable limitation to the tireless aim of moral philosophy to make the world safe for well-disposed people."[27] So tragedies are both illuminating and corrective. By showing us an ethically relevant space over which we lack control, Williams argues, they show us what we must cede to nature, fate, and the capricious gods.

It is this set of claims about Greek tragedies that I want to scrutinize, sympathetically but rather critically, for the remainder of this chapter. We need to begin by observing that Williams' view of tragedy lies very close to that of Schopenhauer. Schopenhauer believed that all art presents suffering human beings with detached aesthetic representations of the life of the "Will," that is, the life we lead when we allow our desires to propel us into practical engagement with our uncertain world. Different art-forms perform that task differently. But because the life we lead when we are in the grip of desire is a life of unending suffering, tragedy plays a particularly central and valuable role among the art forms:

> The purpose of this highest poetical achievement is the description of the terrible side of life. The unspeakable pain, the wretchedness and misery of mankind, the triumph of wickedness, the scornful mastery of chance, and the irretrievable fall of the good and the innocent are all here presented to us; and here is to be found a significant hint as to the nature of the world and of existence ... The motives that were previously so powerful now lose their force, and instead of them the complete knowledge of the real nature of the world, acting as a quieter of the will, produces resignation, the giving up not merely of life, but of the whole will-to-live.[28]

Williams does not endorse Schopenhauer's claim that watching tragedies leads to resignation – although he does not deny it either. He does, however, fully endorse Schopenhauer's view that the significance of tragedy lies in its capacity to offer us the truth about the horrors of existence, in a form that we can watch and understand, as we cannot understand them while we are practically engaged with them. Williams connects this understanding with a new level of honesty about our practical engagements. If moral philosophy deludes us by making the world seem "safe for well-disposed people," tragedies pull off the mask of safety, and allow us to see what sort of world it really is in which we must spend our brief time.

Schopenhauer's view of tragedy is undergirded by his specific psychology, which offers an account of the painfulness of erotic striving, its constant frustration, and in general the misery of being an erotic being in a world that is not set up to satisfy us in a stable way. I see no signs of these misogynistic and anti-erotic elements of Schopenhauer in Williams. But if those elements are not in the background, we need to ask more precisely just what Williams himself does mean by "the horrors." For Schopenhauer, what we see when we see "the horrors" is the absurd and ineluctably painful life into which erotic striving propels us. What does Williams mean, if he doesn't quite mean that?

It would seem that the "horrors" of human life, the events that make it painful and frustrating, are of two distinct, albeit overlapping, sorts. Some really are the products of chance and/or necessity. The condition of mortality and subjection to pain, as well as the (related) operations of a whole host of natural disasters seem to be such "horrors." These "horrors" seem uppermost in Williams' mind, as they are uppermost in the play, and I think really that it is the fact of our subjection to pain and, ultimately, death that lies at the heart of his argument.[29] On the other hand, when one thinks about human suffering, one sees that quite a lot of it is inflicted by human beings, sometimes acting accidentally or ignorantly (as is the case with Sophocles' heroine Deianeira), but all too often acting culpably – maliciously, or collaboratively, or negligently. Wars, murders, betrayals, political upheavals – all these events, ubiquitous in tragedies, seem to have human authors. Thus, it seems at least in principle possible for them to be stopped in the future, or very much diminished. It isn't stupid to think about the Holocaust and to say, "Never again."

When we begin thinking in this way, we see that in reality – and in today's world more than ever – the line between one sort of "horror" and the other is a very hard one to draw. Most of the actual "horrors" people experience have elements of both chance/necessity and human bad behavior in their causal history. When there is an earthquake in a rich American city, it will do little damage, because buildings have been built in order to withstand earthquakes. If they don't, it is someone's fault, and legal penalties will follow. When an earthquake happens in a poor developing country, the loss of life is likely to be great. Often we can still blame people on the scene, who did not build buildings up to building code standards (such was the case with the Gujarat earthquake of 2001). But even when the local inhabitants were doing the best they could with their available resources, obeying the best standards that they thought they could set for themselves, that doesn't dispose of the question of bad behavior: for surely the asymmetry between San Francisco and Ahmedabad ought to trouble us, and we ought to think it outrageous that being born in Gujarat, rather than California, should have exposed one to "horrors" that are spared wealthy Californians. The fact that Gujarat just didn't have the resources to protect people against calamity is outrageous, while Americans enjoy expensive ski vacations and many other unnecessary luxuries. Again, when people die of HIV/AIDS in Africa, in one way, this is a natural calamity. Surely, however, there is bad behavior afoot as well, in the reluctance of pharmaceutical companies to make life-saving medications available at a reasonable cost, and, more generally, in the unwillingness of rich nations to support the development of an adequate health infrastructure in Africa.[30]

As we think along these lines, we see that even "the condition of mortality" is not something fixed and given. What we can cure and what we can't are constantly changing, and what we at least know is that most of the world's people don't get all the care that would bring their life expectancy up to the level of life expectancy in the developed countries. Life expectancy at birth in the U.S. is approximately 79 years; in Sierra Leone it is approximately 34 years. So there is mortality and mortality. And surely there is a great deal that human beings concerned with justice can do to make lives in other parts of the world less disfigured by chance and necessity at an early age.

I have said that Williams, unlike Schopenhauer, does not counsel resignation. Nonetheless, a focus on chance and necessity as the causes of the "horrors" of human life cannot help affecting one's practical engagements in some way. If the Williamsian agent does not adopt detachment and resignation as a response, what other attitude remains open to him? Perhaps the sort of practical engagement urged by Camus: an ongoing commitment to action for the sake of action, in the face of the absurdity of all such engagements. Like Sisyphus pushing his boulder, the agent may remain active, but bereft of any hope of ever achieving his goal. That attitude might not be the best way to confront the world, however, if its "horrors" contain a large admixture of human bad behavior that dedicated human action can in fact alter.

More generally, if one looks at the world's "horrors" thinking, "All that is chance and necessity," then, I suggest, one is likely to think rather badly about one's practical options. Surely Cicero is correct when he observes that the person who does no active wrong cannot take credit for justice, if what he has done is to sit by idle when he could be helping human beings who have been assaulted or harmed.[31] We might even wonder whether he could take credit for justice if what he had done was to plunge into the world in the existentialist way, without a real hope of altering what is bad about it. If virtuous action must be pursued for its own sake, it remains unclear whether the actions recommended by Camus can count as just actions, since they seem to be actions in which the goal of a just world has been silenced, and action is performed more or less for the sake of being active. If Williams has an account of how the agent he envisages can act for the sake of the just, without hope of progress, he has not presented that account here, and he strongly discourages his reader from supplying such an account.

What good, responsible practical choice requires is a delicate set of deliberations in which we ask ourselves, "What can we change, and how far, and by what means? What operations of chance are intolerable for a decent world?" We need, then, to think about the boundary between the two types of "horrors," how elusive and how unstable it is, and what this means for our practical political engagements. The fact that Williams nowhere mentions the distinction between two types of horrors, and never suggests that a good response to them might be to work as hard as one can for justice, is, to me, a serious shortcoming in his article, and perhaps in other writings of his as well. What, indeed, is wrong with trying to "make the world safe for well-disposed people" – where that means, in concrete terms, trying to make sure that every child gets decent nutrition, access to education and other basics of a decent dignified human life, that all children and adults have access to high quality health care and needed pharmaceuticals, that rape and child sexual abuse do not disfigure the lives of women and children, and so forth? (In fact, I'm inclined to adopt Williams' tag, "to make the world safe for well-disposed people," as a motto for my "capabilities approach.")[32] Williams does not endorse Schopenhauer's resignationism or the existentialist idea of the absurd, but he surely comes rather close to these notions, in his utter silence about constructive practical responses that might emerge from our confrontation with the world as it really is.[33]

Another way of putting the point is this: Williams imagines us looking at the world as it really is, and his picture is that we are looking into a black chasm not of our own making. We stare at that chasm and, through the detachment from our own lives that art makes possible, we see clearly just how black it is. My picture of "looking at the world as it really is" is different. I imagine that we are looking into a mirror and seeing the ugly faces of human beings, their humanity distorted by greed, fear, and sloth. At least our own all-too-familiar faces loom up at us this side of the black chasm. To be sure, the black chasm is still there in the distance, in the form of inevitable death for each and every one of us. But unless Williams has some further argument that he hasn't given, as to why mortality makes all our moral efforts meaningless, I think he simply has not shown that an intensification of moral and political effort, to "make the world safe for well-intentioned people," is not the best imaginable outcome of our confrontation with the real nature of existence. It seems to me obvious that there is a big difference between dying of malnutrition at age 4 and dying of cancer at age 90. At any rate, he has not argued that there is no such difference. And there is no doubt that we can do a great deal more than we currently do to move all the children in the world closer to the better death and away from the worse death. If we can do more and don't, then it isn't chance or necessity, it is us, and its name is injustice, a word that does not occur in Williams' article.

The idea that we must just face the way the world really is, including its "horrors," leads to different reactive attitudes in Williams' view and in mine. For Williams, the confrontation with reality leaves room for resignation, for an elegant cynical world-weariness, for a rebellious Nietzschean cheerfulness, for existentialist commitment, for ineluctable grief, for a kind of compassion that is closely linked to grief. It leaves no room, however, for anger, an attitude that I also found oddly absent, or suppressed, in Williams the man. Nor does it leave room for a type of compassion that is closely linked to anger and constructive action, a compassion that says, "This is intolerable, and it must never be allowed to happen again." On my view, human bad behavior and neglect are always appropriate objects of anger, resentment, and blame. It would be inappropriate to greet these "horrors" with resignation, or elegant cynical world-weariness, or Nietzschean cheerfulness, or even existentialist commitment, insofar as that commitment fails to pursue the just for its own sake, as an achievable goal. Much the same is true for mixed events, events co-caused by chance/necessity and human bad behavior. Some portion of such events might be the appropriate object of Williamsian attitudes, but it seems to me that it would be inappropriate to give these attitudes free play, since we never know how much we can do to prevent such disasters until we try with all our might. Sadly, however, we human beings never have tried with all our might to give other human beings the prerequisites of decent living.

And notice what has now become of the issue of good news and bad. The news that the suffering we witness is the result of distant, unapproachable, implacable, unintelligent necessity would in a sense be bad news: for it would mean that it had to happen, and that similar things will go on happening. We cannot extricate ourselves from such necessities. That is what Williams means by saying that such news is a corrective to overoptimistic offers of "good news." But I think that there is another sense in which that kind of news is good: for it means that there is nobody to blame and nothing more to do. We can sit back and resign ourselves to the world as it is, knowing that we cannot change it.

If, however, we think that malice, ignorance, and callousness may lie behind the suffering we witness, well, that is in one sense good news: for it means that there is a hope of change. But it is in another sense bad news: for it means that the suffering was perhaps not necessary, and that if we had worked harder or thought better we might have prevented it. At the very least it means that we had better get ourselves together to do whatever we can to avoid such things in the future.

III Tragedies, necessity, justice

I have now laid my own cards on the table. What, however, of Greek tragedy? Williams might be wrong about our prospects and responsibilities, but right about the Greeks. I shall now, however, argue that in some very central ways the tragic poets are with me rather than Williams in their sense of what the confrontation with reality involves, and what responses are its appropriate outcome.

In the view I have outlined and endorsed, one of the most important endeavors of human practical reason will be to ask in a practical way (not a deep metaphysical way)[34] about the relationship between natural necessity and human effort, and to try to sort out what kinds of efforts and engagements we need to make the world slightly better. I now claim that tragedies, varied though they are, typically invite us to sharpen our deliberative faculties in just this way, learning how to make the valuable distinction between human bad behavior, which might be altered, and unalterable necessity; between the sphere of chance and fate, and the sphere of justice.

I begin with two historical notes. First is a note about the tragic festivals. Ancient Greek tragedy, as it was performed and lived, was not offered to its spectators as an object of detached or solitary contemplation. The tragic festivals were civic festivals, central parts of the civic religion. The way plays were produced (by companies of citizen actors, trained by yet other citizens), the way the spectators were seated (with pride of place given to young men on the verge of military service),[35] the way plays were routinely assessed (with a strong emphasis on their ethical content), all this heightened the sense that the witnessing of a play was an occasion for solemn civic deliberation. The very structure of the theatre – an amphitheatre across which one could see the faces of one's fellow citizens, as one sat in the bright sunlight – promoted community awareness and discouraged a retreat into private thoughts about human catastrophe. It is now commonplace to underline the deliberative context of the tragedies, and to see them as part of Athens's elaborate construction of civic reason and civic friendship.[36] It would be hard for such an audience to forget about human responsibility and issues of justice. Williams tends to ignore the performance situation of tragedy and to imagine his reader or spectator as isolated from others. He thus omits central aspects of the ancient tragic festivals.

My second contextual note concerns the Greek gods. Williams talks little about the Greek gods; he prefers to talk of impersonal forces such as "chance" and "necessity." The difference is, however, crucial to a proper interpretation of the tragedies. The Greek gods are typically not thought of as pieces of an implacable machine that grinds down humans ineluctably. They are imagined as anthropomorphic agents, and not perfect such agents either. Their unlimited power and their lack of understanding of suffering and limitation are usually taken to make them rather infantile and narcissistic, not fully capable of an ethical response to the world. How to reconcile such a picture of the gods with the thought that the gods are worthy of worship is a tough problem, with which sophists and philosophers – and, presumably, ordinary citizens – wrestled in a variety of ways. What is clear, however, is that ethical blame of the gods is not inappropriate in the Greek world.[37] Questions about the justice of divine actions were live questions, and it was not inappropriate to press such questions. In Judaeo-Christian religion, when people like Job ask questions about God's justice, it always turns out that they have gotten something wrong, or committed an impiety, or tried to understand something that there is no understanding. When Greek humans ask about the justice of divine actions, their accusations may be correct. The Greeks wisely saw that anthropomorphic beings would not necessarily become better by having unlimited power. This thought, central to Olympian religion, entails that a large portion of the "chance/necessity" part of human suffering is actually caused not by necessity at all, but by a different form of quasi-human bad behavior. The gods who cause these things are motivated by greed, jealousy, love, all the usual human motives. There is no necessity about their choices, which are frequently depicted as the outcome of whim and caprice, lacking even the most cursory deliberation. If one forgets about this huge difference between Greek religion and Judaeo-Christian religion, one is likely to misunderstand a lot of what happens in the tragedies.

To go further with the "stark fictions" of the Greeks, I must now turn to some concrete examples. Williams acknowledges that tragedies vary a great deal, but his argument, while focused on the *Trachiniai*, is intended to apply to at least some others. He indicates that Sophocles is central to his analysis. I shall therefore choose one play each of Aeschylus and Euripides (really a trilogy of Aeschylus), but three plays of Sophocles, including the *Trachiniai*.

1 Aeschylus' Oresteia

The conflict between Greeks and Trojans is represented in *Agamemnon* as the outcome of a complex interweaving of divine and human choices. Helen's destructive role is highlighted: she is the charming lion cub who fawns on its keepers and then turns on them savagely. The play represents her as unfaithful by choice, and this infidelity as a prime cause of the war. Agamemnon's dilemma at Aulis, however, is represented as caused by the gods and the grim necessities they throw up in a human life that was doing pretty well. These divine actions themselves, however vaguely they are described in the play, are likely to be seen as not so much necessity/chance as bad anthropomorphic behavior: above all, Artemis' jealousy and vindictiveness. (Alternately, her anger may possibly be caused by a previous bad action on Agamemnon's part, but this version of the story, known elsewhere, is not mentioned in the play.) So there is bad behavior at two levels. Further elements of bad behavior are supplied by Agamemnon when he arrogantly and overweeningly agrees to tread on purple cloth; by Clytemnestra as she first betrays and then murders him; by Aegisthus, as he sleeps with another man's wife and aids her in the murder. Thus, although the men of the Chorus do invoke Zeus as a mysterious unknown cause of their fate, the audience certainly sees that human choices have, at the very least, made things considerably worse. They also see that the divine choices that set up the bad situation are similar in kind to the bad human choices, inspired by bad passions rather than by any grand necessitarian scheme.

The trilogy's end, as I am sure Williams himself would agree, depicts progress in human life, and progress of a sort that, once it has happened, is unlikely to be wholly reversed. The cycle of revenge is superseded by the rule of law. Although some of the characters seem to think that everything lies in the hands of the gods, they are ultimately proven wrong: human beings can take the world into their own hands, through politics, and make at least some difference. The Erinyes (Furies), doglike goddesses who hound those who must assume the burden of a blood-guilt, become humanoid women, now called Eumenides (well-disposed ones).[38] Accepting a promise from Athena, they take their place in the city. A jury of citizens of Athens acquits Orestes, ending the curse upon the house. Aeschylus' myth of the origins of law resembles, indeed, the classical myth of the social contract: people agree to leave the "state of nature" to join a community regulated by law.

Once law is on the scene, it may be corrupted, but it is not likely to disappear utterly. It remains in the world as a hope and a warning. So the trilogy brings "good news" of a kind that is not merely Kantian, showing moral institutions as good in themselves – but virtually Hegelian (or displaying the signs of "improvement" that Kant mentioned, foreshadowing Hegel), showing that these institutions have made things at least a bit better for the future. It is difficult to imagine a future in which the rule of law would utterly disappear from the world and be replaced by family vendettas of the sort Aeschylus depicts.

The forces that wrought havoc in human life have not disappeared with the advent of the rule of law. Aeschylus depicts the Erinyes as remaining on in the city, in an honored place underground. He thus reminds us that law always coexists with the dark human motives that give rise to the need for law. Law's victory is tenuous and insecure. Aeschylus thus invites his audience to think hard about what law can and cannot do to "make the world safe for well-intentioned people." (I note that the new name for the

Erinyes is Eumenides, which means, literally, "well-intentioned ones," and they are so-named because they have the intention of making Athens safe for well-intentioned human beings through their partnership with law.)

Nobody who had followed the entire trilogy would be under the delusion that law had eliminated adultery, murder, the lust for power, and all the conflicts, military and familial, to which these motives give rise. Bad human behavior in this way moves toward the realm of necessity, or at least permanence: we see that it is very likely that human beings will behave horribly to one another again and again, and that even the best laws can't stop this bad behavior totally. The audience would also be reminded that the human body is fragile, capable of being raped (Cassandra), stabbed repeatedly (Agamemnon), even cut up like a sacrificial goat (Iphigeneia). Just to be born with such a body leaves one exposed to calamity on a large scale. So Williams' thoughts do enter the work indirectly: the audience would very likely think that so long as humans are mortal and have bodies, various horrible things can happen to them, and, so long as their desires are roughly as they have been, they will also do various horrible things to one another. These "horrors" can never be completely prevented. The challenge posed by the trilogy, however, is to sort all this out, asking what good laws and good cities can actually contribute to human life. Its conclusion is surely that they can contribute quite a lot.

2 Sophocles' Philoctetes

This play acknowledges chance and necessity as part-causes of human suffering. Philoctetes' suffering comes by chance, when he steps by mistake into the sacred precinct of the goddess Chryse. The wound that is his punishment causes him unbearable pain.[39] His eventual role in the Trojan War is fated, and his return to Troy is thus apparently necessary, come what may. Nonetheless, the accent in the entire drama is on the difference in human life that can be made by friendship, truthfulness, and compassion, working within the outlines of necessity. Unlike Aeschylus and Euripides, who also wrote dramas on this theme, Sophocles chose to make the island of Lemnos uninhabited. Unlike Euripides, he gives Philoctetes no healing herb that would soothe his pain.[40] Sophocles thus magnifies the element of human bad behavior: just because they don't like the stench of an oozing sore, the Greeks have abandoned a loyal member of their expedition to a very miserable and lonely existence. Philoctetes' bitter anger is justified, though perhaps its very bitterness and obsessiveness demean him and harm his prospects for friendship.[41]

As for the action of the drama itself, the accent is squarely placed on moral choice and the prospects of compassion and justice. Neoptolemus, swayed by Odysseus' persuasive rhetoric and his own desire for glory, agrees to deceive Philoctetes, thus compounding one wrong with another.

225

The sight of Philoctetes' attack of pain produces, however, a moral revolution, in which considerations of both justice and compassion figure. (*Eleos* and *oiktos*, and their relatives, suffuse the drama, and the play has been said by both recent and earlier critics to be, in effect, a meditation upon tragic compassion.)[42] Neoptolemus borrows *papai*, the cry that Philoctetes had used to communicate his agony, to express the pain of his own ethical guilt, as he realizes that he has been the accomplice of a great injustice.

Indeed, human justice almost hijacks necessity. Neoptolemus' decision to return the bow to Philoctetes and allow him to remain on his island leaves no way for the Greeks to win the Trojan War, since the oracle has made clear that it cannot be won without him and his bow. At this point, Sophocles has to find some way of bringing his ethical construct into line with the known contours of history, so he uses Heracles as a *deus ex machina*, to tell Philoctetes that he really ought to go to Troy to be healed and help the Greeks win the war. What is fascinating, however, is that even the divine intervention works through ethical choice. Heracles does not simply tell Philoctetes that he'd better knuckle under to chance and necessity. Instead, he firmly reminds him of their friendship, and Philoctetes is persuaded to return out of his love for the man to whose terrible suffering he himself, by building the funeral pyre, put an end. Philoctetes exclaims, "O you who brought to me a voice I longed for," and only then concludes that he will go along with Heracles' suggestions.[43]

Philoctetes shows that justice and ethical choice do not have limitless power in human life. They must operate within the context of chance, necessity, and the gods. The play symbolizes this circumscription at its end, when Philoctetes, bidding farewell to his island, says that he is going "where great destiny sends me, and the judgement of friends, and the all-subduing *daimôn*, who accomplished this."[44] The judgement of friends, like Lemnos, is surrounded by more savage currents; its achievements are, however, real.

Once again, then, the tragic audience is challenged to ponder the interactions of human choice with destiny and chance, asking what friendship and compassion can and cannot achieve. Anger and a constructive compassion (a compassion leading to helpful action) are prominent among the responses cultivated by the play as legitimate and valuable. Justice is among the play's central themes.

3 Sophocles' Antigone[45]

Hegel was especially fond of this play, arguing that it supports his view of progress within history. Each of the protagonists, Hegel said, has too narrow a view of the ethical universe. Creon thinks only about the well-being of the city, ignoring the claims of the family and its religion. Antigone thinks only of the religion of the family, forgetting about the needs of the city. The audience, Hegel argued, would see things in a more complicated way, and would see that both spheres of action deserve respect.[46]

So far, I believe, so good.[47] Hegel then went on to argue that the conflict between city and family religion depicted in the play had been well resolved only in the modern state, which builds into the very idea of the legitimate sphere of state action a respect for the "private" sphere and its religious claims. As to this further claim, I think he is wrong, both about how new this "resolution" is and about how total it is. In his funeral oration, as represented in Thucydides, the great Athenian statesman Pericles already boasted that the Athenian democracy had arranged things in such a way that citizens would not be forced to violate the "unwritten laws" of family piety in order to be good law-abiding citizens. So Hegel's idea, in its general outlines, is not new. Nor, however, does modernity mean the end of trouble. Modern liberal democracies have a very delicate balancing act to conduct when they try to protect the space in which people follow claims of conscience, while still preserving public safety and the rule of law. The tension between these two spheres is the subject of endless litigation in modern democracies, whether the immediate topic be conscientious objection in wartime, or a priest's refusal to testify to information he heard in the confessional, or the right of employees to refuse work that imposes requirements that conflict with those of their religion, or the right of a religious believer to use otherwise illegal drugs in a sacred ceremony.[48]

My first criticism of Hegel, then, is that he makes the conflict look easier than it is. It is actually very tough, and to that extent good human behavior will require delicate deliberation and balancing – of a sort that the play prompts.

My second criticism of Hegel, which is the one I stressed in *The Fragility of Goodness*, is that his reading ignores suggestions within the play that even the best human efforts may be undermined by forces both human and extra-human. The play alludes frequently to human greed, erotic passion, and the desire for power as ongoing forces in human nature that hijack the search for good ethical choice. Even if people are conscientious and do their best, it is relatively unlikely that they will all do so all the time, given the power of these motives, as the play represents them. *Erôs* conquers the minds of both humans and gods, and it can "wrench just men's minds aside from justice, doing them violence."[49] The play is thus in agreement with Aeschylus: what law has to grapple with is the recalcitrant material of human desire, and it is unlikely that it will achieve a total or stable victory. Finally, there are also forces outside of human bad behavior that constrain human action. The troubles that the gods cause for human beings are compared to a huge wave swelling up out of the sea.[50] (Some of these wavelike forces are just plain chance, and some the result of divine jealousy, love, anger, and so forth.)

Good institutions, and good judgement within them, can make the tragedies of human life somewhat less frequent and less dire. It cannot make human life easy or ethically pure. So, once again, we are presented with a question that is also a challenge: what could we do better, and what are we struggling against that might not get better?

4 Sophocles' Trachiniai

This play is indeed bleak. Blameworthy action is in it in the form of Nessus the centaur's machinations, as, reacting resentfully to Deianeira's sexual refusal, he substitutes the poison for a love charm. (I am tempted to call this an early case of quid-pro-quo sexual harassment, a human problem about which Williams showed admirably progressive and feminist concern.) The human agents, however, are dupes and victims, and Williams is right to emphasize Deianeira's vulnerability, as her well-intentioned actions plunge her beloved husband into unbearable pain. Let us, however, consider more closely the play's remarkable ending, which Williams rightly makes central.

Heracles is stricken not by love but by horrible agony. Watching him suffer, his son Hyllus asks for *suggnômosunê*, fellow-feeling, from his companions and, later, from the Chorus – indirectly from the audience – contrasting this sympathy with the callousness of the gods. The famous concluding passage is cited by Williams as his epigraph. I substitute a doggedly literal version for the old and slightly non-literal translation that Williams offers.[51] (I note that Williams begins with the third line in my version, leaving out the appeal to sympathy.)[52]

> Lift him up, friends, showing great sympathy (*suggnômosunê*)
> with me in what has happened,
> and knowing of the great indifference (*agnômosunê*) of the gods
> displayed in these events,
> gods who begat us and are called our fathers
> but who look on such sufferings as these.
> What is to come no one can see,
> but what is here now is pitiable for us
> and shameful for them,
> but of all men hardest for the man
> who is enduring this calamity.
> [He now addresses the leader of the Chorus]
> Do not be left behind in the house, young woman.
> You have lately seen terrible deaths
> And many unprecedented sufferings,
> and there is not one of these things that is not Zeus.

Williams sees in these lines a truthful recognition of the inevitable limitations of human projects. Hyllus recognizes and accepts that the universe is fundamentally unjust and arbitrary, and that there is nothing to be done about that. Thus the "stark fiction" confronts us squarely with "the horrors" and immunizes us against the philosophers' "good news." But there are two problems with such a reading.

First, Williams' reading ignores the extent to which human moral judgement is prized and asserted, even in the face of disaster: the pity and fellow-feeling of the human community have a nobility that, in Aristotle's words, "shines through" despite the horror, contrasting favorably with the indifference of the gods.[53] That is not exactly the same as Kant's good news about the will beset by the "accidents of stepmotherly nature," but it is surely closer to Kant than Williams acknowledges.

Second, Williams' reading makes too little, I believe, of Hyllus's anger. As I have said, Williams does not exactly counsel resignation, but anger does not appear to be on the menu of attitudes suggested by his perspective. Resignation to tragic necessity, however, is certainly not what is conveyed by the words *megalên theôn agnômosunên*, "great indifferent-thoughtlessness of the gods," nor yet by the characterization of the gods as so-called parents who sat by while terrible events transpired.

Think of an Indian onlooker, surveying the carnage after General Dyer's massacre of thousands of innocent civilians at Amritsar. He might well have spoken such a speech, ending it with the line, "And there is nothing here that is not the Raj." In other words, how dare these powerful people come here claiming to be our superiors and parents, and then conduct themselves in this disgraceful and evil way? The power of the Raj, like the power of the gods, is so far beyond the power of a few thousand Indian civilians that it looks invincible. Nonetheless, one can protest it.[54] In the case of India and Britain, one may ultimately prevail. In the case where the disparity of power between victims and perpetrators is as absolute as that between mortals and gods, it is not very clear what can be done, although withdrawal of worship is at least one thing that is regularly tried, in both tragedy (the end of the *Trojan Women*) and comedy (*The Birds*); short of that, angry demands for acknowledgment and reparation must be pursued and pursued again. Even if the gods are relatively obtuse, they are not altogether deaf to human accusations. Given that their obtuseness frequently seems to arise not from profound malice but from a real lack of understanding of what mortal beings experience, making the cost of their actions clear to them is at least a hopeful stratagem.

The gods, moreover, are paradigms for human conduct. The Greeks noted again and again that bad humans often rationalize their own questionable actions by pointing to the fact that the gods do similar things. (Plato's *Republic* makes this a central theme in the critique of myth; Aristophanes makes grim humor out of the practice in *Clouds*, where a young man justifies violence against his father in just this way.) So even if the gods themselves will not be changed, Hyllus offers a solemn warning to humans: don't behave like that. Have compassion with human suffering, rather than culpable neglect. As in *Philoctetes*, then, compassion is seen as something good in human life, and something that is always within our power, even when many other things are not.

5 Euripides' Troades

This play is filled with blameworthy action. Its female protagonists suffer rape, child-murder, enslavement, husband-murder, and the destruction of their city by fire. Throughout, they protest with dignified and justified anger against the callousness and rapacity of the Greeks. It looks as if there is quite a lot that human beings might do to prevent such atrocities: indeed, preventing them has been a good part of the story of modern international law.

Even in the ancient Greek world, it was understood that some types of conduct by victors in war were morally unacceptable. The debate recorded by Thucydides over the fate of the rebellious colony of Mytilene shows that the question of killing all the adult males in a city and enslaving the women and children was highly controversial in Athens, a subject of intense ethical struggle. Cleon swayed the populace to vote for such a course, and a ship was sent to execute the grim command. Diodotus then persuaded them that the course they had chosen was unacceptable. They reversed their judgement and sent out a second ship to catch the first. Only because, by sheer chance, the first ship had been becalmed at sea did the second ship manage to catch up and stop the atrocities. (Here's an intersection between chance and blameworthy human action that worked, for once, in a positive direction.) The story of Mytilene is highly relevant to Euripides' drama, because just before it was staged the Athenians had voted to exact a similar penalty from the rebellious colony of Melos; having no Diodotus to stop them, they had already put their decision into effect. The drama surely asks Athenians to contemplate the human cost of their political choices, choices that could be changed, as they were well aware. It is not every victorious imperial power that represents its own history as one of deeply guilty rapacity and crime, at a solemn civic festival where all adult citizens are invited to ponder future courses of conduct. (Would that the United States had such a festival.)

The play, then, puts the accent on blameworthy human action. And yet there is a sense in which it is bleaker, even, than Sophocles. The human passions that caused the Trojan War are displayed as permanent features of human nature, which are almost certain to prompt similar events in the future. Moreover, as the chorus addressed to Eros shows, the gods themselves are motivated by similar passions, and those large extremely powerful quasi-human beings will no doubt continue to wreak havoc in human life.

Could the power of reason help? The centerpiece of the drama is one of those displays of sophistic argument for which Euripides was so famous, an extended debate between Hecuba and Helen about Helen's proper punishment, carried out before Menelaus as judge. Hecuba clearly has the better of the argument. Is Menelaus listening at all? Clearly, he is looking. In one of the most bizarre moments in all Greek tragedy, Hecuba, pleased that Menelaus has condemned Helen to death, warns him not to let her travel home on the same ship with him. He replies: "What's the matter? Has she put on weight?" (*ti d'esti? meizon brithos ê paroith' echei?*) To which Hecuba can only reply, "There is no lover who does not go on loving." The handwriting is on the wall for justice, when passion is on the scene. Euripides has often been seen as a rationalist, who believes in the power of argument to change the world. I'd rather say that he is an extreme pessimist about reason's power to change the world. It can be there in its best form, and yet *erôs* carries the day.

Thus the play draws near to Williams, by portraying a world in which the badness inherent in human beings will continue to create "horrors," and there is virtually nothing to be done about this. It gives an account of the genesis of the "horrors" that is quite different from Williams', placing the accent on human motives, but the pessimism is almost as great.

Nonetheless, I would say that the play does not in the end display human beings as powerless against their own darkest tendencies. First, there is the fact that some people in this play have managed to become good: all the women excepting Helen, and, to some extent, the Greek herald Talthybius, who knuckles under and serves the Greeks' horrendous purposes, but with decency and considerable reluctance. What can these good people do in a world run by powerful bad people? Well, since the characters of the play are all powerless, the whole action of the play, insofar as it is action, is a variegated display of the possibilities of powerless people. They can, as they do, love one another and show one another loyalty and kindness. They can do things with dignity rather than simply falling apart. In the case of Talthybius, they can arrange for the grim events to be carried out a little bit less grimly, with decency and respect for the customs of Trojan burial.

Most of all, they can talk: they can name the wrongs done to them, accuse those who wrong them, and carry those accusations into the record of history.[55] At the play's end, the Chorus says, "The name of our land has been wiped out." But of course it hasn't, and the audience would immediately recognize the fact. The Trojan protest against Greek injustice lingers on, haunting the Greek imagination of a Greek poet, several hundred years after the remembered event, at the Greater Dionysia, most solemn civic festival of the most powerful of Greek cities. When, at the play's very end, Hecuba, addressing her aged body, asks it to move forward, and the Chorus concludes, "Alas for our city, but nonetheless, put your foot forward toward the Greek fleet," (*prophere podos son epi platos Achaiôn*), the very meter, full of resolutions, shows that these women are on the move, a force in history, not dead yet. In the end, then, they carve out a space for something like action, even in their situation of extreme powerlessness. The very fact of the play's performance testifies to their (limited) success.

I would argue, then, broadening and to some extent countering Williams' account, that the "stark fictions" of the Greeks typically challenge their audience to difficult reflections about the causes of disaster: is the cause immutable necessity, or is it malice and folly? Where should we draw the line between the one and the other? We gain understanding from the subtle and frequently indeterminate way in which tragedies pose that question, and from the challenges they give us to confront the role of blameworthy agency even in matters (such as war, and rape, and slavery) that seem as natural as breathing. We must never forget that tragedies were vehicles of political deliberation and reflection at a sacred civic festival – in a city that held its empire as a "tyranny" and killed countless innocent people. For that audience, tragedy did not bring the good news of resignation; it brought the bad news of self-examination and change.

To put it another way, when, with the tragedies, we progress beyond a naively optimistic view of the world, we are not brought directly to pessimism – or, if we are brought there, we are also brought beyond it, into a more complicated ethical terrain, in which we cannot relax our efforts for a moment, since it is never clear in advance what the good will can do to mitigate the "horrors."

In short, instead of conceding the part of ethical space within which tragedies occur to implacable necessity or fate, tragedies often challenge their audience to inhabit it actively, as a contested place of moral struggle, a place in which virtue might possibly in some cases prevail over the caprices of amoral power, and in which, even if it does not prevail, it may still shine through for its own sake. In our contemporary world, in which it is a good assumption that most of the starvation and much of the other misery we witness is the result of culpable negligence by the powerful, resignation would, again, be relatively good news for the powerful, letting them off the hook. But the truthful news of Greek tragedy, for us, as for the Athenians, is far worse than that: for the bad news is that we are as culpable as Zeus in the *Trachiniai*, and the Greek generals in *The Trojan Women*, and Odysseus in *Philoctetes*, and many other gods and mortals at many times and places – unless and until we throw off our laziness and selfish ambition and obtuseness and ask ourselves how the harms we witness might have been prevented. It is this injunction to a socially active compassion, in league with justice, and drawing on the resources of an adult non-naïve sort of hope, that Williams omits from his story of Greek tragedy. And that, for me, means that his story of the bad is just too good to be true.

IV A contemporary stark fiction?

Sometimes the very remoteness of the Greek dramas helps us read them well. At other times, however, remoteness does not help, for distance can mask the element of choice and blameworthy human action, making everything look necessary. I believe that something like this happened in Williams' reading of Sophocles. I turn, then, to a stark fiction set in today's world, the short story "Giribala" by the Bengali writer Mahasweta Devi, first published in 1985.[56] The story fits Williams' category both in style and in content. It is written very sparingly, with little attention devoted to thick details of character and social circumstance, although social attitudes do play a more central role, perhaps, than they do in most tragedies. The protagonists's subjection to the operations of forces outside her control is the story's primary theme. In many respects the story resembles *The Trojan Women*, and might even have been written with that paradigm in view. In another way, her vulnerability resembles that of Deianeira.

Giribala, a girl from a poor rural village, was married off by her parents at the age of 14. We learn that she has no very distinctive qualities excepting her "lovely eyes."[57] People, including her own parents, treat her as an object of economic exchange. "Nobody ever imagined that she could think on her own, let alone act on her own thought."[58] Like the Trojan women, like countless women in many times and places, she is considered to be a pawn of destiny, rather than an agent.

Giri's husband Aulchand turns out to be a weak and venal man, something of a scoundrel, though not profoundly evil. At every stage, she encounters both chance and necessity. She has no choice about whether or whom to marry, she has no choice about where to live and work. She has no choice about whether to have sex with her husband. Nonetheless, at each stage she seizes hold of agency within the narrow confines of her life. Early in the marriage, Giri is preoccupied with hiding her silver ornaments and hoarding her slender savings, so that Aulchand cannot squander them. Later, she takes on extra work at the landlord's home for herself and her daughters. After the birth of the fourth child, she gets herself sterilized without Aulchand's consent. These thin slices of agency do little, however, to shape the larger facts of her life. She is still poor, malnourished, unable to control the family's finances so that their condition would really improve.

When her first daughter reaches adolescence, her husband discovers a new source of money: he sells his own child to a trafficker, under pretense of marriage. Giri discovers the fraud too late, and her efforts to get the police to take interest in the matter are fruitless. Nonetheless, she is determined to shelter the second daughter. Her vigilance only makes the husband's ruses more cunning, and soon the second daughter, too, is gone into the sex trade. Whenever these terrible things happen, people pull out the old Bengali saying, "A daughter born, To husband or death, She's already gone" – and they refuse to take action. The police wouldn't help anyway, they say, and there's really nothing we can do.

Giri, however, won't let her life be utterly determined by the fatalism of those around her. One day she sees her husband eyeing the third daughter, and she begins thinking. "Giri silently held those striking eyes of hers steadily on Aulchand's face, longer than she had ever done before."[59] The next morning she is missing. With the third daughter on her hip and the boy holding her hand, she has walked down the road and caught the morning bus into the city. She leaves her husband a message: she is going to do domestic work in the city to feed and raise the remaining children, and if he ever comes looking for her she will put her neck under a train.

People are stunned. How could a woman do something like that? They decide that she, not her husband, is the bad one. "Arriving at this conclusion seemed to produce some kind of relief for their troubled minds."[60] Here's the end of the story:

> And Giribala? Walking down the unfamiliar roads and holding Maruni on her hip and Rajib by the hand, Giribala only regretted that she had not done this before. If she had left earlier, then Beli would not have been lost, then Pori would not have been lost. If only she had had this courage earlier, her two daughters might have been saved.
>
> As this thought grew insistent and hammered inside her brain, hot tears flooded her face and blurred her vision. But she did not stop even to wipe her tears. She just kept walking.

The story certainly presents us with "horrors" of many kinds, including most of the kinds that *The Trojan Women* depicts, plus the horrors of malnutrition, marriage without consent, and extreme poverty that it does not mention. The fact that, unlike Greek dramas, the story concerns poor people makes it possible, indeed, for it to include a wider range of horrors than tragedies typically can. What is very clear, however, is that the fatalistic response that says, "all this is just the necessity of a woman's life" is a bogus response, one that the story ultimately repudiates as corrupt, an accomplice of malice and cruelty. To think that way about oneself or those close to one is to refuse to be an agent. To say that about women's lives is to refuse to see them as agents.

Now of course the Williamsian agent, as I've said, could still be active. But she would have to be active in a way that accepts, rather than rebuts, the common sayings about a woman's life, namely that it is entirely circumscribed by chance and necessity. She would be active, then, in a Sisyphean way, having understood that there is no changing the parameters of her existence. What the story shows us is that this very attitude is deeply corrupt and corrupting, deforming one's sense of what can be achieved and the motives that strain toward achievement.

Bleak though her lot is, there are pockets of space in Giribala's existence all along, and she sees at the end that she might have made more of them earlier, had she not believed the common clichés about chance and necessity. Finally, she takes the truly radical step of breaking out of her context altogether. It's not as if she's going off to limitless possibility and freedom; her new life will be hard and, in its way, oppressive. But it will not contain her husband's machinations, it will almost certainly contain alternatives other than sex work for Maruni, and it may even include school for both Maruni and Rajib. The story supports Giribala's choice to make the most of her bleak lot, as, rather like the Greek women marching with dignity toward the Greek ships, she marches down the road, too busy to wipe away her tears.

The story prompts further thoughts: how might the grimmer aspects of Giribala's very common story have been prevented by better political deliberation? A reader knowledgeable about the local context would at this point have many useful thoughts. Legal remedies can be of at least some help – aggressive enforcement of laws against trafficking; perhaps the decriminalization and unionization of sex work, which has been tried in West Bengal with some success; better police education; better enforcement of laws regarding marital age and marital consent; more efforts to open education to the working poor. More important than these, the story suggests, will be measures that simply go directly to female agency and try to enhance that. Microcredit schemes that put women in charge of their own economic lives are strongly suggested. I've seen women's banks in West Bengal (and elsewhere) where many young Giris tell their stories, proudly displaying the goats, or other cottage industries, through which they have earned a measure of independence and even gained some education for themselves.

Maybe such practical details, or even the inspiration to ponder them, would suffice to make the story no longer "stark" in Williams' sense. But if "stark" means "so abstract that we cannot think of any useful practical response," then I begin to lose interest in the category of "stark." *The Trojan Women* was not "stark" in that sense, generalized though its predicaments were: as I've said, it was clearly intended to prompt rather concrete reflections about just conduct to the vanquished in wartime, pertinent to the Melos situation.

I believe that Williams would not have liked "Giribala." He had an aesthetic preference for the unalterable, and this story's relentlessly practical questioning, as it asks, and asks us to ask, "What can be changed? How can it be changed? Why aren't we changing it?" would probably have struck him as boring. I do not find it boring. I believe that it is exciting to think how we might create a space for hope in the middle of ugliness. Indeed, it is the contemplation of the unalterable that I find closer to being boring, since what is human life, anyway, but doing the best one can with the options one actually has? This aesthetic difference marks, I believe, a deep difference between Williams' sense of life and my own. To return to our theme, however, I believe that "Giribala" lies far closer to the Greek tragic tradition than Williams would have acknowledged.

Is the story non-tragic because it does not end badly, or, at least, not as badly as it began? Well, that's true of a good many of the plays that the Greeks called "tragedies." Indeed, Aristotle preferred the type where the reversal averted a catastrophe, a type that is prominently found in Euripides.[61] What "tragic" means, indeed, is very likely something just ever so slightly optimistic, even "progressive." If Walter Burkert is correct, "song of the goat" alludes to the fact that the Greeks now sacrifice goats, whereas at some earlier time they sacrificed human beings. Well, that's a type of progress, and, if Burkert is right, tragedy alludes to that progress – while revealing at the same time how easy it is for human beings to slip back into the old ways of atrocity.[62]

V The aesthetics of despair?

Nietzsche wrote that when a philosopher harps very insistently on a theme, that shows us that there is a danger that something else is about to "play the master." Nietzsche was talking about rationalists and their desire to suppress the irrational passions that threatened to take over, by harping again and again on the power of reason. But his insight may be applied elsewhere. When Williams denigrated the aspirations of philosophers to "make the world safe for well-intentioned people" and harped so insistently on the value of an honest confrontation with the hopelessness of it all, what might have been in danger of playing the master? I believe that much of Williams' interest in Nietzschean pessimism and irrationalism, at this period in his work at least, was in the service of warding off a view of human prospects that verged on despair. I have argued that his reaction to "reality" lacked anger, and this is a general feature of his writing, at least at this time. Contempt, world-weariness, an irritability linked to the world-weariness – all this can be seen in his repudiation of the philosophers he criticizes. But we never see plain *anger*, the sense that wrong has been done and that one had better go out and right it. Anger, as Aristotle and the Stoics remind us, is not an entirely painful emotion, because at its root it is hopeful: it looks forward to the righting of the wrong that has taken place. I think Williams' non-angry attitude to tragedy was of a piece with his critique of the Enlightenment in the same essay: doing good for a bad world did not energize him, because his attitude to the world was at some deep level without hope. The world was a mess, and there was no saving or even improving it. It was childish, naïve, to suggest that improvement was possible. (His liberal politics were difficult to reconcile with this view, and this perhaps explains his increasing withdrawal from politics, and even political thinking, in later life, at least until the very end, in *Truth and Truthfulness*.)

Nietzsche called this attitude *amor fati*, and connected this embracing of necessity with a kind of cheerfulness, the cheerfulness that comes when we abandon the hope of real change. Similarly, what seems to energize this Williams essay, to provide its only measure of good cheer, is a kind of elegant, even cheerful, assertion of the hopelessness of things against the good-newsers, a sense that one had been honest where others are dishonest, that one had faced the worst with honesty and it has not destroyed one. This attitude is hard to argue against, since the world is indeed full of bad things. Perhaps Kant was right to say that one simply has to adopt some "practical postulates" of a more hopeful kind if one is to engage constructively in the world of human affairs. Certainly, however, the Greek tragedies I have discussed do not manifest the world as incapable of being changed, or make fun of the attitude that demands justice.

One could never get the better of Bernard Williams in an argument. He was always several steps ahead, modifying his position to circumnavigate the objection. Even now, when he cannot respond, his capacity for response is so powerfully present that all one can do is to pose to him some questions, such as:

Isn't it perhaps all right to try to engage one's philosophical energies so as to make things a little better in the world, and can't one do so without being duped by any teleology of progress? Or: isn't Kant's sort of "good news" worth working for, even if Hegel's sort may indeed be (at least partially) a delusion?

Isn't it not boring but rather exciting to see what one might do under the aegis of anger and hope? Or: Isn't Dickens more exciting, really, than Nietzsche? (I know he would have said "no" to that one: he would have liked Oscar Wilde's dictum, "One would have to have a heart of stone to read the death of Little Nell without laughing.")

Is despair possibly a sin, as well as a psychological problem?

It is but one mark of Williams' depth and greatness, as a philosopher and as a human being (as a philosopher who insisted on bringing his humanity into philosophy) that he understood those objections to himself, their human urgency, and the impossibility of answering them, except by living life and thought in one's own way.

Acknowledgments

I am grateful to John Deigh and Charles Larmore, to faculty members in the consortium for Graduate Study in ancient Greek and Roman Philosophy in the Greater Chicago Area, and to students in my seminar on Contemporary Virtue Ethics at Harvard University, spring 2007, for their comments on an earlier draft of this chapter, and to Valentina Urbanek for an illuminating presentation on the issues in that seminar. I am especially grateful to Daniel Callcut for his perceptive comments. I am sure that I have not answered all the questions they raised.

Notes

1 Related and in some cases overlapping ruminations about Williams are to be found in my "Tragedy and Justice: Bernard Williams Remembered," *The Boston Review* 28 (Oct./Nov. 2003), 35–9.
2 *Morality: An Introduction to Ethics* (New York: Harper Torchbooks, 1972), p. ix.
3 Ibid.
4 In *Problems of the Self* (Cambridge: Cambridge University Press, 1973), pp. 103–24.
5 Princeton, NJ: Princeton University Press, 2002.
6 See Nussbaum, "The Costs of Tragedy: Some Moral Limitations of Cost-Benefit Analysis," in Matthew D. Adler and Eric A. Posner (eds), *Cost-Benefit Analysis: Legal, Economic, and Philosophical Perspectives* (Chicago: University of Chicago Press, 2001), pp. 169–200.
7 "Philosophy," in M. I. Finley (ed.), *The Legacy of Greece: A New Appraisal* (Oxford: Oxford University Press, 1981), pp. 202–55, reprinted as "The Legacy of Greek Philosophy" in Williams, *The Sense of the Part: Essays in the History of Philosophy*, ed. Myles Burnyeat (Princeton, NJ: Princeton University Press, 2006), pp. 3–48.
8 *Moral Luck: Philosophical Papers 1973–1980* (Cambridge: Cambridge University Press, 1981).
9 *Shame and Necessity* (Berkeley, CA: University of California Press, 1993).
10 In *The Greeks and Us*, ed. R. B. Louden and P. Schollmeier (Chicago: University of Chicago Press, 1996), pp. 43–53, reprinted in Bernard Williams, *The Sense of the Past*, pp. 49–59. For ease of reference, I quote from the latter version, citing the essay as "Women of Trachis."
11 Williams, "Women of Trachis," p. 49.
12 See, for example, his famous remarks about the French Revolution in "The Contest of the Faculties," in Hans Reiss (ed.), *Kant's Political Writings* (Cambridge: Cambridge University Press, 1970), p. 182. Kant argues that the "universal yet disinterested sympathy" we see for the struggles of the French people against tyranny

> proves that mankind as a whole shares a certain character in common, and it also proves (because of its disinterestedness) that man has a moral character, or at least the makings of one. And this does not merely allow us to hope for human improvement; it is already a form of improvement in itself.

13 Williams at least appears to reject this idea in "Women of Trachis," p. 52, saying, "No good or bad news can be found in history or the actual balance of things at all." (The view is imputed to Kant, though Kant's actual view is more complicated, see n. 12 above and text below.)
14 Williams, "Women of Trachis," p. 52. Williams also speaks dismissively of Nietzsche's idea of affirming the "eternal recurrence" of the same events, "Women of Trachis," pp. 53–4. What I have called a Nietzschean turn in Williams did not extend to an embrace of this metaphysical fiction.
15 Williams, "Women of Trachis," p. 54.
16 Ibid., p. 55.
17 Williams' example here is Hardy's *Jude the Obscure*. His thought is presumably that novels grounded in the dailiness of social life have a hard time representing large cosmic forces.
18 Williams, "Women of Trachis," p. 56.
19 Ibid.
20 Ibid.

21 Ibid., p. 58, Cf. p. 51.
22 Ibid., p. 56. Cf. "extreme, undeserved, and uncompensated suffering," (Williams, "Women of Trachis," p. 58), "unredeemed and hideous suffering" (Williams, "Women of Trachis," p. 57).
23 Ibid., pp. 58–9.
24 Ibid., p. 59.
25 Ibid.
26 Ibid.
27 Ibid. (This is the last sentence of the article.)
28 A. Schopenhauer, *The World as Will and Representation*, trans. E. J. Payne (New York: Dover, 1969), vol. I, pp. 252–3.
29 Like the play, Williams' account of it focuses on a life that is ending in agonizing pain: the story of Heracles' death, he notes, has been adjusted "in order to remove any hint of glory from it, to leave it as nothing but unredeemed and hideous suffering" (Williams, "Women of Trachis," p. 57). On p. 51, discussing Hegel's view of history, he speaks of "the horrors which underlie every human achievement"; here the focus seems broader, including human bad behavior as well as chance and necessity; Williams never returns, however, to this broader conception of what "horrors" include. And he announces that he has chosen the "Women of Trachis" precisely because it brackets all other complexities in order to focus on "leaving in the starkest relief its extreme, undeserved, and uncompensated suffering" on page 58. What about Williams' well-known views about death in "The Makropulos Case: Reflections on the Tedium of Immortality," (*Problems of the Self* [Cambridge: Cambridge University Press, 1973], pp. 82–100)? The idea that one would lose the will to live out of boredom has always struck me as a strange one, and one can only say that views that make something good out of death tend to become less attractive to their authors over time: see my discussion of Williams in my reply to John Fisher, "Replies," in a special issue on my work, *The Journal of Ethics* 10 (2006), 463–506.
30 Rich countries are not immune from this sort of bad behavior: the inequalities in basic health care in the U.S. cause many people to die who might otherwise live.
31 *De Officiis*, I.28–30.
32 Of course, the tag is hyperbolic, in the sense that we are all mortal and subject to illness and pain; but it seems wrong to stop trying to combat these remaining causes of non-safety.
33 To those who object that Williams the man pursued constructive political engagement in many ways, working on the Royal Commission on Gambling and chairing the Royal Commission on Pornography, I can reply, first, that there need be no harmony between conduct and expressed philosophical views; and, second, that the objectors would do well to ponder chronology. Williams' practical engagements were, by his own account, dismal failures and futilities: the report on pornography that he labored for years to produce was promptly shelved when Thatcher won the election. Certainly that experience might well incline one to a Sisyphean view of political engagement.
34 I mean that we don't have to solve the free-will problem in order to ask the practical question. Of course, that very claim may be thought metaphysical by some.
35 See John J. Winkler, "The Ephebes' Song: *Tragôidia* and *Polis*," *Representations* 11 (1985), 26–62.
36 See, for example, J. Peter Euben, *Corrupting Youth: Political Education and Democratic Culture* (Princeton, NJ: Princeton University Press, 1997); Euben (ed.), *Greek Tragedy and Political Theory* (Berkeley, CA: University of California Press,

1986), a wide-ranging collection of essays; Danielle Allen, *Talking to Strangers* (Chicago: University of Chicago Press, 2004), especially pp. 119–59.

37 Williams briefly acknowledges this point in "Women of Trachis" on p. 59, but he never integrates that remark into his overall discussion of "necessity."

38 We might say that the new name indicates a commitment to make the world safe (or at least safer) for well-disposed people: they won't be hounded for inherited blood-guilt.

39 Not surprisingly, this is Williams' focus in his brief mention of the play in "Women of Trachis," on p. 56, speaking of "its display of hideous and destructive physical agony."

40 As described by Dio Chrysostom, discourses 52 (describing how he read all three plays on a summer afternoon) and 59 (giving a close paraphrase of the opening of Euripides' play). Both plays preceded that of Sophocles in date (Euripides' was in 431, Sophocles' in 409); thus we see Sophocles' choices against the background they established. In both other plays, the Chorus consists of inhabitants of Lemnos; in Sophocles', the Chorus consists of sailors on the arriving ship.

41 See my "Consequences and Character in Sophocles' *Philoctetes*," *Philosophy and Literature* 1 (1972); I return to the play, focusing on the emotion of compassion, in "The Morality of Pity: Sophocles' *Philoctetes* and the European Stoics," forthcoming in Rita Felski (ed.), *Rethinking Tragedy* (Baltimore, MD: Johns Hopkins University Press, 2007).

42 See Stephen Halliwell, *The Aesthetics of Mimesis* (Princeton, NJ: Princeton University Press, 2002), p. 208; an influential earlier discussion of the play is in Gotthold Ephraim Lessing, *Laocoon: An Essay upon the Limits of Painting and Poetry* (originally publication 1766), trans. Ellen Frothingham (New York: Farrar, Straus and Giroux, 1968).

43 Sophocles. *Philoctetes*, lines 1445–7.

44 Ibid., lines 1466–8.

45 My analysis of the play in *The Fragility of Goodness: Luck and Ethics in Greek Tragedy and Philosophy* (Cambridge: Cambridge University Press, 1986, 2nd edn, 2001), Chapter 3, is the basis for these remarks.

46 See my discussion in *The Fragility of Goodness*, Chapter 3.

47 I argue that Hegel's view is not incompatible with seeing Antigone as, in some important ways, morally superior to Creon.

48 See my *Liberty of Conscience: In Defense of America's Tradition of Religious Equality* (New York: Basic Books, 2008), Chapter 4. My analysis of the U.S. law of religion-based "accommodation" in that chapter starts with the *Antigone*.

49 Lloyd-Jones's translation, in *Sophocles*, vol. 2, Loeb Classical Library (Cambridge, MA: Harvard University Press, 1994), pp. 791–2.

50 Ibid., pp. 586–7.

51 In most respects I follow Lloyd-Jones's literal prose version in the new Loeb Sophocles (above n. 49), but I restore the approximate line-divisions of the poetry, for ease of comparison with the version quoted by Williams, and I have changed a few words.

52 He does, however, briefly mention it in "Women of Trachis" on page 58, discussing the non-understanding of the gods.

53 See Aristotle, *Nicomachean Ethics* 1100b30: "Nonetheless, even in the midst of these things [pains and misfortunes], the noble shines through."

54 In his *Autobiography*, Nehru describes an encounter with General Dyer on a train in 1919 (Jawaharlal Nehru, *An Autobiography*, Centenary edition [Delhi: Oxford University Press, 1985, original publication 1936], pp. 42–3). Unobserved, the

young Nehru took the vacant upper berth of a crowded compartment and could not help overhearing the loud conversation of a group of British officers:

> One of them was holding forth in an aggressive and triumphant tone and soon I discovered that he was Dyer, the hero of Jallianwala Bagh, and he was describing his Amritsar experiences. He pointed out how he had the whole town at his mercy and he had felt like reducing the rebellious city to a heap of ashes, but he took pity on it and refrained ... I was greatly shocked to hear his conversation and to observe his callous manner. He descended at Delhi station in pyjamas with bright pink stripes, and a dressing-gown.

If the last touch belongs more to Aristophanes (Poseidon at the end of the *Birds* is about right), the rest is on all fours with Euripides. Indeed, Dyer's speech could have been extracted from the opening dialogue of the gods in *The Trojan Women*. (Once again: think of a play that put Jesus in pink striped pajamas, and you will see the large difference between Greek piety and its Christian analogue.)

55 At least in *Truth and Truthfulness* (Princeton, NJ: Princeton University Press, 2002), Williams appears to think this an important human endeavor.
56 The story is translated by Kalpana Bardhan in her *Of Women, Outcastes, Peasants, and Rebels: A Selection of Bengali Short Stories* (Berkeley, CA: University of California Press, 1990), pp. 272–89.
57 Ibid., p. 272.
58 Ibid.
59 Ibid., p. 289.
60 Ibid.
61 See Anne Pippin Burnett, *Catastrophe Survived: Euripides' Plays of Mixed Reversal* (Oxford: Clarendon Press, 1971).
62 Burkert, "Greek Tragedy and Sacrificial Ritual," *Greek, Roman, and Byzantine Studies* 7 (1966), pp. 87–121.

11

AGAINST POLITICAL LUCK

Christopher Kutz

But what awaits us tomorrow? A hundred millions of the most diverse contingencies, which will determine on the instant whether they run or we do;
whether one man is killed and then another; but all that's being done now is
mere child's play.

(Prince Andrei to Timohin, *War and Peace*)[1]

I Introduction: the ubiquity of luck

Politics is permeated by luck. Political action is messy by nature, involving
the intersecting lives and acts of many people and institutions. As a consequence, policy initiatives and political gambits succeed or fail not simply
on the basis of good intentions and wise planning, but because of the
myriad contingencies that affect any large-scale endeavour. A strong rain in
a swing state can affect the turnout of one set of partisans rather than
another at an election. International crises determine the options open to
political leaders. Domestic policy reform succeeds or fails because chance
alignments of interests and judgements of public sentiment provide either
the force to drive past obstacles, or make those obstacles impassable. And,
more controversially, a general's head cold might cause misjudgements at a
crucial battle, leading to the end of an empire rather than its extension.

To say that politics, then, is a domain of luck is to state a triviality.
Politics is a branch of life, and like all life it is inhabited by fleeting contingency as much (or more) as inevitability. But politics is not just impersonal poll results, military successes, and policy changes. Politics is an
activity of persons – persons with moral concerns and moral character –
and it is impelled and sustained by their concern for their values, goals, and
reputations. To speak of political luck in relation to political agency is not
just to point in the direction of the contingency of outcome, or *fortuna*, to
use Machiavelli's famous term, but in the direction of evaluation, of both
the outcomes and the agents who produce them. Politicians who insist,
despite the disastrous news of the day, that they shall be vindicated by history, gesture hopefully in this direction, that a lucky outcome will save their

legacy; whereas the losers of history seem already to have received luck's judgement. To return to Machiavelli, the question is not just whether a politician's *virtù*, or skill, can dominate *fortuna*, but whether *fortuna*, for its part, can determine *virtù*.

And yet here we seem back to a triviality. Of course, the politician's hopes and fears are well founded. As a matter of brute fact, we heap rewards on the lucky winners of historical gambles (if only posthumously) and scorn on the losers. Some of these rewards and punishments are as direct as triumphal laurels and ritual humiliations. But they also take subtler form, through a form of cognitive error: the over-attribution of success or failure to the inherent qualities and aptitudes of the actor, rather than the situation. While Napoleon may be no hero to his valet, his heroism in the eyes of the many confounds success with virtue.

These observations about our social practices and biases in awarding political honour and disgrace – in reflecting political luck, in this thin sense – mirror our practices in interpersonal morality. The twin papers by Bernard Williams and Thomas Nagel that launched the discussion of luck in morality can be seen as trying to extract strong normative conclusions from these sociological commonplaces, moving from the *is* of moral psychology to the *ought* of moral evaluation. In particular, both Williams and Nagel sought to demonstrate, or at least illuminate, a number of related theses (not all clearly laid out, to be sure). These theses include at least the following:

1   Some acts depend for their justification, or their absence of justification, upon facts which only obtain subsequently and in virtue of contingent outcomes. Thus, luck can retrospectively validate or invalidate agent choice.
2   Among these post-justified acts are those grounded in first-personal practical judgements, whose content involves the basic parameters and motivating ideals of the agent's life. (These two points reflect Williams' particular interests.)
3   Agents' accountability for acts – the degree of praise or blame they are due – depends in part on the actual, contingent consequences of those acts. Thus, a theory of accountability cannot be exclusively intentionalist. (This thesis is emphasized by Nagel.)
4   Since the normative ("ethical", in Williams' preferred sense) values relevant to assessing persons is partly a function of external, contingent factors, exhausted neither by good intentions nor ex ante judgements, a moral theory that vests value solely in internal qualities will be inadequate to ethical reality (and may also be incoherent in its own terms).

Taken together, these theses amount to a radical challenge to intention- or reason based moral theory of a roughly Kantian sort. For if a large class of normative judgements – What should I do? How should I respond to what has happened? How bad is what I have done? – are meant to be products of reason but subject to fortune, then moral theory looks more like the weather forecast than the Ten Commandments. Morality might instead offer good advice for the future, and retrospective rationalizing descriptions, but the moral value of one's acts, hence one's life, remains fortune's hostage. So, at least, Williams and Nagel suggest, in offering instead a less coherent but descriptively more apt account of the interplay of will and circumstance in ethical judgement and response.

My focus in this chapter will be only obliquely on the merits of these theses in relation to the claims of intention-based moral theories. Instead, I want to pursue the particular relation of politics to luck, and in so doing to pay particular attention to Williams' excavation of the concept. First, I offer a charitable construction of the concept of moral luck, and while I will not pretend confidence that the conception can withstand all objections, I believe it can be rendered sufficiently coherent and attractive such that its role in our everyday moral practices can be tolerated. (Indeed, as Nagel and Williams both say, purging everyday morality of luck would be far more disruptive, whatever the force of the arguments for the purge.)

I then turn to the more dramatic form that claims of outcome-dependence can take in politics. In particular, when politicians absorb the possibility of political luck into their own deliberations, they set the scene for great geopolitical gambits, as the predicate for historical grandeur. As such, I want to argue, the concept of political luck is itself deeply pernicious, as it can feed a dangerous monomania all too common in historical tragedy. The problem is not with outcome-dependence itself, but in the way in which contemplation of its possibility skews practical judgement past what reason would demand.

My path to these conclusions is as follows. Sections II and III examine Nagel's and Williams' accounts of moral luck, respectively, with an eye to rendering them plausible as philosophical accounts, and not merely descriptions of our practices. Section IV extends the moral account to political life, and makes extended use of a contemporary foreign policy adventure put in terms of a historical gamble: the 2003 invasion of Iraq. Section V concludes with a caution about the distorting effects of political luck on political agency.

II Luck and blame: Nagel

Williams and Nagel support their claim for the radical character of luck more by example than argument – albeit, examples of quite different character. Nagel's central examples of outcome-dependent moral assessment concern either comparisons between equally reckless actors, only one of whom actually causes harm; or well-intentioned political actors whose gambits, like the Decembrists' failed revolt against the Czar, simply enable tragedy. According to Nagel, while the *mens rea* (intentions, or levels of awareness of the risk) of the reckless actors might be equivalent, the moral value of what they have done is not equivalent: "If one negligently leaves the bath running with the baby in it, one will realize, as one bounds up the stairs toward the bathroom, one has done something awful, whereas if it has not, one has merely been careless."[2] Similarly for the well-intentioned failures:

> If the American Revolution had been a bloody failure resulting in greater repression, then Jefferson, Franklin and Washington would still have made a noble attempt, and might not even have had to regret it on their way to the scaffold, but they would also have had to blame themselves for what they had helped bring on their compatriots.[3]

Nagel is not simply making the point that something worse has happened in the unfortunate cases, namely death. Rather, because something worse has happened, the actor has *done* something worse, and that therefore he warrants greater reproach – at least from himself. Intuitions might well vary with this case, and one might wonder whether the difficulty of psychologically separating the badness of the outcome from the wrongness of the conduct had led Nagel to an erroneous metaphysical conclusion. Let us therefore put aside the difficult metaphysical question whether an act, separated in time from its consequence, can change in normative value as a result of the consequence – say, going from careless to awful. It will certainly be true that reactions to that act – the way it lingers as a shameful memory, or the antipathy it arouses in others – are dramatically inflected by the consequences.

Of course, one can imagine a dialectic seeking to move the two cases together, to the effect that on reflection, one ought to be more horrified by even harmless negligence, or less moved by actual outcomes.[4] On this line of thought, those reckless drivers who actually cause harm give proof positive of the dangerousness of their conduct, while our grounds for judging the potential dangerousness of the harmless driver are usually far weaker. But, as Nagel remarks, the dialectic is likely to leave space between the assessments of the two drivers.[5] If one accepts the controversial point that our reflectively stabilized practices of accountability are, at bottom, the foundation of our norms of accountability, then outcomes will warrant differing responses – that actors' deserts vary with the consequences of their acts. (Below, in Section IV, I will try to make the case for this thesis.) Put aside the merits of the claim for the moment, however. As a matter of social practice, it will be simply true that we respond to agents partly in terms of the outcomes they produce; and any conception of morality that fails to acknowledge this feature of our practice would be revisionary enough of our entrenched reactive attitudes that it could not be accepted as an interpretation of our practices. To be sure, intent and motive might be as relevant to retrospective moral assessments as they are to legal assessments. Discovery, for example, that a lethally reckless driver was rushing a loved one to the hospital would change one's assessment relative to a non-lethal reckless driver who was simply enjoying the imposition of risk on others. In such a case, it would not be true (much less clearly true, ex ante, as Nagel suggests) that the first driver had done something far worse than the second.

Left like this, then, Nagel's account of moral luck is properly a theory of retrospective accountability rather than a guide to practical reasoning. The philosophical implications of the claim still run deep, for to ground accountability even partly on outcome rather than intent is to deny the sufficiency of the usual mentalistic apparatus of normative assessment. And this, as we have seen, is to deny what many have considered a deeply seductive image of morality, as a form of judgement concerning what is up to us, rather than what merely happens. As a normative thesis, Nagel's view might also be seen as underwriting a version of victors' justice, legitimating the celebrations of historical triumphs that conveniently excise the harms and wrongs done along the way. But it is also worth noting what it does not revise: the permissions and constraints that feature ex ante, at the point of decisionmaking. For there is nothing in Nagel's account to suggest that, absent extenuating circumstances, the possibility of mitigated blame in the event of success should make an otherwise impermissible act appropriate. While I might feel relief, say, that my failure to check behind the car before backing out led to no tragedy, there's no symmetrical compensation at the advance end, except in the obvious sense that one can permissibly engage in risky behaviour (driving) but not behaviour that will certainly produce an identifiable harm. But I cannot say to myself in advance that if no harm happens, then the risk I took was clearly justified.

I will discuss below, in Part IV, more direct applications to politics. The first application, however, is straightforward: the practice of assessing political leaders, like other actors, is clearly outcome-dependent. To the extent political leaders concern themselves with their place in historical memory – which is to say, all of them, all the time – they recognize that success washes clean the reputational dirt earned achieving victory. Whether they should make use of this truth is another matter.

III Luck and choice: Williams

Williams situates his discussion of moral luck very differently, not in terms of norms of reproach or the underlying value of acts, but on the question of how, ex ante, first-person practical judgements can be justified and how they can be unjustified. His famous example is a fictionalized painter, Gauguin, who decides that the possibility of realizing "his gifts as a painter" requires him to leave his family to destitution in Paris, while he sails to Tahiti.[6] Gauguin recognizes the cost to his family, and even sees it as a moral cost; but he weighs this cost against the possibility of becoming what he most wants to be. The question for Gauguin, and for Williams, is whether he can justify the choice to himself – that is, justify imposing certain costs on his family, in exchange for uncertain aesthetic and reputational success. (Williams, in a puzzling passage I take up below, says that a justification for Gauguin in terms of these values need not justify him to his family, nor to us.) For Williams stipulates that Gauguin does not know whether he has talent sufficient to justify the act – or even if he can be said, retrospectively, to know that he has the talent, he does not know this before he leaves.

Williams' answer is no less perplexing for its familiarity in the domain of politics: eventual success, and only that, will justify Gauguin's choice. If Gauguin is able to realize the paintings he believes he can produce, then and only then will it have been worthwhile to him to strand his family. But without artistic triumph, Gauguin by his own lights will have unjustifiably betrayed those he loves.[7] On the other hand, according to Williams, there are distinctions among the possibilities of failure. While certain "extrinsic," or coincidental failures in the project, such as an accident en route, or illness, will not undermine the justification for the act, an "intrinsic" basis for the failure – namely, a lack of talent – will cause the initial act to become "unjustified."[8]

How can this be so? It is hardly priggish to wonder, first, how aesthetic triumph can outweigh betraying vulnerable members of one's families – whether any sort of comparability between the values is possible. After all, one might think, as we non-relatives of Gauguin's perhaps do, that he might have been a very bad man and a very good painter.[9] Moralists might go on to wonder in what sense Gauguin's decision could be justified at all, if it could not be justified to those most closely affected by it. Put aside for the moment, however, these concerns about the nature of moral value and the relation to practical justification – below I will offer some defences of these claims. The truly puzzling claim is how a choice can move from being neither justified nor unjustified at the outset, to being justified or unjustified in virtue of its outcome. The question is not whether there is, in the abstract, logical space for "neither-justified-nor-unjustified" verdict; ternary logics are well developed to deal with such possibilities. Although the intermediate verdict is usually interpreted as "unknown" in such logics, and thus as a matter of epistemology, not metaphysics, intermediate truth values are defensible. But it is not clear whether intermediate truth values are consistent with the two models of rational decisionmaking at hand: expected-utility maximization and deontological/principle-based.

Take deontological, principle-based decisionmaking first. Assuming that operative principles can be determined, there would seem to be no problem in applying such a perspective ex ante. Either it will be the case that, even in conditions of uncertainty, it is permissible to inflict certain harms and betray trusts for the sake of possible personal achievements or it will not be permissible. It is hard to see, as Williams says, how the permissibility branch could be maintained: how, that is, conditions could be specified which would render inflicting such harms permissible, ex ante. For example, if what is at stake, per hypothesis, is the thought that some possible aesthetic gains can offset moral injuries, then the argument for permissibility in a deontological framework, no less than in a utilitarian one, must go by way of assumptions about the probability of producing those gains. Such principles would, presumably, license a range of gambles subject to deontic thresholds: one might inflict such and such a harm (but nothing worse), provided the gains to be expected are of such a character, and there is some sufficient likelihood of their being realized. If the conditions are met, and Gauguin can permissibly inflict these harms, then he is warranted in acting as he does, and his eventual triumph is gravy – a matter of supererogatory value. Apart from the issue of value commensurability, the situation is simply like that of any well-intentioned soul whose attempt to act rightly produces a beneficial outcome.

It may well be true, as Williams says, that no set of plausible principles could be defined, for this or any comparable case involving hugely uncertain, ego-driven self-reflexive assessments: can I be a great artist, a hero to my cause, etc? Any such principles would fall prey in their subjective variant to problems of moral hazard (namely, how "reasonably" can one assess one's prospects for greatness) or, on their objective variant of "actual" potential greatness, simply be inapplicable.[10] But if, in fact, no plausible set of permitting conditions can be defined, then the conclusion that most readily follows is that a deontological framework would simply forbid Gauguin's choice, not that deontology must instead struggle to integrate the notion of prior permission based on retrospective justification. (Though one might conclude independently, so much the worse for deontology, if one rejects its insistence on the priority of moral claims.) There seems to be no pressure from within deontology for a suspended judgement, that Gauguin's act is neither justified nor unjustified, nor that it could be unjustified ex ante, and somehow justified ex post. Rather, all pressures in the direction of accommodating Gauguin's choice can be accounted for at the level of reasoning about the operative scope of the relevant principles. There simply is no gap for retrospective justification to fill.

It is also hard to pay mind to a justificatory gap in an expected utility framework. According to expected utility theory, an act is justified when the benefits (utility gains) it could bring, discounted by their improbability, exceed the costs it could impose, discounted by their improbability. The risk of failure ex post is thus calculated into the ex ante judgement. Put aside, again, the problem of commensurating and ranking aesthetic gains against personal betrayals. Assuming, despite the implausibilities mentioned above, that probabilities and values can be assigned to Gauguin's aspirations towards greatness, then it will either be the case, ex ante, that his gamble is rationally justified, or it will not. Nothing that happens once the die is cast can subvert the initial judgement, except insofar as it reveals misestimates of the values or probabilities. One might regret the loss taken on a rational financial gamble, say, an expensive raffle ticket whose discounted potential value nonetheless exceeded its cost. And one might rejoice in the winnings from a raffle ticket, whose expected value is significantly exceeded by its cost. But it would clearly be an error to think that the outcome, either way, affected the justifiability of taking the gamble in the first place – or, more radically – to think that the rationality of the act could be an open question, until matters are resolved.[11]

Williams' specific complaint about utilitarianism, in this context, is confusing. Apart from the important point that any attempt to fit the relevant values into the utilitarian framework will inevitably be either handwaving or vulgar reductionism, he says that utilitarianism also fails, importantly, to distinguish between different types of failures: namely, the "intrinsic" failures I mentioned above, rooted in the agent's own incapacity (despite his hopes), and "extrinsic," accidental failures.[12] Presumably Williams means that an expected utility framework can at best only price out, and thus accommodate, extrinsic failures, which do not "unjustify" the ex ante gamble, but rather treat it as the downside already taken into account. He does not spell out the difference made by intrinsic failures, although the peculiar difficulties in assigning probabilities to such failures, mentioned above, are surely part of the story. To return to the raffle ticket example, one might say that while the failure of a ticket to be drawn is simply the rationally calculated downside of the risk, one's discovery that one has instead bought a counterfeit ticket could be counted as outside the zone of calculated risk, and undermines the project itself.[13] Or, to take Williams' other example, the doomed love affair of Anna Karenina and Vronsky: the lovers might have reckoned the risks of separation, poverty, or accidental death, but perhaps there was no way for them to estimate the actual hazard of the impossibility of a socially isolated love. The problem, in these cases, is not simply a paucity of data on the relevant risk, but the reflexive and even self-fulfilling nature of those risks, all of which go to pre-conditions of the possibility of success. Gauguin's actual shot at greatness is affected, for better or worse, by his ego; the love affair by the anxiety it arises in Anna; and perhaps even the prospect of buying a fake ticket by concerns of being gulled. The non-occurrence of these risks are, in effect, assumed as part of the baseline, and it is only from this baseline that agents can then rationally project their upsides and downsides. This offers an interpretation of

CHRISTOPHER KUTZ

Williams' remark that when a project fails intrinsically, the agent's hopes are "not just negated, but refuted": refuted because the gamble, in hindsight, never made sense at all.[14]

Such a distinction, between inestimable baseline probabilities, and estimable outcome probabilities, could if sustained make sense of Williams' rejection of a utilitarian framework. It is of course open to question whether the distinction can be maintained, or whether these baseline conditions can be subject to some rational estimation as well. In any event, I think there is something more telling to the distinction Williams has in mind, and which goes farther to explain the retrospective effects of the outcome. This is the dimension of reputation. For it is clear that what Gauguin fears is the obverse of what he hopes for: not quite that he will fail to produce great art, but that he will prove himself to be a pompous fool, a *schmuck*. And Anna's place in literary history is as a beautifully limned romantic idiot. What "refutes" the gamble, in these cases, is not the fact that the benefit did not materialize, nor even that the direct costs still have to be paid. Rather, it is the further effect on the self-understanding, as well as the public reputation, of the gambler. And this cost, of appearing foolish or, worse, actually being revealed as a fool, might be thought to lie beyond a utilitarian calculation which might otherwise justify the gamble.

These points might all be disputed, of course. A consequentialist might simply say that the cost of looking foolish is one among many risks to be accounted for, and if it is a bad enough risk, then it provides a reason not to engage in an otherwise rationally justified gamble. If it is bad enough, yet also so uncertain that a probability cannot be assigned, then there is a case for adopting a maximin strategy, precluding such a gamble (or, instead and to the same effect, applying the precautionary principle). But the expressive character of the stakes are nonetheless unruly with a utilitarian framework; and whether or not the costs can be balanced against the anticipated benefits upfront, the actual realization of the cost – the revelation of the failure – is such that it cannot be assuaged by pointing back towards the ex ante justification. Whether this is a consequence of the psychology of regret and shame, or of the nature of justification, is unclear. But Williams' point, and the distinction between intrinsic and extrinsic failure, clearly have some bite.

If Williams is right, then, that principle-based reasoning is too indeterminate, or otherwise inadequate, to accommodate outcome-sensitivity in cases where, intuitively, the prospect of the outcome matters to its ex ante permissibility; and if utilitarian reasoning is unable to accommodate certain kinds of outcomes as well – namely, the intrinsic failures – then it does look as though, at the least, life is capable of presenting us with a range of choices that can be regarded only ex post as clearly justified or unjustified. Of course, even if utilitarianism and deontological frameworks are unable to provide an ex ante justificatory framework for these cases – or, rather, even if the conclusions one might reach about justifiability are subject to ex

250

post revision – it does not follow that the strong thesis is true, that the decision to act, at the time, is neither justified nor unjustified. It could be the case that it is justified (or unjustified) by some further theory of choice, perhaps a non-reductive, all-in form of consequentialism which can also discount future expectations. As formal possibilities, such theories are easily described. But an air of hand-waving must surely accompany claims of their meaningfulness, unless and until the ex ante forms of reasoning are spelled out. At the least, it would seem Williams has shifted the burden of argument to those who would assert that such choices have a determinate form of justification.

But even if Williams has shifted the burden from one who would assert the possibility of an ex ante permission to risk current suffering for future happiness, one might still question whether the freedom of the choice is fully symmetrical. The notion of a radical, self-defining choice is a familiar one in existential literature, and it appeals to romantic longings of self-realization. But it has also often represented a desire to flee the ties of mundane obligation, and the fact that such an escape is fantasized does not mean it is acceptable. Claims of outcome-based justification might reflect nothing more than the desire to transcend those obligations, grounded in a self-absorbed psychology that revels in triumph and ignores the costs. I have already indicated concern that the notion of ex post unjustification has more to do with an agent's focus on his or her reputation, than on the status of norms governing his conduct. The idea of an intrinsic, choice-justifying success, grounded in the agent's own capacities (for art, for love, for remaking a political landscape) looks a lot like a fantasy of repainting an interpersonal normative landscape in the hues of one's own ego.

All that being said, a weaker and perhaps more accurate version of Williams' claim might still be developed. This would be the claim, not that the original act occurs outside a space of objective justification, but that from the point of view of the actor, it must be treated as such. The indeterminacies of system, or uncertainties of prediction, render the choice up for grabs ex ante, and only subject to justification or rejection ex post. Such choices might still be constrained by ex ante principles, prescribing maximin reasoning with regard to the worst extremes, for instance. But there will be a core set of choices for which justification will come subsequently as an epistemic matter, if it comes at all.[15] And it is to this first-personal, epistemically-constrained perspective that Williams' claims about moral luck are addressed. Gauguin, at least, cannot settle in advance the question of permissibility. And since his perspective on his decision is, ultimately, the only determinative view on what he should do, there simply will be no practically effective ex ante perspective which can offer justification in advance.

There is another benefit to construing Williams' claim about the subjective availability of justification. For it is only by rendering Williams' claim about moral luck in subjective terms that we can make sense of his further, equally provocative, claim about the nature of moral justification: that "even if Gauguin can ultimately be justified, that need not provide him with any way of justifying himself to others, or at least to all others."[16] On Williams' view, then, outcomes can justify ex post, but only relative to certain classes of agents – namely, those who give priority to the values inherent in the outcome.

But this is a puzzling position. Surely, one might think, moral justification is non-relative, position independent. This, after all, is the distinguishing feature of moral justification. Prudential justification, by contrast, is positional. An act might make sense for me, given my assessment of its costs and benefits, even though its costs weigh too heavily on you for you to find it reasonable. Indeed, the tradition in contractualism in ethics treats the notion of interpersonal acceptability as the basis for moral justification.[17] Questions of justification are pragmatically relevant when the act in question runs counter to some other party's interests or preferences. The prudential justification for the agent's act is presupposed (assuming this is not a case of irrational, perhaps akratic, behaviour). In such a case, for the aggrieved party to ask for moral justification just is to ask for a reason why she too might see the act as one that ought to be performed – or, alternatively, why some related set of considerations entail that, her preferences notwithstanding, the agent is still entitled to perform the act. For example, someone offering justification for their trespass onto private property in pursuit of a stag might offer respect for traditional patterns of land use as a reason for permission or forgiveness, not – or not just – the hunter's own reason, namely the pleasure of the hunt or the prospect of a meal.

What is puzzling about Williams' remark is that the outcome-relative justification Gauguin offers is not merely prudential, nor does it appear to be moral in any familiar sense of that term. For all the talk I have offered above, of deontological versus consequentialist justifications, Williams himself points to a notion of justification that is distinctly non-moral, when he writes that the Gauguin case illustrates the point that "we have deep and persistent reasons to be grateful that" the world we have is not one in which "morality [is] universally respected."[18] The justification Gauguin comes to have, and which he might not have had, sounds in this broader dimension of non-prudential value, yet it is not a value whose allegiance can be demanded of those hurt by its attainment, or who otherwise deplore the values it realizes.

So Williams here treads a difficult line: avoiding pure relativism, on the one hand, where justification simply reduces to realization of whatever values the agent has, and avoiding the overriding dictate of purely moral values, on the other. His position in this essay thereby calls to mind another famous and related claim of his, in "Internal and External Reasons," along with the concomitant difficulties of his claim in that essay.[19] In that essay, Williams argues that we are properly said to have (normative) reason to act in a certain way when and only when one can construct an argument showing that the act in question would realize some value or desire already held by the agent. Lacking such prior motivations, agents lack reason to act in terms of those values or ends. Thus, more generally, the claim that someone has reason to act is relational (or "internal," in Williams' terms), and cannot necessarily be universalized.

The difficulty with Williams' view that reasons are internal, relative to agents' prior motivations, lies not with its logic, but with its frankly revisionary aim to remove from our moralistic repertoire the charge that an agent who fails to comply with what he himself might acknowledge are the moral considerations at issue thereby fails to act on the reasons he has.[20] As Williams readily acknowledges, to give up on the universalistic language of morality as a source of external reasons, applicable to all agents in virtue of their capacity to think, feel, or act, is to give up on a great deal of the suasive force of morality. We are left with the resources of internal reason, and might for all that be able to show that, indeed, most people actually have prior motivations that, properly construed, would support the course of action morality (in our view) demands. But the claim that morality itself is anchored in reason is instead cast adrift – and once that is so, it is not clear that the remainder is recognizably a moral institution at all. Morality, in other words, might not survive Williams' internalist reduction.

So much the worse for morality, one might say – and the lessons of moral luck provide yet more reason to be sceptical of the institution. The problem, however, is that a central part of the claim of moral luck rests on a notion of justification that is clearly broader than a claim of internal rational support. Williams writes, in reference to political decisions that leave losers as well as winners in their wake, that

> It is not reasonable, in such a case, to expect those particular people who have been cheated, used, or injured to approve of the agent's action, nor should they be subjected to the patronising thought that, while their complaints are not justified in terms of the whole picture, they are too closely involved to be able to see that truth. Their complaints are, indeed, justified, and they may quite properly refuse to accept the agent's justification which the rest of us may properly accept.[21]

On pain of triviality, the language of "proper" acceptance of a justification must go beyond the limited question whether political actors have individual reason to act as they do, or whether victims have reason to voice their objections. Justification is perforce intersubjective and non-individual. But perhaps Williams' notion of justification can be resurrected on collective grounds: in terms of values *we* share, not just in terms of the agent's own motivations. On such an account, Gauguin is justified to us – properly justified – because his acts realize values we endorse, even in competition with morality. That is a real justification, to us, and stands apart from whatever reasons to act he may have had. It calls upon others – us – to assess his reasons in the dimensions of value he puts forward – here, aesthetic and Romantic values – and to weigh those reasons ex post, in light of their attainment (or his failure to attain those values). The ex post perspective is reasonable in this case, for to value a value like aesthetics is to value principally its instantiations. Until the scale of the realized value is actually in play – is concretized in a body of work – there will simply be no way to judge whether the game is worth the candle.

By contrast, while Gauguin's family doubtless also appreciates the value of the beautiful, they likely weigh it differently against the disvalue of poverty. As a result, Gauguin's justification to himself, perhaps to us, is not a moral justification – it makes no moral claim on all others (as moral claims do, simply as a matter of semantics), nor does it provide a basis for seeing his family's supposed resentment as in any way unjustified.[22] But it does amount to an interesting and significant form of ex post justification.

Such a view is also consistent with the point that justification cannot be simply a matter of *cui bono*, for one can value certain values independent of their personal benefit. For example, an aesthete might regard Gauguin as choosing wisely simply on the hearsay claim that Gauguin had produced great art, unseen by the evaluator. Gauguin would be justified in the eyes of the aesthete, though not to those who value hearth and home over gallery success, though neither set of evaluators would either gain or lose in any meaningful sense. Justification may be non-moral, but it operates in the same space of intersubjective argument as morality. It is non-relative individually, while also non-universalistic. The further claim of outcome-dependence supports this limited relativity insofar as it illuminates the gap between the outcome values we third-parties might prefer, as against the intrinsic, deontic values at stake in the sufferings of intimates. But this connection is exegetical, not logical.

IV Ex post justification and political gambling

I now want to turn to the question motivating this chapter, namely whether and how the notion of ex post justification, which we have derived from reflections on interpersonal, moral cases, applies in the domain of politics. First, however, we should take stock of the conceptual equipment in play. Nagel's account of moral luck provided us with the outcome-dependent nature of accountability; and while he did not provide us with a justification for that dependence, his account of its pervasiveness in moral thought indicates its centrality. Williams, meanwhile, has given us an ex ante perspective on ex post dependence: on the way in which certain decisions to act can be taken in light of potential resultant values, without being able to claim the force of those values in advance. On the ex ante face, this means that a straightforward consequentialist justification will be lacking, and that actions aimed at the values at stake will be gambles of a sort – gambles that must produce both the desired outcomes and the justification for the gamble itself.

We can also see some normative support for Nagel's observations on the nature of accountability. While accountability is a moral notion, to be sure, our social practices of accountability need not only reflect moral values, nor need moral values be dominant. I remarked above on the positional character of accountability: Gauguin owes his family one response for his betrayal, and the world quite another; reciprocally, those affected differently are differently warranted in the responses they may mete out to him. If the account I have ascribed to Williams is plausible, that non-moral normative justification can be relative to particular assignments and experiences of value, then assignments of accountability might also vary along these dimensions. If aesthetic values have been realized, even at grave human cost, we bystanders might warrantably respond in one register, while family members might respond in another. Furthermore, our responses as bystanders might well be more outcome-dependent than the responses of family: the wrong of betrayed promises occurs at the moment of the deci-sion, before its fruits are gathered. (Whether our response as bystanders is actually justified can only be settled from within a moral theory; but it will be perforce a moral assessment of that response, not simply a reflection of whether our local interests were served.)

Taken together, then, we have a coherent account of an outcome-dependent form of normative assessment, with logical space for the normative gamble. But we also have been given notice of a set of hazards inherent in this form of normative assessment. Two of them I have noted already. First, while this account does provide a justification for outcome-dependent account-ability, the justification only has force insofar as we can see its values as properly rivalling moral values. When we forgive the bloodied victor his sins, our forgiveness and celebration might reflect nothing more than a temporal myopia, or a discounting of the costs of suffering simply because those costs are not known to us. The fact of value pluralism *might* sup-port the claim of justification, but the justification might also be specious, by our own lights, even without acceding exceptionless priority to moral value. Second, Williams' distinction between intrinsic and extrinsic sources of failure, and the concomitant notions of refuted versus negated hopes, reveals a further degree of egoistic distortion in this decision calculus. While Williams is surely right that Gauguin would have rued the dis-covery of limited talent more than a chance failure to mount his Tahitian expedition, this fact only reveals the degree to which his concern is a dis-covery about himself – whether or not *he* is a great artist – rather than a discovery about whether great art will, in fact, be produced (by him, as it happens).

This combination is a heady mix. Kant warned long ago of the difficulties in accurately assessing the relation of our wills to the moral law.[23] These difficulties are amplified in the domain of politics. The possibility of retrospective justification, coupled with the unconscious prominence of reputational considerations, invites ego to take on the cloak of political heroism. Needless to say, the invitation has often been taken in history. Consider Machiavelli's famous endorsement of incaution:

> I think it is certainly better to be impetuous than incautious, for fortune is a woman, and it is necessary, if you wish to master her, to conquer her by force; and it can be seen that she lets herself be overcome by the bold, rather than by those who proceed coldly.[24]

The confusion of prudence and eros (and, in Platonic terms, thumos) is at the surface in Machiavelli's account, and it points to the pernicious hold the concept of political luck has taken on the political imagination (of men). Whatever the possible truth to outcome-sensitivity in political evaluation, the temptations it offers have been at the root of grand historical follies.

The modern exemplar of political incaution is the invasion of Iraq. While a full account of the deliberations leading to this epic historical disaster is yet to be given, one reason for the invasion seems to have been a desire among a cadre of like-minded political figures – the "Vulcans" as they called themselves – to establish a new geo-political mapping of the Middle East. The Vulcans, whose most famous members were Paul Wolfowitz and Douglas Feith, both of the Department of Defense, saw in the wake of the 9/11 attacks a chance to "sweep the table" in the region, displace the Israeli-Palestine conflict from its pivotal role, to cement an American military presence less dependent on the stability of Saudi Arabia, and to encourage the development of stabilizing democratic political and civic institutions.[25] They aimed, in other words, to wage a grand gamble, with war as the means and a US-friendly coalition of new regimes as the end.[26]

Now, I do not mean to insist on the truth of this particular account of the motivations of the Iraq War. First, whatever the declared justifications for the war, the actual motivations of the policymakers might have been far cruder: the sheer macho thrill of war (especially when fought from the policymaker's perch), or the pursuit of material advantage. Or the motivations may have been more cautious: a preference for a worst-case scenario of an unwarranted invasion as against Iraq's use of weapons of mass destruction. On such a calculus, even a high probability of error in threat-assessment would be dominated by the risks of a nuclear bomb.[27]

All these accounts of the decision to go to war enjoy some support. But I wish to concentrate on the argument of the grand gamble, because of its resonance in longstanding ideals of political leadership. While there are purely calculative politicians, to be sure, the narcissistic motivations that often lie at the heart of political ambition go hand in hand with the ideal of the gambler, each politician a potential Napoleon or Churchill, impetuous as to the future and with the wind of war at his back. To the extent – and it is a great extent – that the glorious future revolves around one's own celebrity, it is hard for the would-be gambler to distinguish genuine consequential calculation from adolescent fantasy. The trope of the gamble offers not just a moralized and romanticized rationalization of cruder motives – for instance, of war as a venue for displays of power – but dresses that rationalization up in heroic garb. Moreover, the cognitive distortions entailed by these layers of fantasy are further evident in the mistaken planning for the post-war period, with its now notoriously inaccurate estimate of direct and indirect costs.[28] If a preferred self-image of the gambler is that of the card-counter, the hard-nosed actuary of chance, the Iraq War presented us with a more realistic image of the fantasist looking for a triumphant score.[29]

The second distorting feature of the concept of political luck lies not in the manifest temptations of the gambler-hero image, but in the difficulty of comparing costs against gains, where both estimates are done under multiple layers of uncertainty. In discussing Gauguin, I suggested that one reason for thinking in consequentialist terms, that ex ante no determinate assessment could be given was the substantial uncertainty of the relevant variables, compounded by the reflexive nature of some of the outcomes. This class of political gambles invites a long and familiar list of biases to the table, including optimistic biases in overestimating success (and hence under-discounting the benefits and over-discount costs), and a general discounting of remote or statistical, but nonetheless real, costs – human suffering and death, in the case of war – against more easily visualized symbols of success.[30] The reflexive nature of the estimating problem is fully present as well, for the prospect of success in waging war, fomenting revolution, and so forth, depends upon the political actor's own future actions and skills of leadership, not just one's courageous act of taking the gamble in the first place. The failures of Iraq policymaking become highly predictable under this lens.

There is a third distorting aspect as well, and it comes from the relativized sense of justification that one must invoke to make sense of Williams' claim. While the justification is not moral – and cannot be moral – the fact that it is also not purely personal allows it to displace moral demands. Williams does not imagine that Gauguin can defeat the grievances of his family by pointing to the glory of his art, but only that he can convince other onlookers to ignore their complaints. By hypothesis, recall, moral justification is simply unavailable. Were the art capable of redressing the moral costs, then that prospect could have been taken into account, as a basis for reasonable assent by the family, or by consequentialist calculation. Instead, the aesthetic success displaces the moral costs.

Imagine what would have to be true for a war like Iraq to be justified in moral terms. Assuming some disregard for international law is compatible with moral justification, it would at least have to be the case that the new political and legal ordering that accommodates pre-emption as an alternative legitimate basis for war is likely to make the world more secure on balance, despite the risks of providing other states with a legal cover for cross-border raids. Second, the direct and indirect human costs of war and national recovery, discounted by their high probability, must be outweighed by the reduction in risks generated by the Hussein regime, and the reduction in the very real costs of that regime's political repression, all discounted by the lower probabilities of reducing the costs in those dimensions.[31] And third, there must be an answer to the deontological challenge whether an external invasion can, even in principle, legitimate a new regime – that is, whether only internal agents of political change have moral standing to engage in these cost-benefit calculations in the first place.

All these are hard questions in moral and political philosophy, and I do not pretend that I know how they must be answered in the case of Iraq, although of course I have made clear my own prejudices. Nor do I want to insinuate that political choices can never be made in the face of uncertainty, in light of the likelihood of bias and distortion. The first would be a recipe for dogmatism, and the second for stagnant conservatism. But there is a continuum between the fearful caution of a Chamberlain, willing to wager nothing, and the rashness of an Alexander, willing to wager everything. Lasting legacies of political leadership fall between the two, with an honest eye directed at the payouts. If questions about uncertain payoffs were properly directed deliberations about the political future, then the concept of political luck would have no purchase: the invasion either could have been justified or shown to be unjustified ex ante, on the basis of the estimates one could make and the principled reason one could engage in. Actual success or failure would be icing. The most pernicious effect, however, of focussing on the possibility of ex post justification is that it renders these questions moot, because justification will be at hand when, and only when, success obtains. One need not account for the real downside costs, as a moral accounting would demand. The only downside cost that looms large for a political gambler is the risk of looking a fool, and that risk is itself probably over-discounted by the unattractiveness of its realization.[32] Moreover, a keen awareness of the outcome-dependency of social accountability, with the realization that the victory will be celebrated and its costs forgotten, means that there is essentially no pressure for an honest moral accounting of the decision at hand. The irony here is that morality will have little purchase on politics not for its lack of realism, as many charge, but precisely because of its realism.

V Rejecting political luck

The elaboration of the role of luck in prospective choice, by Williams, and in retrospective accountability, by Nagel, performed a service for contemporary moral philosophy, by revealing the unreality of the picture of moral assessment it offered. Noting luck's role allows us to understand dimensions of moral assessment that integrate better with our life embedded in a world of chance and mutual vulnerability.[33] Williams' discussion further limits the role of a related philosophical ideal, that of the fully rationalized decision. While Williams' explorations of the notion of justification are puzzling, they do not seem simply confused, but instead genuinely reveal complexities in the nature of agency.

Yet moral luck is, in the end, more modest than political luck. One might accept the coherence of the concept and accommodate oneself to its role in our practices of allocating praise and blame. But political luck presents special dangers, in large part because of the magnifying lenses provided by the imagined audience of history – an audience lacking in the moral realm. Thus, I have sought here to accentuate the negative instead: the dangers that arise when the concept of luck is taken as the lodestar of consequential decisionmaking. Williams did not invite these dangers, of course. But his emphasis on the limited role of moral justification provides more support than is needed for one of the deadliest temptations in political thought, ever since Plato visited Sicily: the desire to rework a political landscape *in toto*, rationalizing a choice that piecemeal analysis would quickly convict of foolhardiness. Actuarial thought in politics may be less stirring than the political morality of a Machiavellian statesman. But it may in the end be more honest both to morality, and to oneself.

Acknowledgments

Some of this work was supported by a research fellowship at the James Fleming Centre for Legal Research at the Australian National University, School of Law. I am grateful to Peter Cane, Ariel Colonomos, Jessica Riskin, and Samuel Scheffler for extended discussion of this essay, to the members of the Bay Area Forum for Law and Ethics for their enormously helpful contributions and criticisms, and to Daniel Callcut for his superb editorial advice.

Notes

1 Leo Tolstoy, *War and Peace*, trans. Constance Garnett (London: Heinemann, 1904), Pt. X, Chapter 25, p. 838.
2 Thomas Nagel, "Moral Luck," reprinted in Daniel Statman (ed.), *Moral Luck* (Albany, NY: SUNY Press, 1993), pp. 57–71, 63.
3 Ibid., p. 62.

4 This equalizing strategy is the heart of a number of responses to Nagel's and Williams' articles. See, for example, Judith Andre, "Nagel, Williams, and Moral Luck," in *Moral Luck*, pp. 123–9.

5 Nagel, pp. 62–3.

6 Bernard Williams, "Moral Luck," reprinted in *Moral Luck*, pp. 38–55.

7 This formulation, of course, begs the question, addressed below, whether betrayal can be justified. Compare E.M. Forster's famous quip in *Two Cheers for Democracy*: "[I]f I had to choose between betraying my country and betraying my friend I hope I should have the guts to betray my country." "What I believe," in *Two Cheers for Democracy* (London: Edward Arnold, 1939).

8 Williams, "Moral Luck," p. 41.

9 And one might, as Williams suggests, be happy that if bad people are the price of good art, that there are some bad people in the world. Ibid, p. 38. It should be said, this seems a dubious proposition in both the particular and the general case. Surely there might have been some way Gauguin could have done more for his family while realizing his talents.

10 Williams, "Moral Luck," p. 39. As Williams says, a principle that permits such harms when and only when one believes oneself to be a great artist (or to be capable of becoming such) is a license for fatuous self-delusion.

11 Of course, if the consumption value of gambling itself – the thrill of risk-seeking – is taken into account, then ex ante even a highly improbable gamble can be justified.

12 Ibid., p. 40.

13 I admit that the analogy is not wholly illuminating, since a raffle ticket's not being drawn seems as intrinsic a form of failure as anything else.

14 Ibid., p. 42.

15 The claim that justification is only epistemically available ex post is, I think, consistent with Williams' somewhat puzzling denial that the luck at play is epistemic rather than metaphysical. Williams' point is that it could not be said, at the time of decision, that Gauguin knew that his choice would be justified. That knowledge, if knowledge it is, is only available retrospectively. Ibid., p. 40.

16 Ibid., p. 38.

17 See, e.g., T.M. Scanlon, "Contractualism and Utilitarianism," in A. Sen and B. Williams (eds), *Utilitarianism and Beyond* (New York: Cambridge University Press, 1982), pp. 103–28. The views of Jürgen Habermas are cognates, see, e.g., his *Moral Consciousness and Communicative Action*, trans. Christian Lenhardt (Cambridge, MA: MIT Press, 2001).

18 Williams, "Moral Luck," p. 38 (I have rearranged the sentential clauses). This sentence rules out one interpretation of the claim of justification, that it is basically consequentialist. If such justifications were adequate in cases like this, then this would be a world in which (consequentialist) morality was respected as well.

19 Bernard Williams, "Internal and External Reasons," in *Moral Luck* (New York: Cambridge University Press, 1981), pp. 101–13.

20 Williams stresses the narrowness of the import of his claim in "Internal Reasons and the Obscurity of Blame," in *Making Sense of Humanity* (New York: Cambridge University Press, 1995), pp. 35–45.

21 Williams, "Moral Luck," p. 51.

22 I also mean to leave open the possibility that we might regard Gauguin's actions as unjustified in any sense, yet still be glad of the outcomes – making the proverbial lemonade. But Williams' rejection of the priority of morality does not encompass this possibility.

23 Immanuel Kant, *Groundwork of the Metaphysics of Morals* 4:407 (1785).

24 Niccolò Machiavelli, *The Prince*, trans. Luigi Ricci (New York: Modern Library, 1950), Ch. XXV, 94.

25 James Mann, *Rise of the Vulcans: The History of Bush's War Cabinet* (New York: Viking Books, 2004), especially pp. 351ff.

26 As a quip of the war planners had it at the time, "Everyone wants to go to Baghdad. Real men go to Tehran." Quoted in David Remnick, "War without end," *The New Yorker* (April 21, 2003).

27 As President George Bush said in a pre-war speech, "Facing clear evidence of peril, we cannot wait for the final proof – the smoking gun – that could come in the form of a mushroom cloud." Speech in Cincinatti, OH (October 7, 2002), available at: http://www.narsil.org/war_on_iraq/bush_october_7_2002.html.

28 For a depressing, account of these distortions, see Thomas E. Ricks, *Fiasco: The American Military Adventure in Iraq* (New York: Penguin, 2007).

29 This discussion owes much to Ariel Colonomos, "Le pari de la guerre," unpublished MS, CERI and Science-Politique, especially his discussion of the role of luck in the rationalization of pre-emptive war.

30 For a list of relevant biases, see Daniel Kahneman and Amos Tversky, "Judgement under Uncertainty: Heuristics and Biases," *Science* 185 (1974), 1124–31.

31 More specifically, the certainties of war's direct costs must be weighed against the risk that substitute risks or substitute repression will arise. The human costs alone have been estimated (as of 2006) at an excess of civilian deaths around 650,000 (with a 95 percent confidence interval from 392–942,000), mostly from direct violence caused by governmental collapse, but also by a damaged infrastructure. Gilbert Burnham, Riyadh Lafta, Shannon Doocy, and Les Roberts, *The Lancet* (October 11, 2006). This also ignores the opportunity cost of using US funds for these purposes rather than others.

32 Moreover, one might think that political actors who have risen high enough to have the authority to make such wagers have already shown themselves to be risk-takers in this dimension.

33 Martha Nussbaum's *The Fragility of Goodness* (New York: Cambridge University Press, 2nd ed., 2001) remains one of the most eloquent explorations of this ideal, in Greek philosophy and literature.

12

POLITICAL AGENCY AND THE ACTUAL

Sharon R. Krause

Political theory these days has far too little to say about political action. The field's defining debates in the last generation have centered instead on the study of justice. What justice means, how it relates to community and to public deliberation, and whether it can accommodate differences of culture and identity are the issues that have most preoccupied political theorists. Our theories of justice do make plenty of assumptions about citizens as agents; in particular, they assume a capacity for rational autonomy. Yet they have not adequately explored the nature and conditions of the agency they assume.[1] In this respect, political agency is very much present in political theory even despite its absence, although it is strikingly undertheorized. One reason for political theory's lack of attention to political action is the belief among many theorists that action is a merely practical affair, grounded primarily in psychological and sociological considerations. Political theory, being a normative enterprise, should focus not on what citizens *do* but on what they *ought* to do, hence not on political action but on political norms.

This view of what political theory is about reflects what Bernard Williams has called "the intense moralism" of the field.[2] The theories of justice that dominate today give strict priority to the moral over the political; in particular, they represent "the continuation of a (Kantian) morality as the framework of the [political] system."[3] They draw unnecessarily sharp divides between "principle and interest, or morality and prudence."[4] Both Rawls and Habermas, the dominant contemporary theorists of justice, manifest this moralism in their work. Even the later work of Habermas, which claims to look for justice "between facts and norms," ultimately privileges "the moral rather than the facts."[5] The upshot is not only that political theory is heavy on normative standards and light on political realities, but that the normative standards it identifies tend to be distorted by its neglect of political and psychological facts, including facts about political agency.

The moralism of political theory in this respect is countered by the realist methods of American political science, which makes the study of political action its business. Locating itself firmly on the other side of the fact–value divide, political science means to describe how citizens and other political actors actually behave, remaining agnostic on the normative question of how they should behave. Yet as an account of agency this view is hobbled by an analytic framework that tends to recognize only interest-based motives. Political behavior so conceived involves little of the deliberative, self-guided action – not to mention moral conviction – that we commonly associate with agency, characterized as it is by unreflective, even mechanistic, reactions to one's own (and others') predetermined interests. As Williams puts it, the realist view of political science and the moralistic view of political theory "are made for each other. They represent a Manichaean dualism of soul and body, high-mindedness and the pork barrel."[6] This dualism in the contemporary study of political life helps explain why political agency is so poorly understood today. Political theory has its head too much in the clouds of normativity to take action seriously while political science tends to reduce action to mere behavior.

There is no small irony in this impoverished discourse. After all, the concept of agency is strongly associated with the Kantian ideal of autonomy that is so central to contemporary liberal theory. The value of autonomy, and with it agency, is a foundational assumption of liberal theory. Thus liberalism champions political freedom and the rights of individuals on the grounds that they establish protected spaces for the exercise of autonomy. Liberal theory would therefore seem to be a natural place for the study of political agency to emerge. Yet to the limited extent that political theorists have addressed this topic, the most interesting work has come not from liberals but from those who stand outside the dominant liberal paradigm: poststructuralists, democratic theorists, and communitarians.[7] Liberal theory ignores agency at its own peril, however, for action is the heart of politics. The study of justice and the theory of norm justification, with which liberal theory is so much concerned today, only matter because the actions of citizens and their representatives need to be guided and coordinated. What kind of agents we are – what it means to be an agent at all – bears directly on the kinds of political order open to us and the kinds of standards that ought to govern us. So without a viable understanding of the nature and conditions of political agency, liberal theory cannot grasp its own subject matter and it runs the risk of misconceiving the nature of justice.

Williams' work on moral agency has much to offer in this regard, although its value for political theory has not been widely explored. The influence on political theory of other aspects of his work has been duly noted elsewhere, such as his account of value pluralism and his early defense of the importance of emotions for moral and political deliberation.[8] Yet his work on agency has gone largely unnoticed by political theorists.[9]

Williams' account combines a subtle moral psychology of agency with a complex understanding of how the exercise of agency is always contingent and often internally conflicted. In contrast to the idyll of agency as rational autonomy that is simultaneously present (because assumed) and absent (because undertheorized) in liberal theory today, this view elaborates agency in light of the many dimensions of what Williams once called "the actual."[10] What actually occurs – both within us and outside us – is a constitutive part of agency. Actual political agency is what one might call "nonsovereign" agency, but it is ripe with potential for principled political action. This is an account that bridges the Manichaean divide between moralism and realism, and that has important implications for normative political theory. Still, Williams was insufficiently attentive to the effects of power on agency, and attending to these effects will require some modifications to his account. When suitably modified, Williams' non-sovereign theory of agency points to a new ethic of responsibility in politics, and it suggests that we should rethink the liberal theory of justice.

I Action and deliberation: the character of agency

Williams identifies "two sides to action," namely deliberation and result.[11] This "two-sides" approach offers a valuable analytic framework for exploring the contours of agency. In this section, we examine the deliberation dimension of action; the section that follows explores the results side of action. The deliberation dimension of action connects agency to character. Agents are more than bodies in motion; they act deliberately, meaning in a way that reflects the desires, beliefs and purposes that establish their characters. Indeed, the presence of such concerns marks intentionality, and therefore is "constitutive of human action."[12] An important feature of character on Williams' account is the defining role that desire plays within it. Who we are, most fundamentally, is given by the fundamental desires we have. Williams emphasizes that the desires that constitute us need not take the form of unreflective appetites. Many of them contain cognitive content. The desires that form one's "motivational set," for instance, may well include such things as "dispositions of evaluation, patterns of emotional reaction, personal loyalties, and various projects, as they may be abstractly called, embodying commitments of the agent."[13] The desire to see justice done, for instance, clearly requires complex cognitive faculties. This example also demonstrates that some of the desires that constitute character have a "self-transcending" quality. Such desires do not have the pleasures of the agent himself as their objects; in fact, they may aim at states of affairs that do not involve the agent at all.[14] Moreover, the desires that constitute character are in principle sensitive to deliberation, insofar as deliberative processes can add desires to or subtract them from the agent's motivational set, provided that these processes engage at least some existing elements in the set.[15] So rational reflection has a role in character, and hence in agency, but for Williams rationality is shot through with desire not sovereign over it, as on Kantian views. Consequently, practical deliberation must engage desires to be meaningful and efficacious.[16]

What this means is that agency, including moral agency, is driven by reflective desire, not by a form of reason that transcends desire. Moreover, the kinds of desires that drive moral agency are not in any significant sense unique. It is "unrealistic" to demand a "sharp distinction" between moral and non-moral motivations.[17] To do so denigrates motivations that are in fact capable of possessing "structural importance in life," or ethical value broadly construed.[18] What Williams found so appealing about Homeric notions of action was precisely that "they did *not* revolve around a distinction between moral and non-moral motivations."[19] His own work aims, he says, to provide a conception of ethics "that will be ... continuous with our understanding of human beings in other respects."[20] Thus moral obligations are not *sui generis* but "relate basically to needs that are very everyday."[21] To be a moral agent is to act from the full range of dispositions that constitute one's ground projects and form one's character. These projects are "the conditions of my existence, in the sense that unless I am propelled forward by the conatus of desire, project, and interest, it is unclear why I should go on at all."[22] We are most fully agents when we act from desires that are most central to our character, for "to be an expression of character is perhaps the most substantial way in which an action can be one's own."[23] The moral psychology of agency that Williams offers here reflects his commitment to "the actual." It grounds agency in a realistic account of who we are, psychologically speaking. It rejects the idealized account of autonomy implicit in much liberal theory, which associates moral agency with a faculty of practical reason that is sovereign over desire and with a notion of persons that is independent of character.

Character as the source of action constrains as much as it enables, and this is another way in which moral agency embodies the actual. As Williams emphasizes, we are not free to abandon or abstract from the dispositions that constitute our characters and the ground projects that make us who we are.[24] Nor do we choose our characters in any wholesale way, although we are certainly capable of reflecting on them and striving for the cultivation of new virtues or the eradication of old vices. Yet, for the most part, one is thrown into one's character, which imposes itself through the influences of parents, social groups, and experiences one neither chooses nor controls. In these ways character itself reflects agency's immersion in the actual. More than that, the claims of character rule out some possible actions and make others necessary. Character grounds practical necessity, the feeling that there are some things that one simply *must* (or must not) do.[25] In this respect, character-based necessity is marked by an aspect of passivity. Ethical conviction, Williams insists, "must in some sense come to you" rather than being the product of conscious choice.[26] What it means to have an ethical conviction is to feel that one's decision is "inescapable."[27] As a form of practical necessity, ethical conviction presses itself upon us precisely because we cannot escape who we are. Martin Luther's "Here I stand; I can do no other" is an instance of necessity in this form. Williams also mentions Sophocles' Ajax in this regard. Shamed by actions of his own that brought a "grotesque humiliation" upon him, Ajax finds that he can no longer live "the only kind of life his *ethos* demands."[28] His solution is to commit suicide, saying, "Now I am going where my way must go."[29] Ajax's character, as Williams sees it, determines his path. Ironically, character enables agency by imposing necessities on us. The more fully an agent one is – the more an action is one's own – the less choice is involved in one's decision. The common idea that agency is above all the exercise of free choice is therefore deeply misguided.

As the parting words of Ajax indicate, one way of exercising agency is to claim as one's own a decision that presents itself under the guise of practical necessity. The story of Aeschylus's *Agamemnon* offers another illustration. Having offended the gods, Agamemnon is asked to sacrifice his daughter to placate them and thereby assure the success of the military expedition to Troy under his command. As Williams presents the case, Agamemnon's character imposes necessity on him by demanding fidelity to his role as the commander of the expedition and the responsibilities this role entails. When he decides to sacrifice his daughter, the Chorus says of him that he "put on the harness of necessity."[30] Williams draws attention to the active quality of this phrase. Far from passively submitting to necessity, Agamemnon "is said to have put on the harness of necessity as someone puts on armour."[31] In putting it on, Agamemnon "takes something that is a necessity, and makes it his own."[32] Laying claim to actions that elude one's will is, of course, an act of will. Yet the will is not the main player here. Instead, Agamemnon's agency consists in shouldering responsibility for an action that he did not will. In a similar way, when Martin Luther King decided in 1959 to leave Dexter Church in Montgomery for a new position in Atlanta, he told his congregation, "I can't stop now, History has thrust something upon me which I cannot turn away."[33] One commentator has called this speech in Montgomery the moment in King's public life "when freedom and necessity, choice and calling, seemed to coincide."[34] What history thrust on King was a collection of unchosen effects. Some of these effects had emanated indirectly from his own (and others') acts of civil disobedience beginning with the Montgomery bus boycott of 1955, but most of them were not in any way the products of his will. In responding to them, King was honoring the claims of his character, responding to the practical necessities that it imposed on him in light of historical events. In effect, he put on the "harness" of history. By answering the call that history made to his conscience, he made the thrust of history his own, and in doing so he transformed his necessities into an exercise of his agency.

The relationship between agency and character may seem to suggest a notion of personal identity that is marked by a high degree of internal harmony. Williams does sometimes point in this direction. In one place, for instance, he insists that we need to be able to interpret a person's actions as part of a "pattern" that establishes "unity" in his behavior.[35] Such unity appears to be important to the ideal of integrity. One who displays integrity "acts from those dispositions and motives which are most deeply his."[36] In this respect, his actions stand in harmony with his identity, where his identity is itself characterized by enough inner consistency to make the use of the word "his" meaningful.[37] Bonnie Honig has criticized Williams on this score, challenging what she sees as the "primacy of the unitary subject of integrity" in his work.[38] His ideal of integrity, she says, represents "a phantasmatic yearning for a clear central principle, commitment, or disposition, upon which a singular (individual or group) subjectivity can be grounded and secured."[39] This ideal stands in tension with Williams' own commitment to value conflict, and to the irreducible moral remainders that such conflict generates. Honig approves of the latter dimension of his work, seeing it as implying a valuable affirmation of "difference" within individual subjectivity, or personal identity. Intrasubjective difference is too often elided by liberal pluralists and multiculturalists, who "tend to domesticate or conceal this sort of difference" by assuming that value conflict exists only between persons and groups not within them.[40] To the extent that Williams makes moral conflict and the remainders it generates a regular feature of the deliberative life of moral agents, Honig welcomes his contribution and thinks it holds great promise as a corrective to liberal and multiculturalist notions of the unitary subject. It stresses "unruliness, contingency, luck, and struggle at the center" of moral experience.[41] As she sees it, however, Williams effectively reneges on this promise, ultimately relegating "dilemmas to the margins of ethics and politics in order to protect the boundaries of agentic integrity from the disruption, danger, and harm with which he associates dilemmas."[42] Thus he treats tragedy, the dramatic embodiment of inner conflict, as "peculiar" and peripheral to moral life rather than constitutive of it.[43] Honig wants to show, by contrast, that the "radical undecidability" of the tragic dilemma is actually central to moral agency itself.

Honig is right to find a tension here, and right to insist on the centrality of conflict within moral life. Yet the weight of Williams' thought seems to me to support the view that the intrasubjective conflict associated with tragedy reflects a common and ineradicable feature of moral agency. He makes it clear that one's deepest commitments are not always mutually consistent, and that they may call for diverse, even contrary, courses of action. The value pluralism he defends infuses character and personal identity, and he

267

regards internal value-conflict as a regular feature of human experience.[44] Moral conflicts are ineliminable, he says, "neither systematically avoidable, nor all soluble without remainder."[45] It is true that Williams refers to tragic conflicts as "peculiar," saying that they lie "beyond the ordinary routes of moral thought."[46] Conflicts count as tragic when "an agent can justifiably think that whatever he does will be wrong: that there are conflicting moral requirements and that neither of them succeeds in overriding or out-weighing the other."[47] Their peculiarity is a function of the fact that they present us with extreme forms of conflict. In tragedy both options are simply bad (and extreme in the kinds of harm they entail), and neither one clearly outweighs the other. By contrast, most of the time the options we face in moral conflicts are more mixed and the harms they entail are not so serious. And often we do have grounds for thinking that one outweighs the other, all things considered. But even when all this is true, whatever choice one makes will come at some cost and will generate moral remainders and reasonable regrets. The difference between tragedy and normal life is not a difference of kind but one of degree. The basic structure of intrasubjective conflict is common to both. This commonality explains why we can still relate to the Greek tragedies and why Williams made these tragedies the centerpiece of *Shame and Necessity*, perhaps his most powerful work. Tragedy is not marginalized in Williams' account but central to it, precisely because tragedy reflects in dramatic form universal aspects of moral agency.[48]

So internal dividedness on moral questions and the feeling of regret are common. Even integrity is sometimes marked by internal division. Under certain circumstances, integrity will consist in navigating one's intrasubjec-tive conflict without fully bringing the competing claims of one's character into harmony. In such cases, a person of integrity will have regrets; indeed, her regret will be a mark of her integrity because it demonstrates the depth of her commitments and her responsiveness to the various moral claims in play. Honig interprets Williams as counseling subjects to withdraw from moral conflict, however, so as to preserve their integrity and avoid regrets.[49] She sees his famous discussion of George the chemist, in "A Critique of Utilitarianism," as an example of this tendency. The dilemma George faces is whether to accept a job at a company that would allow him to support his family but would involve him personally in the promotion of biochemical warfare, something which he strongly opposes on moral grounds. If George refuses the job, someone else – in fact, a zealous advo-cate of biochemical warfare – is likely to take it. Williams means to dispute what he takes to be the utilitarian answer to the dilemma, which is that George "obviously" should take the job because doing so is likely to bring about the best end state. For Williams there is nothing obvious here because the moral values in play are all forceful. What he most objects to, however, is the fact that the utilitarian's exclusive focus on end states, to the neglect of agency, leaves out what is in fact a crucial consideration for any moral agent, namely the distinctive role of one's own agency in bringing about a particular outcome. The utilitarian approach fails to distinguish between my doing something, such as "killing someone, and its coming about because of what I do that someone else kills them."[50] This way of thinking about moral dilemmas alienates the agent "from his actions and the source of his action in his own convictions."[51] The point of the example, then, is to show that our own actions matter in a special way to us, that what *we* do – and not merely what happens – is of moral importance. Yet there is no suggestion here that one's actions should or could be totally free of conflict. So although Williams suggests that George should refuse the job (so as to prevent his own action from contributing to the promotion of biochemical warfare), he never says that doing so will save George from inner conflict or preserve him from regret. After all, there is still his unmet obligation to support his wife and children. This is a real moral remainder that his decision does not dissolve.[52]

It is true, as Honig insists, that moral "withdrawal is not an option," and that the effort to secure integrity by avoiding intrasubjective conflict would risk "an agency whose integrity depends upon a problematic political quiescence and/or withdrawalism."[53] The political value of recognizing intrasubjective conflict as a constitutive feature of moral agency is that doing so presses us to attend to the moral remainders of all our decisions. From this perspective we must continually ask how best to position ourselves, given our "complicity with and resistance to the discourses, practices, and institutions that [we] seek to overcome or transform."[54] So the effort to secure integrity by withdrawing from conflict would be bad for political agency and for democratic politics. But the thrust of Williams' thought does not support Honig's worries in this respect. Against withdrawalism, Williams maintained that "the notion of a moral claim is of something that I may not ignore: hence it is not up to me to give myself a life free from conflict by withdrawing my interest from such claims."[55] The whole point of integrity, in fact, is that the person of integrity refuses to withdraw from conflict. She faces up to moral conflict by answering to the convictions that constitute her character, and when these convictions conflict she feels the moral remainders of her decisions.[56] Agency does not entail intrasubjective harmony in any simple sense. Although it involves action that is patterned with reference to some enduring (but certainly not fixed) beliefs, dispositions, and desires, there is nothing to say that these characteristics and the actions they inspire will be fully consistent with one another or reducible to a single overarching principle. And in this way, Williams' account disputes another feature of the liberal ideal of agency as autonomy, namely the notion that moral agency consists in acting from rationally derived (hence unified) standards of right, and that the exercise of moral agency should therefore be unconflicted and free of regret.

SHARON R. KRAUSE

Williams' account of the deliberative dimension of agency rests on a realistic moral psychology, then, one that means to show how agency is both enlivened and constrained by the actual. It honors the actual place of desires within human motivations (including moral motivations); it recognizes the actual embeddedness of agency in the unchosen but powerfully animating claims of character; and it acknowledges the actual experience of moral conflict that regularly impacts the exercise of agency. In all these respects, Williams contests assumptions about agency implicit in liberal theory, especially the neo-Kantian strains of liberalism that dominate political theory today. He rejects the rationalism that associates agency with a form of reason that transcends desire; he denies that agency is primarily a matter of unconstrained choice or the adoption of a characterless impartiality; and he disputes the equation of agency with a perfectly unified or unconflicted subjectivity. These challenges to liberal assumptions map onto some familiar critiques of liberalism posed by communitarians and others in recent years. In elaborating the second dimension of agency – agency as result – Williams raises a very different set of considerations, however. Here the actual is represented not by a realistic moral psychology but by a realistic account of the contingencies that constrain and in some respects constitute agency.

II Agency and result: contingency in action

The deliberative dimension of agency cannot stand alone for it is also in the nature of agency to issue in some result, or to cause an effect. Consequently there is a common association between agency and efficacy or control. In view of this association, the tradition of modern liberalism has tended to regard agency as "mastery, independence, or sovereignty."[57] This view of agency extends beyond liberal theorists as well, as Patchen Markell notes. Even the communitarian critics of liberalism, who have powerfully disputed the idea that agency consists in the "unencumbered" choice of one's ends, have in their own ways perpetuated the ideal of agency as a form of self-sovereignty. Although they acknowledge that one's ends tend to be given rather than freely chosen, they too see agency as "a matter of control or efficacy in carrying out one's purposes – wherever those purposes come from."[58] Michael Sandel's civic republicanism and Charles Taylor's politics of recognition, in which encumbered selves act so as to bring about the unchosen ends or projects that establish their identities, exemplify this view. Even within "accounts of the self as encumbered," then, "the fantasy of sovereign agency" persists.[59] As we have seen, Williams shares some of the communitarian convictions about the encumbered self. But he contests the ideal of agency as mastery at a much deeper level than do the communitarians by infusing agency with contingency.

Williams' discussion of agent-regret about the involuntary is one illustration of how contingency permeates agency. Agent-regret is a species of regret that a person feels toward past acts of his own that have turned out badly. The truck driver who unintentionally runs over a small child in the street is likely to feel regret of this kind.[60] Crucially, agent-regret is not limited to voluntary and intentional action. The deliberative dimension of agency entails that intention is a part of agency, but agent-regret suggests that agency extends beyond intention. Results matter too. The truck driver who feels agent-regret recognizes his own agency in the terrible event and accepts a kind of responsibility for it. True, his responsibility in this instance is different than it would be if he had run over the child intentionally, but the absence of malicious intent does not let him off the hook entirely, either in his own eyes or in ours. And his regret is natural, even salutary. As Williams points out, "it would be a kind of insanity never to experience sentiments of this kind towards anyone."[61] It would be insane because we know that agency is more than the enactment of our projects. Indeed, the reason we can relate to tragic heroes such as Ajax or Oedipus is that "we know that in the story of one's life there is an authority exercised by what one has done, and not merely by what one has intentionally done."[62] The Greeks understood that "the responsibilities we have to recognize extend in many ways beyond our normal purposes and what we intentionally do."[63] Our projects get us moving, but once in motion we find ourselves in a field of actual results that often bear little relation to these projects. As Markell has said, "Action projects human beings into a world of causality, initiating sequences of events that, once begun, proceed without necessarily respecting the agent's intentions."[64] Hence there is "a necessary gap," in Williams' words, between the two sides of action in deliberation and result.[65]

Yet the exercise of agency involves reaching across this gap. We cannot "entirely detach ourselves from the unintentional aspects of our actions ... and yet still retain our identity and character as agents."[66] To a significant degree, we become aware of ourselves in the world – aware of who and what we are – by observing the effects we have. A major part of childhood development involves coming to comprehend oneself as a cause. Think of all the things that 3-year olds do to get a reaction from those around them, which means to experience themselves as causes. Identity develops and is sustained in part as the effects of our own causality are reflected back to us through the responses of other people. The effects we unintentionally cause also contribute to this feedback loop. Indeed, it is a part of the experience of agency to realize that one's effects on the world sometimes overreach one's intentions. Moral maturity and political awareness involve being sensitive to the effects that aspects of our identity and personality have on others, independently of our intentions. Does one's brashness intimidate others? Is one's whiteness alienating in this group, given its racial profile? Does one's habit of self-deprecation invite domination? To be aware in these ways is to experience the scope of one's agency as it outruns one's will, and to claim one's effects on the world even when they are unintended. This experience can be deeply satisfying. It is a good feeling to learn that one has unwittingly helped another or touched someone's life in a meaningful way. I am my sister's "rock of Gibraltar," or so she tells me, although I never set out to be. The potency of our actions exceeds whatever power there is in our own aspirations. And even when our effects are not positive, we nevertheless have a stake in them. Consider the truck driver again. What would it mean for him to walk away from the scene of the accident without regret, to tell himself – and to really believe – that he had no responsibility for what happened because he did not mean to do it? It would be to say that he is nothing more than his will, and therefore to deny a major part of the power he actually exercises in the world, power that is not directed by his will. This reductionistic view is antithetical to the experience of agency, which is the experience of occupying space in the world that goes beyond the bounds of one's intentions. This is another way in which agency is constituted by the actual. To take responsibility for one's actual but unintended effects on the world is to claim them, and this act of claiming is an important part of what agency is.

Contingency figures in agency with respect to the meaning of one's actions as well. One way that agency differs from random motion is that it issues in deeds that are meaningful. Part of the meaning of an action is given by the intentions of the agent and part of it comes from the way in which the action fits into the larger pattern of the agent's character. In considering the action of the truck driver who unintentionally ran down a child, we know to classify it as an accident rather than an instance of malice by referring to the agent's intentions. Similarly, when you come to me bearing gifts I interpret your action with reference to what I know about your character. I know, let us say, that you are a loyal and generous person and not the manipulative type, and consequently there are no grounds for me to think that you are just buttering me up for some purposes of your own. In these respects, the content or meaning of actions is drawn from the agent herself. Not all the meaning in one's effects comes from the agent, however. Some of this meaning derives from contingent conditions that are beyond the agent's control.

These contingent conditions constitute what Williams called "moral luck," or "those elements which are essential to the outcome but lie outside" the agent's control.[67] The notion of moral luck is ostensibly focused on considerations of moral justification and value but there are important implications here for agency. Consider Williams' well-known discussion of Gauguin, who abandoned his wife and children to pursue his art unfettered in the South Pacific. Gauguin's decision will be morally justified, Williams argues, only if he succeeds as a painter. If he fails, "then he did the wrong thing ... in the sense that ... he has no basis for the thought that he was justified in acting as he did."[68] Success or failure will depend significantly (although not entirely) on luck – the luck that Gaugin turns out to be a gifted painter, the luck of avoiding the kinds of injury or accident that would prevent him from realizing his gifts, and so on. The idea of moral luck may seem to be deeply disruptive of moral agency. The meaningfulness of action, as we have seen, is crucial to distinguishing exertions of agency from instances of random motion. Yet moral luck suggests that the meaning of an act is not drawn solely from the act itself. Moral luck entails that actions can only be justified retrospectively, in light of what happens later, which implies that their full meaning only emerges in a way that is partially independent of what the agent did. The meaning of our actions to some extent eludes our grasp; agency extends not only beyond intentions but even beyond the agent herself.

The Kantian view that Williams challenges here seats agency exclusively in the will, or in the deliberative rather than results dimension of action. It regards agency as being at least partly immune to luck – and to contingency more generally – by virtue of the moral will, which Kant calls the only thing that "can be regarded as good without qualification."[69] If agency is defined strictly in terms of individual will, then it can be constructed as immune to factors that are outside the control of the will. This view makes the moral agent sovereign over his action, treating agency itself as a kind of sovereignty. If instead agency is defined in terms of both will (or deliberation, in Williams' terms) and result, then the Kantian claim of immunity fails. There are good reasons to follow Williams here because the meaning and value that our actions hold for us typically do rest partly on their results. The experience of agent-regret is once again illuminating. We understand the truck driver's regret because we know that our actions do not stop being *ours* when contingent factors intervene. It was bad luck that the child ran out in front of the driver's truck too quickly for him to brake, but still *he* was the cause of her death. He is not immune to regret because his agency is not immune to luck.

It is important to see here that luck is not merely an external limitation on agency. The thrust of Williams' discussion is not to suggest that individual agency dissolves when luck enters the picture. That view would retain an element of the Kantian perspective, which strictly separates agency from luck and other contingencies. It holds that *"what I most fundamentally am"* is beyond the influence of luck, that there is a fully sovereign agent somewhere in every moral being.[70] For Williams, agency is not a matter of sovereignty in this sense. Agency is not sovereign because luck sometimes affects our effects on the world. The meaning of our actions is partly given by the meaning they turn out to have, and this meaning is somewhat beyond our control. It is also sensitive to social and political factors, including the configurations of power that pertain in a particular society, although (as Honig notes) Williams failed to elaborate this point. A more political perspective on moral luck would reveal the ways in which the meaning that one's actions turn out to have is partly dependent on a larger field of power relations. Whether Gauguin's paintings of Tahitian women will come to be seen as successful, for instance, depends to some extent on the degree to which they resonate with prevailing relations of power between men and women, and between white European and brown native peoples, among other things.[71] Likewise, a woman who abandoned her children for her art, as Gaugin did, would likely face a far higher hurdle in justifying her action to others and to herself, given women's traditional obligations with respect to childrearing and the prevalent belief (even stronger in Gauguin's day) that women's function is to serve the needs of others rather than to pursue ambitious projects of their own, both of which reflect gender-based inequalities of power. We shall have more to say presently about Williams' neglect of power within moral luck, but for now it is enough to notice that the exercise of agency is pervaded by luck, and that moral luck represents one more way in which agency incorporates the actual.

The meaning of our actions depends on another kind of contingency as well, namely the social context of interpretation. This meaning is inter-subjective in significant measure. Williams did not explore this dimension of agency at much length, so in pressing the point I go beyond his analysis. The work of Hannah Arendt is useful in this regard. She maintains that one reason for the "inherent unpredictability" of human action is that action as meaningful motion is always part of a story that is at least partly scripted by persons other than the agent. "Action reveals itself fully only to the story-teller," Arendt says, or "to the backward glance of the historian." Consequently, "all accounts given by the actors themselves ... become mere useful source material in the historian's hands and can never match his story in significance."[72] One reason for this is that human action involves more than just the doer. Action is comprised of two parts, "the beginning made by a single person" and "the achievement in which many join by 'bearing' and 'finishing' the enterprise."[73] Think of Rosa Parks and her refusal to relinquish her seat on the bus. She began an action that was only fully achieved through the recognition and subsequent acts of many other people, in the civil rights movement and beyond. We tend to think of what she did as a spontaneous act of individual resistance: she was sick and tired of Jim Crow and one day she just refused to abide it any longer. In fact, her action that day was part of a carefully orchestrated collective effort on the part of civil rights activists.[74] It was in large part because others were there to name what she did, to give it a determinate interpretation and articulate its public significance, that her action was "achieved" in Arendt's sense of the word. They gave the otherwise mundane act of holding one's seat its power and effectiveness as the distinctive action it was, as a forceful defense of freedom and human dignity. In this respect, one might say that those who took part in "bearing" what Rosa Parks began were co-participants in the exercise of her agency. Her ability to affect the world would have been much different without them. Arendt's account suggests that individual political agency is actually a collective enterprise.

The "bearers" of Rosa Parks' agency were not limited to civil rights workers, either, or the participants in the collective action that constituted the civil rights movement. Other members of the public – the media, local authorities, white segregationists, northern liberals, and so on – who saw what she did and understood it to be a principled act of resistance to racial inequality were also the bearers of her action. All actions require bearers as interpreters in this sense. Drawing on Arendt, Markell has argued that "the *meaning* of our deeds is not wholly at our disposal, for the very terms through which we make assessments of significance are not exclusively our own, but intersubjective."[75] This is surely right, and it has important political implications. The intersubjective character of meaning makes our interpretations of action vulnerable to prevailing prejudices and inequalities of power within society. Consider, for example, the way in which the gender of agents influences our common interpretations of their actions. A promiscuous woman is morally suspect, even "out of control," while a promiscuous man is seen to be exercising a kind of mastery. Or again, public displays of affection by gay couples are frequently interpreted by heterosexuals as an aggressive "flaunting" of an overly sexualized lifestyle, while among straight couples similar deeds carry the very different meaning of romance, bonding, even mutual commitment. These differences of interpretation have powerful effects on the results of the actions. And the differences go beyond the *evaluations* we attach to the deeds; they include what we understand the actions themselves to *be*. We are the bearers of one another's acts, and as such we participate in constituting these acts in the sense of determining both their meaning and their impact.

The point is that our ability to effect results, which is a crucial aspect of agency, is partly dependent on how others understand and respond to what it is that we are doing. The gay couple who kiss each other in public for the purpose of demonstrating their committed bond will face difficulties in effecting this result if what observers "see" is instead an aggressive assertion of decadence. Moreover, to the extent that their action is interpreted in this way, it may inadvertently contribute to the very patterns of prejudice and domination that prevent them from being fully successful in achieving their goal in this instance.[76] They are agents all right, but not necessarily in the way they wanted to be. From one perspective, the effect that the intersubjective interpretation of action has on agency appears to be a constraint. If agency were nothing more than enacting results that reflect the individual will, then it would be correct to say that agency is constrained by the intersubjective character of action's meaning. Yet we have seen that there are reasons to resist the simple equation of agency with will. Even the deliberative dimension of agency contains elements that are not the product of individual will alone, including character itself, and the results dimension of agency contains many more contingencies that elude the control of the will.

When the exercise of agency is interpreted by its bearers in a way that reverses its actual effects relative to the agent's intentions, agency is subject to a double dilemma. There is first the absence of bearers who can help connect the intention behind the action to its results, which generates a certain failure of agency. Second, insofar as the actual results reinforce the prevailing perspectives that refuse to bear the action, and so assure its continued failure into the future, they double the damage. This double damage reflects existing conditions of social and political inequality, and it threatens to reproduce them. There is a common inclination, at least in liberal democracies, to deny the depth of this dilemma. As liberals, we are partial to the ideal of sovereign agency. We want to believe that we can achieve our acts on our own, that what we are capable of accomplishing is not dependent on the opinions (sometimes false, often biased) of others. This is a noble aspiration in many ways. Yet in light of what we have seen so far, the ideal of agency as mastery is an idyll. It is falsified by elements in both the deliberative and the results dimensions of agency, as our analysis of Williams has shown. And the dream of mastery clouds our vision by obscuring the subtle ways that power inequities and injustice can affect agency. Patterns of domination and oppression not only shape character but they influence moral luck and affect the intersubjective interpretation of action. The "non-sovereign" model of agency suggested by Williams opens the door to this understanding.[77] It illuminates the effects of injustice not only on but within agency, and it has important implications for liberal-democratic politics.

III The politics of non-sovereign agency

Williams never elaborated directly the political implications of his non-sovereign model of agency. He did gesture toward a political "ethic of responsibility" in his late writings, and he periodically indicated an affinity for "radical politics," but he did not spell out the meaning of either one in any detail nor identify the connections between them and his understanding of moral agency. This section sketches very briefly a vision of how non-sovereign agency might contribute to an ethic of responsibility for a progressive liberal-democratic politics. In doing so, it goes beyond anything that Williams himself said, and it draws on insights from other contemporary theorists, but it is intended to chart a course that is consistent with the view of agency Williams lays out and that suggests how his work might be fruitfully appropriated for contemporary political theory.

What Williams called his "ethic of responsibility" for politics means to express a "realistic view of the powers, opportunities, and limitations of political actors."[78] It was inspired by the ethic of responsibility found in

Max Weber's "Politics as a Vocation." Weber contrasted this ethic with an "ethic of ultimate ends," in which the agent feels responsible "only for seeing to it that the flame of pure intentions is not quelched."[79] He does the right thing and then leaves the results to God (or chance). This agent is also willing to undertake morally dubious, or at least "dangerous," means to achieve his ends. The ethic of ultimate ends implicitly construes agency exclusively in terms of deliberation and will, with no acknowledgement of the results dimension of moral agency. In Weber's ethic of responsibility, by contrast, one must "give an account of the foreseeable results of one's action," including unintended results.[80] This ethic involves attentiveness not only to the means used but to the realities of the situation more generally. In fact, it requires a "trained relentlessness in viewing the realities of life, and the ability to face such realities and to measure up to them inwardly."[81] The notion of moral agency implicit here incorporates contingency and emphasizes results as well as intention. Williams recommends the ethic of responsibility for politicians and political leaders. He wants to turn them away from moralism and utopianism in their political action so as to encourage forms of political agency that are ethical but nevertheless politically prudent and sensitive to unintended consequences.

The model of non-sovereign agency clearly underwrites this ethic. It suggests that the exercise of agency is potent in ways that agents themselves do not choose and cannot control. Markell has argued persuasively that acknowledgement of how our own action is inevitably exposed to "an unpredictable and uncontrollable future" can be politically valuable, specifically with respect to justice. The reason, he says, is that "dominative social relations … may be supported in part by the (impossible) aspiration to achieve sovereign agency."[82] Structures of inequality reflect this aspiration insofar as the power, status, and resources they shore up help to insulate some persons and groups from the fact that sovereign agency eludes their grasp.[83] Dominating others does not actually make you a sovereign agent but it obscures from your view the limits of your sovereignty. A high status position in society, for instance, helps ensure that there will be many attentive others to bear your actions and help bring them to fruition. When your actions are dependably borne by others, you may never experience the actual contingency that pervades them, or be aware of how dependent you really are. Acknowledgement of our non-sovereignty as agents, Markell suggests, would mean coming to terms with "the uncertainty and risk that mark social interaction," and it would involve relinquishing the social structures of inequality that support our misguided efforts to secure mastery and that obstruct justice.[84]

Markell's argument is a powerful one, but we could take the politics of non-sovereign agency even further, beyond what either Markell or Williams articulates. The fact of non-sovereignty should inspire a kind of humility in us, not unlike the recognition of interdependence and connectedness that grounds the feminist ethics of care.[85] It demonstrates that we are responsible for far more than we thought, and far more than liberal theory suggests. Liberal theory tells us that our main responsibility as citizens is to avoid willfully violating the rights of other persons, rights that in theory protect the sovereignty of persons as agents. Rights are tremendously valuable in politics, of course. But the realities of non-sovereign agency suggest that our political responsibilities go well beyond respect for rights. What we have seen is that responsibility is not to be identified narrowly with intention. The exercise of agency consists partly in claiming as our own aspects of our actions that we did not intend. Likewise, as the bearers of one another's agency, we each have some responsibility for the degree to which others can successfully enact the claims of their character, or the degree to which others can be free. The model of non-sovereign agency suggests that we are responsible for a much wider range of injustices than most of us have ever imagined insofar as we bear a measure of responsibility for many injustices that we did not intentionally commit. To be sure, the degree of responsibility one bears will be greater when injustice is willful than when it is unintended, but the fact that it is not always willful is not enough to fully discharge our responsibility in relation to it. In sending one's children to private school on account of the poor quality of the local public schools, one may not intend to make things worse for the (largely poor, largely minority) students who cannot afford to buy their way out of the public schools. Yet when public schools are abandoned by the professional classes, they do tend to get worse. And since the public school system, at least in American society, is the gateway to opportunity and to the promises of freedom and equality for all, inadequate schools represent real injustice. By abandoning the schools, one contributes to this injustice, however indirectly, and hence bears some responsibility for it. Clearly, there are many other factors that figure here too, most of them beyond one's control. But to the extent that agency often includes results that outrun intentions, this fact will not let one off the hook. A form of the agent-regret felt by the truck driver who unwittingly ran down a child is appropriate here. The political ethic of responsibility inspired by recognition of the non-sovereign character of agency will cultivate appropriate regret among citizens, and encourage them to act on their regret for the purpose of changing the conditions that give rise to it. So the ethic of responsibility suggested by non-sovereign agency calls for citizens and public officials to face the injustice of their own actions in a more comprehensive way than does the liberal paradigm, and to take a more active role in changing it.

Another implication of non-sovereign agency in politics concerns the way we think about what injustice is. Contemporary liberal theory tends overwhelmingly to conceive of justice according to a distributive paradigm. Following Rawls, justice is theorized in terms of the correct distribution of rights, goods, and opportunities. These resources are understood to be for the use of persons as sovereign or autonomous agents, the assumption being that so long as the distribution is fair, these sovereign agents should be equally capable of making use of them. Injustice happens when things are not distributed properly, and so long as improper distributions are avoided we need not inquire any more deeply into the conditions of agency. Yet in the light cast by the reality of non-sovereign agency, the distributive paradigm of justice proves to be limited. Above all, it does not adequately address our vulnerability as agents to the social interpretation of action, the fact that our actions must be borne by others to reach fruition. The distribution of resources is indeed relevant to how well or badly we mutually bear one another's agency, but it does not tell the whole story. Factors such as beliefs, desires, and dispositions, which cannot be distributed, are also crucial. Domination and oppression concern more than simply the allocation of resources; they also involve how we feel about and how we treat one another, and they enter into the constitution of agency itself. They therefore deeply affect the degree to which persons are able to make good use of the resources that are distributed to them. For this reason, Iris Marion Young has argued for "displacing the distributive paradigm" in favor of one that makes the non-distributive issues of domination and oppression central to justice.[86] Whereas the distributive paradigm focuses on the "allocation of entities" among "antecedently existing individuals" – or in our terms, sovereign agents – her alternative approach makes primary the institutional processes and informal practices that shape these individuals and that influence their ability to make use of the entities allocated to them.[87]

For example, the still frequent depiction of women in movies and television as hapless victims of violence, too inept to avoid obvious danger and too weak or panicked to mount effective physical resistance once it strikes, constitutes an injustice that cannot be described distributively. It attacks not what women *have* but *how we are* in the world. For more than a generation now feminists have been articulating the damage done by depictions of violence against women, damage not only to women but to children and men as well. This damage is real precisely because agency is non-sovereign. Such depictions not only shape the dispositions and desires that are the sources of agency among women but they also undercut the possibility of a wider community of co-participants who can "bear" (i.e., recognize, accept, expect) the non-victimized agency of women. The qualities that American society recognizes as feminine also make it easy to victimize women. And as much as this victimization holds women back in many ways, nevertheless in our society more doors open – the potential scope of agency is widest – for women who have mastered the traditional norms of femininity. There are many bearers for traditionally feminine exertions of agency but few bearers for forms of agency on the part of women that do not fit this mold. A

woman whose presence is physically imposing, whose voice is command-
ing, who defends herself forcefully against slights, who aggressively makes
her needs and views known, who tells you directly when you have crossed
the line with her – in short, a woman who is nobody's victim – is in some
ways less fully an agent in American society today than a more conventional (meaning more victim-like) woman. Because there is relatively little
community to bear novel forms of agency, non-traditional women may in
practice have fewer opportunities to rise and a more limited scope of
options for the exercise of their action, even despite the equal distribution
of liberal rights. The subtle but very powerful effects of non-sovereign
agency in this regard help us to see aspects of injustice that the liberal
paradigm obscures from view.

The importance of non-distributive justice points back to the ethic of
responsibility. Patterns of domination and oppression are in large measure
the byproducts of actions that aim in other directions (toward self-interest,
say, or security, or status) but for which agents nevertheless bear responsibility. These forms of injustice cannot be resolved simply through a new
allocation of resources. What is needed are changes in the dispositions,
desires, and beliefs that constitute character and form the basis for the
deliberative dimension of agency. Also important is the cultivation of what
Markell calls "acknowledgement," or a recognition of the ways in which the
results of our action exceed and sometimes counteract our intentions – and
the regret that properly accompanies this recognition. However, acknowledgement and regret alone will not be enough if they do not generate political action aimed at reform. And change in the direction of justice will
require the cultural transformation that gives rise to new communities of
bearers, reforming conventional prejudices and expectations, and empow-
ering those once marginalized to fully achieve the agency they initiate. The
two dimensions of the politics of non-sovereignty thus come together. They
point to a form of political life that is perhaps more "progressive" than
liberalism but by no means utopian. Although Williams resisted utopianism, he sometimes wrote as if "radical social action" were important,[88] and
he declared himself open to "explore what more radical and ambitious
forms" of political order might be available.[89] He also insisted that "we
have constantly to reinvent the political framework – in part, through our
attitudes to our fellow citizens" if we are to move closer to justice.[90]

In talking of radical social action, Williams raised the question of how it
might be combined with a pluralistic theory of values.[91] If we believe that
values are plural, conflicting, incommensurable, and historically contingent,
as Williams held them to be, how can we remain committed enough to the
values we (happen to) hold to take up radical social action on their behalf,
and run the risks it entails? A similar question could be posed with respect
to the notion of non-sovereign agency itself. I have argued that understanding
the non-sovereign quality of agency is crucial to realizing non-distributive

justice and the ethic of responsibility. The progressive politics we should be aiming for hinges on this understanding. But isn't the reality of non-sovereign agency bound to be a bit demoralizing? In confronting the actual, defined as all the ways that our own agency eludes our grasp, we are faced with a multitude of reasons for not acting at all. Insofar as our exertions of agency are constituted by contingency and disrupted by luck, reflect a character we did not choose, elude the control of what we think of as our will, subject us to the opinions of those who bear out our actions, and sometimes embroil us in tragedy, what could possibly be the point of making the effort? If cynicism about the authenticity and the efficacy of one's action leads to passivity, there may be reason to worry about the idea of non-sovereign agency. Even though the dream of sovereignty is illusory, and although the pursuit of this dream may give rise to the kinds of domination and inequality that Markell has identified, still the costs of relinquishing the dream may not be negligible either. We may need it, if only to save agency from the potentially deadening force of the actual, and so to protect the possibility of radical social action.

Williams' non-sovereign model of agency raises another danger as well. This one is a function of the fact that he did not think enough about the *politics* of non-sovereign agency. He generally treats "the actual" within agency as something inevitable that we ought to resign ourselves to living with. He faults Kantianism for offering false solace against contingency,[92] and he criticizes liberalism for its effort to control necessity and chance by imposing a framework of social justice on politics.[93] Yet if contingency, necessity, and chance are in fact infused with politics, if they contribute to domination and oppression by enacting relations of power, then it is not at all clear that acceptance is the right attitude to take. Martha Nussbaum has remarked along similar lines that much of the suffering that Williams associates with tragedy (and hence contingency) is actually the product of human vice.[94] A more political perspective on non-sovereign agency would resist the quietism that haunts Williams' account. But it would in principle further Williams' own ambition to articulate the real "powers, opportunities, and limitations of political actors," and hence illuminate the nature of political agency more fully.

Despite the deficits and missteps in his account, the model of non-sovereign agency that Williams developed holds great value for political theory today. It presses us to think beyond the limits of liberal autonomy and distributive justice. It reminds us how deeply interdependent we are, but also how potent. Indeed, the notion of non-sovereign agency illuminates the ways that our power to affect the world exceeds our intentions, sometimes disrupting and even reversing them. It thus reveals the scope of our agency to be wider than we knew even as it undermines our sense of mastery. It makes us conscious of our responsibility not only for the unintended results of our own actions but also for bearing out the agency of

SHARON R. KRAUSE

others. It shows us that the sources of agency are to be found in character and desire rather than in a form of reason that transcends them. And finally, it teaches us that the exercise of agency is frequently riven by conflict and that the idea of the unitary subject is a myth, and it reminds us to look for the moral remainders that we generate. In all these ways, Williams has opened up terrain that demands to be explored further, and explored with a distinctively political lens. Above all, he has given us valuable resources for correcting the present absence of political agency in political theory today – and for doing so in a way that eschews the sometimes excessive moralism of much contemporary theory in favor of an account that attends to what is actual about agency.

Notes

1 Jürgen Habermas may seem to be an exception to this rule, insofar as his account of justice is rooted in what he calls the theory of communicative action. Yet Habermas' "discourse ethics" and his "discourse theory of democracy," like John Rawls' theory of justice, focus mainly on the procedures of norm justification and the practice of deliberation, rather than on political action *per se*. See Habermas, *Moral Consciousness and Communicative Action*, trans. Christian Lenhardt and Shierry Weber Nicholsen (Cambridge, MA: MIT Press, 1990); *Justification and Application*, trans. Ciaran P. Cronin (Cambridge, MA: MIT Press, 1994); *The Inclusion of the Other: Studies in Political Theory*, trans. Ciaran Cronin and Pablo De Greiff (Cambridge, MA: MIT Press, 1998); and *Between Facts and Norms*, trans. William Rehg (Cambridge, MA: MIT Press, 1998). See also John Rawls, *A Theory of Justice* (Cambridge, MA: Harvard University Press, 1971); and *Political Liberalism* (New York: Columbia University Press, 1993).
2 Bernard Williams, *In the Beginning Was the Deed* (Princeton, NJ: Princeton University Press, 2005), p. 12.
3 Ibid., p. 2.
4 Ibid., p. 2.
5 Ibid., p. 16.
6 Ibid., p. 12.
7 I have in mind poststructuralists such as Judith Butler, communitarians such as Michael Sandel, Charles Taylor, and Michael Walzer, and democratic theorists influenced by Hannah Arendt, such as Bonnie Honig and Patchen Markell. Judith Butler, *Gender Trouble: Feminism and the Subversion of Identity* (New York: Routledge, 1990) and *Bodies that Matter: On the Discursive Limits of "Sex"* (New York: Routledge, 1993); Michael Sandel, *Liberalism and the Limits of Justice* (New York: New York University Press, 1984) and *Democracy's Discontent: America in Search of a Public Philosophy* (Cambridge, MA: Harvard University Press, 1996); Charles Taylor, "Cross-Purposes: The Liberal-Communitarian Debate," in Nancy L. Rosenblum (ed.), *Liberalism and the Moral Life* (Cambridge, MA: Harvard University Press, 1989), pp. 159–82; Michael Walzer, *Exodus and Revolution* (New York: Basic Books, 1985) and *Politics and Passion: Toward a More Egalitarian Liberalism* (New Haven, CT: Yale University Press, 2004); Bonnie Honig, *Political Theory and the Displacement of Politics* (Ithaca, NY: Cornell University Press, 1993); and Patchen Markell, "Tragic Recognition: Action and Identity in *Antigone* and Aristotle," *Political Theory* 31(1) (2003), 6–38. See also Don Herzog, "Romantic Anarchism and Pedestrian Liberalism," *Political Theory*

35(3) (2007), 313–33. For recent work on political agency within the liberal paradigm, see Philip Pettit, *A Theory of Freedom: From the Psychology to the Politics of Agency* (Oxford: Oxford University Press, 2001); and Mika LaVaque-Manty, *Arguments and Fists: Political Agency and Justification in Liberal Theory* (New York: Routledge, 2002).

8 Bonnie Honig draws attention to the importance for political theory of Williams' work on value pluralism, although she also criticizes certain aspects of his view, as we shall see in what follows. Bonnie Honig, "Difference, Dilemmas, and the Politics of Home," in Seyla Benhabib (ed.), *Democracy and Difference* (Princeton, NJ: Princeton University Press), pp. 257–77. Mark Jenkins credits Williams with having resuscitated interest in the role of emotions in practical deliberation and moral psychology more generally. See Mark P. Jenkins, *Bernard Williams* (Montreal: McGill-Queens, 2006), p. 61. Williams' late work on politics proper, published posthumously, has arrived on the scene too recently to have yet had much effect on the field. So far, however, it is his account of political legitimacy that has attracted most attention from political theorists.

9 An exception is Bonnie Honig, whose discussion of Williams is treated below. Patchen Markell, also discussed below, mentions him briefly in a footnote in the context of a discussion about agency. Patchen Markell, "Tragic Recognition: Action and Identity in *Antigone* and Aristotle," *Political Theory* 31(1) (2003), 32, n. 18.

10 Bernard Williams, "Moral Luck," in *Moral Luck: Philosophical Papers 1973–1980* (Cambridge: Cambridge University Press, 1981), p. 30.

11 Williams, *Shame and Necessity* (Berkeley, CA: University of California Press, 1993), p. 69.

12 Ibid., p. 34.

13 Williams, "Internal and External Reasons," in *Moral Luck*, p. 105.

14 Williams, *Ethics and the Limits of Philosophy* (Cambridge, MA: Harvard University Press, 1985), p. 50.

15 Williams, "Internal and External Reasons," p. 104.

16 Ibid., pp. 108, 109.

17 Williams, "Ethical Consistency," in *Problems of the Self* (Cambridge: Cambridge University Press, 1973), p. 174.

18 Williams, "Persons, Character, and Morality," in *Moral Luck*, p. 2.

19 Williams, *Shame and Necessity*, p. 41; original emphasis.

20 Williams, "Replies," in J.E.J. Altham and Ross Harrison (eds), *World, Mind and Ethics: Essays on the Ethical Philosophy of Bernard Williams* (Cambridge: Cambridge University Press, 1995), p. 203.

21 Ibid., p. 205.

22 Williams, "Persons, Character, and Morality," p. 12.

23 Williams, "Practical Necessity," in *Moral Luck*, p. 130.

24 Williams, "A Critique of Utilitarianism," in J.J.C. Smart and Bernard Williams (eds.), *Utilitarianism For and Against* (Cambridge: Cambridge University Press, 1973), p. 116f.

25 Williams, *Shame and Necessity*, p. 103; see also Williams, "Practical Necessity," p. 130f.

26 Williams, *Ethics and the Limits of Philosophy*, p. 169.

27 Ibid.

28 Williams, *Shame and Necessity*, pp, 72–3.

29 Williams, "Practical Necessity," p. 131.

30 Ibid., p. 132.

31 Ibid., p. 133.

32 Ibid., p. 136.

SHARON R. KRAUSE

33 Quoted in David Lewis, *King: A Critical Biography* (Baltimore, MD: Penguin, 1971), p. 109.
34 Richard H. King, *Civil Rights and the Idea of Freedom* (Athens, GA: University of Georgia Press, 1996), p. 92f.
35 Williams, "Morality and the Emotions," in *Problems of the Self*, p. 222.
36 Williams, "Utilitarianism and Moral Self-indulgence," in *Moral Luck*, p. 49.
37 Jenkins remarks along these lines that Williams is keen to sustain, against Utilitarianism, "the wholeness and satisfactions of a transparent practical agency." Jenkins, *Bernard Williams*, p. 42.
38 Honig, "Difference, Dilemmas, and Politics of Home," p. 258.
39 Ibid., p. 271.
40 Ibid., p. 258.
41 Ibid., p. 261.
42 Ibid., p. 259.
43 Ibid., p. 262.
44 Williams, "Conflicts of Values," p. 72f.
45 Williams, "Ethical Consistency," p. 179.
46 Williams, "Conflicts of Values," p. 75.
47 Ibid., p. 74.
48 Williams, *Shame and Necessity*, pp. 69, 164–6.
49 Honig, "Difference, Dilemmas, and the Politics of Home," p. 259.
50 Williams, "A Critique of Utilitarianism," p. 117.
51 Ibid., p. 116.
52 It is also worth noting that Williams did not intend the examples of George and Jim to fully illustrate the complex structure and moral psychology of integrity. As he later emphasized, the examples were only meant to show that direct utilitarianism could not accommodate our sense of the moral importance to us of our own actions in bringing about states of affairs, over and above the importance of the states of affairs themselves. His specific answers to the questions of what George and Jim should have done "was not the main point." The main point instead lay "in an invitation to think about the notions and styles of thought that one can bring to bear on such questions." Williams, "Replies," p. 213.
53 Honig, "Difference, Dilemmas, and the Politics of Home," p. 272.
54 Ibid., p. 166.
55 Williams, "Ethical Consistency," p. 178.
56 It is true that Williams does not discuss the ways in which this awareness of the moral remainders in one's life might be given expression in political action. It is one thing to feel the moral remainders of one's decisions and another to take up political action that could put them to right. Williams's account leaves the latter possibility untapped, and this represents a serious limitation of his view. Honig's critique is very much on the mark in this regard.
57 Markell, "Tragic Recognition," p. 8.
58 Ibid.
59 Ibid.
60 Williams, "Moral Luck," p. 28.
61 Ibid., p. 29.
62 Williams, *Shame and Necessity*, p. 69.
63 Ibid., p. 74. This passage and the one cited immediately above further support the idea that for Williams tragedy is not marginal to moral experience but expressive of deep and common features of it.
64 Markell, "Tragic Recognition," p. 19. See also Hannah Arendt, *The Human Condition* (Chicago, IL: University of Chicago Press, 1958), pp. 190–2.

65 Williams, *Shame and Necessity*, p. 69.
66 Williams, "Moral Luck," p. 29.
67 Ibid., p. 30.
68 Ibid., p. 23.
69 Immanuel Kant, *Grounding for the Metaphysics of Morals*, trans. James W. Ellington (Indianapolis: Hackett, 1981), pp. 7, 383.
70 Williams, "Moral Luck," p. 38; original emphasis.
71 In a similar vein, Honig wants to show that power relations affect the nature and frequency of the moral dilemmas (and tragedies) that we face. See Honig, *Political Theory and the Displacement of Politics* (Ithaca, NY: Cornell University Press, 1993), pp. 264, 234.
72 Arendt, *The Human Condition*, p. 192.
73 Ibid., p. 189.
74 See Aldon Morris, *The Origins of the Civil Rights Movement* (New York: Free Press, 1984), pp. 51–3; and King, *Civil Rights and the Idea of Freedom*, p. 40.
75 Markell, "Tragic Recognition," p. 20. As Markell notes, Seyla Benhabib has referred to this aspect of action as its "interpretive indeterminacy." Benhabib, *Critique, Norm and Utopia* (New York: Columbian University Press, 1986), p. 136.
76 I do not mean to suggest that any of this is the fault of the gay couple, or to imply that there is nothing to be gained for gay people through public displays of affection. Over time, efforts by gay couples to rearticulate the intended meaning of such displays may have an impact on how they are received by a prejudiced public. Social change often transpires in just this way. In such cases, activists function as intermediary bearers of their own actions, carrying the meaning of the action, as they see it, to the wider community whose response partly determines the actual results the action can achieve. Even here, however, individuals do not bear their agency alone. They depend on partial communities of interest and identity, what one recent writer has called "subaltern counterpublics" to provide the recognition and support needed to achieve the action before a larger public. Nancy Fraser, "Rethinking the Public Sphere: A Contribution to the Critique of Actually Existing Democracy," in Craig Calhoun (ed.), *Habermas and the Public Sphere* (Cambridge, MA: MIT Press, 1993), p. 123.
77 The term "non-sovereignty" as applied to agency comes from Arendt rather than Williams, but it expresses aspects of agency that Williams powerfully articulates. See Arendt, *The Human Condition*, pp. 234–5; and see also Markell, who uses the term "impropriety" to capture the idea of non-sovereignty in agency. Markell, "Tragic Recognition," p. 31, note 3.
78 Williams, *In the Beginning was the Deed*, p. 12.
79 Max Weber, "Politics as a Vocation," in H.H. Gerth and C. Wright Mills, *From Max Weber* (New York: Oxford University Press, 1946), p. 121.
80 Ibid., p. 120.
81 Ibid., p. 126f.
82 Markell, "Tragic Recognition," p. 30.
83 Ibid., p. 30.
84 Ibid., p. 30.
85 For discussions of the ethic of care, see, for example, Carol Gilligan, *In a Different Voice: Psychological Theory and Women's Development* (Cambridge, MA: Harvard University Press, 1982); Joan C. Tronto, *Moral Boundaries: A Political Argument for an Ethic of Care* (New York: Routledge, 1994); Nel Noddings, *Caring: A Feminine Approach to Ethics* (Berkeley, CA: University of California Press, 1984); and Virginia Held (ed.), *Justice and Care: Essential Readings in Feminist Ethics* (Boulder, CO: Westview Press, 1995).

86 Iris Marion Young, *Justice and the Politics of Difference* (Princeton, NJ: Princeton University Press, 1990), p. 15.
87 Young herself did not possess as well-developed a view of non-sovereign agency as what we find in Williams. Sometimes, in fact, she sounds as if she retains a residual attachment to the liberal ideal of sovereignty. For instance, she holds that justice should make possible "self-development" and "self-determination" (Young, *Justice and the Politics of Difference*, p. 37). Still, her discussion of the non-distributive dimensions of justice is instructive and is basically compatible with the non-sovereign model of agency.
88 Williams, "Conflicts of Values," p. 71.
89 Williams, *In the Beginning Was the Deed*, p. 17.
90 Ibid., p. 126.
91 Williams, "Conflicts of Values," p. 71.
92 Williams, "Moral Luck," pp. 20–1.
93 Williams, *Shame and Necessity*, p. 128.
94 See Martha Nussbaum's chapter in this volume. See also Jenkins, *Bernard Williams*, p. 180.

INDEX

Related titles from Routledge

Descartes
The Project of Pure Enquiry
Bernard Williams

'For someone who wanted to understand what Descartes *meant*, what problems he was actually struggling to solve, it must be absolutely indispensable reading. And there can be no one interested in philosophy at all who is not interested in Descartes in this sense.'

Mary Warnock, New Society

'Excellent.'

The Times Educational Supplement

'His biographical digest is as succinct as his philosophical analysis is thorough.'

The Sunday Times

'Bernard Williams is arguably the greatest philosopher of his era.'

The Guardian

'One of the most brilliant figures of his generation.'

Glasgow Herald

'*Descartes – The Project of Pure Enquiry*, first published in 1978 and repackaged here with a foreword by the Cartesian scholar John Cottingham, is a good deal more than just a survey of one of the landmarks in the history of philosophy. It is itself a work of substantive philosophical analysis and a reminder of just what British philosophy lost when Williams died in 2003.'

New Humanist

'This is a powerful book that illuminates not only the work of a great historical thinker, but also fundamental philosophical questions'

The Philosophers' Magazine Online

ISBN 10: 0-415-35626-1 (hbk)
ISBN 10: 0-415-35627-X (pbk)

Available at all good bookshops
For ordering and further information please visit:
www.routledge.com